Children's Jukebox

Second Edition

The Select Subject Guide to Children's Musical Recordings

Rob Reid

American Library Association
Chicago   2007

While extensive effort has gone into ensuring the reliability of information appearing in this book, the publisher makes no warranty, express or implied, on the accuracy or reliability of the information, and does not assume and hereby disclaims any liability to any person for any loss or damage caused by errors or omissions in this publication.

Composition in Minion and Gill Sans by ALA Editions using InDesign CS on a PC platform.

The paper used in this publication meets the minimum requirements of American National Standard for Information Sciences—Permanence of Paper for Printed Library Materials, ANSI Z39.48-1992.∞

Library of Congress Cataloging-in-Publication Data
Reid, Rob.
  Children's jukebox : the select subject guide to children's musical recordings / Rob Reid. — 2nd ed.
    p. cm.
  ISBN 0-8389-0940-X (alk. paper)
  1. Children's songs—Discography—Indexes. 2. Children's songs—Reviews. I. Title.
  ML156.4.C5R45 2007
  016.78242083'0266—dc22

                                                                    2006103175

ISBN-13: 978-0-8389-0940-9
ISBN-10: 0-8389-0940-X

Printed in the United States of America
11 10 09 08 07   5 4 3 2 1

For Jayne, Laura, Julia, Alice, and Sam

Contents

Introduction   xi

Discography of Featured Recordings   1

A Recommended Core Collection   17

Rob's Favorite Original Children's Songs   23

The Subject Listings

Accidents   29
Alphabet/Letters   29
Amusement Parks/
   Playgrounds   31
Angels   32
Animals   32
Alligators/Crocodiles   36
Armadillos   37
Bats   37
Bears   37
Beavers   38
Bison   38
Camels   39
Cats   39
Chipmunks   40
Clams   40
Cows/Bulls   40
Coyotes   41
Deer   41
Dogs   41

Dolphins   43
Donkeys/Mules   43
Elephants   44
Elk   44
Foxes   44
Frogs/Toads   45
Giraffes   46
Gnus   46
Goats   46
Gorillas   47
Groundhogs   47
Hermit Crabs   47
Hippopotamuses   47
Horned Toads   48
Horses   48
Jellyfish   48
Kangaroos   48
Koalas   48
Lions   48
Lizards   49
Llamas   49

Lobsters   49
Manatees   49
Mice   49
Monkeys/Chimpanzees   50
Moose   51
Octopus   52
Opossums   52
Otters   52
Pigs   52
Platypuses   53
Porcupines   53
Rabbits   53
Raccoons   54
Rats   54
Rhinoceroses   54
Salamanders/Newts   54
Sea Anemones   55
Sheep   55
Skunks   55
Slugs   55
Snails   55

Snakes   56
Squids   56
Squirrels   56
Starfish   56
Tigers   56
Turtles   56
Wallabies   57
Weasels   57
Whales   57
Wolves   57
Worms   58
Zebras   58

Appliances   58
Arguing/Fighting   58
Babies   59
Babysitters   60
Backwards/
   Upside Down   61
Balloons   61
Bathtime   61
Bedtime   62
Birds   66
Blackbirds   67
Bluebirds   67
Chickadees   67
Chickens/Roosters   68
Cranes   69
Crows   69
Cuckoos   69
Ducks   69
Eagles   70
Flamingos   70
Geese   70
Kookaburras   70
Loons   71
Nightingales   71
Owls   71
Parrots   71
Pelicans   71
Penguins   71
Pigeons   71
Puffins   72
Quails   72
Robins   72
Seagulls   72
Sparrows   72

Swans   72
Toucans   72
Turkeys   72
Warblers   73
Woodpeckers   73

Birthdays   73
Blankets/Quilts   74
Body   74
Books/Reading   77
Boredom   78
Brotherhood/
   Sisterhood   78
Bubbles   80
Bullying   80
Burping   81
Celebration   81
Childhood   83
Circus   84
Cities/Neighborhoods/
   Towns   84
Cleverness   85
Clocks/Time   85
Clothing   86
Hats   87
Mittens   87
Pajamas   87
Pants   88
Shoes   88
Socks   89
Underwear   89

Clumsiness   89
Collecting Things   89
Colors   89
Continents   91
Africa   91
Australia   92

Computers   92
Consumerism   92
Cooking/Baking   92
Cooperation/
   Sportsmanship   93
Counting/
   Numbers   94

Countries   98
Algeria   98
Argentina   98
Austria   99
Benin   99
Bolivia   99
Bosnia and
   Herzegovina   99
Brazil   99
Cambodia   99
Cameroon   99
Canada   99
Chile   100
China   100
Colombia   100
Congo   100
Cuba   100
Denmark   100
Ecuador   101
England   101
Ethiopia   101
Finland   101
France   101
Germany   102
Ghana   102
Greece   102
Guyana   102
Haiti   102
India   103
Indonesia   103
Iran   103
Ireland   103
Israel   103
Italy   103
Jamaica   104
Japan   104
Kenya   104
Korea   104
Madagascar   105
Malaysia   105
Martinique   105
Mexico   105
The Netherlands   105
New Zealand   105
Nigeria   106
Norway   106
Peru   106
The Philippines   106

Puerto Rico   106
The Republic of
    Cape Verde   106
Russia   106
Scotland   107
Senegal   107
South Africa   107
Spain   107
Sweden   107
Switzerland   108
Tatarstan   108
Tibet   108
Tonga   108
Trinidad and Tobago   108
Turkey   108
Uganda   108
Ukraine   108
Uruguay   108
Venezuela   108
Vietnam   109
Yugoslavia   109
Zaire   109

Cowboys/
    Cowgirls   109
Days of the Week   111
Death   112
Differences   112
Digging   113
Dinosaurs   113
Disabilities   114
Divorce   115
Dolls   115
Drawing/Painting   115
Dreams   116
Earth   117
Earthquakes   118
Ecology/Nature   118
Emotions   119
Anger   120
Embarrassment   121
Fear   121
Happiness   122
Love   123
Sadness   125

Family   126
Aunts   127
Brothers   127
Cousins   128
Fathers   128
Grandfathers   128
Grandmothers   129
Grandparents   129
Mothers   129
Parents   130
Sisters   130
Uncles   131

Farms   131
Fish   133
Flying   134
Food   135
Beverages   137
Bread/Buns/
    Sandwiches   138
Cakes/Donuts   138
Candy   138
Cookies   139
Crackers   139
Fruit   139
Gum   141
Honey   141
Ice Cream   141
Jam/Jelly   142
Macaroni and Cheese   142
Meat   142
Pancakes   142
Pasta/Spaghetti   142
Peanut Butter   143
Peanuts   143
Pickles   143
Pie   143
Pizza   144
Popcorn   144
Soup/Stew   144
Vegetables   145

Forgetfulness   146
Freedom   146
Friendship   147
Furniture   149
Gardens   149

Gluttony   150
Good-bye Songs   150
Growing   152
Hair   153
Health/Nutrition   153
Hello Songs   154
Heroes/
    Superheroes   156
Hiccupping   156
Home/Houses   156
Hugs   156
Hurrying   157
Illness   157
Imaginary Characters/
    Creatures   158
Aliens   158
Dragons   158
Elves/Fairies/
    Leprechauns   159
Ghosts   159
Giants   160
Mermaids   160
Monsters   160
Ogres/Trolls   160
Sasquatch   161
Unicorns   161
Vampires   161
Witches   161
Wizards   161

Imaginary Friends   161
Imaginary Places   162
Imagination   162
Insects   164
Ants   164
Bees   165
Beetles   165
Boll Weevils   166
Butterflies/Moths/
    Caterpillars   166
Cockroaches   166
Crickets   167
Fireflies   167
Flies/Fleas   167
Grasshoppers   167

Ladybugs 168
Mosquitoes 168
Islands 168
Jokes and Riddles 168
Jungles/
    Rainforests 169
Kindness 169
Kisses 169
Kites 170
Languages 170
    African Languages 171
    American Indian 173
    Arabic 173
    Bahasa Indonesia 173
    Bararra 173
    Basque 174
    Cantonese 174
    Creole 174
    Danish 174
    Dutch 174
    Finnish 174
    French 174
    German 176
    Greek 176
    Hawaiian 176
    Hebrew 176
    Hindi 177
    Icelandic 177
    Italian 177
    Japanese 177
    Korean 178
    Ladino 178
    Malagasy 178
    Malaysian 178
    Mandarin 178
    Maori 178
    Maya 178
    Norwegian 178
    Patua (Brazil and
        French Guiana) 178
    Pitjantjatjara (Australian
        Aboriginal) 179
    Portuguese 179
    Russian 179
    Spanish 179
    Swedish 183

    Swiss German 183
    Tamil (India) 183
    Tatar 183
    Tibetan 183
    Turkish 183
    Tzotzil (Mexico) 183
Laziness 183
Libraries 184
Literary/Folklore
    Characters 184
Losing Things 187
Luck 187
Lullabies 187
Mail 191
Making Things 192
Manners 192
Messiness 192
Misbehavior 193
Money 194
Months of the
    Year 194
Morningtime 195
Mountains 196
Movement 197
    Dancing 204
Moving 206
Music 206
    Musical Instruments 207
    Singing 209
    Yodeling 211
Names 212
Nighttime 213
Noise 214
Nonsense 214
Nursery Rhymes 216
Occupations 220
Opposites 220
Optimism 221
Outer Space 221
    Aurora Borealis 222
    Moon 222

    Planets 223
    Stars 223
    Sun 224
Patience 224
Peace 225
Perseverance 225
Pirates 226
Plants 227
    Flowers 227
    Mushrooms 228
    Pumpkins 228
    Trees 228
Playing 230
Pollution 231
Procrastination 231
Questions 231
Radio 232
Rainbows 232
Recreation/
    Sports 233
    Baseball 233
    Basketball 234
    Bowling 234
    Camping/Camps 234
    Fishing 234
    Hiking/Walking 235
    Hunting 235
    Juggling 236
    Riding 236
    Skateboarding 237
    Skating 237
    Soccer 237
    Surfing 237
    Swimming 237
Recycling 238
Rivers 238
Robots 239
Rocks and
    Minerals 239
Rounds 239
Royalty 241
Safety 242
Schools 243

Sea and Seashore
  245
Seasons 246
  Autumn/Fall 246
  Spring 247
  Summer 247
  Winter 248
Self Concept/
  Self-Esteem 248
Senses 251
  Hearing 251
  Sight 252
  Smell 252
Shadows 252
Shapes 252
Sharing 252
Shyness 253
Size 253
Special Places 254
Spiders 254
Spiritual 255
Stores/Markets/
  Restaurants 256
Storytelling 257

Teddy Bears 257
Teeth 258
Telephones 259
Television 259
Thankfulness 260
Tickling 260
Tools 260
Toys 261
Transportation/
  Travel 262
  Airplanes 262
  Automobiles 262
  Ballooning 264
  Bicycles 264
  Boats 265
  Buses 265
  *Construction
    Equipment 266*
  Jeeps 266
  Motorcycles 266
  Subways 266
  Taxis 266
  Tractors 266
  Trains 266
  Trucks 269
Treehouses 270

Twins/Triplets 270
The United States
  of America 270
  California 270
  Florida 270
  Hawaii 270
  Idaho 271
  Illinois 271
  Louisiana 271
  New York 271
  Ohio 271
  Texas 271
  Wisconsin 272
  Wyoming 272
Video Games 272
Volcanoes 272
Wagons 272
Water 272
Weather 273
  Clouds 273
  Rain 273
  Snow 275
  Wind 275
Wishes 276
Wordplay 277
Zoos 279

Resources 281

Introduction

I truly believe I've listened to more children's musical recordings than anyone in the history of humankind.

I heard more than 650 recordings in 2006; 547 made it into this book. The first edition of *Children's Jukebox* contained 308 recordings and several practical programming ideas. This new edition has been expanded to cover 170 subject headings (and more subcategories), while the programming ideas have been moved to the companion book *Something Musical Happened at the Library*.

There have been many changes in children's recorded music since the first edition. Cassettes were the most common format then, and only a few businesses sold the recordings through print catalogs. Today, all of the recordings listed in this book are available in compact disc format and available for purchase on the Internet, some from the artists themselves through their personal websites. More and more recordings are also available as downloads from various websites (see the Resources list at the end of this book).

The recordings listed in this book represent the finest children's recordings on the market. Many are Parent's Choice Award winners, ALA Notable Recordings, Grammy Award winners, and recordings I discovered from my years of reviewing for *School Library Journal* and *Booklist*. This is a select index of songs. The individual song titles are the best recordings for each category.

Recordings not included in the book are original soundtracks, recordings featuring show tunes and contemporary pop hits, and recordings featuring popular licensed characters, such as those from Sesame Street and Barney.

Many traditional songs can be found under a variety of titles. For example, the song "Bought Me a Cat" shows up on various recordings as "The Barnyard Song," "Fiddle I Fee," "Had a Bird," "Had a Cat," and "I Had a Cat." When I was able to identify such songs, I listed them separately with a reference to the other versions. In the case of some songs where the difference in titles was slight, such as "Frog Went A-Courtin'" versus "Froggie Went A-Courtin'," I grouped all of the recordings under one title, which I hope will not cause too much confusion for the person trying to match the title in the book to the title on the recording in her hand.

My thanks go out to all of the artists who helped this project with their support. They responded to my correspondence with enthusiasm and have filled up my house with their wonderful recordings. A special thank you goes to Beth Blenz-Clucas of Sugar Mountain PR for introducing me to many artists for the first time.

Children's musical recordings are still a largely untapped resource for library programs and classroom activities. It is my hope that they will be embraced by parents and adults who work with children.

Discography of
Featured Recordings

Abell, Timmy. *The Farmer's Market*. Upstream, 1989.

———. *I Know an Old Lady*. Upstream, 1995.

———. *Little Red Wagon*. Upstream, 2005.

Allard, Peter and Ellen. *Good Kid*. Peter and Ellen Allard, 2000.

———. *Pizza Pizzaz*. 80-Z Music, 2006.

———. *Raise the Children*. Peter and Ellen Allard, 1996.

———. *Sing It! Say It! Stamp It! Sway It!* vol. 1. 80-Z Music, 1999.

———. *Sing It! Say It! Stamp It! Sway It!* vol. 2. 80-Z Music, 1999.

———. *Sing It! Say It! Stamp It! Sway It!* vol. 3. 80-Z Music, 2002.

Alsop, Peter. *Pluggin' Away*. Moose School, 1990.

———. *Stayin' Over*. Moose School, 1987.

———. *Take Me with You*. Moose School, 1986.

———. *Uh-Oh!* Moose School, 2002.

———. *Wha' D'Ya Wanna Do?* Moose School, 1983.

Arnold, Linda. *Circus Magic*. Youngheart, 1998.

———. *Favorites in the Key of Fun*. Ariel, 1996.

———. *Happiness Cake*. Ariel, 1988.

———. *Make Believe*. Ariel, 1986.

———. *Peppermint Wings*. Ariel, 1990.

———. *Sing Along Stew*. Ariel, 1995.

———. *Splash Zone*. Youngheart, 2000.

Atkinson, Lisa. *The Elephant in Aisle Four*. A Gentle Wind, 2000.

———. *I Wanna Tickle the Fish*. A Gentle Wind, 1987.

————. *The One and Only Me*. A Gentle Wind, 1989.

Avni, Fran. *Artichokes and Brussel Sprouts*. Music for Little People, 1988.

————. *I'm All Ears: Sing into Reading*. Starfish Music, 1999.

————. *Little Ears: Songs for Reading Readiness*. Leapfrog School House, 2000.

————. *Tuning into Nature*. Lemonstone, 2002.

Banana Slug String Band. *Adventures on the Air Cycle*. Music for Little People, 1989.

————. *Dirt Made My Lunch*. Music for Little People, 1987.

————. *Goin' Wild*. Slug Music, 1999.

————. *Penguin Parade*. Music for Little People, 1995.

————. *Singing in Our Garden*. Slug Music, 2002.

————. *Slugs at Sea*. Music for Little People, 1991.

————. *Wings of Slumber*. Slug Music, 2004.

Barchas, Sarah. *Bridges across the World*. High Haven, 1999.

————. *Get Ready, Get Set, Sing!* High Haven, 1994.

————. *If I Had a Pony*. High Haven, 1996.

————. *¡Piñata! and More*. High Haven, 1997.

Bartels, Joanie. *Bathtime Magic*. BMG, 1990.

————. *Morning Magic*. BMG, 1987.

————. *Put On Your Dancing Shoes*. Purple Frog, 2001.

————. *Sillytime Magic*. BMG, 1989.

————. *Travelin' Magic*. BMG, 1988.

Beall, Pamela, and Susan Nipp. *Wee Sing and Play*. Price Stern Sloan, 1981.

————. *Wee Sing and Pretend*. Price Stern Sloan, 2001.

————. *Wee Sing Animals, Animals, Animals*. Price Stern Sloan, 1999.

————. *Wee Sing around the World*. Price Stern Sloan, 1994.

————. *Wee Sing Children's Songs and Fingerplays*. Price Stern Sloan, 1977.

————. *Wee Sing for Baby*. Price Stern Sloan, 1996.

————. *Wee Sing Fun 'n' Folk*. Price Stern Sloan, 1989.

————. *Wee Sing Games, Games, Games*. Price Stern Sloan, 1986.

————. *Wee Sing in the Car*. Price Stern Sloan, 1999.

————. *Wee Sing Nursery Rhymes and Lullabies*. Price Stern Sloan, 1985.

————. *Wee Sing Silly Songs*. Price Stern Sloan, 1982.

————. *Wee Sing Sing-Alongs*. Price Stern Sloan, 1982.

Berkner, Laurie. *Buzz Buzz*. Two Tomatoes, 1998.

————. *Under a Shady Tree*. Two Tomatoes, 2002.

————. *Victor Vito*. Two Tomatoes, 1999.

———. *Whaddaya Think of That?* Two Tomatoes, 2000.

Big Jeff. *Big Jeff.* Big Jeff, 2000.

———. *Big Jeff and His Middle-Sized Band.* Big Jeff, 2004.

Boynton, Sandra. *Dog Train.* Boynton, 2005.

———. *Philadelphia Chickens.* Boynton, 2002.

———. *Rhinoceros Tap.* Boynton, 1996.

Brown, Greg. *Bathtub Blues.* Red House, 1993.

Buchman, Rachel. *Baby and Me.* A Gentle Wind, 1991.

———. *Hello Everybody!* A Gentle Wind, 1986.

———. *Sing a Song of Seasons.* Rounder, 1997.

Byers, Kathy. *Do You Wish You Could Fly?* KT Music, 2000.

———. *'Round the Campfire.* KT Music, 2004.

Cassidy, Nancy. *Nancy Cassidy's KidsSongs.* Klutz Press, 2004.

Chapin, Tom. *Around the World and Back Again.* Sony, 1996.

———. *Billy the Squid.* Sony, 1992.

———. *Family Tree.* Sony, 1992.

———. *Great Big Fun for the Very Little One.* Sundance, 2001.

———. *In My Hometown.* Sony, 1998.

———. *Making Good Noise.* Sundance, 2003.

———. *Moonboat.* Sundance, 1989.

———. *Mother Earth.* Sundance, 1990.

———. *Some Assembly Required.* Razor & Tie, 2005.

———. *This Pretty Planet.* Sony, 2000.

———. *Zag Zig.* Sony, 1994.

Charette, Rick. *Alligator in the Elevator.* Pine Point, 1985.

———. *Bubble Gum.* Educational Activities, 1983.

———. *Chickens on Vacation.* Pine Point, 1990.

———. *King Kong Chair.* Pine Point, 2004.

———. *A Little Peace and Quiet.* Pine Point, 1993.

———. *Popcorn and Other Songs to Munch On.* Pine Point, 1994.

———. *Toad Motel.* Pine Point, 1999.

———. *Where Do My Sneakers Go at Night?* Pine Point, 1987.

The Chenille Sisters. *The Big Picture and Other Songs for Kids.* Red House, 1992.

———. *1, 2, 3 for Kids.* Red House, 1990.

———. *Teaching Hippopotami to Fly!* Can Too Records, 1996.

Coffey, James. *Animal Groove.* Blue Vision, 1999.

———. *Come Ride Along with Me.* Blue Vision, 1997.

———. *I Love Toy Trains*. Blue Vision, 2005.

———. *My Mama Was a Train*. Blue Vision, 2002.

Colleen and Uncle Squaty. *Fingerplays, Movement and Story Songs*. Colleen and Uncle Squaty, 1993.

———. *Movin' Party*. Colleen and Uncle Squaty, 2001.

———. *1, 2, 3, Four-Ever Friends*. Colleen and Uncle Squaty, 1995.

———. *Rumble to the Bottom*. Colleen and Uncle Squaty, 1997.

———. *Sing-a-Move-a-Dance*. Colleen and Uncle Squaty, 2005.

Cosgrove, Jim. *Bop Bop Dinosaur*. Hiccup, 1998.

———. *Mr. Stinky Feet's Road Trip*. Warner Brothers, 2005.

———. *Ooey Gooey*. Hiccup, 2001.

———. *Pick Me! Pick Me!* Hiccup, 2003.

———. *Stinky Feet*. Hiccup, 2002.

Craig n Co. *Rock n Together*. Craig n Co, 1998.

Crow, Dan. *Dan Crow Live*. Allshouse, 1992.

———. *A Friend, a Laugh, a Walk in the Woods*. Allshouse, 2000.

———. *The Giggling Dragon*. Allshouse, 2005.

———. *Oops!* Rounder, 1988.

Daddy A Go Go. *Big Rock Rooster*. Boyd's Tone, 2002.

———. *Cool Songs for Cool Kids*. Boyd's Tone, 1998.

———. *Eat Every Bean and Pea on Your Plate*. Boyd's Tone, 2006.

———. *Mojo A Go Go*. Boyd's Tone, 2004.

———. *Monkey in the Middle*. Boyd's Tone, 2000.

Dana. *Dana's Best Rock and Roll Fairy Tales*. RMFK, 1999.

———. *Dana's Best Sing and Play-a-Long Tunes*. RMFK, 1995.

———. *Dana's Best Sing and Swing-a-Long Tunes*. RMFK, 1997.

———. *Dana's Best Travelin' Tunes*. RMFK, 1995.

Del Bianco, Lou. *A Little Bit Clumsy*. Storymaker, 1995.

———. *Lost in School*. Storymaker, 2000.

———. *When I Was a Kid*. Storymaker, 1993.

Diamond, Charlotte. *Charlotte Diamond's World*. Hug Bug, 2000.

———. *Diamond in the Rough*. Hug Bug, 1986.

———. *Diamonds and Daydreams*. Hug Bug, 1996.

———. *Diamonds and Dragons*. Hug Bug, 1988.

———. *My Bear Gruff*. Hug Bug, 1992.

———. *10 Carrot Diamond*. Hug Bug, 1985.

The Dream Project. *We've All Got Stories*. Rounder, 1996.

Feldman, Jean. *Dr. Jean and Friends.* Jean Feldman, 1998.

———. *Dr. Jean Sings Silly Songs.* Jean Feldman, n.d.

———. *Is Everybody Happy?* Jean Feldman, 2001.

———. *Just for Fun!* Jean Feldman, 2005.

———. *Keep On Singing and Dancing with Dr. Jean.* Jean Feldman, 1999.

———. *Nursery Rhymes and Good Ol' Times.* Jean Feldman, 2002.

Fink, Cathy. *Grandma Slid down the Mountain.* Rounder, 1987.

———. *When the Rain Comes Down.* Rounder, 1988.

Fink, Cathy, and Marcy Marxer. *Air Guitar.* High Windy, 1993.

———. *All Wound Up!* Rounder, 2001.

———. *Blanket Full of Dreams.* Rounder, 1996.

———. *Bon Appétit!* Rounder, 2003.

———. *A Cathy & Marcy Collection for Kids.* Rounder, 1994.

———. *Changing Channels.* Rounder, 1996.

———. *Help Yourself.* Rounder, 1990.

———. *Nobody Else like Me.* Rounder, 1998.

———. *Pillow Full of Wishes.* Rounder, 2000.

———. *Pocket Full of Stardust.* Rounder, 2002.

———. *Scat like That.* Rounder, 2005.

Fite, Stephen. *Cool to Be in School.* Melody House, 2004.

———. *Gobs of Fun.* Melody House, 2005.

———. *Havin' Fun and Feelin' Groovy.* Melody House, 2001.

———. *Monkey Business.* Melody House, 1998.

———. *We're Just like Crayons.* Melody House, 1990.

———. *Wiggles, Jiggles, and Giggles.* Melody House, 2000.

Foote, Norman. *Foote Prints.* Disney, 1991.

———. *If the Shoe Fits.* Disney, 1992.

———. *1000 Pennies.* Norman Foote, 2001.

———. *Pictures on the Fridge.* Casablanca Kids, 1997.

———. *Shake a Leg.* Casablanca Kids, 1995.

Frezza, Rebecca. *Music in My Head.* Big Truck, 2002.

———. *Road Trip.* Big Truck, 2003.

———. *Tall and Small.* Big Truck, 2006.

Garcia, Jerry, and David Grisman. *Not for Kids Only.* Acoustic Disc, 1993.

Gemini. *The Best of Gemini.* Gemini, 1998.

———. *The Best of Gemini,* vol. 2. Gemini, 2005.

Gill, Jim. *Jim Gill Makes It Noisy in Boise, Idaho.* Jim Gill, 1995.

————. *Jim Gill Sings Do Re Mi on His Toe Leg Knee.* Jim Gill, 1999.

————. *Jim Gill Sings the Sneezing Song and Other Contagious Tunes.* Jim Gill, 1993.

————. *Jim Gill's Irrational Anthem.* Jim Gill, 2001.

————. *Moving Rhymes for Modern Times.* Jim Gill, 2006.

Grammer, Red. *Be Bop Your Best!* Red Note, 2005.

————. *Can You Sound Just like Me?* Smilin' Atcha, 1983.

————. *Down the Do-Re-Mi.* Red Note, 1991.

————. *Hello World.* Red Note, 1995.

————. *Red Grammer's Favorite Sing Along Songs.* Red Note, 1993.

————. *Teaching Peace.* Red Note, 1986.

Green Chili Jam Band. *Coconut Moon.* Squeaky Wheel, 1997.

————. *Magic Bike.* Green Chili Jam, 1991.

————. *Starfishing.* Green Chili Jam, 1993.

Greg and Steve. *Fun and Games.* Youngheart, 2002.

————. *Kidding Around.* Youngheart, 1985.

————. *Kids in Motion.* Youngheart, 1987.

————. *Playing Favorites.* Youngheart, 1991.

————. *Ready, Set, Move!* Greg and Steve, 2004.

————. *Rockin' down the Road.* Youngheart, 1995.

————. *We All Live Together,* vol. 1. Youngheart, 1975.

————. *We All Live Together,* vol. 2. Youngheart, 1978.

————. *We All Live Together,* vol. 3. Youngheart, 1979.

————. *We All Live Together,* vol. 4. Youngheart, 1980.

————. *We All Live Together,* vol. 5. Youngheart, 1994.

Grunsky, Jack. *Dancing Feet.* Casablanca Kids, 2004.

————. *Follow the Leader.* Casablanca Kids, 2002.

————. *Jack in the Box 1.* Casablanca Kids, 2001.

————. *Jack in the Box 2.* Casablanca Kids, 2001.

————. *Like a Flower to the Sun.* Casablanca Kids, 2003.

————. *Playground.* Casablanca Kids, 2001.

————. *Sing and Dance.* Casablanca Kids, 2000.

————. *World Safari.* Casablanca Kids, 2004.

Guthrie, Woody. *Nursery Days.* Smithsonian Folkways, 1992.

————. *Songs to Grow On for Mother and Child.* Smithsonian Folkways, 1991.

————. *Woody's 20 Grow Big Songs.* Warner Brothers, 1992.

Guthrie, Woody and Arlo. *This Land Is Your Land.* Rounder, 1997.

Harley, Bill. *Big Big World*. A&M, 1993.

———. *Down in the Backpack*. Round River, 2001.

———. *50 Ways to Fool Your Mother*. Round River, 1986.

———. *I Wanna Play*. Round River, 2007.

———. *Monsters in the Bathroom*. Round River, 1984.

———. *One More Time*. Round River, 2005.

———. *Play It Again*. Round River, 1999.

———. *There's a Pea on My Plate*. Round River, 1997.

———. *The Town around the Bend*. Round River, 2003.

———. *You're in Trouble*. Round River, 1988.

Harper, Jessica. *40 Winks*. Alacazam, 1998.

———. *Hey, Picasso*. Rounder, 2004.

———. *Inside Out*. Rounder, 2001.

———. *Nora's Room*. Alacazam, 1996.

———. *Rhythm in My Shoes*. Rounder, 2000.

———. *A Wonderful Life*. Alacazam, 1994.

Harper, Monty. *The Great Green Squishy Mean Concert CD*. Monty Harper, 2005.

———. *Imagine That*. Monty Harper, 1996.

———. *Jungle Junk!* Monty Harper, 1992.

———. *Take Me to Your Library*. Monty Harper, 2003.

Haynes, Sammie. *Nature's ABCs*. A Gentle Wind, 2004.

Herdman, Priscilla. *Daydreamer*. Music for Little People, 1993.

———. *Stardreamer*. Alacazam, 1988.

Hinojosa, Tish. *Cada Niño: Every Child*. Rounder, 1996.

Hinton, Sam. *Whoever Shall Have Some Good Peanuts*. Smithsonian Folkways, 2006.

Howdy, Buck. *Giddyup!* Prairie Dog Entertainment, 2005.

———. *Skidaddle!* MCA, 2003.

Hullabaloo. *Sing Along with Sam*. Hullabaloo, 2006.

Ives, Burl. *Burl Ives Sings Little White Duck*. Columbia, 1974.

Jenkins, Ella. *Growing Up with Ella Jenkins*. Smithsonian Folkways, 2002.

———. *Sharing Cultures with Ella Jenkins*. Smithsonian Folkways, 2003.

———. *Songs Children Love to Sing*. Smithsonian Folkways, 1996.

Jonas, Billy. *What Kind of Cat Are You?!* Bang-a-Bucket, 2002.

Kaldor, Connie. *A Duck in New York City*. Folle Avoine, 2003.

———. *A Poodle in Paris*. Folle Avoine, 2004.

Kaye, Mary. *I Sang It Just for You*. Mary Kaye, 2003.

———. *Mouse Jamboree*. Mary Kaye, 2004.

———. *Spin Your Web*. Mary Kaye, 2006.

Kimmy Schwimmy. *Kimmy Schwimmy Music*, vol. 1. North Corner, 2005.

Kinder, Brian. *Again*. Brian Kinder, 2003.

———. *A Kid like You*. Brian Kinder, 2002.

———. *One More Time*. Brian Kinder, 2004.

Kinnoin, Dave. *Daring Dewey*. Song Wizard, 1990.

———. *Dunce Cap Kelly*. Song Wizard, 1993.

———. *Getting Bigger*. Song Wizard, 1997.

Kirk, John, and Trish Miller. *The Big Rock Candy Mountain*. A Gentle Wind, 2004.

Knight, Tom. *The Classroom Boogie*. Tom Knight, 2003.

———. *Don't Kiss a Codfish/When I Grow Up*. Tom Knight, 2005.

———. *Easy as Pie*. Tom Knight, 1992.

———. *The Library Boogie*. Tom Knight, 2001.

Ladysmith Black Mambazo. *Gift of the Tortoise*. Music for Little People, 1994.

LaFond, Lois. *I Am Who I Am*. Zoom Express, 1985.

———. *Lois LaFond and the Rockadiles*. Rockadile, 1998.

———. *One World*. Rockadile, 1989.

———. *Turning It Upside Down*. Rockadile, 1994.

The Learning Station. *All-Time Children's Favorites*. Monopoli/Learning Station, 1993.

———. *Children Love to Sing and Dance*. Monopoli/Learning Station, 1987.

———. *Get Funky and Musical Fun*. Monopoli/Learning Station, 2003.

———. *Here We Go Loopty Loo*. Monopoli/Learning Station, 1998.

———. *La Di Da La Di Di Dance with Me*. Monopoli/Learning Station, 2004.

———. *Literacy in Motion*. Monopoli/Learning Station, 2005.

———. *Rock n' Roll Songs That Teach*. Monopoli/Learning Station, 1997.

———. *Seasonal Songs in Motion*. Monopoli/Learning Station, 2001.

———. *Singing, Moving, and Fun*. Monopoli/Learning Station, 1986.

———. *Tony Chestnut and Fun Time Action Songs*. Monopoli/Learning Station, 1997.

Lithgow, John. *Farkle and Friends*. Kid Rhino, 2002.

———. *Singin' in the Bathtub*. Sony, 1999.

Livingston, Bob. *Open the Window*. A Gentle Wind, 1991.

Lonnquist, Ken. *The Circus Kenlando*. Kenland, 1996.

———. *Earthy Songs*. Kenland, 2006.

———. *The Lost Songs of Kenland*. Kenland, 1998.

———. *Sci-Fi Hi-Fi*. Kenland, 1999.

———. *The Switcher-On of Stars*. Kenland, 2000.

———. *Welcome 2 Kenland*. Kenland, 1992.

Madsen, Gunnar. *Ants in My Pants!* G-Spot, 2001.

———. *Old Mr. Mackle Hackle*. G-Spot, 1999.

Magical Music Express. *Friendship Stew*. A Gentle Wind, 2001.

———. *Music Is Magic*. Magical Music Express, 2002.

Marxer, Marcy. *Jump Children*. Rounder, 1997.

Mayer, Hans. *Just a Little Hug*. Myther, 1996.

———. *See You Later, Alligator*. Myther, 1997.

———. *Stars of the Swing Set*. Myther, 1999.

McCutcheon, John. *Autumnsongs*. Rounder, 1998.

———. *Bigger Than Yourself*. Rounder, 1997.

———. *Family Garden*. Rounder, 1993.

———. *Howjadoo*. Rounder, 1986.

———. *Mail Myself to You*. Rounder, 1988.

———. *Springsongs*. Rounder, 1999.

———. *Summersongs*. Rounder, 1995.

———. *Wintersongs*. Rounder, 1995.

McGrath, Bob. *Sing Along with Bob #1*. Golden Books, 1985.

———. *Sing Along with Bob #2*. Golden Books, 1990.

McGrath, Bob, and Katherine Smithrim. *Songs and Games for Toddlers*. Kids' Records, 1985.

McMahon, Elizabeth. *Blue Sky Sparklin' Day*. Rosie Rhubarb, 1993.

———. *Magic Parade*. Mrs. McPuppet, 2006.

———. *Tea Party Shuffle*. Rosie Rhubarb, 1997.

———. *Waltzing with Fireflies*. Rosie Rhubarb, 1999.

Milkshake. *Bottle of Sunshine*. Milkshake, 2004.

———. *Happy Songs*. Milkshake, 2002.

———. *Play!* Milkshake, 2007.

Miss Amy. *Underwater*. Ionian, 2004.

———. *Wide, Wide World*. Ionian, 2005.

———. *You Are My Flower*. Last Affair, 1998.

———. *You Are My Little Bird*. Smithsonian Folkways, 2006.

———. *You Are My Sunshine*. Last Affair, 2002.

Moo, Anna. *Anna Moo Crackers*. Moosic, 1994.

———. *Making Moosic*. Good Moo's, 1992.

———. *Moochas Gracias*. Good Moo's, 2002.

———. *When I Was a Child*. Good Moo's, 1996.

Mr. Al. *Dance like This*. Cradle Rock, 2000.

———. *Mr. Al a Carte*. Cradle Rock, 1998.

———. *Mr. Al Concert Live*. Cradle Rock, 2004.

———. *Put Your Groove On*. Cradle Rock, 2002.

———. *Rockin' the Alphabet*. Cradle Rock, 1998.

———. *Sing Me a Color*. Cradle Rock, 2001.

Mr. Al and Stephen Fite. *Back to School Again*. Melody House, 1996.

Muldaur, Maria. *Animal Crackers in My Soup*. Music for Little People, 2002.

———. *On the Sunny Side*. Music for Little People, 1990.

———. *Swingin' in the Rain*. Music for Little People, 1998.

Nagler, Eric. *Improvise with Eric Nagler*. Rounder, 1989.

Ode, Eric. *Grandpa's Truck*. Deep Rooted, 2003.

———. *I Love My Shoes*. Deep Rooted, 2005.

———. *Trash Can*. Deep Rooted, 2002.

Old Town School of Folk Music. *Wiggleworms Love You*. Old Town School, 2005.

Palmer, Hap. *Can a Cherry Pie Wave Goodbye?* Hap-Pal, 1991.

———. *Can a Jumbo Jet Sing the Alphabet?* Hap-Pal, 1998.

———. *Can Cockatoos Count by Twos?* Hap-Pal, 1996.

———. *One Little Sound*. Hap-Pal, 2002.

———. *Peek-a-Boo*. Hap-Pal, 1990.

———. *So Big*. Hap-Pal, 1994.

———. *Turn On the Music*. Hap-Pal, 1997.

———. *Two Little Sounds*. Hap-Pal, 2003.

Parachute Express. *Doctor Looney's Remedy*. Trio Lane, 1998.

———. *Don't Blink*. Trio Lane, 2004.

———. *Feel the Music*. Disney, 1991.

———. *Friends, Forever Friends*. Trio Lane, 1996.

———. *Sunny Side Up*. Disney, 1991.

———. *Who's Got a Hug?* Trio Lane, 1998.

Paxton, Tom. *Goin' to the Zoo*. Rounder, 1997.

———. *I've Got a Yo-Yo*. Rounder, 1997.

———. *Your Shoes, My Shoes*. Red House, 2002.

Pease, Tom. *Boogie! Boogie! Boogie!* Tomorrow River, 1986.

———. *Daddy Starts to Dance*. Tomorrow River, 1996.

———. *I'm Gonna Reach!* Tomorrow River, 1989.

———. *Wobbi-Do-Wop!* Tomorrow River, 1993.

Pelham, Ruth. *Under One Sky*. A Gentle Wind, 1982.

Penner, Fred. *Fred's Favourites*. Casablanca Kids, 2004.

———. *My First Adventure*. Casablanca Kids, 2002.

———. *Rhyme a Word or Two*. Casablanca Kids, 2004.

———. *Sing with Fred*. Casablanca Kids, 2002.

———. *Storytime*. Casablanca Kids, 2002.

———. *What a Day!* Casablanca Kids, 1994.

Peter, Paul, and Mary. *Peter, Paul, and Mommy*. Warner Brothers, 1969.

———. *Peter, Paul, and Mommy, Too*. Warner Brothers, 1993.

Peterson, Carole. *H.U.M.—All Year Long*. Macaroni Soup, 2003.

———. *Sticky Bubble Gum*. Macaroni Soup, 2002.

———. *Stinky Cake*. Macaroni Soup, 2005.

———. *Tiny Tunes*. Macaroni Soup, 2005.

Pirtle, Sarah. *Heart of the World*. A Gentle Wind, 2002.

———. *Magical Earth*. A Gentle Wind, 1993.

———. *Two Hands Hold the Earth*. A Gentle Wind, 1984.

———. *The Wind Is Telling Secrets*. A Gentle Wind, 1988.

Polisar, Barry Louis. *Family Concert*. Rainbow Morning, 1993.

———. *Family Trip*. Rainbow Morning, 1993.

———. *Juggling Babies*. Rainbow Morning, 1993.

———. *Naughty Songs for Boys and Girls*. Rainbow Morning, 1993.

———. *Old Dog, New Tricks*. Rainbow Morning, 1993.

———. *Old Enough to Know Better*. Rainbow Morning, 2005.

———. *Teacher's Favorites*. Rainbow Morning, 1993.

Pullara, Steve. *A Big Bowl of Musicroni*. Cool Beans, 2005.

———. *Hop like a Frog*. Cool Beans, 1997.

———. *One Potato, Two Potato*. Cool Beans, 1995.

———. *Spinning Tails*. Cool Beans, 2001.

Raffi. *Baby Beluga*. Troubadour, 1980.

———. *Bananaphone*. Troubadour, 1994.

———. *Corner Grocery Store*. Troubadour, 1979.

———. *Evergreen, Everblue*. Troubadour, 1990.

———. *Everything Grows*. Troubadour, 1987.

———. *Let's Play*. Troubadour, 2002.

————. *More Singable Songs*. Troubadour, 1977.

————. *One Light One Sun*. Troubadour, 1987.

————. *Quiet Time*. Rounder, 2006.

————. *Raffi in Concert*. Troubadour, 1989.

————. *Raffi Radio*. Troubadour, 1995.

————. *Rise and Shine*. Troubadour, 1982.

————. *Singable Songs for the Very Young*. Troubadour, 1976.

Ralph's World. *The Amazing Adventures of Kid Astro*. Mini Fresh, 2004.

————. *At the Bottom of the Sea*. Mini Fresh, 2002.

————. *Green Gorilla, Monster, and Me*. Disney, 2006.

————. *Happy Lemon*. Mini Fresh, 2002.

————. *Peggy's Pie Parlor*. Mini Fresh, 2003.

————. *Ralph's World*. Mini Fresh, 2001.

Raven, Nancy. *Friends and Family*. Lizard's Rock, 2003.

————. *Hop, Skip, and Sing/Singing in a Circle and Activity Songs*. Lizard's Rock, 2003.

————. *The House We Live In*, vols. 1 and 2. Lizard's Rock, 2003.

————. *Jambalaya!* Lizard's Rock, 2003.

————. *Nancy Raven Sings Her Favorites*. Lizard's Rock, 2003.

————. *People and Animal Songs/Lullabies and Other Children's Songs*. Lizard's Rock, 2003.

————. *Singing, Prancing, and Dancing*. Lizard's Rock, 2003.

————. *You Gotta Juba*. Lizard's Rock, 2003.

Riders in the Sky. *Harmony Ranch*. Sony, 1991.

————. *Saddle Pals*. Rounder, 1987.

Roberts, Justin. *Great Big Sun*. Justin Roberts, 1997.

————. *Meltdown!* Justin Roberts, 2006.

————. *Not Naptime*. Justin Roberts, 2002.

————. *Way Out*. Justin Roberts, 2004.

————. *Yellow Bus*. Justin Roberts, 2001.

Rosen, Gary. *Cookin'*. GMR, 1996.

————. *Pet Sounds*. GMR, 2005.

————. *Teddy Bears' Picnic*. GMR, 1999.

————. *Tot Rock*. Lightyear, 1993.

Rosenshontz. *Family Vacation*. Lightyear, 1992.

————. *Rock 'n Roll Teddy Bear*. Lightyear, 1992.

————. *Rosenshontz Greatest Hits*. Lightyear, 1994.

————. *Share It*. RS, 1982.

————. *Tickles You!* Lightyear, 1991.

————. *Uh-Oh!* Lightyear, 1991.

Rosenthal, Phil. *Animal Songs*. American Melody, 1996.

————. *Folksongs and Bluegrass for Children*. Rounder, 2000.

————. *The Green Grass Grew All Around*. American Melody, 1995.

————. *The Paw Paw Patch*. American Melody, 1987.

————. *Turkey in the Straw*. American Melody, 1997.

Roth, Kevin. *Dinosaurs and Dragons*. Sony, 1992.

————. *Train Songs and Other Tracks*. Marlboro, 1994.

————. *Travel Song Sing Alongs*. Marlboro, 1994.

————. *Unbearable Bears*. Marlboro, 1985.

Rudnick, Ben. *Blast Off!* Ben Rudnick, 2004.

————. *Emily Songs*. Ben Rudnick, 2000.

————. *Fun and Games*. Listen Up, 2002.

Rymer, Brady. *Every Day Is a Birthday*. Bumblin' Bee, 2006.

————. *I Found It!* Bumblin' Bee, 2004.

————. *Look at My Belly*. Bumblin' Bee, 2002.

Scruggs, Joe. *Abracadabra*. Educational Graphics, 1986.

————. *Ants*. Educational Graphics, 1994.

————. *Bahamas Pajamas*. Educational Graphics, 1990.

————. *Deep in the Jungle*. Educational Graphics, 1987.

————. *Even Trolls Have Moms*. Educational Graphics, 1988.

————. *Late Last Night*. Educational Graphics, 1984.

————. *Traffic Jams*. Educational Graphics, 1985.

Seeger, Pete. *For Kids and Just Plain Folks*. Sony, 1997.

————. *Pete Seeger's Family Concert*. Sony, 1992.

Sharon, Lois, and Bram. *Everybody Sing!* Casablanca Kids, 2002.

————. *Great Big Hits*. Elephant, 1992.

————. *Great Big Hits 2*. Elephant, 2002.

————. *Mainly Mother Goose*. Elephant, 1984.

————. *Name Games*. Casablanca Kids, 2002.

————. *One Elephant, Deux Éléphants*. Elephant, 1980.

————. *School Days*. Casablanca Kids, 2004.

————. *Sing A to Z*. Elephant, 1990.

————. *Sleepytime*. Casablanca Kids, 2002.

Shontz, Bill. *Animal Tales*. Lightyear, 1993.

———. *The Day I Read a Book.* Bearspaw, 1998.

———. *Teddy Bear's Greatest Hits.* Bearspaw, 1997.

Silberg, "Miss Jackie." *The Complete Sniggles, Squirrels, and Chicken Pox.* Miss Jackie, n.d.

———. *Joining Hands with Other Lands.* Kimbo, 1993.

———. *Lollipops and Spaghetti.* Miss Jackie, 1979.

———. *Peanut Butter, Tarzan, and Roosters.* Miss Jackie, 1981.

———. *Sing about Martin.* Miss Jackie, 2005.

———. *Sing It Again Please.* Miss Jackie, n.d.

———. *Touched by a Song.* Miss Jackie, 2004.

Simmons, Al. *The Celery Stalks at Midnight.* Casablanca Kids, 1996.

———. *Something Fishy at Camp Wiganishie.* Casablanca Kids, 1995.

———. *The Truck I Bought from Moe.* Casablanca Kids, 1997.

Sprout, Jonathan. *Dr. Music.* Sprout, 1993.

———. *Kid Power.* Sprout, 1991.

———. *On the Radio.* Sprout, 1986.

Staines, Bill. *The Happy Wanderer.* Red House, 1993.

———. *One More River.* Red House, 1998.

SteveSongs. *Little Superman.* SteveSongs, 2003.

———. *Marvelous Day!* Rounder, 2006.

———. *Morning til Night.* Steve Roslonek, 1998.

———. *On a Flying Guitar.* SteveSongs, 2000.

Stotts, Stuart. *Are We There Yet?* Tomorrow River, 1991.

———. *One Big Dance.* Tomorrow River, 1996.

Stotts, Stuart, and Tom Pease. *Celebrate: A Song Resource.* Tomorrow River, 2000.

Strausman, Paul. *Blue Jay, Blue Jay!* A Gentle Wind, 1997.

———. *Camels, Cats, and Rainbows.* A Gentle Wind, 1982.

———. *Rainbows, Stones, and Dinosaur Bones.* A Gentle Wind, 1984.

———. *The World's Big Family.* A Gentle Wind, 1987.

Sweet Honey in the Rock. *All for Freedom.* Music for Little People, 1989.

———. *I Got Shoes.* Music for Little People, 1994.

———. *Still the Same Me.* Rounder, 2000.

Thaddeus Rex. *Martian Television Invasion.* Thaddeus Rex, 2005.

———. *We Wanna Rock.* Thaddeus Rex, 2006.

They Might Be Giants. *Here Come the ABCs.* Disney, 2005.

Tickle Tune Typhoon. *All of Us Will Shine.* A Gentle Wind, 1987.

———. *Circle Around.* Tickle Tune Typhoon, 1983.

————. *Healthy Beginnings*. Tickle Tune Typhoon, 1993.

————. *Hearts and Hands*. Music for Little People, 1991.

————. *Patty-Cakes and Peek-a-Boos*. Music for Little People, 1994.

————. *Singing Science*. Music for Little People, 2000.

Troubadour. *On the Trail*. A Gentle Wind, 1990.

Trout Fishing in America. *Big Trouble*. Trout, 1991.

————. *Family Music Party*. Trout, 1998.

————. *InFINity*. Trout, 2001.

————. *It's a Puzzle*. Trout, 2003.

————. *Mine!* Trout, 1994.

————. *My Best Day*. Trout, 2006.

————. *My World*. Trout, 1997.

Tucker, Nancy. *Escape of the Slinkys*. A Gentle Wind, 2005.

————. *Glad That You Asked*. A Gentle Wind, 1988.

————. *Happy as a Clam*. Nancy Tucker, 1989.

Ungar, Jay, and Lyn Hardy. *A Place to Be*. A Gentle Wind, 1981.

Various Artists. *African Playground*. Putumayo, 2003.

————. *Asian Dreamland*. Putumayo, 2006.

————. *Caribbean Playground*. Putumayo, 2004.

————. *cELLAbration! A Tribute to Ella Jenkins*. Smithsonian Folkways, 2004.

————. *A Child's Celebration of Folk Music*. Music for Little People, 1996.

————. *A Child's Celebration of Silliest Songs*. Music for Little People, 1999.

————. *A Child's Celebration of Song*. Music for Little People, 1992.

————. *A Child's Celebration of Song 2*. Music for Little People, 1996.

————. *A Child's Celebration of the World*. Music for Little People, 1998.

————. *Dreamland*. Putumayo, 2003.

————. *Folk Playground*. Putumayo, 2006.

————. *French Playground*. Putumayo, 2005.

————. *Grandma's Patchwork Quilt*. American Melody, 1987.

————. *Hear and Gone in 60 Seconds*. Rounder, 2003.

————. *I'm Gonna Let It Shine*. Round River, 1991.

————. *Latin Playground*. Putumayo, 2002.

————. *Peace Is the World Smiling*. Music for Little People, 1989.

————. *The Planet Sleeps*. Sony, 1997.

————. *Reggae Playground*. Putumayo, 2006.

————. *Sing Along with Putumayo*. Putumayo, 2004.

————. *World Playground*. Putumayo, 1998.

———. *World Playground 2.* Putumayo, 2001.

Vitamin L. *Every Moment!* Lovable Creature, 1994.

———. *Everyone's Invited!* Lovable Creature, 1991.

———. *Swingin' in the Key of L.* Lovable Creature, 1992.

———. *Walk a Mile.* Lovable Creature, 1989.

Walker, Graham. *Cats' Night Out.* Laughing Fox, 1986.

———. *Fiddlesticks.* Laughing Fox Music, 2005.

———. *Jumpety Jump.* Graham Walker, 2001.

———. *Knobbledee Knees.* Laughing Fox, 2003.

Walker, Mary Lu. *The Frog's Party.* A Gentle Wind, 1989.

Yosi. *Monkey Business.* Yosi, 2002.

———. *Under a Big Bright Yellow Umbrella.* Yosi, 2004.

———. *What's Eatin' Yosi?* Yosi, 2006.

Zanes, Dan. *Catch That Train!* Festival Five, 2006.

———. *Family Dance.* Festival Five, 2001.

———. *House Party.* Festival Five, 2003.

———. *Night Time!* Festival Five, 2002.

———. *Rocket Ship Beach.* Festival Five, 2000.

A Recommended Core Collection

Few individuals or institutions are going to invest in the 547 recordings featured in this index. This list of forty-six children's musical recordings is a good starting point from which to build a collection. There is something magical and creative about each of the selections, from the simple delivery for infants and toddlers in Rachel Buchman's *Hello Everybody!* to the creative, complex arrangements of Tom Chapin's *Some Assembly Required*.

Allard, Peter and Ellen. *Sing It! Say It! Stamp It! Sway It!* vol. 2.
All three volumes of this series are great. Highlights of the very practical second volume include the body movement songs "Glad to See You," "That's the Way It Goes," and "Wiggle Your Fingers."

Alsop, Peter. *Wha' D'Ya Wanna Do?*
Alsop wrote some of the best original children's songs ever. Some appear here, such as "I Am a Pizza," "Don't Trick Your Dad," and "You Get a Little Extra When You Watch T.V."

Banana Slug String Band. *Penguins on Parade.*
This band's specialty is nature and ecology songs; this recording finds them at the top of their game. Highlights include "Noses," "Croak-a-Ribit," and the hilarious "Moose."

Barchas, Sarah. *Bridges across the World.*
One of the best multicultural recordings ever produced for children. Get a glimpse of the world and different languages with songs such as "Children of the World Say Hello" and "Happy Birthday around the World."

Beall, Pamela, and Susan Nipp. *Wee Sing Silly Songs.*
The Wee Sing series makes a wealthy treasury of traditional children's songs. Nonsensical highlights in this volume include "Little Bunny Foo Foo," "My Hat It Has Three Corners," and "One Bottle o' Pop."

Big Jeff. *Big Jeff.*
Big Jeff's easy-going yet funny manner will get the kids involved, with playful songs such as "A New Way to Say Hello," "Down the Sidewalk," and the hilarious "The Orange Song."

Buchman, Rachel. *Hello Everybody!*
This is my favorite recording for the toddler set. I've gotten a lot of mileage out of sharing Buchman's versions of "Hello Ev'rybody!" and "I Think I'll Try Some."

Chapin, Tom. *Some Assembly Required.*
Pick any Chapin recording for your core collection. The highlights of this particular recording are the hilarious "Don't Make Me Dance" and the amazingly inspirational "Walk the World Now, Children."

The Dream Project. *We've All Got Stories.*
Listen to the energetic "Welcome to My World" and "We've All Got Stories" (off-key notes and all), as well as a soulful "Old MacDonald" that will knock your socks off.

Fink, Cathy, and Marcy Marxer. *A Cathy & Marcy Collection for Kids.*
This collection highlights the best of this veteran duo's early works, such as "When the Rain Comes Down," "Jump Children," "Grandma Slid down the Mountain," and "It's a Beautiful Day."

Garcia, Jerry, and David Grisman. *Not for Kids Only.*
A truer title has never been issued. All ages will enjoy these traditional tunes, such as "There Ain't No Bugs on Me" and "Teddy Bears' Picnic," as well as Elizabeth Cotton's "Freight Train."

Gill, Jim. *Jim Gill Makes It Noisy in Boise, Idaho.*
Gill gets things started with "List of Dances," which will not only get kids moving, but spark their creativity, too. The fun continues with "Oh Hey Oh Hi Hello" and "The Sound Effects Song."

Grammer, Red. *Down the Do-Re-Mi.*
Grammer's powerful voice is showcased on both cover songs, such as Bill Staines's "A Place in the Choir," and original Grammer compositions, such as "The ABCs of You" and the stunning "Brothers and Sisters."

Grunsky, Jack. *Jack in the Box 1.*
Many of Grunsky's songs have been repackaged in the Jack in the Box series. This volume contains his two best songs—the beautiful "With My Own Two Hands" and "Songbirds."

Guthrie, Woody. *Woody's 20 Grow Big Songs.*
Is there anyone who has created better children's songs than Woody Guthrie? Original Guthrie recordings are woven around contemporary recordings by members of the Guthrie family. Highlights include "Needle Sing" and the tongue-twister "Mailman."

Harley, Bill. *Big, Big World.*
Harley is also in the top echelon of children's recording artists. Highlights here include covers of "Walk a Mile" and "Turn the World Around" and his original composition "Sittin' Down to Eat."

Harper, Jessica. *Rhythm in My Shoes.*
Actress Harper is a natural children's songwriter, singer, and arranger. Listen to her smooth, pleasant renditions of "I'm Not Going to Chase the Cat Today," "My Baby Is a Genius," and "Girlquake."

Herdman, Priscilla. *Daydreamer.*
Herdman delivers crystal-clear interpretations of modern-day children's classics, such as John McCutcheon's "Kindergarten Wall," Carol Johnson's "Love Grows One by One," and the classic standard "What a Wonderful World."

Hinton, Sam. *Whoever Shall Have Some Good Peanuts.*
This reissue by Smithsonian Folkways showcases Hinton's wonderful interpretations of traditional songs ranging from "Old Dan Tucker" and "A Horse Named Bill" to "Mr. Rabbit" and "Frog Went A-Courtin'."

Jonas, Billy. *What Kind of Cat Are You?!*
Jonas specializes in percussion, with songs such as "Tongo" and "Old St. Helen," a song about the volcano. The wordplay and child interaction of the title song is precious.

Kinder, Brian. *A Kid like You.*
Kinder is a creative songwriter with a great, unique voice. Everyone will be gyrating with the inventive "Must Be Working" and singing along to the infectious call-and-response song "Echo Gecko."

Kirk, John, and Trish Miller. *The Big Rock Candy Mountain.*
The highlights of this solid collection include the duo's "I Read It in a Book" and a fun version of "Old MacDonald" that blends snippets of traditional songs, such as "Bingo" and "The Little Skunk's Hole."

The Learning Station. *Literacy in Motion.*
Each of these twenty songs was developed around a specific children's book. Examples include the song "No No No" for David Shannon's book *No David*, and "Wild Things" for Maurice Sendak's *Where the Wild Things Are.*

Lithgow, John. *Singin' in the Bathtub.*
Actor Lithgow shares several standard classics, such as "A You're Adorable" and "Everyone Eats When They Come to My House," as well as a fun, over-the-top rendition of "I Had a Rooster."

Livingston, Bob. *Open the Window.*
The title track of this fun bunch of songs should be considered a modern-day classic. Other highlights include "What Do You Want (To Know)" and the playful, noisy "Dog Songs."

McCutcheon, John. *Mail Myself to You.*
McCutcheon gives his unique delivery on several classics, including "I'm a Little Cookie," "Somos El Barco," and "Turn Around," as well as his original modern-day classic "Kindergarten Wall."

Mitchell, Elizabeth. *You Are My Little Bird.*
Mitchell's gorgeous vocals are the focus of this delightful collection of traditional and contemporary children's songs. Highlights include Woody Guthrie's "Who's My Pretty Baby" and the magical "If You Listen."

Nagler, Eric. *Improvise with Eric Nagler.*
Here it is—my favorite children's recording! Nagler opens with a lively version of "Howjadoo" and keeps up the creative energy through "Cluck Old Hen," "Super Mom," "Jumping in the Leaves," "You Just Improvise," and the closer "Lulu Lullaby."

Paxton, Tom. *Goin' to the Zoo.*
Many of Paxton's most popular songs can be found on this recording, including the title cut, "The Marvelous Toy," "My Dog's Bigger Than Your Dog," "Englebert the Elephant," and "Jennifer's Rabbit."

Pease, Tom. *Boogie! Boogie! Boogie!*
I've seen Pease in concert several times and believe he has enough energy to power the world. Pick up on his enthusiasm through such songs as "World Citizen," "Many Cows," and even the quiet closer "Sabonana Kusasa."

Pelham, Ruth. *Under One Sky.*
The title song is a beautiful, simple, catchy sing-along and one of the best children's songs ever. So are her songs "If I Could Be Anything," "Rainbow 'round Me," "Wake You in the Morning," and "What Do I Do?"

Penner, Fred. *Fred's Favourites.*
This best-of collection showcases Penner's career through songs such as "What a Day," "Trans Canadian Super Continental Special Express," and his best song, "I Am the Wind."

Pirtle, Sarah. *Magical Earth.*
Pirtle's recording is a wonderful showcase of our global music community, and that is reflected through songs like "The Other Side of the World," "Paz y Libertad," "Walls and Bridges," and "Follow the Voice."

Polisar, Barry Louis. *Old Dog, New Tricks.*
This recording features many of Polisar's best animal songs, such as "I Wanna Be a Dog," "I've Got a Dog and My Dog's Name Is Cat," and the catchy "I'm a Three-Toed, Triple-Eyed, Double-Jointed Dinosaur."

Raffi. *Singable Songs for the Very Young.*
This is the touchstone recording that revolutionized the children's music industry. Sing along with "Down by the Bay," "Spider on the Floor," "Mr. Sun," and other trademark Raffi songs. And then buy all of his other recordings.

Ralph's World. *Peggy's Pie Parlor.*
Meet the new Raffi! Ralph Covert has quickly become one of the most popular new children's entertainers of the new century. His "Puppy Dog" song is an instant classic, and "I Never See Maggie Alone" is hilarious.

Roberts, Justin. *Way Out.*
Roberts is another popular newcomer who shows that the children's music industry is in good shape. Highlights of this particular recording include "Roller in the Coaster" and "Bigger."

Rosenshontz. *Rosenshontz Greatest Hits.*
This duo created magic together. This recording is just a small sample of their work together—including "These Are the Questions," "Share It," and "Sleep Sleep"—as well as songs from their respective solo careers. Buy their entire inventory.

Rosenthal, Phil. *Folksongs and Bluegrass for Children.*
Rosenthal does the best job of introducing traditional songs for today's child. This is a nice representation of his work, frequently featuring his family. Listen to the wonderful renditions of "Hop High, Ladies" and "The Paw Paw Patch."

Sharon, Lois, and Bram. *Great Big Hits.*
This trio regularly developed the most inventive arrangements to traditional songs. Listen to what they did to "How Much Is That Doggie in the Window?" Also featured are their trademark songs "One Elephant" and "Skinnimarink."

Silberg, "Miss Jackie." *Peanut Butter, Tarzan, and Roosters.*
Along with Buchman's *Hello Everybody!* this is a fantastic model recording for anyone working with very young children. Listen to the effective deliveries of "I See a Horsie" and "Old MacDonald Had a 'Whzz.'"

Staines, Bill. *The Happy Wanderer.*

Staines wrote one of the best children's songs ever with "A Place in the Choir." Enjoy this and another strong Staines composition, "First Lullaby," plus his treatment of several classics, such as "Little Brown Dog."

Trout Fishing in America. *My World.*

Everyone will be laughing at "Six," "Beans and Weenies," "Baby's Got the Car Keys," and "My Hair Had a Party Last Night." Add "Science Fair" to the list of best-ever children's songs.

Various Artists. *Caribbean Playground.*

You can't go wrong with any of the Putumayo Kids recordings. This particular album will have your toes tapping to "Jamaica Farewell," "Three Little Birds," and Taj Mahal's great version of "Great Big Boat."

Various Artists. *cELLAbration! A Tribute to Ella Jenkins.*

Tom Chapin, Bill Harley, and many more artists gathered together to honor the music of Ella Jenkins. Cathy Fink starts the party off with my favorite Jenkins song, "You'll Sing a Song and I'll Sing a Song."

Zanes, Dan. *Family Dance.*

Zanes is my favorite of the recent slate of children's artists. Buy all of his recordings. This particular recording contains the lively "Jump Up," "All around the Kitchen," and "Water for the Elephants," which may be the best circus song ever.

Rob's Favorite Original Children's Songs

This list features my favorite contemporary, original children's songs. The song's composer(s) is listed in parentheses along with one recording on which the song appears. Check them all out, including my favorite children's song—"Walk a Mile" by Jan Nigro.

"All across This Wide Wide World" (Sarah Barchas)—Barchas, Sarah, *Bridges across the World*.

"All around the World" (Cathy Fink)—Fink, Cathy, and Marcy Marxer, *A Pillow Full of Wishes*.

"All Work Together" (Woody Guthrie)—Guthrie, Woody, *Woody's 20 Grow Big Songs*.

"Alligator Stomp" (Anna Moo)—Moo, Anna, *Anna Moo Crackers*.

"A Beautiful Day" (Gary Rosen)—Rosenshontz, *Tickles You!*

"Bedtime Round" (John Forster, Tom Chapin)—Chapin, Tom, *Billy the Squid*.

"Bigger" (Justin Roberts)—Roberts, Justin, *Way Out*.

"Bling Blang" (Woody Guthrie)—Guthrie, Woody, *Woody's 20 Grow Big Songs*.

"Brothers and Sisters" (Kathy Grammer, Red Grammer)—Grammer, Red, *Down the Do-Re-Mi*.

"Calling All Children" (Jessica Harper)—Harper, Jessica, *40 Winks*.

"Come On Down" (Joe Scruggs)—Scruggs, Joe, *Ants*.

"Cowgirl Song" (Ben Rudnick, Emily Rudnick)—Rudnick, Ben, *Emily Songs*.

"The Crow's Toes" (Tom Paxton)—Paxton, Tom, *I've Got a Yo-Yo*.

"Dance Around" (Woody Guthrie)—Guthrie, Woody, *Nursery Days*.

"Deepest Africa" (Jan Harmon)—The Chenille Sisters, *Teaching Hippopotami to Fly!*

♪ 23 ♪

"Dogs" (Dan Crow)—Crow, Dan, *Oops!*

"Don't Make Me Dance" (John Forster, Tom Chapin)—Chapin, Tom, *Some Assembly Required*.

"Don't Make Me Sing Along" (Lisa Lambert)—Simmons, Al, *The Celery Stalks at Midnight*.

"Don't Trick Your Dad" (Peter Alsop)—Alsop, Peter, *Wha' D'Ya Wanna Do?*

"Dreams of Harmony" (Joanne Olshansky Hammil)—Various Artists, *A Child's Celebration of the World*.

"Dreamtime Rendezvous" (Kathy Grammer, Red Grammer)—Grammer, Red, *Down the Do-Re-Mi*.

"11 Easy Steps" (Keith Grimwood, Ezra Idlet)—Trout Fishing in America, *Family Music Party*.

"Evergreen, Everblue" (Raffi)—Raffi, *Evergreen, Everblue*.

"Everything Grows" (Raffi)—Raffi, *Everything Grows*.

"Excuses" (Judith Steinberg, Victor Cockburn)—Troubadour, *On the Trail*.

"First Lullaby" (Bill Staines)—Staines, Bill, *The Happy Wanderer*.

"Follow the Voice" (Sarah Pirtle)—Pirtle, Sarah, *Magic Earth*.

"For Who I Am" (Ken Lonnquist)—Lonnquist, Ken, *Sci-Fi Hi-Fi*.

"Garden Song" (David Mallett)—Peter, Paul, and Mary, *Peter, Paul, and Mommy, Too*.

"Get off the Computer" (John Boydston)—Daddy A Go Go, *Big Rock Rooster*.

"Goin' to the Zoo" (Tom Paxton)—Paxton, Tom, *Goin' to the Zoo*.

"Grandma's Patchwork Quilt" (Larry Penn)—Various Artists, *Grandma's Patchwork Quilt*.

"Happy Day" (Jack Grunsky)—Grunsky, Jack, *Sing and Dance*.

"Hello Ev'rybody!" (Charity Bailey)—Buchman, Rachel, *Hello Everybody!*

"Here's One Wish" (Marcy Marxer)—Fink, Cathy, and Marcy Marxer, *Bon Appétit!*

"House at Pooh Corner" (Kenny Loggins)—Shontz, Bill, *Teddy Bear's Greatest Hits*.

"House Party Time" (Dan Zanes)—Zanes, Dan, *House Party*.

"Howja Do" (Woody Guthrie)—Guthrie, Woody, *Woody's 20 Grow Big Songs*.

"I Am a Pizza" (Peter Alsop)—Alsop, Peter, *Wha' D'Ya Wanna Do?*

"I Am the Wind" (Fred Penner)—Penner, Fred, *Fred's Favourites*.

"I Don't Wanna Go to School" (Barry Louis Polisar)—Polisar, Barry Louis, *Teacher's Favorites*.

"I Had an Old Coat" (Paul Kaplan)—Allard, Peter and Ellen, *Good Kid*.

"I Like to Sing" (Bill Harley)—Harley, Bill, *I Wanna Play*.

"I Love Mud" (Rick Charette)—Charette, Rick, *Alligator in the Elevator*.

"I Never See Maggie Alone" (Ralph Covert)—Ralph's World, *Peggy's Pie Parlor*.

"I Wanna Be a Dog" (Barry Louis Polisar)—Polisar, Barry Louis, *Old Dog, New Tricks*.

"I'd Like to Visit the Moon" (Jeff Moss)—The Chenille Sisters, *1, 2, 3 for Kids*.

"If I Could Be Anything" (Ruth Pelham)—Pelham, Ruth, *Under One Sky*.

"If You Love a Hippopotamus" (Connie Kaldor)—Kaldor, Connie, *A Duck in New York City*.

"I'm a Little Cookie" (Larry Penn)—Pease, Tom, *Boogie! Boogie! Boogie!*

"I'm a Three-Toed, Triple-Eyed, Double-Jointed Dinosaur" (Barry Louis Polisar)—Polisar, Barry Louis, *Old Dog, New Tricks*.

"It's Better Than That" (Peter Berryman, Lou Berryman)—Trout Fishing in America, *InFINity*.

"It's OK" (Gary Rosen, Christa Faust)—Rosenshontz, *Tickles You!*

"Jig Along Home" (Woody Guthrie)—Guthrie, Woody, *Woody's 20 Grow Big Songs*.

"Kids in Motion" (Eric Lowen, Dan Navarro, Rick Boston)—Greg and Steve, *Kids in Motion*.

"Kids' Peace Song" (Peter Alsop)—Alsop, Peter, *Take Me with You*.

"Kindergarten Wall" (John McCutcheon)—McCutcheon, John, *Mail Myself to You*.

"Lisa Lee Elizabeth" (Monty Harper)—Harper, Monty, *Imagine That*.

"Listen to the Horses" (David Eddleman)—Raffi, *More Singable Songs*.

"Listen to the Water" (Bob Schneider)—Allard, Peter and Ellen, *Raise the Children*.

"The Little Red Hen" (Elizabeth McMahon)—McMahon, Elizabeth, *Blue Sky Sparklin' Day*.

"The Little White Duck" (Bernard Zaritzky, Walt Barrows)—Ives, Burl, *Burl Ives Sings Little White Duck*.

"Lizzie's Do's and Don'ts" (Jessica Harper)—Harper, Jessica, *Inside Out*.

"Look out Your Window" (Bill Harley)—Harley, Bill, *The Town around the Bend*.

"Looking for a Planet" (Barney Fuller)—Green Chili Jam Band, *Coconut Moon*.

"Love Grows One by One" (Carol Johnson)—Herdman, Priscilla, *Daydreamer*.

"Love Is a Special Way of Feeling" (Fran Avni)—Avni, Fran, *Artichokes and Brussel Sprouts*.

"Love Makes a Family" (Marcy Marxer)—Fink, Cathy, and Marcy Marxer, *Blanket Full of Dreams*.

"Lullaby for Teddy-O" (Eileen Packard)—Herdman, Priscilla, *Stardreamer*.

"Magic Penny" (Malvina Reynolds)—Tickle Tune Typhoon, *Circle Around*.

"Mail Myself to You" (Woody Guthrie)—McCutcheon, John, *Mail Myself to You*.

"The Marvelous Toy" (Tom Paxton)—Paxton, Tom, *Goin' to the Zoo*.

"The Mitten" (Elizabeth McMahon)—McMahon, Elizabeth, *Blue Sky Sparklin' Day*.

"The Moon's Lullaby" (Sarah Pirtle)—Pirtle, Sarah, *Two Hands Hold the Earth*.

"Morningtown Ride" (Malvina Reynolds)—Raffi, *Baby Beluga*.

"Must Be Working" (Brian Kinder)—Kinder, Brian, *A Kid like You*.

"My Mama Was a Train" (James Coffey)—Coffey, James, *My Mama Was a Train*.

"My Roots Go Down" (Sarah Pirtle)—Pirtle, Sarah, *Two Hands Hold the Earth*.

"Nature's All around Us" (Sammie Haynes)—Haynes, Sammie, *Nature's ABCs*.

"Needle Sing" (Woody Guthrie)—Guthrie, Woody, *Woody's 20 Grow Big Songs*.

"The Night the Froggies Flew" (Desquaw Woody, Colleen Hannafin)—Colleen and Uncle Squaty, *Fingerplays, Movement and Story Songs*.

"Nocturnal" (Billy Jonas)—Jonas, Billy, *What Kind of Cat Are You?!*

"On the Day You Were Born" (Kathy Grammer, Red Grammer)—Grammer, Red, *Hello World*.

"On Top of Spaghetti" (Tom Glazer)—Yosi, *What's Eatin' Yosi?*

"1, 2, 3 Four-Ever Friends" (Desquaw Woody)—Colleen and Uncle Squaty, *1, 2, 3 Four-Ever Friends*.

"Open the Window" (Bob Livingston, Reade Wood, Albert Hirschprung)—Livingston, Bob, *Open the Window*.

"The Other Side of the World" (Sarah Pirtle)—Pirtle, Sarah, *Magical Earth*.

"Owl Moon" (Bruce O'Brien)—Pease, Tom, *Daddy Starts to Dance*.

"Part of the Family" (Lois LaFond, L. L. Carton Bacon, Glenn Taylor)—LaFond, Lois, *One World*.

"Peace on Earth" (Stuart Stotts)—Stotts, Stuart, *One Big Dance*.

"A Place in the Choir" (Bill Staines)—Staines, Bill, *The Happy Wanderer*.

"Place to Be" (Malvina Reynolds)—Ungar, Jay, and Lyn Hardy, *A Place to Be*.

"Preacher Herman" (John Forster, Michael Mark)—Chapin, Tom, *Billy the Squid*.

"Puff (The Magic Dragon)" (Lenny Lipton, Peter Yarrow)—Peter, Paul, and Mary, *Peter, Paul, and Mommy*.

"Puppy Dog" (Ralph Covert)—Ralph's World, *Peggy's Pie Parlor*.

"Rainbow 'round Me" (Ruth Pelham)—Pelham, Ruth, *Under One Sky*.

"Read a Book to Me" (Tom Pease)—Pease, Tom, *I'm Gonna Reach!*

"Rubber Blubber Whale" (Si Kahn)—McCutcheon, John, *Howjadoo*.

"Safe at Home" (Steve Van Zandt)—McCutcheon, John, *Bigger Than Yourself*.

"Sandwiches" (Bob King)—Alsop, Peter, *Wha' D'Ya Wanna Do?*

"Science Fair" (Ezra Idlet, Keith Grimwood)—Trout Fishing in America, *My World*.

"Sittin' Down to Eat" (Bill Harley)—Harley, Bill, *Big Big World*.

"Skateboard" (Joe Scruggs)—Scruggs, Joe, *Deep in the Jungle*.

"Sleepytime Swing" (Paul Strausman, Carole Anne Coogan)—Strausman, Paul, *Rainbows, Stones, and Dinosaur Bones*.

"Somos El Barco" (Lorre Wyatt)—Pease, Tom, *I'm Gonna Reach!*

"Songbirds" (Jack Grunsky)—Grunsky, Jack, *Jack in the Box 1*.

"Spider on the Floor" (Bill Russell)—Raffi, *Singable Songs for the Very Young*.

"Spider's Web" (Charlotte Diamond)—Diamond, Charlotte, *10 Carrot Diamond*.

"Summer Time Winter Time" (Desquaw Woody)—Colleen and Uncle Squaty, *Fingerplays, Movement and Story Songs*.

"Sun in My Eyes" (Ralph Covert)—Ralph's World, *The Amazing Adventures of Kid Astro*.

"The Teddy Bears' Picnic" (Jimmy Kennedy, John W. Bratton)—Garcia, Jerry, and David Grisman, *Not for Kids Only*.

"These Are the Questions" (Gary Rosen, Bill Shontz, Michael Thaler)—Rosenshontz, *Tickles You!*

"This Land Is Your Land" (Woody Guthrie)—Guthrie, Woody and Arlo, *This Land Is Your Land*.

"This Pretty Planet" (John Forster, Tom Chapin)—Chapin, Tom, *Family Tree*.

"This Shall Forever Be" (Ken Lonnquist)—Lonnquist, Ken, *Earthy Songs*.

"Time to Sleep" (Marcy Marxer)—Fink, Cathy, and Marcy Marxer, *Blanket Full of Dreams*.

"Turning and Turning" (Rebecca Frezza)—Frezza, Rebecca, *Tall and Small*.

"Under One Sky" (Ruth Pelham)—Pelham, Ruth, *Under One Sky*.

"The Unicorn" (Shel Silverstein)—Various Artists, *A Child's Celebration of the World*.

"Wake You in the Morning" (Ruth Pelham)—Pelham, Ruth, *Under One Sky*.

"Walk a Mile" (Jan Nigro)—Vitamin L, *Walk a Mile*.

"Walk the World Now, Children" (John Forster, Michael Mark, Tom Chapin)—Chapin, Tom, *Some Assembly Required*.

"Waltzing with Bears" (Dale Marxsen)—Herdman, Priscilla, *Stardreamer*.

"Welcome to My World" (Jane Sapp, The Dream Project)—The Dream Project, *We've All Got Stories*.

"We've All Got Stories" (Jane Sapp, The Dream Project)—The Dream Project, *We've All Got Stories*.

"What Do I Do?" (Ruth Pelham)—Pelham, Ruth, *Under One Sky*.

"What Do You Do on a Rainy Day?" (Gary Rosen, George Storey)—Rosen, Gary, *Tot Rock*.

"What Does Your Mama Do?" (Si Kahn)—Pease, Tom, *Boogie! Boogie! Boogie!*

"When the Rain Comes Down" (Bob Devlin)—Fink, Cathy, and Marcy Marxer, *A Cathy & Marcy Collection for Kids*.

"With My Own Two Hands" (Jack Grunsky)—Grunsky, Jack, *Jack in the Box 1*.

"World Citizen" (Stuart Stotts)—Stotts, Stuart, *One Big Dance*.

"Wynken, Blynken, and Nod" (Eugene Field, Lucy Simon)—Various Artists, *A Child's Celebration of Song*.

"You Can't Make a Turtle Come Out" (Malvina Reynolds)—Ungar, Jay, and Lyn Hardy, *A Place to Be*.

"You Get a Little Extra When You Watch T.V." (Peter Alsop)—Alsop, Peter, *Wha' D'Ya Wanna Do?*

"You Might as Well Sleep" (Greg Brown)—Brown, Greg, *Bathtub Blues*.

"You'll Sing a Song and I'll Sing a Song" (Ella Jenkins)—Raffi, *Corner Grocery Store*.

The Subject Listings

Accidents

"Boo Boo Bunny." Rosen, Gary, *Tot Rock*.

"The Boo Boo Song." Byers, Kathy, *Do You Wish You Could Fly?*

"The Boo Boo Truck." Green Chili Jam Band, *Starfishing*.

"Boo Boo Waltz." Silberg, "Miss Jackie," *Touched by a Song*.

"Disaster." Avni, Fran, *Artichokes and Brussel Sprouts*.

"I Think I'll Need a Bandaid." Trout Fishing in America, *Big Trouble*.

"Jennie Fell Down." Ungar, Jay, and Lyn Hardy, *A Place to Be*.

"Look Ma, No Hands." Rosenshontz, *Uh-Oh!*

"My Name Is Burt." Rudnick, Ben, *Blast Off!*

"Oops!" Crow, Dan, *Oops!*

"Oops." Paxton, Tom, *I've Got a Yo-Yo*.

"Oops Oops Bang Bang." Kaldor, Connie, *A Poodle in Paris*.

"Scabs." Cosgrove, Jim, *Ooey Gooey*.

"Uh-Oh!" Alsop, Peter, *Uh-Oh!*

"Uh Oh!" Rosenshontz, *Rosenshontz Greatest Hits*; Rosenshontz, *Uh-Oh!*

"Uh-Oh, Accident." Chapin, Tom, *Family Tree*; Chapin, Tom, *Great Big Fun for the Very Little One*.

"You Know It Got Better." Ungar, Jay, and Lyn Hardy, *A Place to Be*.

Alphabet/Letters

"A, B, C, D, E." Roberts, Justin, *Great Big Sun*.

"'A' for the Ant." Abell, Timmy, *I Know an Old Lady*.

"'A' I Ate an Apple." Kinder, Brian, *One More Time*.

"'A' You're Adorable." The Chenille Sisters, *Teaching Hippopotami to Fly!*; Lithgow, John, *Singin' in the Bathtub*; Muldaur, Maria, *Swingin' in the Rain*; Sharon, Lois, and Bram, *Great Big Hits*.

"ABC." Avni, Fran, *Little Ears: Songs for Reading Readiness*; Ralph's World, *Ralph's World*. (Same song as "ABC Song" and "The Alphabet Song.")

"ABC." Scruggs, Joe, *Abracadabra*.

"ABC Nursery Rhyme Game." Beall, Pamela, and Susan Nipp, *Wee Sing in the Car*.

"ABC of Me." Milkshake, *Bottle of Sunshine*.

"ABC Rock." Greg and Steve, *We All Live Together*, vol. 1.

"ABC Song." Barchas, Sarah, *Get Ready, Get Set, Sing!* (Same song as "ABC" and "The Alphabet Song.")

"ABC Train." Barchas, Sarah, *Get Ready, Get Set, Sing!*

"ABCs." Mayer, Hans, *Stars of the Swing Set*.

"The ABC's of You." Grammer, Red, *Down the Do-Re-Mi*; Penner, Fred, *What a Day!*

"The Alfabet Song." Polisar, Barry Louis, *Teacher's Favorites*.

"The Alphabet Boogie." Fink, Cathy, *When the Rain Comes Down*.

"Alphabet Dub." Mitchell, Elizabeth, *You Are My Sunshine*.

"Alphabet Forwards and Backwards." Feldman, Jean, *Keep On Singing and Dancing with Dr. Jean*.

"Alphabet in Motion." Palmer, Hap, *Can a Jumbo Jet Sing the Alphabet?*

"Alphabet Medley." Sharon, Lois, and Bram, *Sing A to Z*.

"Alphabet of Nations." They Might Be Giants, *Here Come the ABCs*.

"Alphabet Rag." Harper, Monty, *Imagine That*.

"The Alphabet Song." Bartels, Joanie, *Sillytime Magic*.

"The Alphabet Song." Beall, Pamela, and Susan Nipp, *Wee Sing Children's Songs and Fingerplays*; Beall, Pamela, and Susan Nipp, *Wee Sing in the Car*. (Same song as "ABC" and "ABC Song.")

"Alphabet Soup." Chapin, Tom, *Moonboat*.

"Alphabet Soup." Various Artists, *Hear and Gone in 60 Seconds*.

"Alphabet Train." Feldman, Jean, *Just for Fun!*

"The 'B' Song." The Chenille Sisters, *1, 2, 3 for Kids*.

"Bean Bag Alphabet Rag." Palmer, Hap, *Can a Cherry Pie Wave Goodbye?*

"Before the ABC's." Lonnquist, Ken, *Sci-Fi Hi-Fi*.

"Can a Jumbo Jet Sing the Alphabet?" Palmer, Hap, *Can a Jumbo Jet Sing the Alphabet?*

"The Cowboy's ABC." Riders in the Sky, *Saddle Pals*.

"E Eats Everything." They Might Be Giants, *Here Come the ABCs*.

"Everything Else Starts with 'E.'" Roberts, Justin, *Great Big Sun*.

"Flying V." They Might Be Giants, *Here Come the ABCs*.

"Funky Backwards Alphabet." Mr. Al, *Rockin' the Alphabet*.

"Go for G!" They Might Be Giants, *Here Come the ABCs*.

"I-C-A-B." Walker, Graham, *Fiddlesticks*.

"Let's Alphabecise." Fite, Stephen, *Monkey Business*.

"Letter Dance." Feldman, Jean, *Is Everybody Happy?*

"Letter Game." Strausman, Paul, *Blue Jay, Blue Jay!*

"Letter Tales." Feldman, Jean, *Just for Fun!*

"Lettercise." Feldman, Jean, *Is Everybody Happy?*

"Moving around the Alphabet." Palmer, Hap, *One Little Sound*.

"Nature's ABC's." Haynes, Sammie, *Nature's ABCs*.

"Peter's ABC's." Alsop, Peter, *Uh-Oh!*

"Piggy Letter Boogie." LaFond, Lois, *Turning It Upside Down*.

"Pocket Full of B's." Palmer, Hap, *Can a Cherry Pie Wave Goodbye?*

"Q U." They Might Be Giants, *Here Come the ABCs*.

"Rockin' the Alphabet." Mr. Al, *Rockin' the Alphabet*.

"Seven Little Letters." Feldman, Jean, *Is Everybody Happy?*

"Sounds from A to Z." Rosenshontz, *Share It*.

"We're Great!" Feldman, Jean, *Just for Fun!*

"Who Put the Alphabet in Alphabetical Order?" They Might Be Giants, *Here Come the ABCs*.

"Z Y X." They Might Be Giants, *Here Come the ABCs*.

Amusement Parks/Playgrounds

"At the Swing Set." Mr. Al, *Dance like This*.

"Mary-Go-Round." Knight, Tom, *Easy as Pie*.

"The Merry-Go-Round." Beall, Pamela, and Susan Nipp, *Wee Sing and Play*.

"Merry Go Round." Guthrie, Woody, *Nursery Days*; Guthrie, Woody, *Woody's 20 Grow Big Songs*; Raven, Nancy, *Singing, Prancing, and Dancing*.

"Merry-Go-Round." Palmer, Hap, *Peek-a-Boo*.

"The Swing." Buchman, Rachel, *Sing a Song of Seasons*.

"A Swing Tune." The Chenille Sisters, *The Big Picture and Other Songs for Kids*.

"Take Us on the Rides." Foote, Norman, *Shake a Leg*.

"Wonder Wheel." Zanes, Dan, *Family Dance*.

Angels

"Rachel's Garden." Cosgrove, Jim, *Stinky Feet*.
"Three Little Angels." Byers, Kathy, *'Round the Campfire*.

Animals (see also Birds; Farms; Insects; Spiders; Zoos)

"'A' for the Ant." Abell, Timmy, *I Know an Old Lady*.
"All God's Critters." McCutcheon, John, *Howjadoo*. (Same song as "A Place in the Choir.")
"Animal Fair." Beall, Pamela, and Susan Nipp, *Wee Sing Silly Songs*; Berkner, Laurie, *Whaddaya Think of That?*; Muldaur, Maria, *Swingin' in the Rain*; Rosenthal, Phil, *Animal Songs*; Roth, Kevin, *Travel Song Sing Alongs*.
"Animal Friends." Ralph's World, *Ralph's World*.
"Animal Groove." Coffey, James, *Animal Groove*.
"Animal Groups." Rosen, Gary, *Pet Sounds*.
"The Animal Song." Tucker, Nancy, *Happy as a Clam*.
"Animal Tales." Shontz, Bill, *Animal Tales*.
"Animals Are Dancing." Banana Slug String Band, *Penguin Parade*.
"Animals Down Under." Tickle Tune Typhoon, *Singing Science*.
"Animals in the Big Woods." Lonnquist, Ken, *Earthy Songs*.
"As I Was Walking to Town One Day." Peterson, Carole, *Stinky Cake*.
"Baa, Neigh, Cock-a-Doodle-Doo." Howdy, Buck, *Giddyup!*
"Backyard Safari." Tickle Tune Typhoon, *Singing Science*.
"The Barnyard Song." Hinton, Sam, *Whoever Shall Have Some Good Peanuts*. (Same song as "Bought Me a Cat," "Fiddle I Fee," "Had a Bird," "I Had a Bird," and "I Had a Cat.")
"Bats Eat Bugs." Banana Slug String Band, *Dirt Made My Lunch*.
"Betty Is Convinced that She's a Buffalo." Kaldor, Connie, *A Poodle in Paris*.
"Blue Jay." Strausman, Paul, *Blue Jay, Blue Jay!*
"Bought Me a Cat." Beall, Pamela, and Susan Nipp, *Wee Sing Animals, Animals, Animals*; Beall, Pamela, and Susan Nipp, *Wee Sing Fun 'n' Folk*; Magical Music Express, *Music Is Magic*. (Same song as "The Barnyard Song," "Fiddle I Fee," "Had a Bird," "I Had a Bird," and "I Had a Cat.")
"Bringing Home a Baby Bumble Bee." Feldman, Jean, *Dr. Jean Sings Silly Songs*. (Same song as "Baby Bumblebee" and "Gifts for Mommy.")
"Brown Bear, Brown Bear, What Do You See?" Greg and Steve, *Playing Favorites*.
"Bye Bye Dodo." Chapin, Tom, *Billy the Squid*.
"Cluck, Cluck, Red Hen." Cassidy, Nancy, *Nancy Cassidy's KidsSongs*; Raffi, *Corner Grocery Store*.

"Counting Cows." Cosgrove, Jim, *Mr. Stinky Feet's Road Trip.*

"Cow in the Car." Dana, *Dana's Best Travelin' Tunes.*

"Deepest Africa." The Chenille Sisters, *Teaching Hippopotami to Fly!*; Pease, Tom, *Wobbi-Do-Wop!*

"Different Way of Talking." McMahon, Elizabeth, *Waltzing with Fireflies.*

"Dinosaur in Your Backpack." Trout Fishing in America, *InFINity.*

"Do the Pet Sounds." Rosen, Gary, *Pet Sounds.*

"Down by the Bay." Arnold, Linda, *Sing Along Stew*; Barchas, Sarah, *If I Had a Pony*; Beall, Pamela, and Susan Nipp, *Wee Sing in the Car*; Beall, Pamela, and Susan Nipp, *Wee Sing Silly Songs*; Cassidy, Nancy, *Nancy Cassidy's KidsSongs*; Greg and Steve, *Playing Favorites*; Pullara, Steve, *One Potato, Two Potato*; Raffi, *Singable Songs for the Very Young*; Roth, Kevin, *Dinosaurs and Dragons*; Roth, Kevin, *Travel Song Sing Alongs.*

"Down in the Glen." Ralph's World, *The Amazing Adventures of Kid Astro.*

"Down the Sidewalk." Big Jeff, *Big Jeff.*

"Eatin' Animal Crackers." Rymer, Brady, *I Found It!*

"Everybody's Got to Have a Home." Shontz, Bill, *Animal Tales.*

"Fiddle I Fee." McMahon, Elizabeth, *Waltzing with Fireflies*; Old Town School of Folk Music, *Wiggleworms Love You.* (Same song as "The Barnyard Song," "Bought Me a Cat," "Had a Bird," "I Had a Bird," and "I Had a Cat.")

"Fifteen Animals." Boynton, Sandra, *Philadelphia Chickens.*

"Fish Are Orderly." Paxton, Tom, *I've Got a Yo-Yo.*

"Frog on a Log." McCutcheon, John, *Springsongs.*

"Gifts for Mommy." Peterson, Carole, *Sticky Bubble Gum.*

"Go into the Night." Banana Slug String Band, *Penguin Parade.*

"Had a Bird." Raven, Nancy, *Hop, Skip, and Sing.* (Same song as "The Barnyard Song," "Bought Me a Cat," "Fiddle I Fee," "I Had a Bird," and "I Had a Cat.")

"Had a Little Rooster." Beall, Pamela, and Susan Nipp, *Wee Sing Fun 'n' Folk*; Raven, Nancy, *People and Animal Songs.* (Same song as "I Had a Rooster" and "I Love My Rooster.")

"Hundreds of Chicks." Barchas, Sarah, *If I Had a Pony.*

"I Had a Bird." Feldman, Jean, *Dr. Jean and Friends.* (Same song as "The Barnyard Song," "Bought Me a Cat," "Fiddle I Fee," "Had a Bird," and "I Had a Cat.")

"I Had a Cat." Abell, Timmy, *I Know an Old Lady.* (Same song as "The Barnyard Song," "Bought Me a Cat," "Fiddle I Fee," "Had a Bird," and "I Had a Bird.")

"I Had a Rooster." Allard, Peter and Ellen, *Raise the Children*; Barchas, Sarah, *If I Had a Pony*; Buchman, Rachel, *Hello Everybody!*; Lithgow, John, *Singin' in the Bathtub*; McMahon, Elizabeth, *Magic Parade*; Silberg, "Miss Jackie,"

Peanut Butter, Tarzan, and Roosters. (Same song as "Had a Little Rooster" and "I Love My Rooster.")

"I Know an Old Lady." Abell, Timmy, *I Know an Old Lady*; Feldman, Jean, *Keep On Singing and Dancing with Dr. Jean*; The Learning Station, *Here We Go Loopty Loo*; The Learning Station, *Literacy in Motion*; Peter, Paul, and Mary, *Peter, Paul, and Mommy, Too*; Roth, Kevin, *Travel Song Sing Alongs*; Roth, Kevin, *Unbearable Bears*; Silberg, "Miss Jackie," *Lollipops and Spaghetti.*

"I Love My Rooster." Berkner, Laurie, *Whaddaya Think of That?* (Same song as "Had a Little Rooster" and "I Had a Rooster.")

"I Wouldn't Be Scared, Not Me." Stotts, Stuart, *One Big Dance.*

"If Animals Could Dance." The Learning Station, *La Di Da La Di Di Dance with Me.*

"If I Were a Dog." Cosgrove, Jim, *Pick Me! Pick Me!*

"I'm Not Going to Chase the Cat Today." Harper, Jessica, *Rhythm in My Shoes.*

"I've Got a Dog and My Dog's Name Is Cat." Polisar, Barry Louis, *Family Concert*; Polisar, Barry Louis, *Old Dog, New Tricks.*

"Jump like a Kangaroo." Barchas, Sarah, *If I Had a Pony.*

"Jumpin' Beans." Grunsky, Jack, *Follow the Leader*; Grunsky, Jack, *Sing and Dance.*

"Kiss a Cow." Crow, Dan, *Oops!*

"Last Night I Had a Dream." Berkner, Laurie, *Whaddaya Think of That?*

"Let's Be Little Animals." Yosi, *Monkey Business.*

"A Little Brown Dog Named Joe." Harper, Jessica, *Inside Out.*

"A Little Red Jeep." Charette, Rick, *Toad Motel.*

"Little White Duck." Abell, Timmy, *I Know an Old Lady*; Bartels, Joanie, *Bathtime Magic*; Ives, Burl, *Burl Ives Sings Little White Duck*; Raffi, *Everything Grows*; Rosenthal, Phil, *Animal Songs.*

"The Littlest Duck." Kaldor, Connie, *A Poodle in Paris.*

"Lizards." Banana Slug String Band, *Adventures on the Air Cycle.*

"Miranda the Panda." Shontz, Bill, *Teddy Bear's Greatest Hits.*

"The Mitten." McMahon, Elizabeth, *Blue Sky Sparklin' Day.*

"Mole in the Ground." Staines, Bill, *One More River*; Zanes, Dan, *Rocket Ship Beach.*

"Movin' round the Room." Colleen and Uncle Squaty, *Sing-a-Move-a-Dance.*

"Night Creatures." Tickle Tune Typhoon, *Singing Science.*

"Nobody's Chasin' Nobody." Harper, Jessica, *A Wonderful Life.*

"Nocturnal." Jonas, Billy, *What Kind of Cat Are You?!*

"Nocturnal." Lonnquist, Ken, *Earthy Songs.*

"Nocturnal Animals." Banana Slug String Band, *Dirt Made My Lunch.*

"Noses." Banana Slug String Band, *Penguin Parade.*

"One Little Coyote." Riders in the Sky, *Harmony Ranch.*

"Oo Ee." Magical Music Express, *Music Is Magic*.

"Ooh There's a Lion." Kimmy Schwimmy, *Kimmy Schwimmy Music*, vol. 1.

"Our Dog Bernard." Polisar, Barry Louis, *Family Concert*.

"Over in the Meadow." Beall, Pamela, and Susan Nipp, *Wee Sing Nursery Rhymes and Lullabies*; Feldman, Jean, *Dr. Jean Sings Silly Songs*; McCutcheon, John, *Mail Myself to You*; Old Town School of Folk Music, *Wiggleworms Love You*; Raffi, *Baby Beluga*.

"A Pair O' Barracudas." Ode, Eric, *I Love My Shoes*.

"Pet Sounds." Rosenshontz, *Share It*.

"The Pets." Ungar, Jay, and Lyn Hardy, *A Place to Be*.

"Pets Go to the Vet." Charette, Rick, *King Kong Chair*.

"Pig on Her Head." Berkner, Laurie, *Buzz Buzz*.

"A Place in the Choir." Abell, Timmy, *The Farmer's Market*; Grammer, Red, *Down the Do-Re-Mi*; Knight, Tom, *Don't Kiss a Codfish*; Staines, Bill, *The Happy Wanderer*. (Same song as "All God's Critters.")

"Quack, Quack, Quack." Kaldor, Connie, *A Duck in New York City*.

"Rabbit on My Shoulder." Alsop, Peter, *Uh-Oh!*

"Reptile World." Polisar, Barry Louis, *Old Enough to Know Better*.

"Safe at Home." Banana Slug String Band, *Penguin Parade*.

"Say Good Day!" Peterson, Carole, *Tiny Tunes*. (Same song as "When Cats Get Up in the Morning.")

"Say Hi to the Animals." Ralph's World, *Happy Lemon*.

"Scooby Dooby." McMahon, Elizabeth, *Blue Sky Sparklin' Day*.

"Sing in the Spring." Diamond, Charlotte, *Diamond in the Rough*.

"Sittin' Down to Eat." Harley, Bill, *Big Big World*; Harley, Bill, *Play It Again*.

"Skidaddle!" Howdy, Buck, *Skidaddle!*

"Slither like a Snake." Avni, Fran, *Little Ears: Songs for Reading Readiness*; Avni, Fran, *Tuning into Nature*.

"Slithery Snake." McGrath, Bob, and Katherine Smithrim, *Songs and Games for Toddlers*.

"Song about a Duck." Kirk, John, and Trish Miller, *The Big Rock Candy Mountain*.

"Spin Your Web." Kaye, Mary, *Spin Your Web*.

"Stop at the Petshop." Barchas, Sarah, *If I Had a Pony*.

"Swinging on a Star." Bartels, Joanie, *Sillytime Magic*; Lithgow, John, *Singin' in the Bathtub*; Pease, Tom, *Boogie! Boogie! Boogie!*; Rudnick, Ben, *Fun and Games*. (Same song as "Would You Like to Swing on a Star?")

"Taking My Cat down the Slide." Charette, Rick, *Chickens on Vacation*.

"There's a Dog in School." Peterson, Carole, *H.U.M.—All Year Long*; Stotts, Stuart, and Tom Pease, *Celebrate: A Song Resource*.

"There's a Hippo in My Tub." Bartels, Joanie, *Bathtime Magic*.

"Three Little Pigs." Avni, Fran, *Artichokes and Brussel Sprouts*.

"Two Kinds of Seagulls." Chapin, Tom, *Mother Earth*; Chapin, Tom, *This Pretty Planet*.

"Way Down Yonder." The Learning Station, *Tony Chestnut and Fun Time Action Songs*.

"We Are Wildlife Too!" Banana Slug String Band, *Goin' Wild*.

"What Do Animals Need?" Banana Slug String Band, *Penguin Parade*.

"What Kind of Animal." Kinder, Brian, *One More Time*.

"When a Big Fat Hippopotamus Is Yawning." Barchas, Sarah, *If I Had a Pony*.

"When Cats Get Up in the Morning." Old Town School of Folk Music, *Wiggleworms Love You*. (Same song as "Say Good Day!")

"When I Went Out." Avni, Fran, *Artichokes and Brussel Sprouts*; Avni, Fran, *Tuning into Nature*.

"Where Has My Little Dog Gone?" Barchas, Sarah, *Get Ready, Get Set, Sing!*

"Wiggle." Alsop, Peter, *Uh-Oh!*

"Woodland Chorus." Shontz, Bill, *Animal Tales*.

"A World of Colors." Barchas, Sarah, *If I Had a Pony*.

"The World's Biggest Zoo." Green Chili Jam Band, *Starfishing*.

"Would You Like to Swing on a Star?" Muldaur, Maria, *On the Sunny Side*; Various Artists, *A Child's Celebration of Folk Music*. (Same song as "Swinging on a Star.")

"You're an Animal, Too!" Moo, Anna, *Anna Moo Crackers*.

"Zebra in the Kitchen." Daddy A Go Go, *Monkey in the Middle*.

Alligators/Crocodiles

"Allen Gator." Paxton, Tom, *Goin' to the Zoo*.

"The Alligator Chant." Feldman, Jean, *Dr. Jean Sings Silly Songs*.

"Alligator in the Elevator." Charette, Rick, *Alligator in the Elevator*.

"Alligator Jump." Knight, Tom, *Easy as Pie*.

"Alligator Pie." Magical Musical Express, *Music Is Magic*; Peterson, Carole, *H.U.M.—All Year Long*.

"The Alligator Rag." Lonnquist, Ken, *The Lost Songs of Kenland*.

"Alligator Stomp." Grunsky, Jack, *Dancing Feet*; Grunsky, Jack, *Jack in the Box 1*.

"Alligator Stomp." Moo, Anna, *Anna Moo Crackers*.

"The Alligator Waltz." Kaldor, Connie, *A Duck in New York City*.

"Amos the Alligator Dude." Palmer, Hap, *Turn On the Music*.

"The Crocodile." Beall, Pamela, and Susan Nipp, *Wee Sing Silly Songs.*

"Deep in the Jungle." Scruggs, Joe, *Deep in the Jungle.*

"Five Frogs." Moo, Anna, *Anna Moo Crackers.*

"I Got an Alligator." Yosi, *Monkey Business.*

"Jaws of a Crocodile." Lonnquist, Ken, *The Circus Kenlando.*

"Monkeys and the Alligator." Feldman, Jean, *Dr. Jean and Friends.*

"The Monkey's New Shoes." Mayer, Hans, *Just a Little Hug.*

"Road Alligator." Miss Amy, *Wide Wide World.*

"Six Little Monkeys." Yosi, *Under a Big Bright Yellow Umbrella.*

"The Smile on the Crocodile." Sharon, Lois, and Bram, *Everybody Sing!*; Sharon, Lois, and Bram, *Great Big Hits.*

"Susie and the Alligator." Fink, Cathy, *When the Rain Comes Down*; Fink, Cathy, and Marcy Marxer, *A Cathy & Marcy Collection for Kids.*

"Ten Little Monkeys." Palmer, Hap, *Two Little Sounds.* (Similar to "Five Little Monkeys" and "No More Monkeys.")

Armadillos

"Armadillo." Strausman, Paul, *The World's Big Family.*

"Little Armadillos." Foote, Norman, *Foote Prints.*

"Thundering Armadillos." Lonnquist, Ken, *The Circus Kenlando.*

Bats

"Bat." Lonnquist, Ken, *The Circus Kenlando*; Lonnquist, Ken, *Earthy Songs.*

"Bring Back the Bat." Avni, Fran, *I'm All Ears: Sing into Reading*; Avni, Fran, *Tuning into Nature.*

Bears

"Baby Bear's Chicken Pox." Avni, Fran, *Artichokes and Brussel Sprouts*; Silberg, "Miss Jackie," *The Complete Sniggles, Squirrels, and Chicken Pox.*

"The Bear." Beall, Pamela, and Susan Nipp, *Wee Sing Fun 'n' Folk.*

"The Bear and the Mountain." Foote, Norman, *Shake a Leg.*

"The Bear Hunt." The Learning Station, *Here We Go Loopty Loo.*

"Bear Hunt." SteveSongs, *On a Flying Guitar.*

"The Bear That Snores." Roth, Kevin, *Unbearable Bears.* (Same song as "The Snoring Bear.")

"The Bear Went over the Mountain." Beall, Pamela, and Susan Nipp, *Wee Sing Animals, Animals, Animals*; Beall, Pamela, and Susan Nipp, *Wee Sing Silly*

Songs; Feldman, Jean, *Dr. Jean Sings Silly Songs*; Greg and Steve, *Ready, Set, Move!*; McGrath, Bob, *Sing Along with Bob #1*.

"Bears Dance 'round My Head." Buchman, Rachel, *Baby and Me*.

"Boogie Woogie Dancin' Bear." Coffey, James, *Animal Groove*.

"Cinnamon Bear." Walker, Graham, *Fiddlesticks*.

"The Cool Bear Hunt." Feldman, Jean, *Dr. Jean Sings Silly Songs*.

"Dear Old Woolly Bear." McMahon, Elizabeth, *Waltzing with Fireflies*.

"Goldilocks and the 3 Bears." The Learning Station, *La Di Da La Di Di Dance with Me*; The Learning Station, *Literacy in Motion*.

"Goldilocks Rap." Shontz, Bill, *Teddy Bear's Greatest Hits*.

"The Goldilocks Rock." Dana, *Dana's Best Rock and Roll Fairy Tales*.

"Grizzly Bear." Beall, Pamela, and Susan Nipp, *Wee Sing Animals, Animals, Animals*; Beall, Pamela, and Susan Nipp, *Wee Sing Fun 'n' Folk*.

"Grizzly Bear Paradise." Banana Slug String Band, *Goin' Wild*.

"Honey Bear." Roth, Kevin, *Unbearable Bears*.

"Honey, Honey, Honey." Kaldor, Connie, *A Duck in New York City*.

"Just Right." Knight, Tom, *The Library Boogie*.

"One Shoe Bear." Rosenshontz, *Rosenshontz Greatest Hits*.

"The Polar Bear Stomp." The Chenille Sisters, *1, 2, 3 for Kids*.

"Sleepy Bear." Raven, Nancy, *People and Animal Songs*.

"The Snoring Bear." Roth, Kevin, *Travel Song Sing Alongs*. (Same song as "The Bear That Snores.")

"That Bear Makes Me Crazy." Roth, Kevin, *Travel Song Sing Alongs*; Roth, Kevin, *Unbearable Bears*.

"There's a Bear in There." Ode, Eric, *Trash Can*.

"Three Bears." Rosen, Gary, *Teddy Bears' Picnic*.

"The Three Boppin Bears Rap." Feldman, Jean, *Dr. Jean Sings Silly Songs*.

"Waltzing with Bears." Herdman, Priscilla, *Stardreamer*; Knight, Tom, *Don't Kiss a Codfish*; Rosen, Gary, *Teddy Bears' Picnic*.

"You're a Bear." Shontz, Bill, *Teddy Bear's Greatest Hits*.

Beavers

"The Beaver Call." Feldman, Jean, *Dr. Jean Sings Silly Songs*; Peterson, Carole, *Sticky Bubble Gum*.

"I'm Proud to Be a Beaver." Banana Slug String Band, *Goin' Wild*.

Bison

"Bison." Banana Slug String Band, *Goin' Wild*.

Camels

"Alice the Camel." The Learning Station, *All-Time Children's Favorites*.

"Cameling." Chapin, Tom, *Billy the Squid*; Chapin, Tom, *Great Big Fun for the Very Little One*.

"Emil, the Camel." Strausman, Paul, *Camels, Cats, and Rainbows*.

Cats

"Barn Cat." Ode, Eric, *Grandpa's Truck*.

"Barn Cat." Walker, Graham, *Fiddlesticks*.

"Black Cat." Silberg, "Miss Jackie," *The Complete Sniggles, Squirrels, and Chicken Pox*; Silberg, "Miss Jackie," *Sing about Martin*.

"The Cat Came Back." Berkner, Laurie, *Whaddaya Think of That?*; Penner, Fred, *Fred's Favourites*; Penner, Fred, *Storytime*; Trout Fishing in America, *Big Trouble*.

"Cat Song." Gemini, *The Best of Gemini*. (Same song as "My Cat Can.")

"Cats." Strausman, Paul, *Camels, Cats, and Rainbows*.

"A Cat's like That." Crow, Dan, *The Giggling Dragon*.

"Cats' Night Out." Walker, Graham, *Cats' Night Out*.

"Chainsaw." Stotts, Stuart, *Are We There Yet?*

"Dagger." Lonnquist, Ken, *The Lost Songs of Kenland*.

"Emily Miller." Ralph's World, *Ralph's World*.

"Here, Kitty, Kitty." Barchas, Sarah, *Get Ready, Get Set, Sing!*

"I Love Little Kitty." Beall, Pamela, and Susan Nipp, *Wee Sing Animals, Animals, Animals*.

"I Sold My Cat." Lonnquist, Ken, *The Switcher-On of Stars*; Lonnquist, Ken, *Welcome 2 Kenland*.

"I Wanna Purple Kitty for My Birthday, Mom." Diamond, Charlotte, *Diamonds and Dragons*.

"A Kitten." Barchas, Sarah, *If I Had a Pony*.

"Kitty Cat Shuffle." Mayer, Hans, *See You Later, Alligator*.

"Kitty Kat, Kitty Kat." Roberts, Justin, *Great Big Sun*.

"Kitty Kitty." Kinder, Brian, *Again*.

"The Library Cat." Charette, Rick, *King Kong Chair*.

"Little Cat." Knight, Tom, *Don't Kiss a Codfish*.

"Long Time Ago." Raven, Nancy, *People and Animal Songs*.

"Malcolm McGillikitty." Ralph's World, *At the Bottom of the Sea*.

"Max the Cat." The Chenille Sisters, *The Big Picture and Other Songs for Kids*.

"My Cat Can." Colleen and Uncle Squaty, *Fingerplays, Movement and Story Songs*. (Same song as "Cat Song.")

"My Grandma's Cat." Pirtle, Sarah, *Magical Earth*.

"My Pussycat." McMahon, Elizabeth, *Tea Party Shuffle*.

"No, You May Not Eat My Kitty." Kinnoin, Dave, *Daring Dewey*.

"Once There Was a Little Kitty." Buchman, Rachel, *Sing a Song of Seasons*.

"Porky." Charette, Rick, *Where Do My Sneakers Go at Night?*

"Raining Cats and Dogs." Foote, Norman, *Foote Prints*.

"Raining Cats and Dogs." LaFond, Lois, *One World*.

"There's a Bowl of Milk in the Moonlight." Various Artists, *Hear and Gone in 60 Seconds*.

"There's No Substitute for a Cat." Polisar, Barry Louis, *Old Enough to Know Better*.

"Three Little Kittens." Beall, Pamela, and Susan Nipp, *Wee Sing Nursery Rhymes and Lullabies*; Feldman, Jean, *Nursery Rhymes and Good Ol' Times*.

"What Kind of Cat Are You?!" Jonas, Billy, *What Kind of Cat Are You?!*

Chipmunks

"Anilae, Anilae (Chipmunk, Chipmunk)." Beall, Pamela, and Susan Nipp, *Wee Sing around the World*.

Clams

"Calypso Clam." Coffey, James, *Animal Groove*.

Cows/Bulls

"A Bull Named Bob." Paxton, Tom, *Your Shoes, My Shoes*.

"The Cow." McMahon, Elizabeth, *Blue Sky Sparklin' Day*.

"Cow Planet." Boynton, Sandra, *Dog Train*.

"Cowlit Night." Raffi, *Bananaphone*.

"Cows." Boynton, Sandra, *Philadelphia Chickens*.

"Cowtown." Yosi, *Monkey Business*.

"Did You Feed My Cow?" Various Artists, *cELLAbration! A Tribute to Ella Jenkins*.

"Little Black Bull." Raven, Nancy, *People and Animal Songs*.

"Making Moosic." Moo, Anna, *Making Moosic*.

"Many Cows." Pease, Tom, *Boogie! Boogie! Boogie!*

"Purple Cow." Charette, Rick, *Popcorn and Other Songs to Munch On*.

"Rosie the Cow." Walker, Graham, *Knobbledee Knees*.

"Thelma the Cow." Kaldor, Connie, *A Poodle in Paris*.

"3 Happy Cows." Lonnquist, Ken, *Sci-Fi Hi-Fi*.

"Wake Up, You Lazybones!" Peterson, Carole, *Tiny Tunes*.

Coyotes

"Coyotes." Lonnquist, Ken, *The Circus Kenlando*.

Deer

"We Weary Deer." Trout Fishing in America, *Family Music Party*; Trout Fishing in America, *My World*.

Dogs

"Alice the Beagle." Colleen and Uncle Squaty, *Sing-a-Move-a-Dance*.

"Barnyard Stomp." Polisar, Barry Louis, *Old Enough to Know Better*.

"The Bee and the Pup." Beall, Pamela, and Susan Nipp, *Wee Sing Fun 'n' Folk*.

"Best of Companions." Chapin, Tom, *Zag Zig*.

"Bingo." Beall, Pamela, and Susan Nipp, *Wee Sing Animals, Animals, Animals*; Beall, Pamela, and Susan Nipp, *Wee Sing Children's Songs and Fingerplays*; Coffey, James, *Animal Groove*; Feldman, Jean, *Nursery Rhymes and Good Ol' Times*; Fite, Stephen, *Monkey Business*; Greg and Steve, *We All Live Together*, vol. 4; McGrath, Bob, *Sing Along with Bob #2*; Old Town School of Folk Music, *Wiggleworms Love You*; Peterson, Carole, *H.U.M.—All Year Long*; Raven, Nancy, *Hop, Skip, and Sing*; Rosenthal, Phil, *Turkey in the Straw*; Sharon, Lois, and Bram, *Great Big Hits 2*; Sharon, Lois, and Bram, *Name Games*.

"Bird Dog." McCutcheon, John, *Autumnsongs*.

"Bobo and Fred." Rosen, Gary, *Pet Sounds*; Rosenshontz, *Rock 'n Roll Teddy Bear*.

"Ding Dong Dog." Harper, Jessica, *Nora's Room*.

"Disappearing Dog." Walker, Graham, *Knobbledee Knees*.

"D-O-G." Roberts, Justin, *Not Naptime*.

"A Dog Named Boomer." Daddy A Go Go, *Cool Songs for Cool Kids*.

"Dog Olympics." Lonnquist, Ken, *The Circus Kenlando*.

"Dog Rules." Chapin, Tom, *In My Hometown*.

"Dog Songs." Livingston, Bob, *Open the Window*.

"The Dog That Went to Yale." Simmons, Al, *The Truck I Bought from Moe*.

"Dog Train." Boynton, Sandra, *Dog Train*.

"Dogs." Crow, Dan, *Dan Crow Live*; Crow, Dan, *Oops!*

"Dog's Life." McCutcheon, John, *Springsongs*.

"Doggie." Grammer, Red, *Can You Sound Just like Me?*

"Don't Listen to My Dog." Ode, Eric, *Trash Can*.

"Everybody Walks a Dog." Pullara, Steve, *Hop like a Frog*.

"Fred." Paxton, Tom, *Goin' to the Zoo*.

"The Great Big Dog." Berkner, Laurie, *Whaddaya Think of That?*

"He Likes to Bark." Sprout, Jonathan, *Kid Power*.

"The Hound Dog Song." Staines, Bill, *The Happy Wanderer*.

"How Much Is That Doggie in the Window?" Sharon, Lois, and Bram, *Great Big Hits*.

"Howling at the Moon." Gemini, *The Best of Gemini*.

"I Got Two Dogs." Lithgow, John, *Farkle and Friends*.

"I Love That Dog." Kaldor, Connie, *A Poodle in Paris*.

"I Think I Might Be a Dog." Daddy A Go Go, *Big Rock Rooster*.

"I Wanna Be a Dog." Alsop, Peter, *Wha' D'Ya Wanna Do?*; Diamond, Charlotte, *10 Carrot Diamond*; Polisar, Barry Louis, *Family Concert*; Polisar, Barry Louis, *Old Dog, New Tricks*.

"Lonely Dog Tango." Madsen, Gunnar, *Ants in My Pants!*

"Monster." Ralph's World, *Green Gorilla, Monster, and Me*.

"My Dog." Charette, Rick, *Where Do My Sneakers Go at Night?*

"My Dog." Kinder, Brian, *A Kid like You*.

"My Dog Pepper." Colleen and Uncle Squaty, *Rumble to the Bottom*.

"My Dog Rags." Cassidy, Nancy, *Nancy Cassidy's KidsSongs*; McGrath, Bob, *Sing Along with Bob #1*. (Same song as "Rags.")

"My Dog Sam." Harley, Bill, *50 Ways to Fool Your Mother*; Harley, Bill, *One More Time*.

"My Little Puppy." Thaddeus Rex, *Martian Television Invasion*.

"My Neighbor's Dog." Foote, Norman, *Shake a Leg*.

"My Puppy Dog." McMahon, Elizabeth, *Blue Sky Sparklin' Day*.

"Nikky, Terror of the Family." Del Bianco, Lou, *When I Was a Kid*.

"Oh Where, Oh Where Has My Little Dog Gone?" Beall, Pamela, and Susan Nipp, *Wee Sing Nursery Rhymes and Lullabies*.

"Ol' Blue." Hinton, Sam, *Whoever Shall Have Some Good Peanuts*; Staines, Bill, *One More River*.

"Old Mother Hubbard." Silberg, "Miss Jackie," *The Complete Sniggles, Squirrels, and Chicken Pox*.

"Our Dog Bernard." Polisar, Barry Louis, *Old Dog, New Tricks*.

"Piccolo the Dog." Pullara, Steve, *A Big Bowl of Musicroni*.

"Pickup Hiccup Truck." Cosgrove, Jim, *Bop Bop Dinosaur*.

"A Poodle in Paris." Kaldor, Connie, *A Poodle in Paris*.

"A Puppy." Barchas, Sarah, *If I Had a Pony*.

"Puppy at the Pound." Chapin, Tom, *Some Assembly Required*.

"Puppy Dog." Ralph's World, *Peggy's Pie Parlor*.

"Puppy Kisses." Atkinson, Lisa, *The Elephant in Aisle Four*.

"Puppy Love." Gemini, *The Best of Gemini.*

"Rags." Sharon, Lois, and Bram, *Great Big Hits.* (Same song as "My Dog Rags.")

"Raining Cats and Dogs." Foote, Norman, *Foote Prints.*

"Raining Cats and Dogs." LaFond, Lois, *One World.*

"Sammy the Dog." Ralph's World, *Happy Lemon.*

"Snuggle Puppy." Boynton, Sandra, *Philadelphia Chickens.*

"So Long, Doggies." Boynton, Sandra, *Rhinoceros Tap.*

"Softest Dog." Foote, Norman, *Pictures on the Fridge.*

"Space Dog." Frezza, Rebecca, *Road Trip.*

"The Tale of a Dog." Kaye, Mary, *Mouse Jamboree.*

"Walkin' the Dog." Knight, Tom, *Easy as Pie.*

"Wild Dog on the Farm." Pease, Tom, *Boogie! Boogie! Boogie!*

"You'll Be Sorry." Chapin, Tom, *Billy the Squid*; Chapin, Tom, *Great Big Fun for the Very Little One.*

Dolphins

"Dolphin Dance." Tickle Tune Typhoon, *Hearts and Hands.*

"Dolphin Drummers." Pirtle, Sarah, *Magical Earth.*

"Dolphins." Charette, Rick, *Chickens on Vacation.*

"The Dolphins and the Mermaid." Lonnquist, Ken, *The Lost Songs of Kenland*; Lonnquist, Ken, *The Switcher-On of Stars.*

Donkeys/Mules

"Chester the Donkey." Walker, Graham, *Cats' Night Out.*

"Come My Little Donkey." Moo, Anna, *Anna Moo Crackers.*

"Donkey Riding." Allard, Peter and Ellen, *Sing It! Say It! Stamp It! Sway It!* vol. 1; Raven, Nancy, *Hop, Skip, and Sing.*

"Erie Canal." Berkner, Laurie, *Buzz Buzz*; Grammer, Red, *Red Grammer's Favorite Sing Along Songs*; Hullabaloo, *Sing Along with Sam*; Zanes, Dan, *Rocket Ship Beach.*

"Mi Burro (My Burro)." Beall, Pamela, and Susan Nipp, *Wee Sing around the World.*

"Mules." Beall, Pamela, and Susan Nipp, *Wee Sing Silly Songs.*

"Sweetly Sings the Donkey." Beall, Pamela, and Susan Nipp, *Wee Sing Animals, Animals, Animals*; Beall, Pamela, and Susan Nipp, *Wee Sing Sing-Alongs.*

"Tingalayo." Beall, Pamela, and Susan Nipp, *Wee Sing Animals, Animals, Animals*; Beall, Pamela, and Susan Nipp, *Wee Sing around the World*; Berkner, Laurie, *Victor Vito*; Cassidy, Nancy, *Nancy Cassidy's KidsSongs*; Raffi, *One Light One*

Sun; Raffi, *Raffi in Concert*; Sharon, Lois, and Bram, *Great Big Hits*; Sharon, Lois, and Bram, *Name Games*; Sharon, Lois, and Bram, *One Elephant, Deux Éléphants*.

"Whoa Nellie." Arnold, Linda, *Favorites in the Key of Fun*.

Elephants

"Chew a Cherry." Lonnquist, Ken, *Welcome 2 Kenland*.

"Elephant Hide and Seek." SteveSongs, *Marvelous Day!*

"The Elephant in Aisle Four." Atkinson, Lisa, *The Elephant in Aisle Four*.

"Elephant Train." Fite, Stephen, *Wiggles, Jiggles, and Giggles*.

"The Elephant Who Couldn't Pay Rent." Pullara, Steve, *One Potato, Two Potato*.

"Elephants Have Wrinkles." Colleen and Uncle Squaty, *Sing-a-Move-a-Dance*.

"The Elephant's Lullaby." Knight, Tom, *The Library Boogie*.

"Englebert the Elephant." Paxton, Tom, *Goin' to the Zoo*.

"In an Elephant World." Chapin, Tom, *Around the World and Back Again*.

"One Elephant." Beall, Pamela, and Susan Nipp, *Wee Sing Animals, Animals, Animals*; Beall, Pamela, and Susan Nipp, *Wee Sing Children's Songs and Fingerplays*; Sharon, Lois, and Bram, *Great Big Hits*; Sharon, Lois, and Bram, *One Elephant, Deux Éléphants*; Sharon, Lois, and Bram, *School Days*. (Same song as "One Little Elephant.")

"One Little Elephant." Raven, Nancy, *Nancy Raven Sings Her Favorites*; Raven, Nancy, *You Gotta Juba*. (Same song as "One Elephant.")

"Peculiar to the Pachyderm." Lonnquist, Ken, *The Circus Kenlando*.

"Push the Elephant." Harper, Jessica, *Nora's Room*.

"Willoughby Wallaby Woo." Cassidy, Nancy, *Nancy Cassidy's KidsSongs*; McGrath, Bob, *Sing Along with Bob #1*; Raffi, *Singable Songs for the Very Young*.

"Zousan (Little Elephant)." Mitchell, Elizabeth, *You Are My Little Bird*.

Elk

"Baby Wapiti." Banana Slug String Band, *Goin' Wild*.

Foxes

"The Fox." Abell, Timmy, *I Know an Old Lady*; Cassidy, Nancy, *Nancy Cassidy's KidsSongs*; Colleen and Uncle Squaty, *Fingerplays, Movement and Story Songs*; Kirk, John, and Trish Miller, *The Big Rock Candy Mountain*; Penner, Fred, *Storytime*; Peter, Paul, and Mary, *Peter, Paul, and Mommy, Too*; Raven, Nancy, *People and Animal Songs*; Rosenthal, Phil, *Animal Songs*; Rudnick, Ben, *Blast Off!*; Staines, Bill, *One More River*.

Frogs/Toads

"All the Little Pollywogs." Avni, Fran, *Tuning into Nature*.

"Blue Frog." Penner, Fred, *What a Day!*

"El Coquí (The Frog)." Beall, Pamela, and Susan Nipp, *Wee Sing around the World*.

"Croak-a-Ribit." Banana Slug String Band, *Penguin Parade*.

"Down by the River/Bullfrog." Harper, Jessica, *Inside Out*.

"Five Frogs." Moo, Anna, *Anna Moo Crackers*.

"Five Little Frogs." Raffi, *Singable Songs for the Very Young*.

"The Foolish Frog." Diamond, Charlotte, *Diamond in the Rough*.

"Freddy the Fly Eating Frog." Harley, Bill, *Monsters in the Bathroom*.

"The Frog in the Bog." Beall, Pamela, and Susan Nipp, *Wee Sing Fun 'n' Folk*.

"Frog in the Bog." Cosgrove, Jim, *Stinky Feet*.

"Frog Round." Beall, Pamela, and Susan Nipp, *Wee Sing Sing-Alongs*.

"The Frog Song." Harper, Monty, *The Great Green Squishy Mean Concert CD*.

"The Frog Song." Hinton, Sam, *Whoever Shall Have Some Good Peanuts*.

"Frog Went A-Courtin'." Beall, Pamela, and Susan Nipp, *Wee Sing Fun 'n' Folk*; Berkner, Laurie, *Victor Vito*; Feldman, Jean, *Nursery Rhymes and Good Ol' Times*; Hinton, Sam, *Whoever Shall Have Some Good Peanuts*; Kirk, John, and Trish Miller, *The Big Rock Candy Mountain*; Mitchell, Elizabeth, *You Are My Sunshine*; Rosenthal, Phil, *The Green Grass Grew All Around*; Various Artists, *Folk Playground*. (Same song as "Mr. Froggie Went A-Courtin'.")

"Frogs in the Road." Charette, Rick, *Bubble Gum*.

"The Frog's Party." Walker, Mary Lu, *The Frog's Party*.

"The Garden." Roth, Kevin, *Unbearable Bears*.

"Gatgoon." Sharon, Lois, and Bram, *Sing A to Z*. (Same song as "Little Green Frog.")

"Great Big Frog." Walker, Graham, *Knobbledee Knees*.

"Here's to Cheshire." McCutcheon, John, *Howjadoo*; Seeger, Pete, *For Kids and Just Plain Folks*.

"Hippity-Hop." Avni, Fran, *Artichokes and Brussel Sprouts*; Avni, Fran, *Tuning into Nature*.

"Hop like a Frog." Pullara, Steve, *Hop like a Frog*.

"I've Got a Toad." McMahon, Elizabeth, *Magic Parade*.

"Jumpety Jump." Walker, Graham, *Jumpety Jump*.

"Keemo Kymo." Beall, Pamela, and Susan Nipp, *Wee Sing Fun 'n' Folk*.

"Kiddy Kum Kimo." Sharon, Lois, and Bram, *Great Big Hits 2*; Sharon, Lois, and Bram, *Sing A to Z*.

"King Kong Kitchie." Zanes, Dan, *Rocket Ship Beach*.

"Lick a Frog." Charette, Rick, *King Kong Chair*.

"Little Bitty Frog." Lonnquist, Ken, *Earthy Songs*.

"Little Green Frog." Beall, Pamela, and Susan Nipp, *Wee Sing Animals, Animals, Animals*; Beall, Pamela, and Susan Nipp, *Wee Sing Children's Songs and Fingerplays*. (Same song as "Gatgoon.")

"Me and Froggy Are Friends." Strausman, Paul, *Blue Jay, Blue Jay!*

"Metamorphosis." Diamond, Charlotte, *Diamond in the Rough*.

"Mr. Froggie Went A-Courtin'." Ives, Burl, *Burl Ives Sings the Little White Duck*. (Same song as "Frog Went A-Courtin'.")

"Mr. Froggy." Livingston, Bob, *Open the Window*.

"Newts, Salamanders and Frogs." Banana Slug String Band, *Dirt Made My Lunch*.

"The Night the Froggies Flew." Colleen and Uncle Squaty, *Fingerplays, Movement and Story Songs*.

"One Day My Best Friend Barbara Turned into a Frog." Polisar, Barry Louis, *Old Dog, New Tricks*.

"Peepers." Walker, Mary Lu, *The Frog's Party*.

"Polliwogs." Avni, Fran, *Little Ears: Songs for Reading Readiness*.

"Slimy, Green and Kind of Funny." Thaddeus Rex, *We Wanna Rock*.

"Små Grodorna (Little Frogs)." Beall, Pamela, and Susan Nipp, *Wee Sing around the World*.

"Speckled Frogs." Old Town School of Folk Music, *Wiggleworms Love You*.

"Toad Motel." Charette, Rick, *Toad Motel*.

"Wish Me a Lot of Muck." Kinnoin, Dave, *Dunce Cap Kelly*.

Giraffes

"The Giraffe." Beall, Pamela, and Susan Nipp, *Wee Sing Animals, Animals, Animals*.

"Giraffe/Nightingale." Roberts, Justin, *Yellow Bus*.

"Joshua the Giraffe." Raffi, *Baby Beluga*.

"My Giraffe." Paxton, Tom, *Your Shoes, My Shoes*.

Gnus

"Gned the Gnu." Rosen, Gary, *Tot Rock*.

"The Gnu Song." Lithgow, John, *Singin' in the Bathtub*.

Goats

"Bill Grogan's Goat." Beall, Pamela, and Susan Nipp, *Wee Sing Animals, Animals, Animals*; Beall, Pamela, and Susan Nipp, *Wee Sing Silly Songs*.

"Billy Goat Walk." Kimmy Schwimmy, *Kimmy Schwimmy Music*, vol. 1.

"Billy Goats Gruff." McMahon, Elizabeth, *Magic Parade*.

"Go Out and Get Your Own Goat." Avni, Fran, *Little Ears: Songs for Reading Readiness*; Avni, Fran, *Tuning into Nature*.

"The Goat." Ives, Burl, *Burl Ives Sings Little White Duck*.

"A Kid and a Goat." Foote, Norman, *If the Shoe Fits*.

"The Potato Goat." Crow, Dan, *Oops!*

"Rockabilly Goats Gruff." Knight, Tom, *The Classroom Boogie*.

"Three Billy Goats Groove." Dana, *Dana's Best Rock and Roll Fairy Tales*.

"Three Billy Goats Gruff." Greg and Steve, *Rockin' down the Road*.

Gorillas

"Red Banana." Ralph's World, *Green Gorilla, Monster, and Me*.

Groundhogs

"Groundhog." Hinton, Sam, *Whoever Shall Have Some Good Peanuts*.

"Groundhog Day." McCutcheon, John, *Wintersongs*.

Hermit Crabs

"Tide Pool Heroes." Arnold, Linda, *Splash Zone*.

Hippopotamuses

"Hey Hippopotamus." Roberts, Justin, *Yellow Bus*.

"Hippo Hurray." Arnold, Linda, *Favorites in the Key of Fun*; Arnold, Linda, *Happiness Cake*.

"The Hippopotamus and the Rhinoceros." Beall, Pamela, and Susan Nipp, *Wee Sing Animals, Animals, Animals*.

"Hippopotamus Rock." Rosen, Gary, *Pet Sounds*; Rosenshontz, *Rosenshontz Greatest Hits*; Rosenshontz, *Tickles You!*

"The Hippopotamus Song." Lithgow, John, *Farkle and Friends*; Lithgow, John, *Singin' in the Bathtub*.

"The Hippopotamus Song." Ode, Eric, *I Love My Shoes*.

"How the Hippo Got So Hip." Lonnquist, Ken, *Sci-Fi Hi-Fi*.

"If You Love a Hippopotamus." Alsop, Peter, *Stayin' Over*; Kaldor, Connie, *A Duck in New York City*.

"My Baby Hippo." McMahon, Elizabeth, *Blue Sky Sparklin' Day*.

Horned Toads

"Horny Toad." Harper, Monty, *The Great Green Squishy Mean Concert CD*.
"The Legend of Old Rip." Harper, Monty, *The Great Green Squishy Mean Concert CD*.

Horses

"Goodbye Old Paint." Zanes, Dan, *Rocket Ship Beach*.
"A Happy Horse." Crow, Dan, *A Friend, a Laugh, a Walk in the Woods*.
"Horse Blues." Tucker, Nancy, *Happy as a Clam*.
"The Horse Went Around." Beall, Pamela, and Susan Nipp, *Wee Sing Silly Songs*.
"Horsey Horsey." Rosenthal, Phil, *The Paw Paw Patch*.
"I Have a Horse." Barchas, Sarah, *Get Ready, Get Set, Sing!*
"If I Had a Pony." Barchas, Sarah, *If I Had a Pony*.
"Listen to the Horses." Raffi, *More Singable Songs*; Raffi, *Quiet Time*.
"Little Pony Hoo." Green Chili Jam Band, *Starfishing*.
"The Old Gray Mare." Beall, Pamela, and Susan Nipp, *Wee Sing Animals, Animals, Animals*; Beall, Pamela, and Susan Nipp, *Wee Sing Fun 'n' Folk*.
"The Pony." Charette, Rick, *Alligator in the Elevator*.
"Starbright." Moo, Anna, *Anna Moo Crackers*.

Jellyfish

"Jellyfish." Tucker, Nancy, *Escape of the Slinkys*.
"Jellyfish Jump." Coffey, James, *Animal Groove*.

Kangaroos

"Katie the Kangaroo." Atkinson, Lisa, *The Elephant in Aisle Four*.
"Marsupial Sue." Lithgow, John, *Farkle and Friends*.

Koalas

"Koala." Green Chili Jam Band, *Magic Bike*.
"Koala Bear Diner." Roberts, Justin, *Meltdown!*

Lions

"The Lion." Beall, Pamela, and Susan Nipp, *Wee Sing Animals, Animals, Animals*.
"The Lion Sleeps Tonight." Grunsky, Jack, *Jack in the Box 2*; Howdy, Buck, *Skidaddle!* (Same song as "Mbube [The Lion Sleeps Tonight]" and "Wimoweh.")

"Mbube (The Lion Sleeps Tonight)." Ladysmith Black Mambazo, *Gift of the Tortoise*. (Same song as "The Lion Sleeps Tonight" and "Wimoweh.")

"Signifyin' Monkey." Dana, *Dana's Best Sing and Swing-a-Long Tunes*.

"Wimoweh." Berkner, Laurie, *Whaddaya Think of That?*; Grammer, Red, *Red Grammer's Favorite Sing Along Songs*; Seeger, Pete, *For Kids and Just Plain Folks*; Various Artists, *A Child's Celebration of Song 2*. (Same song as "The Lion Sleeps Tonight" and "Mbube [The Lion Sleeps Tonight].")

Lizards

"Echo Gecko." Kinder, Brian, *A Kid like You*.

Llamas

"Mama Llama." Hullabaloo, *Sing Along with Sam*.

Lobsters

"Lincoln the Lobster." Charette, Rick, *Toad Motel*.

Manatees

"Pink Floyd Saves Hugh Manatee." Daddy A Go Go, *Eat Every Bean and Pea on Your Plate*.

Mice

"Country Mouse and the City Mouse." McMahon, Elizabeth, *Magic Parade*.

"Frog Went A-Courtin'." Beall, Pamela, and Susan Nipp, *Wee Sing Fun 'n' Folk*; Berkner, Laurie, *Victor Vito*; Feldman, Jean, *Nursery Rhymes and Good Ol' Times*; Hinton, Sam, *Whoever Shall Have Some Good Peanuts*; Kirk, John, and Trish Miller, *The Big Rock Candy Mountain*; Mitchell, Elizabeth, *You Are My Sunshine*; Rosenthal, Phil, *The Green Grass Grew All Around*; Various Artists, *Folk Playground*. (Same song as "Mr. Froggie Went A-Courtin'.")

"Grey Little Mouse." Allard, Peter and Ellen, *Sing It! Say It! Stamp It! Sway It!* vol. 3.

"Here's to Cheshire." McCutcheon, John, *Howjadoo*; Seeger, Pete, *For Kids and Just Plain Folks*.

"Hickory Dickory Dock." Barchas, Sarah, *Get Ready, Get Set, Sing!*; Beall, Pamela, and Susan Nipp, *Wee Sing Children's Songs and Fingerplays*; Beall, Pamela, and Susan Nipp, *Wee Sing for Baby*; Beall, Pamela, and Susan Nipp, *Wee Sing Nursery Rhymes and Lullabies*; Feldman, Jean, *Nursery Rhymes and Good Ol' Times*.

"Hickory Dickory Dock." SteveSongs, *On a Flying Guitar*.

"Inside and Outside." Jenkins, Ella, *Growing Up with Ella Jenkins*.

"King Kong Kitchie." Zanes, Dan, *Rocket Ship Beach*. (Similar to "Mr. Froggie Went A-Courtin'.")

"Little Bunny Foo Foo." Beall, Pamela, and Susan Nipp, *Wee Sing Animals, Animals, Animals*; Beall, Pamela, and Susan Nipp, *Wee Sing Silly Songs*. (Same song as "Little Rabbit Foo Foo.")

"The Little Mouse Goes Creeping." Peterson, Carole, *Tiny Tunes*.

"Little Rabbit Foo Foo." Sharon, Lois, and Bram, *Great Big Hits*; Sharon, Lois, and Bram, *Mainly Mother Goose*; Sharon, Lois, and Bram, *Name Games*. (Same song as "Little Bunny Foo Foo.")

"Long Time Ago." Raven, Nancy, *People and Animal Songs*.

"The Mouse." Rosenthal, Phil, *Animal Songs*; Rosenthal, Phil, *Folksongs and Bluegrass for Children*.

"The Mouse and the Clock." Colleen and Uncle Squaty, *Fingerplays, Movement and Story Songs*.

"The Mouse Band." Grunsky, Jack, *Sing and Dance*.

"Mouse in the House." Various Artists, *Reggae Playground*.

"Mouse Jamboree." Kaye, Mary, *Mouse Jamboree*.

"Mr. Froggie Went A-Courtin'." Ives, Burl, *Burl Ives Sings Little White Duck*. (Same song as "Frog Went A-Courtin'.")

"Once There Was a Little Kitty." Buchman, Rachel, *Sing a Song of Seasons*.

"The Tailor and the Mouse." Ives, Burl, *Burl Ives Sings Little White Duck*.

"Three Blind Mice." Beall, Pamela, and Susan Nipp, *Wee Sing Sing-Alongs*; McGrath, Bob, *Sing Along with Bob #2*; Various Artists, *Grandma's Patchwork Quilt*.

Monkeys/Chimpanzees

"The Aba Daba Honeymoon." Bartels, Joanie, *Sillytime Magic*; The Chenille Sisters, *The Big Picture and Other Songs for Kids*; Muldaur, Maria, *Swingin' in the Rain*.

"B-Banana/Monkey See, Monkey Do!" Peterson, Carole, *Stinky Cake*.

"Bongo Bong." Various Artists, *World Playground*.

"Coconut Café." Parachute Express, *Friends, Forever Friends*.

"Deep in the Jungle." Scruggs, Joe, *Deep in the Jungle*.

"Five Little Monkeys." Barchas, Sarah, *If I Had a Pony*; Greg and Steve, *Ready, Set, Move!*; The Learning Station, *Literacy in Motion*; The Learning Station, *Tony Chestnut and Fun Time Action Songs*; McGrath, Bob, *Sing Along with Bob #1*; Palmer, Hap, *So Big*; Yosi, *Monkey Business*. (Similar to "No More Monkeys" and "Ten Little Monkeys.")

"Here Sits a Monkey." Raffi, *Corner Grocery Store*.

"Jabu the Little Monkey." Coffey, James, *Animal Groove*.

"Jane Jane." Raffi, *Let's Play*.

"Jaws of a Crocodile." Lonnquist, Ken, *The Circus Kenlando*.

"Just like the Monkeys." Ralph's World, *The Amazing Adventures of Kid Astro*.

"Mary and Melvin." Palmer, Hap, *One Little Sound*.

"Mikey the Monkey." Beall, Pamela, and Susan Nipp, *Wee Sing and Pretend*.

"Monkey and the Engineer." Rudnick, Ben, *Emily Songs*.

"The Monkey and the Zebra." Beall, Pamela, and Susan Nipp, *Wee Sing Animals, Animals, Animals*.

"Monkey Can Do." Raven, Nancy, *Nancy Raven Sings Her Favorites*; Raven, Nancy, *You Gotta Juba*.

"Monkey Dance." Walker, Graham, *Knobbledee Knees*.

"Monkey in the Middle." Daddy A Go Go, *Monkey in the Middle*.

"Monkey Monkey Monkey." Knight, Tom, *Easy as Pie*.

"Monkey Talk." Lonnquist, Ken, *The Lost Songs of Kenland*.

"Monkeys and the Alligator." Feldman, Jean, *Dr. Jean and Friends*.

"Monkeys in the Trees in India." Kaldor, Connie, *A Poodle in Paris*.

"Monkey's New Shoes." Mayer, Hans, *Just a Little Hug*.

"My Sister's a Monkey." Pullara, Steve, *One Potato, Two Potato*.

"No More Monkeys." Mr. Al, *Mr. Al Concert Live*; Mr. Al, *Put Your Groove On*. (Similar to "Five Little Monkeys" and "Ten Little Monkeys.")

"Pop! Goes the Weasel." Barchas, Sarah, *If I Had a Pony*; Beall, Pamela, and Susan Nipp, *Wee Sing and Play*; Beall, Pamela, and Susan Nipp, *Wee Sing Children's Songs and Fingerplays*; Beall, Pamela, and Susan Nipp, *Wee Sing for Baby*; Old Town School of Folk Music, *Wiggleworms Love You*; Sharon, Lois, and Bram, *Great Big Hits*; Sharon, Lois, and Bram, *Mainly Mother Goose*; Walker, Graham, *Jumpety Jump*.

"Seven Monkeys Up in a Tree." Ralph's World, *Ralph's World*.

"Six Little Monkeys." Yosi, *Under a Big Bright Yellow Umbrella*.

"Ten Little Monkeys." Palmer, Hap, *Two Little Sounds*. (Similar to "Five Little Monkeys" and "No More Monkeys.")

Moose

"Gypsy Moose." Simmons, Al, *The Truck I Bought from Moe*.

"Moose." Banana Slug String Band, *Goin' Wild*; Banana Slug String Band, *Penguin Parade*.

"A Moose Named Amos." Charette, Rick, *Popcorn and Other Songs to Munch On*.

"The Vegetarian Barbeque Moose." Charette, Rick, *Toad Motel*.

Octopus

"Deep in the Water." Kaye, Mary, *I Sang It Just for You*.

Opossums

"Brother Possum." Pirtle, Sarah, *Two Hands Hold the Earth*.

"Raccoon Has a Bushy Tail." Beall, Pamela, and Susan Nipp, *Wee Sing Animals, Animals, Animals*. (Same song as "Raccoon's Tail.")

"Raccoon's Tail." Barchas, Sarah, *If I Had a Pony*; Raven, Nancy, *People and Animal Songs*. (Same song as "Raccoon Has a Bushy Tail.")

Otters

"California Sea Otter." Banana Slug String Band, *Penguin Parade*.

Pigs

"Eight Piggies in a Row." Raffi, *Everything Grows*.

"The Evelyn Way." Madsen, Gunnar, *Old Mr. Mackle Hackle*.

"Little Piggy." Roth, Kevin, *Travel Song Sing Alongs*.

"Lots of Little Wolves." Berkner, Laurie, *Buzz Buzz*.

"My Playful Pig." Palmer, Hap, *Two Little Sounds*.

"The Old Sow." Sharon, Lois, and Bram, *One Elephant, Deux Éléphants*.

"Perfect Piggies." Boynton, Sandra, *Rhinoceros Tap*.

"Pig Island." Boynton, Sandra, *Philadelphia Chickens*.

"Pig Party." Kaye, Mary, *Spin Your Web*.

"Piggy Letter Boogie." LaFond, Lois, *Turning It Upside Down*.

"Priscilla Pig." Walker, Graham, *Cats' Night Out*.

"The Skinny Pig." Crow, Dan, *Oops!*

"Susannah's a Funny Old Man." Sharon, Lois, and Bram, *Great Big Hits*; Sharon, Lois, and Bram, *Name Games*; Sharon, Lois, and Bram, *Sing A to Z*.

"This Little Pig Went to Market." Beall, Pamela, and Susan Nipp, *Wee Sing for Baby*; Beall, Pamela, and Susan Nipp, *Wee Sing Nursery Rhymes and Lullabies*.

"Three Foolish Piglets." Hinton, Sam, *Whoever Shall Have Some Good Peanuts*.

"Three Lil Pigs." Roberts, Justin, *Great Big Sun*.

"The Three Little Pig Blues." Greg and Steve, *Playing Favorites*.

"Three Little Piggies." Beall, Pamela, and Susan Nipp, *Wee Sing Animals, Animals, Animals*.

"3 Little Piggies." Miss Amy, *Underwater*.

"Three Little Piggies." Strausman, Paul, *Blue Jay, Blue Jay!*

"Who's Afraid of the Big Bad Wolf?" Rosenshontz, *Share It*; Shontz, Bill, *The Day I Read a Book*.

Platypuses

"Gus the Platypus." Shontz, Bill, *Animal Tales*.

Porcupines

"Porcupine Path." Kaye, Mary, *Spin Your Web*.
"With a Porcupine." Kinnoin, Dave, *Dunce Cap Kelly*.

Rabbits

"Big Eye Rabbit." Raven, Nancy, *Hop, Skip, and Sing*.
"John the Rabbit." Allard, Peter and Ellen, *Sing It! Say It! Stamp It! Sway It!* vol. 3; McGrath, Bob, and Katherine Smithrim, *Songs and Games for Toddlers*; Mitchell, Elizabeth, *You Are My Flower*; Raven, Nancy, *The House We Live In*, vols. 1 and 2. (Same song as "Old John the Rabbit.")
"Little Bunny Foo Foo." Beall, Pamela, and Susan Nipp, *Wee Sing Animals, Animals, Animals*; Beall, Pamela, and Susan Nipp, *Wee Sing Silly Songs*. (Same song as "Little Rabbit Foo Foo.")
"Little Cabin in the Wood." Beall, Pamela, and Susan Nipp, *Wee Sing Children's Songs and Fingerplays*.
"Little Peter Rabbit." Beall, Pamela, and Susan Nipp, *Wee Sing Animals, Animals, Animals*; Beall, Pamela, and Susan Nipp, *Wee Sing Children's Songs and Fingerplays*; McGrath, Bob, *Sing Along with Bob #2*.
"Little Rabbit Foo Foo." Sharon, Lois, and Bram, *Great Big Hits*; Sharon, Lois, and Bram, *Mainly Mother Goose*; Sharon, Lois, and Bram, *Name Games*. (Same song as "Little Bunny Foo Foo.")
"Little Rabbit, Where's Your Mammy?" Fink, Cathy, *Grandma Slid down the Mountain*.
"Mr. Rabbit." Beall, Pamela, and Susan Nipp, *Wee Sing Animals, Animals, Animals*; Fink, Cathy, and Marcy Marxer, *A Cathy & Marcy Collection for Kids*; Hinton, Sam, *Whoever Shall Have Some Good Peanuts*; Ives, Burl, *Burl Ives Sings Little White Duck*; Ralph's World, *The Amazing Adventures of Kid Astro*; Raven, Nancy, *Hop, Skip, and Sing*; Roth, Kevin, *Travel Song Sing Alongs*; Staines, Bill, *One More River*.
"Mr. Rabbit." Fite, Stephen, *Wiggles, Jiggles, and Giggles*.
"Oh Yes, He Did It." Shontz, Bill, *Animal Tales*.
"Old John the Rabbit." Raven, Nancy, *Hop, Skip, and Sing*. (Same song as "John the Rabbit.")

"Rabbit Ain't Got No Tail." Beall, Pamela, and Susan Nipp, *Wee Sing Animals, Animals, Animals*; Beall, Pamela, and Susan Nipp, *Wee Sing Silly Songs*.

"Rabbit Habit." Knight, Tom, *The Library Boogie*.

"Rabbit in the Hollow." Beall, Pamela, and Susan Nipp, *Wee Sing Games, Games, Games*.

"Rabbits Dance." Raven, Nancy, *Nancy Raven Sings Her Favorites*.

"Rabbit's Ramble." Strausman, Paul, *The World's Big Family*.

"Raccoon Has a Bushy Tail." Beall, Pamela, and Susan Nipp, *Wee Sing Animals, Animals, Animals*. (Same song as "Raccoon's Tail.")

"Raccoon's Tail." Barchas, Sarah, *If I Had a Pony*; Raven, Nancy, *People and Animal Songs*. (Same song as "Raccoon Has a Bushy Tail.").

"Run Bunny Run." Hullabaloo, *Sing Along with Sam*.

"Wascawy Wabbit." LaFond, Lois, *One World*.

"Ya Wanna Buy a Bunny." Bartels, Joanie, *Sillytime Magic*.

Raccoons

"Black Patches." Banana Slug String Band, *Penguin Parade*.

"Mrs. Tuckaway." Grunsky, Jack, *Jack in the Box 2*; Grunsky, Jack, *World Safari*.

"Rabbits Dance." Raven, Nancy, *You Gotta Juba*.

"Raccoon Has a Bushy Tail." Beall, Pamela, and Susan Nipp, *Wee Sing Animals, Animals, Animals*. (Same song as "Raccoon's Tail.")

"Raccoon's Tail." Barchas, Sarah, *If I Had a Pony*; Raven, Nancy, *People and Animal Songs*. (Same song as "Raccoon Has a Bushy Tail.").

Rats

"Matt the Pack Rat." Walker, Graham, *Cats' Night Out*.

"Norman." McMahon, Elizabeth, *Tea Party Shuffle*.

Rhinoceroses

"Don't Be Rude to a Rhinoceros." Paxton, Tom, *I've Got a Yo-Yo*.

"The Hippopotamus and the Rhinoceros." Beall, Pamela, and Susan Nipp, *Wee Sing Animals, Animals, Animals*.

"Our Imaginary Rhino." Roberts, Justin, *Meltdown!*

"Rhino." Lonnquist, Ken, *The Lost Songs of Kenland*.

"You're a Rhino!" Lonnquist, Ken, *Welcome 2 Kenland*.

Salamanders/Newts

"Newts, Salamanders and Frogs." Banana Slug String Band, *Dirt Made My Lunch*.

"Sally Salamander." Rudnick, Ben, *Fun and Games*.

Sea Anemones

"Anemone." Arnold, Linda, *Splash Zone*.

"Let's Be Friends." Arnold, Linda, *Splash Zone*.

Sheep

"Baa Baa Black Sheep." Beall, Pamela, and Susan Nipp, *Wee Sing Animals, Animals, Animals*; Beall, Pamela, and Susan Nipp, *Wee Sing Nursery Rhymes and Lullabies*; McGrath, Bob, *Sing Along with Bob #1*; Raffi, *Singable Songs for the Very Young*; Ralph's World, *At the Bottom of the Sea*.

"Little Bo-Peep." Beall, Pamela, and Susan Nipp, *Wee Sing Nursery Rhymes and Lullabies*.

"Mary Had a Little Lamb." Beall, Pamela, and Susan Nipp, *Wee Sing Nursery Rhymes and Lullabies*; Feldman, Jean, *Nursery Rhymes and Good Ol' Times*; McGrath, Bob, *Sing Along with Bob #2*; Old Town School of Folk Music, *Wiggleworms Love You*; Rosenthal, Phil, *The Paw Paw Patch*; Sharon, Lois, and Bram, *Mainly Mother Goose*; Sharon, Lois, and Bram, *Name Games*.

"Sheep." Various Artists, *Folk Playground*.

"Ten Sleepy Sheep." Harper, Jessica, *40 Winks*.

"Three Little Sheep." Kinder, Brian, *Again*.

Skunks

"Bobby Brought a Skunk to the Pet Parade." Ode, Eric, *Trash Can*.

"The Little Skunk's Hole." Beall, Pamela, and Susan Nipp, *Wee Sing Animals, Animals, Animals*; Beall, Pamela, and Susan Nipp, *Wee Sing Silly Songs*.

Slugs

"Banana Slug." Banana Slug String Band, *Dirt Made My Lunch*.

"Banana Slug." Pease, Tom, *Boogie! Boogie! Boogie!*

"Slimy Slugs." Charette, Rick, *Toad Motel*.

"Slimy the Slug." Diamond, Charlotte, *Diamonds and Dragons*.

"Slug Opera." Kaldor, Connie, *A Duck in New York City*.

Snails

"Sammy the Snail." Cosgrove, Jim, *Pick Me! Pick Me!*

"The Snail." Beall, Pamela, and Susan Nipp, *Wee Sing Animals, Animals, Animals*; Beall, Pamela, and Susan Nipp, *Wee Sing Games, Games, Games*.

Snakes

"Boa Constrictor." The Chenille Sisters, *1, 2, 3 for Kids*; Diamond, Charlotte, *Diamond in the Rough*; Peter, Paul, and Mary, *Peter, Paul, and Mommy*.
"Rattle, Rattle, Rattle and Shake, Shake, Shake." Barchas, Sarah, *If I Had a Pony*.
"Rattlesnake." The Learning Station, *Tony Chestnut and Fun Time Action Songs*.
"The Snake." Beall, Pamela, and Susan Nipp, *Wee Sing Animals, Animals, Animals*.
"With a Wiggle and a Hiss." Barchas, Sarah, *If I Had a Pony*.

Squids

"Billy the Squid." Chapin, Tom, *Billy the Squid*.

Squirrels

"Danger Below." Kinnoin, Dave, *Getting Bigger*.
"Grey Squirrel." Allard, Peter and Ellen, *Sing It! Say It! Stamp It! Sway It!* vol. 3.
"Little Squirrel Came Home." Knight, Tom, *The Library Boogie*.
"Seven Silly Squirrels." Avni, Fran, *Little Ears: Songs for Reading Readiness*.
"Squirrel, Squirrel." Beall, Pamela, and Susan Nipp, *Wee Sing Animals, Animals, Animals*.

Starfish

"I'm a Sea Star." Arnold, Linda, *Splash Zone*.

Tigers

"Do You?" Lonnquist, Ken, *Sci-Fi Hi-Fi*.
"Tiger Island." Knight, Tom, *Easy as Pie*.

Turtles

"Myrtle the Turtle." Atkinson, Lisa, *The One and Only Me*.
"Oh Yes, He Did It." Shontz, Bill, *Animal Tales*.
"Spyrtle the Turtle." SteveSongs, *Marvelous Day!*
"Tiny Tim." Various Artists, *A Child's Celebration of Silliest Songs*.
"Tiny Tim the Turtle." Feldman, Jean, *Dr. Jean Sings Silly Songs*.
"Turtle Rock Boogie." Strausman, Paul, *The World's Big Family*.
"Yertle the Turtle." Various Artists, *A Child's Celebration of Song 2*.
"You Can't Make a Turtle Come Out." Raven, Nancy, *Singing, Prancing, and Dancing*; Ungar, Jay, and Lyn Hardy, *A Place to Be*; Various Artists, *Grandma's Patchwork Quilt*.

Wallabies

"Wacky Wallaby Waltz." Bartles, Joanie, *Put On Your Dancing Shoes*.

Weasels

"Pop! Goes the Weasel." Barchas, Sarah, *If I Had a Pony*; Beall, Pamela, and Susan Nipp, *Wee Sing and Play*; Beall, Pamela, and Susan Nipp, *Wee Sing Children's Songs and Fingerplays*; Beall, Pamela, and Susan Nipp, *Wee Sing for Baby*; Old Town School of Folk Music, *Wiggleworms Love You*; Sharon, Lois, and Bram, *Great Big Hits*; Sharon, Lois, and Bram, *Mainly Mother Goose*; Walker, Graham, *Jumpety Jump*.

Whales

"Baby Beluga." Cassidy, Nancy, *Nancy Cassidy's KidsSongs*; Raffi, *Baby Beluga*; Raffi, *Raffi in Concert*; Various Artists, *A Child's Celebration of Song*.

"The Blue Mammal Waltz." Tickle Tune Typhoon, *Singing Science*.

"Rubber Blubber Whale." Diamond, Charlotte, *Diamonds and Dragons*; McCutcheon, John, *Howjadoo*.

"Sarah the Whale." Sharon, Lois, and Bram, *Name Games*. (Same song as "The Whale.")

"Sing a Whale Song." Chapin, Tom, *Moonboat*.

"The Song of the Whales." Rosenthal, Phil, *Animal Songs*.

"Watching the Whales." Pullara, Steve, *Hop like a Frog*.

"The Whale." Ives, Burl, *Burl Ives Sings Little White Duck*. (Same song as "Sarah the Whale.")

"White Whales." Pirtle, Sarah, *Magical Earth*.

Wolves

"Big Bad Wolf." Kaye, Mary, *I Sang It Just for You*.

"Jiggy Jiggy Bum." Guthrie, Woody, *Nursery Days*.

"Lots of Little Pigs." Berkner, Laurie, *Buzz Buzz*.

"Three Lil Pigs." Roberts, Justin, *Great Big Sun*.

"The Three Little Pig Blues." Greg and Steve, *Playing Favorites*.

"3 Little Piggies." Miss Amy, *Underwater*.

"Three Little Piggies." Strausman, Paul, *Blue Jay, Blue Jay!*

"Who's Afraid of the Big Bad Wolf?" Rosenshontz, *Share It*; Shontz, Bill, *The Day I Read a Book*.

"Wolf Dream." Banana Slug String Band, *Goin' Wild*.

Worms

"Herman the Worm." Mr. Al, *Mr. Al Concert Live*.

"Hole in the Ground." Yosi, *Under a Big Bright Yellow Umbrella*.

"The Littlest Worm." Byers, Kathy, *'Round the Campfire*.

"Nobody Likes Me." Beall, Pamela, and Susan Nipp, *Wee Sing Animals, Animals, Animals*; Beall, Pamela, and Susan Nipp, *Wee Sing Silly Songs*.

"Ten Wiggle Worms." Palmer, Hap, *So Big*.

"200 Worms on the Sidewalk." Walker, Mary Lu, *The Frog's Party*.

"Wonderful Wiggly Worms." Atkinson, Lisa, *The Elephant in Aisle Four*.

"The Worm Song." Pullara, Steve, *Hop like a Frog*.

"Worms." Silberg, "Miss Jackie," *The Complete Sniggles, Squirrels, and Chicken Pox*; Silberg, "Miss Jackie," *Sing about Martin*.

Zebras

"The Monkey and the Zebra." Beall, Pamela, and Susan Nipp, *Wee Sing Animals, Animals, Animals*.

Appliances

"Clothes Encounter." Simmons, Al, *The Celery Stalks at Midnight*.

"Greetings Earthlings." Lonnquist, Ken, *Sci-Fi Hi-Fi*.

"I Took a Bath in a Washing Machine." Gill, Jim, *Jim Gill Sings the Sneezing Song and Other Contagious Tunes*.

"In the Freezer." Scruggs, Joe, *Traffic Jams*.

"Oh When." Beall, Pamela, and Susan Nipp, *Wee Sing and Pretend*.

"Pictures on the Fridge." Foote, Norman, *Pictures on the Fridge*.

"Refrigerator Picture." Scruggs, Joe, *Deep in the Jungle*.

"The Washing Machine." The Chenille Sisters, *The Big Picture and Other Songs for Kids*.

Arguing/Fighting

"Dear Mr. President." Alsop, Peter, *Stayin' Over*.

"Don't You Push Me." Guthrie, Woody, *Nursery Days*; Guthrie, Woody, *Woody's 20 Grow Big Songs*; Raven, Nancy, *Nancy Raven Sings Her Favorites*; Raven, Nancy, *Singing, Prancing, and Dancing*; Various Artists, *Sing Along with Putumayo*.

"Early Sunday Morning." Polisar, Barry Louis, *Family Trip*.

"The Hound Dog Song." Staines, Bill, *The Happy Wanderer*.

"Is Not, Is Too!" Fink, Cathy, and Marcy Marxer, *Scat like That*; Harley, Bill, *Play It Again*.

"On and On and On." Del Bianco, Lou, *Lost in School*.

"Someone Else Decide." McCutcheon, John, *Bigger Than Yourself*.

"Use a Word." Grammer, Red, *Teaching Peace*.

"When Suzie Sneezed." Polisar, Barry Louis, *Old Enough to Know Better*.

"Who's the Winner?" Ralph's World, *The Amazing Adventures of Kid Astro*.

"You're Not the Bossa Nova Me." Daddy A Go Go, *Monkey in the Middle*.

Babies (see also Family)

"Airplane of Food." Roberts, Justin, *Way Out*.

"As You Sleep So Peacefully (A Father's Day Nightmare)." Polisar, Barry Louis, *Juggling Babies*.

"Baby." Sprout, Jonathan, *Dr. Music*.

"Baby Bye." Beall, Pamela, and Susan Nipp, *Wee Sing for Baby*.

"Baby Face." Sharon, Lois, and Bram, *Sing A to Z*.

"Baby Swing." Buchman, Rachel, *Baby and Me*.

"Baby (Why Are You Crying So?)." Simmons, Al, *The Celery Stalks at Midnight*.

"Baby's First." Palmer, Hap, *Peek-a-Boo*.

"Baby's Got the Car Keys." Trout Fishing in America, *Family Music Party*; Trout Fishing in America, *My World*.

"Bad Babies." Boynton, Sandra, *Rhinoceros Tap*.

"Bouncin' Baby." Roberts, Justin, *Great Big Sun*.

"But They'll Never Have a Baby as Nice as Me." Polisar, Barry Louis, *Juggling Babies*.

"Bye-O-Bye." Buchman, Rachel, *Baby and Me*.

"Cartwheels and Somersaults." Roberts, Justin, *Meltdown!*

"Daddy's Diaper Blues." Daddy A Go Go, *Cool Songs for Cool Kids*.

"Diaper Bag Boogie." Cosgrove, Jim, *Stinky Feet*.

"Diaper Rash." Polisar, Barry Louis, *Family Concert*; Polisar, Barry Louis, *Juggling Babies*.

"Diaper Wrap." Stotts, Stuart, *Are We There Yet?*

"Don't Wake Up the Baby (Or the Baby Will Get You)." Polisar, Barry Louis, *Juggling Babies*.

"Getting Up Time." Palmer, Hap, *Peek-a-Boo*.

"Go and Hush the Baby." Polisar, Barry Louis, *Family Trip*.

"Goo Goo Ga Ga." Scruggs, Joe, *Traffic Jams*.

"Goo-Goo-Giggley-I-Oh." Parachute Express, *Sunny Side Up*.

"The Great Big Dog." Berkner, Laurie, *Whaddaya Think of That?*

"His Majesty the Baby." Foote, Norman, *Foote Prints.*

"I Wanna Be Your Baby." Polisar, Barry Louis, *Juggling Babies.*

"John Brown's Baby." Beall, Pamela, and Susan Nipp, *Wee Sing Silly Songs.*

"Kiss the Baby Goodnight." Allard, Peter and Ellen, *Sing It! Say It! Stamp It! Sway It!* vol. 3.

"Little Brand New Baby." Paxton, Tom, *Goin' to the Zoo.*

"Love This Baby." Harper, Monty, *The Great Green Squishy Mean Concert CD.*

"Mister Penn." Rosenshontz, *Uh-Oh!*

"My Baby Is . . ." Buchman, Rachel, *Baby and Me.*

"Natural Disaster." McCutcheon, John, *Autumnsongs.*

"New Baby." Scruggs, Joe, *Bahamas Pajamas.*

"No More Crying." Buchman, Rachel, *Baby and Me.*

"One Day Old." Guthrie, Woody, *Songs to Grow On for Mother and Child.*

"1 Day, 2 Days, 3 Days Old." Mitchell, Elizabeth, *You Are My Flower.*

"Peek-a-Boo." Mayer, Hans, *Stars of the Swing Set.*

"She's a Baby." Penner, Fred, *What a Day!*

"Swinging." Rosenshontz, *Uh-Oh!*

"That's What Babies Do." Moos, Anna, *When I Was a Child.*

"To Babyland." Beall, Pamela, and Susan Nipp, *Wee Sing for Baby*; Beall, Pamela, and Susan Nipp, *Wee Sing Nursery Rhymes and Lullabies.*

"Trouble . . . What Trouble?" Polisar, Barry Louis, *Juggling Babies.*

"The Turning Over Song." Buchman, Rachel, *Baby and Me.*

"Waiting for a Baby." Arnold, Linda, *Make Believe.*

"What Are We Going to Do about the Baby?" Polisar, Barry Louis, *Juggling Babies.*

"What Do You Do With a Crying Baby?" Polisar, Barry Louis, *Juggling Babies.*

"What'cha Gonna Do with the Baby-O?" Raven, Nancy, *People and Animal Songs.* (Same song as "What'll I Do with the Baby-O?")

"What'll I Do with the Baby-O?" Rosenthal, Phil, *The Green Grass Grew All Around.* (Same song as "What'cha Gonna Do with the Baby-O?")

"Who's My Pretty Baby." Mitchell, Elizabeth, *You Are My Little Bird.*

"Who's My Pretty Baby (Hey Pretty Baby)." Guthrie, Woody, *Songs to Grow On for Mother and Child.*

"Why Do I Love You?" Polisar, Barry Louis, *Juggling Babies.*

Babysitters

"Baby Sitter." Craig n Co., *Rock n Together.*

"Babysitter." Frezza, Rebecca, *Road Trip.*

"Babysitter." McCutcheon, John, *Howjadoo*.

"Da Babysitter." Chapin, Tom, *In My Hometown*.

"Still the Ones for Me." McCutcheon, John, *Bigger Than Yourself*.

"When the House Is Dark and Quiet." Polisar, Barry Louis, *Family Concert*; Polisar, Barry Louis, *Family Trip*.

Backwards/Upside Down

"Backwards." Lonnquist, Ken, *The Lost Songs of Kenland*.

"The Backwards Birthday Party." Chapin, Tom, *Zag Zig*.

"Backwards Day." Gill, Jim, *Moving Rhymes for Modern Times*.

"Backwards Land." Palmer, Hap, *Turn On the Music*.

"Peter's ABC's." Alsop, Peter, *Uh-Oh!*

"Upside Down Boy." Rymer, Brady, *Look at My Belly*.

"Zag Zig." Chapin, Tom, *Great Big Fun for the Very Little One*; Chapin, Tom, *Zag Zig*.

Balloons

"Balloon-alloon-alloon." Paxton, Tom, *I've Got a Yo-Yo*.

"Balloons, Balloons." Barchas, Sarah, *Get Ready, Get Set, Sing!*

"Blowing Up Balloons." Crow, Dan, *A Friend, a Laugh, a Walk in the Woods*.

"My Blue Balloon." Beall, Pamela, and Susan Nipp, *Wee Sing and Pretend*.

"Red Balloon." Harper, Jessica, *40 Winks*.

Bathtime

"Away, Mommy, Away." Abell, Timmy, *The Farmer's Market*.

"Bath Time." Gemini, *The Best of Gemini*, vol 2.

"Bathtime." Bartels, Joanie, *Bathtime Magic*; Raffi, *Everything Grows*; Raffi, *Raffi in Concert*.

"Bathtub Blues." Brown, Greg, *Bathtub Blues*.

"Bathtub Blues." Scruggs, Joe, *Bahamas Pajamas*.

"Bathtub Song." Arnold, Linda, *Make Believe*.

"The Bathtub Song." Peterson, Carole, *Tiny Tunes*. (Same song as "Clean-O.")

"Bathtub Soup." Rymer, Brady, *I Found It!*

"Boogie Woogie Washrag Blues." Palmer, Hap, *Peek-a-Boo*.

"Bubba Dubba." Pullara, Steve, *Hop like a Frog*.

"Bubble Bath." Bartels, Joanie, *Bathtime Magic*.

"Bubble Bath." Kaye, Mary, *I Sang It Just for You*.

"Bubble Bath Blues." Frezza, Rebecca, *Music in My Head*.

"Bubblin' in the Bath." Chapin, Tom, *Great Big Fun for the Very Little One*.

"Clean-O." Guthrie, Woody, *Nursery Days*; Guthrie, Woody, *Woody's 20 Grow Big Songs*. (Same song as "The Bathtub Song.")

"Clean-O." Rymer, Brady, *Look at My Belly*.

"Don't Drink the Water." Atkinson, Lisa, *The One and Only Me*.

"Head, Shoulders, Knees, and Toes." Bartels, Joanie, *Bathtime Magic*.

"I Took a Bath in a Washing Machine." Gill, Jim, *Jim Gill Sings the Sneezing Song and Other Contagious Tunes*.

"If You're Gonna Be a Grub." Harley, Bill, *You're in Trouble*.

"In That Bubble." Crow, Dan, *Oops!*

"Miss Lucy." Sharon, Lois, and Bram, *Great Big Hits 2*; Sharon, Lois, and Bram, *Name Games*.

"My Bathtub's Got a Lot of Class/The Bathtub Queen." Atkinson, Lisa, *I Wanna Tickle the Fish*.

"My Trip down the Drain." Charette, Rick, *Where Do My Sneakers Go at Night?*

"Rub-a-Dub." Bartels, Joanie, *Bathtime Magic*.

"Sailing." Fink, Cathy, and Marcy Marxer, *Pillow Full of Wishes*.

"The Shower Song." Sprout, Jonathan, *On the Radio*.

"Showers in the Rain." Allard, Peter and Ellen, *Raise the Children*.

"Singing in the Bathtub." The Chenille Sisters, *1, 2, 3 for Kids*; Lithgow, John, *Singin' in the Bathtub*; Simmons, Al, *Something Fishy at Camp Wiganishie*.

"The Skatter Brak Flath Who Lives in My Bath." Polisar, Barry Louis, *Old Dog, New Tricks*.

"Soap." McGrath, Bob, *Sing Along with Bob #2*.

"Splashing in the Bath." Beall, Pamela, and Susan Nipp, *Wee Sing for Baby*.

"Splashing in the Tub." Charette, Rick, *King Kong Chair*.

"There's a Hippo in My Tub." Bartels, Joanie, *Bathtime Magic*.

"This Is the Way We Take a Bath." Beall, Pamela, and Susan Nipp, *Wee Sing for Baby*.

"Underwater." Miss Amy, *Underwater*.

"Wash-y Wash Wash." Guthrie, Woody, *Songs to Grow On for Mother and Child*.

"You Can Never Go down the Drain." Bartels, Joanie, *Bathtime Magic*.

Bedtime (see also Nighttime)

"All around the World." Fink, Cathy, and Marcy Marxer, *Pillow Full of Wishes*.

"All in a Night." Fink, Cathy, and Marcy Marxer, *Blanket Full of Dreams*.

"All Night All Day." Byers, Kathy, *'Round the Campfire*.

"Bebe Moke (Baby So Small)." Beall, Pamela, and Susan Nipp, *Wee Sing around the World.*

"Bed in Summer." Buchman, Rachel, *Sing a Song of Seasons.*

"Bedtime Round." Chapin, Tom, *Billy the Squid*; Chapin, Tom, *Great Big Fun for the Very Little One.*

"Betty Beep." Palmer, Hap, *Can Cockatoos Count by Twos?*

"Blanketville." Chapin, Tom, *Family Tree*; Chapin, Tom, *Great Big Fun for the Very Little One.*

"Boogedy Blues." Lonnquist, Ken, *The Lost Songs of Kenland.*

"Boogie! Boogie! Boogie!" Pease, Tom, *Boogie! Boogie! Boogie!*

"The Boogieman." Pullara, Steve, *Hop like a Frog.*

"By 'n By." Buchman, Rachel, *Sing a Song of Seasons.*

"Calling All Children." Harper, Jessica, *40 Winks.*

"Cellar Door." Kinnoin, Dave, *Getting Bigger.*

"Close Your Eyes." Milkshake, *Happy Songs.*

"Come On Down." Scruggs, Joe, *Ants.*

"Count Ten." Raven, Nancy, *Singing, Prancing, and Dancing.*

"Count Your Blessings." Alsop, Peter, *Uh-Oh!*

"Countin' Cars on the Sleepytime Train." Fink, Cathy, and Marcy Marxer, *Pocket Full of Stardust.*

"Day Is Done." Sprout, Jonathan, *On the Radio.*

"Diddle Diddle Dumpling." Silberg, "Miss Jackie," *The Complete Sniggles, Squirrels, and Chicken Pox*; Silberg, "Miss Jackie," *Sing about Martin.*

"Down at the Sea Hotel." Brown, Greg, *Bathtub Blues.*

"Down the Lullaby Trail." Riders in the Sky, *Saddle Pals.*

"DreamDreamDream." Harper, Jessica, *Hey, Picasso.*

"Dreams of Harmony." Pease, Tom, *Daddy Starts to Dance*; Various Artists, *A Child's Celebration of the World.*

"Dreamtime Rendezvous." Grammer, Red, *Down the Do-Re-Mi.*

"Drifting." Abell, Timmy, *The Farmer's Market.*

"Drip Drip Drip." Simmons, Al, *The Truck I Bought from Moe.*

"The Farmer's Son." Harper, Jessica, *40 Winks.*

"40 Winks." Harper, Jessica, *40 Winks.*

"Gingerbread Man." Scruggs, Joe, *Bahamas Pajamas.*

"Go to Sleep You Little Creep." Alsop, Peter, *Stayin' Over.*

"Goin' to Bed Early Blues." Cosgrove, Jim, *Stinky Feet.*

"Good Night Moon." Parachute Express, *Feel the Music.*

"Goodnight." Berkner, Laurie, *Victor Vito.*

"Goodnight." Foote, Norman, *Pictures on the Fridge.*

"Goodnight, Goodnight." Fink, Cathy, and Marcy Marxer, *Blanket Full of Dreams.*

"Goodnight, Irene." Herdman, Priscilla, *Stardreamer*; Mitchell, Elizabeth, *You Are My Sunshine*; Raffi, *Corner Grocery Store.*

"Goodnight Moon." Milkshake, *Happy Songs.*

"Goodnight Serenade." Fink, Cathy, and Marcy Marxer, *Pocket Full of Stardust.*

"Goodnight Story Time." Palmer, Hap, *Peek-a-Boo.*

"Grandma's Sleeping in My Bed Tonight." Scruggs, Joe, *Late Last Night.*

"Grasshopper Sittin' on a Sweet Potato Vine." Fink, Cathy, and Marcy Marxer, *Blanket Full of Dreams.*

"Hibernation." McCutcheon, John, *Wintersongs.*

"I Need a Nap." Boynton, Sandra, *Dog Train.*

"I Thought It Was a Monster." Roberts, Justin, *Yellow Bus.*

"I Wouldn't Be Scared, Not Me." Stotts, Stuart, *One Big Dance.*

"I'm Not Afraid of the Dark." Charette, Rick, *A Little Peace and Quiet.*

"I'm Not Tired." Various Artists, *Hear and Gone in 60 Seconds.*

"I'm Your Pillow." Harley, Bill, *The Town around the Bend.*

"It's Been a Big Day." Foote, Norman, *If the Shoe Fits.*

"It's OK." Rosen, Gary, *Cookin'.*

"It's Time to Go to Bed." Charette, Rick, *Chickens on Vacation.*

"Jiggle and Tickle." Fink, Cathy, and Marcy Marxer, *Pocket Full of Stardust.*

"Jim Gill's Lullaby." Gill, Jim, *Jim Gill Makes It Noisy in Boise, Idaho.*

"Kiss the Baby Goodnight." Allard, Peter and Ellen, *Sing It! Say It! Stamp It! Sway It!* vol. 3.

"The Laffy Dullabye." Tucker, Nancy, *Escape of the Slinkys.*

"Lamplighter." Lonnquist, Ken, *The Switcher-On of Stars.*

"A Little Night Light." Parachute Express, *Doctor Looney's Remedy.*

"Magical Waltz." Miss Amy, *Underwater.*

"Maybe the Monster." Roberts, Justin, *Meltdown!*

"Monsters in the Bathroom." Harley, Bill, *Monsters in the Bathroom*; Harley, Bill, *Play It Again.*

"The Moon Is Rising." Thaddeus Rex, *We Wanna Rock.*

"Moonboat." Chapin, Tom, *Moonboat.*

"Morningtown Ride." Cassidy, Nancy, *Nancy Cassidy's KidsSongs*; Diamond, Charlotte, *Diamonds and Daydreams*; Raffi, *Baby Beluga*; Raven, Nancy, *Nancy Raven Sings Her Favorites*; Raven, Nancy, *Singing, Prancing, and Dancing.*

"Mr. Bed Bug." Roth, Kevin, *Travel Song Sing Alongs.*

"My Friend's Sleepin' over Tonight." Magical Music Express, *Music Is Magic*.

"My Mother's Snoring." Lonnquist, Ken, *The Lost Songs of Kenland*.

"Nightlight." Roberts, Justin, *Not Naptime*.

"Night-Light." Scruggs, Joe, *Ants*.

"Not Naptime." Roberts, Justin, *Not Naptime*.

"Off to Bed." Rymer, Brady, *Look at My Belly*.

"One Glass of Water." Fink, Cathy, and Marcy Marxer, *Air Guitar*.

"Quiet Time." Chapin, Tom, *Some Assembly Required*.

"Rock-a-Bye Boogie." Marxer, Marcy, *Jump Children*.

"Rock-A My Dolly." Beall, Pamela, and Susan Nipp, *Wee Sing for Baby*.

"Roll Over." Barchas, Sarah, *Get Ready, Get Set, Sing!* (Same song as "Six on the Bed" and "Ten in the Bed.")

"Safe at Home." Banana Slug String Band, *Penguin Parade*.

"The Sandman." Pease, Tom, *Wobbi-Do-Wop!*

"Say Goodnight, I've Gone to Bed." Atkinson, Lisa, *I Wanna Tickle the Fish*.

"Scary Things." Raven, Nancy, *Nancy Raven Sings Her Favorites*; Raven, Nancy, *You Gotta Juba*.

"Six on the Bed." The Learning Station, *Here We Go Loopty Loo*. (Same song as "Roll Over" and "Ten in the Bed.")

"Sleep Sleep." Rosenshontz, *Rosenshontz Greatest Hits*; Rosenshontz, *Share It*.

"Sleepy Little Town." Yosi, *Under a Big Bright Yellow Umbrella*.

"Sleepyheads (Spencer's Song)." Fink, Cathy, and Marcy Marxer, *Pillow Full of Wishes*.

"Sleepytime Swing." Strausman, Paul, *Rainbows, Stones, and Dinosaur Bones*.

"Sleepytown." Milkshake, *Bottle of Sunshine*.

"Snoozers." Boynton, Sandra, *Philadelphia Chickens*.

"Stayin' Over." Alsop, Peter, *Stayin' Over*.

"The Summer Slumber Party." Palmer, Hap, *Turn On the Music*.

"Swimming with Whales." Banana Slug String Band, *Wings of Slumber*.

"Take a Nap." Scruggs, Joe, *Deep in the Jungle*.

"Teddy Bear Lullaby." Mayer, Hans, *Just a Little Hug*.

"Ten in the Bed." Allard, Peter and Ellen, *Sing It! Say It! Stamp It! Sway It!* vol. 3; Arnold, Linda, *Sing Along Stew*; Beall, Pamela, and Susan Nipp, *Wee Sing Silly Songs*; Penner, Fred, *Rhyme a Word or Two*; Sharon, Lois, and Bram, *Great Big Hits 2*; Sharon, Lois, and Bram, *Sleepytime*. (Same song as "Roll Over" and "Six on the Bed.")

"Ten Sleepy Sheep." Harper, Jessica, *40 Winks*.

"This Little Island." Banana Slug String Band, *Wings of Slumber*.

"Time for Bed." Allard, Peter and Ellen, *Pizza Pizzaz*.

"Time for Little Ones." Fink, Cathy, and Marcy Marxer, *Pillow Full of Wishes.*

"Time to Sleep." Fink, Cathy, and Marcy Marxer, *Blanket Full of Dreams*; Herdman, Priscilla, *Stardreamer*; Marxer, Marcy, *Jump Children.*

"T.I.R.E.D." Stotts, Stuart, and Tom Pease, *Celebrate: A Song Resource.*

"Under Your Bed." Scruggs, Joe, *Traffic Jams.*

"Up They Get to My Sunset." Banana Slug String Band, *Wings of Slumber.*

"Wee Willie Winkie." Silberg, "Miss Jackie," *The Complete Sniggles, Squirrels, and Chicken Pox.*

"When the Darkness Comes." Byers, Kathy, *Do You Wish You Could Fly?*

"Whole Bed." Scruggs, Joe, *Bahamas Pajamas.*

"Who's Been Sleeping in My Bed?" Fink, Cathy, and Marcy Marxer, *Pocket Full of Stardust.*

"Why Kids Sing to Their Parents." Harley, Bill, *The Town around the Bend.*

"Winter Sleep." Rosenthal, Phil, *Animal Songs.*

Birds

"Baby Bird." Beall, Pamela, and Susan Nipp, *Wee Sing Children's Songs and Fingerplays.*

"The Bird." Kaye, Mary, *Mouse Jamboree.*

"The Bird Medley." Fink, Cathy, and Marcy Marxer, *Air Guitar.*

"The Bird Song." Rosenthal, Phil, *Animal Songs.*

"Bird Tales." Foote, Norman, *Shake a Leg.*

"Birdie's Cradle." Beall, Pamela, and Susan Nipp, *Wee Sing for Baby.*

"Buckeye Jim." Mitchell, Elizabeth, *You Are My Little Bird.*

"Chi Chi Bud (Chi Chi Bird)." Beall, Pamela, and Susan Nipp, *Wee Sing around the World.*

"Counting Feathers." Simmons, Al, *Something Fishy at Camp Wiganishie.*

"Do the Bird." Grunsky, Jack, *Follow the Leader*; Grunsky, Jack, *Jack in the Box 2.*

"Flying." Dana, *Dana's Best Travelin' Tunes.*

"Gertie's Birdseed Diner." Chapin, Tom, *In My Hometown.*

"Goodbye Little Birdie." Lonnquist, Ken, *The Circus Kenlando.*

"Hey Little Red Bird." Zanes, Dan, *House Party.*

"Hey! What Did the Blue Jay Say?" Muldaur, Maria, *Animal Crackers in My Soup.*

"If You Want to Fly." SteveSongs, *Marvelous Day!*

"Island Rock." Banana Slug String Band, *Slugs at Sea.*

"Kanyoni Kanja (Little Bird Outside)." Beall, Pamela, and Susan Nipp, *Wee Sing around the World.*

"Little Bird." Beall, Pamela, and Susan Nipp, *Wee Sing Animals, Animals, Animals.*

"Little Bird." Guthrie, Woody, *Woody's 20 Grow Big Songs*; Raven, Nancy, *Hop, Skip, and Sing*.

"Little Bird, Little Bird." Mitchell, Elizabeth, *You Are My Little Bird*.

"Little Birdie." Seeger, Pete, *For Kids and Just Plain Folks*.

"The Little House." Raffi, *Everything Grows*.

"Mary Wore Her Red Dress (Mary Was a Bird)." Raffi, *Everything Grows*; Raffi, *Quiet Time*; Raven, Nancy, *People and Animal Songs*.

"Mocking Bird Hill." Muldaur, Maria, *On the Sunny Side*.

"Mother Gooney Bird." Feldman, Jean, *Dr. Jean and Friends*.

"Pom Na Tu Ri (Springtime Outing)." Mitchell, Elizabeth, *You Are My Little Bird*.

"Red Bird." Barchas, Sarah, *Get Ready, Get Set, Sing!*; Barchas, Sarah, *¡Piñata! and More*.

"Songbirds." Grunsky, Jack, *Follow the Leader*; Grunsky, Jack, *Jack in the Box 1*.

"This Song Is for the Birds." Staines, Bill, *The Happy Wanderer*.

"Three Little Birds." Mitchell, Elizabeth, *You Are My Little Bird*; Various Artists, *Caribbean Playground*; Various Artists, *World Playground*.

"Tweet Tweet." Moo, Anna, *Making Moosic*.

"Up, Up in the Sky." Beall, Pamela, and Susan Nipp, *Wee Sing Animals, Animals, Animals*.

"Wild Bird Round." Lonnquist, Ken, *The Circus Kenlando*; Lonnquist, Ken, *Earthy Songs*; Lonnquist, Ken, *The Switcher-On of Stars*.

"Winter's Come and Gone." Mitchell, Elizabeth, *You Are My Little Bird*.

"Wounded Bird." Diamond, Charlotte, *My Bear Gruff*.

Blackbirds

"Bye Bye Blackbird." Foote, Norman, *Pictures on the Fridge*.

"Sing a Song of Sixpence." Beall, Pamela, and Susan Nipp, *Wee Sing Nursery Rhymes and Lullabies*.

"Two Little Blackbirds." Peterson, Carole, *Sticky Bubble Gum*.

Bluebirds

"Bluebird." Beall, Pamela, and Susan Nipp, *Wee Sing and Play*.

"Bluebird, Bluebird." Sharon, Lois, and Bram, *Mainly Mother Goose*.

Chickadees

"Five Little Chickadees." Allard, Peter and Ellen, *Sing It! Say It! Stamp It! Sway It!* vol. 2.

"Little Chickadee." The Chenille Sisters, *Teaching Hippopotami to Fly!*

Chickens/Roosters

"Ain't Nobody Here but Us Chickens." Nagler, Eric, *Improvise with Eric Nagler*. (Same song as "There Ain't Nobody Here but Us Chickens.")

"All the Colors." Barchas, Sarah, *Bridges across the World*; Barchas, Sarah, *¡Piñata! and More*.

"Baby Chickie." Palmer, Hap, *So Big*.

"The Ballad of Rueben Rooster." Crow, Dan, *Oops!*

"Barnyard Boogie." Grammer, Red, *Teaching Peace*.

"Big Rock Rooster." Daddy A Go Go, *Big Rock Rooster*.

"Chick Chick Chicken." Walker, Graham, *Jumpety Jump*.

"C-H-I-C-K-E-N." Paxton, Tom, *Your Shoes, My Shoes*.

"Chicken Medley." Sharon, Lois, and Bram, *Great Big Hits 2*; Sharon, Lois, and Bram, *Sing A to Z*.

"Chicken Road." Madsen, Gunnar, *Old Mr. Mackle Hackle*.

"The Chicken Song." Beall, Pamela, and Susan Nipp, *Wee Sing in the Car*.

"Chickens for Peace." Alsop, Peter, *Take Me with You*.

"Chickens on Vacation." Charette, Rick, *Chickens on Vacation*.

"The Chicken's Speech." Crow, Dan, *Oops!*

"Chickery Chick." Bartels, Joanie, *Sillytime Magic*; Marxer, Marcy, *Jump Children*.

"Cluck Old Hen." Nagler, Eric, *Improvise with Eric Nagler*.

"Cock-a-Doodle-Doo." The Learning Station, *Here We Go Loopty Loo*.

"Doin' the Chicken." Mr. Al, *Dance like This*.

"Hickety, Pickety, My Black Hen." Beall, Pamela, and Susan Nipp, *Wee Sing Nursery Rhymes and Lullabies*.

"I Know a Chicken." Berkner, Laurie, *Whaddaya Think of That?*

"Little Chicks." Barchas, Sarah, *If I Had a Pony*.

"The Little Red Hen." Avni, Fran, *Artichokes and Brussel Sprouts*.

"The Little Red Hen." Greg and Steve, *Fun and Games*.

"Little Red Hen." Stotts, Stuart, and Tom Pease, *Celebrate: A Song Resource*.

"Mio Galletto (My Little Rooster)." Beall, Pamela, and Susan Nipp, *Wee Sing around the World*.

"New Chicken Dance." The Learning Station, *La Di Da La Di Di Dance with Me*.

"Old Mr. Mackle Hackle." Madsen, Gunnar, *Old Mr. Mackle Hackle*.

"Philadelphia Chickens." Boynton, Sandra, *Philadelphia Chickens*.

"Los Pollitos (The Little Chicks)." Barchas, Sarah, *¡Piñata! and More*; Beall, Pamela, and Susan Nipp, *Wee Sing around the World*; Mitchell, Elizabeth, *You Are My Little Bird*; Old Town School of Folk Music, *Wiggleworms Love You*.

"There Ain't Nobody Here but Us Chickens." Pease, Tom, *I'm Gonna Reach!* (Same song as "Ain't Nobody Here but Us Chickens.")

"Why'd the Chicken Cross the Road." Rudnick, Ben, *Blast Off!*

Cranes

"One Crane." Pease, Tom, *Wobbi-Do-Wop!*; Stotts, Stuart, *Are We There Yet?*

Crows

"Caw Caw Caw." McMahon, Elizabeth, *Magic Parade.*

"Crow Song." Beall, Pamela, and Susan Nipp, *Wee Sing in the Car.*

"The Crow That Wanted to Sing." Paxton, Tom, *I've Got a Yo-Yo.*

"Mama Crow." Pirtle, Sarah, *The Wind Is Telling Secrets.*

"On a Cold and Frosty Morning." Buchman, Rachel, *Sing a Song of Seasons.* (Same song as "Three Craw.")

"Three Craw." Raven, Nancy, *The House We Live In*, vols. 1 and 2; Raven, Nancy, *People and Animal Songs.* (Same song as "On a Cold and Frosty Morning.")

Cuckoos

"The Cuckoo." Beall, Pamela, and Susan Nipp, *Wee Sing Animals, Animals, Animals*; Raven, Nancy, *People and Animal Songs.*

Ducks

"Alle Meine Entchen (All My Little Darlings)." Beall, Pamela, and Susan Nipp, *Wee Sing around the World.*

"Baby Duck/Duckie Countdown." Peterson, Carole, *Sticky Bubble Gum.*

"Be Kind to Your Web-Footed Friends." Beall, Pamela, and Susan Nipp, *Wee Sing Silly Songs*; Various Artists, *A Child's Celebration of Silliest Songs.*

"Be Like a Duck." Boynton, Sandra, *Philadelphia Chickens.*

"Butts Up." Banana Slug String Band, *Slugs at Sea.*

"Donald Duck." Allard, Peter and Ellen, *Sing It! Say It! Stamp It! Sway It!* vol. 2.

"A Duck in New York City." Kaldor, Connie, *A Duck in New York City.*

"A Duck Named Earl." Various Artists, *Grandma's Patchwork Quilt.*

"Duckie Duddle." Peterson, Carole, *Tiny Tunes.*

"Ducks Hatching." SteveSongs, *Marvelous Day!*

"Ducks Like Rain." Peterson, Carole, *H.U.M.—All Year Long*; Raffi, *Rise and Shine.*

"Five Little Ducks." Barchas, Sarah, *Get Ready, Get Set, Sing!*; Beall, Pamela, and Susan Nipp, *Wee Sing Animals, Animals, Animals*; Buchman, Rachel, *Hello Everybody!*; McGrath, Bob, and Katherine Smithrim, *Songs and Games for Toddlers*; Raffi, *Raffi in Concert*; Raffi, *Rise and Shine*; Trout Fishing in America, *Mine!* (Same song as "Four Little Ducks.")

"Four Little Duckies." Ralph's World, *Ralph's World*.

"Four Little Ducks." Pullara, Steve, *One Potato, Two Potato*. (Same song as "Five Little Ducks.")

"Mama Duck." Allard, Peter and Ellen, *Sing It! Say It! Stamp It! Sway It!* vol. 3.

"Six Little Ducks." Arnold, Linda, *Sing Along Stew*; Avni, Fran, *Tuning into Nature*; Bartels, Joanie, *Bathtime Magic*; Beall, Pamela, and Susan Nipp, *Wee Sing Animals, Animals, Animals*; Beall, Pamela, and Susan Nipp, *Wee Sing Nursery Rhymes and Lullabies*; McGrath, Bob, *Sing Along with Bob #1*; Raffi, *More Singable Songs*; Raffi, *Raffi Radio*; Rosenthal, Phil, *Folksongs and Bluegrass for Children*; Rosenthal, Phil, *The Paw Paw Patch*.

"Three Little Fishies." Various Artists, *A Child's Celebration of Silliest Songs*.

"The Ugly Duckling." Greg and Steve, *We All Live Together*, vol. 4; Various Artists, *A Child's Celebration of Song*.

Eagles

"Soaring Eagle." Fite, Stephen, *Wiggles, Jiggles, and Giggles*.

Flamingos

"Pink Floyd Saves Hugh Manatee." Daddy A Go Go, *Eat Every Bean and Pea on Your Plate*.

Geese

"Cry of the Wild Goose." Simmons, Al, *The Celery Stalks at Midnight*.

"Go Tell Aunt Rhody." Abell, Timmy, *I Know an Old Lady*; Raven, Nancy, *People and Animal Songs*.

"Grey Goose." Ives, Burl, *Burl Ives Sings Little White Duck*; Zanes, Dan, *Catch That Train!*

"Why Shouldn't My Goose?" Beall, Pamela, and Susan Nipp, *Wee Sing Sing-Alongs*.

Kookaburras

"Kookaburra." Barchas, Sarah, *Bridges across the World*; Beall, Pamela, and Susan Nipp, *Wee Sing Animals, Animals, Animals*; Beall, Pamela, and Susan Nipp, *Wee Sing around the World*; Beall, Pamela, and Susan Nipp, *Wee Sing Sing-Alongs*; Staines, Bill, *The Happy Wanderer*; Walker, Graham, *Jumpety Jump*.

Loons

"The Loon and the Boy." Charette, Rick, *A Little Peace and Quiet.*

Nightingales

"Giraffe/Nightingale." Roberts, Justin, *Yellow Bus.*

Owls

"Little Owlet." Tickle Tune Typhoon, *Patty-Cakes and Peek-a-Boos.*
"Mr. Owl." Kimmy Schwimmy, *Kimmy Schwimmy Music*, vol. 1.
"Night Owl." Zanes, Dan, *Night Time!*
"Owl Lullaby." Raven, Nancy, *Nancy Raven Sings Her Favorites*; Raven, Nancy, *You Gotta Juba*; Sharon, Lois, and Bram, *Sing A to Z.*
"Two Little Owls." Ives, Burl, *Burl Ives Sings Little White Duck.*

Parrots

"Polly the Parrot." Grunsky, Jack, *Follow the Leader*; Grunsky, Jack, *Jack in the Box 2.*
"Simone's Song (The Parrot Song)." Gill, Jim, *Jim Gill Sings the Sneezing Song and Other Contagious Tunes.*

Pelicans

"Pelican Will." Shontz, Bill, *Animal Tales.*

Penguins

"Flying through the Sea." Arnold, Linda, *Splash Zone.*
"It's a Penguin Party/A La Fiesta De Pingüinos." Arnold, Linda, *Splash Zone.*
"Penguin Dance." Miss Amy, *Wide Wide World.*
"Penguin in Rio." Charette, Rick, *King Kong Chair.*
"Penguin Lament." Boynton, Sandra, *Dog Train.*
"Penguin Parade." Banana Slug String Band, *Penguin Parade.*
"The Penguin Song." Peterson, Carole, *Stinky Cake.*
"Waddle Penguin." Coffey, James, *Animal Groove.*
"Walk like a Penguin." Charette, Rick, *King Kong Chair.*

Pigeons

"Three Blue Pigeons." Beall, Pamela, and Susan Nipp, *Wee Sing Animals, Animals, Animals*; Beall, Pamela, and Susan Nipp, *Wee Sing Children's Songs and Fingerplays.*

Puffins

"The Puffin Song." Knight, Tom, *Don't Kiss a Codfish*.

Quails

"Quail." Banana Slug String Band, *Dirt Made My Lunch*.

Robins

"The North Wind." Mitchell, Elizabeth, *You Are My Little Bird*.
"Robin in the Rain." Raffi, *Singable Songs for the Very Young*.
"Robin Song." Kinder, Brian, *One More Time*.
"Welcome Back, Mrs. Robin." McMahon, Elizabeth, *Magic Parade*.
"Young Robin." Brown, Greg, *Bathtub Blues*.

Seagulls

"Gordie, the Miserable Seagull." Foote, Norman, *If the Shoe Fits*.
"Sea Gulls." Charette, Rick, *Where Do My Sneakers Go at Night?*

Sparrows

"Five Little Sparrows." Diamond, Charlotte, *My Bear Gruff*.

Swans

"The Swan." Beall, Pamela, and Susan Nipp, *Wee Sing Animals, Animals, Animals*.
"The Ugly Duckling." Greg and Steve, *We All Live Together*, vol. 4; Various
    Artists, *A Child's Celebration of Song*.

Toucans

"Toucan." Lonnquist, Ken, *Earthy Songs*; Lonnquist, Ken, *Sci-Fi Hi-Fi*.

Turkeys

"Corny." Tucker, Nancy, *Glad That You Asked*.
"The Turkey Hop." Peterson, Carole, *H.U.M.—All Year Long*.
"Turkey Love Song." Boynton, Sandra, *Rhinoceros Tap*.
"Turkey Talk." Silberg, "Miss Jackie," *The Complete Sniggles, Squirrels, and
    Chicken Pox*.
"Twenty Pumpkins." Barchas, Sarah, *Get Ready, Get Set, Sing!*

Warblers

"Kirtland's Warbler." Lonnquist, Ken, *Earthy Songs*.

Woodpeckers

"The Woodpecker Song." Simmons, Al, *Something Fishy at Camp Wiganishie*.

Birthdays

"The Backwards Birthday Party." Chapin, Tom, *Zag Zig*.

"Billy Blotsky's Birthday Bash." Palmer, Hap, *Turn On the Music*.

"Birthday Boogaloo." Harper, Monty, *Jungle Junk!*

"Birthday Cake." Parachute Express, *Sunny Side Up*.

"Birthday Medley." Mr. Al and Stephen Fite, *Back to School Again*.

"Birthday Song." Daddy A Go Go, *Monkey in the Middle*.

"The Birthday Waltz." Knight, Tom, *The Classroom Boogie*.

"Birthdays around the World." Silberg, "Miss Jackie," *Joining Hands with Other Lands*.

"Celebrate the Day." Palmer, Hap, *One Little Sound*.

"Cut the Cake." McCutcheon, John, *Howjadoo*.

"Every Day Is a Birthday." Rymer, Brady, *Every Day Is a Birthday*.

"The Flu." Craig n Co., *Rock n Together*.

"Glad You're Here!" Lonnquist, Ken, *Sci-Fi Hi-Fi*.

"Happy Birthday." Chapin, Tom, *Great Big Fun for the Very Little One*; Chapin, Tom, *Moonboat*.

"Happy Birthday around the World." Barchas, Sarah, *Bridges across the World*.

"'Happy Birthday' around the World." Rymer, Brady, *Every Day Is a Birthday*.

"A Happy Birthday to You." Allard, Peter and Ellen, *Good Kid*.

"I Wanna Purple Kitty for My Birthday, Mom." Diamond, Charlotte, *Diamonds and Dragons*.

"It's Your Birthday." Roberts, Justin, *Meltdown!*

"Lorilei's Birthday." Colleen and Uncle Squaty, *Sing-a-Move-a-Dance*.

"Las Mañanitas." Barchas, Sarah, *¡Piñata! and More*.

"Mary Kate's Birthday Cake." Cosgrove, Jim, *Pick Me! Pick Me!*

"On My Birthday." Stotts, Stuart, and Tom Pease, *Celebrate: A Song Resource*.

"A Pair O' Barracudas." Ode, Eric, *I Love My Shoes*.

"A Very Special Day." Lonnquist, Ken, *The Lost Songs of Kenland*.

"Waiting." Walker, Mary Lu, *The Frog's Party*.

"The Zoo Was Having a Party." Kaldor, Connie, *A Poodle in Paris*.

Blankets/Quilts

"Buddy Green." Cosgrove, Jim, *Bop Bop Dinosaur.*

"Don't Wash My Blanket." Palmer, Hap, *Peek-a-Boo.*

"On My Grandma's Patchwork Quilt." Various Artists, *Grandma's Patchwork Quilt.*

"Warm, Woolly Blanket." Parachute Express, *Over Easy.*

Body

"All Filled Up." Gill, Jim, *Jim Gill Makes It Noisy in Boise, Idaho.*

"Bean Bag Alphabet Rag." Palmer, Hap, *Can a Cherry Pie Wave Goodbye?*

"Belly Button." Kaldor, Connie, *A Duck in New York City*; Pease, Tom, *I'm Gonna Reach!*

"Belly Button." Ralph's World, *Happy Lemon.*

"Belly Button." Scruggs, Joe, *Late Last Night.*

"Belly Button Dance." Stotts, Stuart, *One Big Dance.*

"Belly Button (Round)." Boynton, Sandra, *Philadelphia Chickens.*

"Bellybutton Song." Various Artists, *Sing Along with Putumayo.*

"Big Strong Muscles." Fink, Cathy, and Marcy Marxer, *Bon Appétit!*

"The Body Song." Nagler, Eric, *Improvise with Eric Nagler.*

"Boney Little Knees." Green Chili Jam Band, *Magic Bike.*

"Brains." Tickle Tune Typhoon, *Hearts and Hands.*

"Can't Sit Still." Greg and Steve, *Rockin' down the Road.*

"Cheerio." Sharon, Lois, and Bram, *Everybody Sing!*; Sharon, Lois, and Bram, *Great Big Hits 2.*

"Do Your Ears Hang Low?" Bartels, Joanie, *Sillytime Magic*; Beall, Pamela, and Susan Nipp, *Wee Sing in the Car*; Beall, Pamela, and Susan Nipp, *Wee Sing Silly Songs*; McGrath, Bob, *Sing Along with Bob #2*; Sharon, Lois, and Bram, *Great Big Hits 2.*

"Doctor Knickerbocker." Sharon, Lois, and Bram, *Name Games.*

"Don't Put Your Finger up Your Nose." Polisar, Barry Louis, *Family Concert*; Polisar, Barry Louis, *Naughty Songs for Boys and Girls.*

"Dr. Dingle." Magical Music Express, *Music Is Magic.*

"Dry Bones." Beall, Pamela, and Susan Nipp, *Wee Sing Silly Songs*; Roth, Kevin, *Dinosaurs and Dragons.*

"Elephants Have Wrinkles." Colleen and Uncle Squaty, *Sing-a-Move-a-Dance.*

"Everybody Has a Face." Peterson, Carole, *Tiny Tunes.*

"Everybody Knows I Love My Toes." Allard, Peter and Ellen, *Sing It! Say It! Stamp It! Sway It!* vol. 1.

"Face in the Mirror." Walker, Graham, *Cats' Night Out*.

"Face to Face." Avni, Fran, *Little Ears: Songs for Reading Readiness*.

"Finger Dance." Ladysmith Black Mambazo, *Gift of the Tortoise*.

"Finger Family." Colleen and Uncle Squaty, *1, 2, 3, Four-Ever Friends*.

"Fingers and Toes." Milkshake, *Happy Songs*.

"Fleas." Colleen and Uncle Squaty, *Rumble to the Bottom*.

"Hands." Fink, Cathy, and Marcy Marxer, *Air Guitar*.

"Hello Everybody, Yes Indeed." Peterson, Carole, *H.U.M.—All Year Long*.

"Horns to Toes." Boynton, Sandra, *Rhinoceros Tap*.

"I Can Hold On." Colleen and Uncle Squaty, *Sing-a-Move-a-Dance*.

"I Like My Hat." Peterson, Carole, *Stinky Cake*.

"I Love Your Eyes." Polisar, Barry Louis, *Teacher's Favorites*.

"Icky Sticky and Ooey Gooey." Peterson, Carole, *Stinky Cake*.

"I'm All Ears." Avni, Fran, *I'm All Ears: Sing into Reading*; Avni, Fran, *Little Ears: Songs for Reading Readiness*.

"The Itch Song." Green Chili Jam Band, *Magic Bike*.

"Knuckles Knees." Gill, Jim, *Jim Gill Sings Do Re Mi on His Toe Leg Knee*.

"Little Flea." Beall, Pamela, and Susan Nipp, *Wee Sing for Baby*.

"Look at My Belly." Rymer, Brady, *Look at My Belly*.

"Mary and Marvin." Palmer, Hap, *One Little Sound*.

"Muscle Shuffle." Green Chili Jam Band, *Magic Bike*.

"My Body." Alsop, Peter, *Wha' D'Ya Wanna Do?*

"My Face." Chapin, Tom, *Some Assembly Required*.

"My Gal's a Corker." Magical Music Express, *Music Is Magic*.

"My Hand on My Head." Beall, Pamela, and Susan Nipp, *Wee Sing Silly Songs*; Feldman, Jean, *Dr. Jean and Friends*. (Same song as "Wiggle the Wool.")

"My Mouth." Crow, Dan, *Oops!*

"Nobody Else like Me." Walker, Mary Lu, *The Frog's Party*.

"The Nose Song." Kaldor, Connie, *A Duck in New York City*.

"Noses." Banana Slug String Band, *Penguin Parade*.

"Noses." Rosenshontz, *Tickles You!*

"Nutty Thumbkin." The Learning Station, *Get Funky and Musical Fun*.

"Oohh, There You Are!" Buchman, Rachel, *Hello Everybody!*

"Parts of Me." Mayer, Hans, *Stars of the Swing Set*.

"Piggy Toes." Palmer, Hap, *Peek-a-Boo*.

"Rabbit on My Shoulder." Alsop, Peter, *Uh-Oh!*

"Safari into My Sister's Nose." Alsop, Peter, *Pluggin' Away*.

"Shakin' Hands." Fink, Cathy, *When the Rain Comes Down*.

"She Waded in the Water." Beall, Pamela, and Susan Nipp, *Wee Sing Silly Songs*.

"Smart Parts." Roberts, Justin, *Great Big Sun*.

"Smelly Feet." Foote, Norman, *Shake a Leg*.

"Smelly Jellies." Kinnoin, Dave, *Getting Bigger*.

"Song in My Tummy." Berkner, Laurie, *Under a Shady Tree*.

"Spider on the Floor." Raffi, *Singable Songs for the Very Young*.

"S'pose My Toes Were Noses." Paxton, Tom, *Goin' to the Zoo*.

"Sticky Bubble Gum." Peterson, Carole, *Sticky Bubble Gum*.

"Stinky Feet." Cosgrove, Jim, *Stinky Feet*.

"Tail Bone." Pease, Tom, *Daddy Starts to Dance*.

"Take Care of Your Body." Stotts, Stuart, and Tom Pease, *Celebrate: A Song Resource*.

"Ten Fingers." Moo, Anna, *Making Moosic*.

"These Hands." Parachute Express, *Feel the Music*.

"This Little Piggy." Scruggs, Joe, *Traffic Jams*.

"Tickle My Toes." Roberts, Justin, *Yellow Bus*.

"Tickle Toe." Gill, Jim, *Jim Gill Makes It Noisy in Boise, Idaho*.

"Tiny Toes." Rosenshontz, *Uh-Oh!*

"Toe Leg Knee." Gill, Jim, *Jim Gill Sings Do Re Mi on His Toe Leg Knee*.

"Toe Town." Colleen and Uncle Squaty, *1, 2, 3, Four-Ever Friends*.

"Toes." Tucker, Nancy, *Glad That You Asked*.

"Two Hands." Ode, Eric, *Grandpa's Truck*.

"Two Hands Four Hands." Grammer, Red, *Down the Do-Re-Mi*.

"Two Thumbs Date." Scruggs, Joe, *Ants*.

"Two Tired Toddlers." Avni, Fran, *I'm All Ears: Sing into Reading*.

"Ukulele Blue Yodel." Colleen and Uncle Squaty, *Sing-a-Move-a-Dance*.

"Wake Up Toes." Bartels, Joanie, *Morning Magic*.

"Way Down Deep Inside." LaFond, Lois, *Turning It Upside Down*.

"We're All in This Together." Grammer, Red, *Hello World*.

"What a Miracle." Palmer, Hap, *Peek-a-Boo*.

"Wiggle the Wool." Colleen and Uncle Squaty, *Fingerplays, Movement and Story Songs*. (Same song as "My Hand on My Head.")

"Wobbi-Do-Wop." Pease, Tom, *Wobbi-Do-Wop!*

"Wonderful Machine." Arnold, Linda, *Favorites in the Key of Fun*.

"You Gotta Have Skin." Lithgow, John, *Singin' in the Bathtub*.

"Your Face Will Surely Show It." Gill, Jim, *Jim Gill Makes It Noisy in Boise, Idaho*.

"Your Hands." Grunsky, Jack, *Follow the Leader*; Grunsky, Jack, *Playground*.
"Zip Zip." Scruggs, Joe, *Abracadabra*.

Books/Reading (see also Libraries; Storytelling)

"Big Books, Little Books." Barchas, Sarah, *Get Ready, Get Set, Sing!*
"Blast Into Books." Harper, Monty, *Take Me to Your Library*.
"Book Book." Knight, Tom, *Don't Kiss a Codfish*.
"Books, Ahoy!" Harper, Monty, *Take Me to Your Library*.
"The Day I Read a Book." Shontz, Bill, *The Day I Read a Book*.
"Four Little Sailors." Staines, Bill, *The Happy Wanderer*.
"Grandma (Tell Me a Story)." Moos, Anna, *When I Was a Child*.
"I Can Read." Grunsky, Jack, *Follow the Leader*; Grunsky, Jack, *Jack in the Box 1*.
"I Like Reading." Charette, Rick, *Where Do My Sneakers Go at Night?*
"I Like to Read." Mayer, Hans, *See You Later, Alligator*.
"I Love to Read." Kinder, Brian, *A Kid like You*.
"I Need to Read." Mr. Al, *Rockin' the Alphabet*.
"If You Couldn't Read." Shontz, Bill, *The Day I Read a Book*.
"I'm a Book." Foote, Norman, *Foote Prints*.
"In Books, in Books." Barchas, Sarah, *Bridges across the World*.
"Just One More Book." Pease, Tom, *Wobbi-Do-Wop!*
"The Library Book." Kaye, Mary, *Mouse Jamboree*.
"My Books." Shontz, Bill, *The Day I Read a Book*.
"My Favorite Books." Stotts, Stuart, and Tom Pease, *Celebrate: A Song Resource*.
"Oh Fiddlesticks." Thaddeus Rex, *We Wanna Rock*.
"One More Time." Kinder, Brian, *One More Time*.
"One Word at a Time." Stotts, Stuart, and Tom Pease, *Celebrate: A Song Resource*.
"Open a Book." Lonnquist, Ken, *Sci-Fi Hi-Fi*.
"Open Up a Book." Stotts, Stuart, and Tom Pease, *Celebrate: A Song Resource*.
"Pages." Crow, Dan, *The Giggling Dragon*.
"The Princess and the Farmer's Son." Harper, Monty, *Imagine That*.
"Read a Book." Arnold, Linda, *Peppermint Wings*.
"Read a Book." Feldman, Jean, *Just for Fun!*
"Read a Book." Fink, Cathy, and Marcy Marxer, *Help Yourself*.
"Read a Book." The Learning Station, *Rock n' Roll Songs That Teach*.
"Read a Book." Scruggs, Joe, *Deep in the Jungle*.
"Read a Book." Shontz, Bill, *The Day I Read a Book*.

"Read a Book to Me." Pease, Tom, *I'm Gonna Reach!*; Stotts, Stuart, and Tom Pease, *Celebrate: A Song Resource.*

"Read a Little Bit More." Stotts, Stuart, and Tom Pease, *Celebrate: A Song Resource.*

"Read around the World." Ode, Eric, *I Love My Shoes.*

"Read It in a Book." Kirk, John, and Trish Miller, *The Big Rock Candy Mountain.*

"Read Me a Story." Mr. Al, *Rockin' the Alphabet.*

"Read to Me." The Chenille Sisters, *The Big Picture and Other Songs for Kids.*

"Reading a Book." Rudnick, Ben, *Blast Off!*

"Reading Books." Thaddeus Rex, *Martian Television Invasion.*

"Seven Nights to Read." Stotts, Stuart, *Are We There Yet?*

"These Are My Glasses." Berkner, Laurie, *Whaddaya Think of That?*

"Tommy Hook." Shontz, Bill, *The Day I Read a Book.*

"Two Books." Diamond, Charlotte, *My Bear Gruff.*

Boredom

"Bored, Bored, Bored." Alsop, Peter, *Wha' D'Ya Wanna Do?*

"I'm Bored." Del Bianco, Lou, *Lost in School.*

"I'm Bored." Polisar, Barry Louis, *Old Enough to Know Better.*

"Nothin' to Do." Fite, Stephen, *Gobs of Fun.*

"Preacher Herman." Chapin, Tom, *Billy the Squid.*

"Puddle of Mud." Ralph's World, *Happy Lemon.*

"Stuck at Home Sitting Down." Moos, Anna, *When I Was a Child.*

Brotherhood/Sisterhood

"The African Village Song." Feldman, Jean, *Dr. Jean Sings Silly Songs.*

"All across This Wide Wide World." Barchas, Sarah, *Bridges across the World.*

"All Mixed Up." Diamond, Charlotte, *Charlotte Diamond's World.*

"All People." LaFond, Lois, *Lois LaFond and the Rockadiles.*

"All the World." Gemini, *The Best of Gemini.*

"Around the Block." Parachute Express, *Sunny Side Up.*

"Bigger Than Yourself." McCutcheon, John, *Bigger Than Yourself.*

"Bridges across the World." Barchas, Sarah, *Bridges across the World.*

"Brothers and Sisters." Grammer, Red, *Down the Do-Re-Mi.*

"Children All over the World." Atkinson, Lisa, *The One and Only Me.*

"The Colors of the Earth." Pirtle, Sarah, *The Wind Is Telling Secrets.*

"Dreams of Harmony." Various Artists, *A Child's Celebration of the World.*

"Everybody Makes a Difference." The Dream Project, *We've All Got Stories.*

"Family Feeling." Vitamin L, *Walk a Mile.*

"Friends." Sprout, Jonathan, *On the Radio.*

"Friends around the World." Yosi, *Under a Big Bright Yellow Umbrella.*

"Friendship." McCutcheon, John, *Bigger Than Yourself.*

"Greetings." Green Chili Jam Band, *Coconut Moon.*

"Hands." Fink, Cathy, and Marcy Marxer, *Air Guitar.*

"Harambe." Various Artists, *Reggae Playground.*

"Hearts and Hands." Tickle Tune Typhoon, *Hearts and Hands.*

"Here's One Wish." Fink, Cathy, and Marcy Marxer, *Bon Appétit!*

"Honey in the Rock." Stotts, Stuart, *Are We There Yet?*

"If Only." Chapin, Tom, *Zag Zig.*

"Is My Family." McCutcheon, John, *Family Garden.*

"It Takes a Lot of People." Pease, Tom, *I'm Gonna Reach!*

"It's a Long Way." Harley, Bill, *Down in the Backpack.*

"It's Gonna Take Us All." Kinder, Brian, *A Kid like You.*

"Just like You." Lonnquist, Ken, *The Lost Songs of Kenland.*

"Kids' Peace Song." Various Artists, *Peace Is the World Smiling.*

"Like Me and You." Raffi, *One Light One Sun*; Raffi, *Quiet Time*; Raffi, *Raffi in Concert*; Various Artists, *A Child's Celebration of the World.*

"Listen." Grammer, Red, *Teaching Peace.*

"Living Together." Kinnoin, Dave, *Getting Bigger.*

"Look a Little Deeper." Vitamin L, *Everyone's Invited!*

"Look through the Kaleidoscope." Diamond, Charlotte, *Charlotte Diamond's World.*

"Mama's Kitchen." Raffi, *Evergreen, Everblue.*

"Members of the Family." Raven, Nancy, *Friends and Family*; Raven, Nancy, *Nancy Raven Sings Her Favorites.*

"My Town Is a Salad Bowl." Chapin, Tom, *In My Hometown.*

"Myself, My People, My World." Barchas, Sarah, *Bridges across the World.*

"One Dream." Diamond, Charlotte, *Diamonds and Daydreams.*

"The Other Side of the World." Pirtle, Sarah, *Magical Earth.*

"Part of One Family." Allard, Peter and Ellen, *Pizza Pizzaz.*

"Part of the Family." LaFond, Lois, *Lois LaFond and the Rockadiles*; LaFond, Lois, *One World.*

"Peace to the Children." Cosgrove, Jim, *Pick Me! Pick Me!*

"People Are a Rainbow." Vitamin L, *Walk a Mile.*

"A Place for Us." Zanes, Dan, *House Party.*

"Side by Side." Rymer, Brady, *Every Day Is a Birthday*.

"Take Good Care of Each Other." Penner, Fred, *Fred's Favourites*; Penner, Fred, *What a Day!*

"To Everyone in All the World." Raffi, *Baby Beluga*.

"Under One Sky." Harley, Bill, *50 Ways to Fool Your Mother*; Pelham, Ruth, *Under One Sky*.

"Up They Get to My Sunset." Banana Slug String Band, *Wings of Slumber*.

"Walk a Mile." Harley, Bill, *Big Big World*; Pease, Tom, *Wobbi-Do-Wop!*; Vitamin L, *Walk a Mile*.

"We Are All Alike." Palmer, Hap, *Can Cockatoos Count by Twos?*

"We Are an African People." The Dream Project, *We've All Got Stories*.

"Welcome to My World." The Dream Project, *We've All Got Stories*.

"We're All in This Together." Grammer, Red, *Hello World*.

"We're Just like Crayons." Fite, Stephen, *We're Just like Crayons*.

"When the Rain Comes Down." Fink, Cathy, *When the Rain Comes Down*; Fink, Cathy, and Marcy Marxer, *A Cathy & Marcy Collection for Kids*; Herdman, Priscilla, *Daydreamer*; Pease, Tom, *Wobbi-Do-Wop!*

"Where Do We Come From?" Stotts, Stuart, and Tom Pease, *Celebrate: A Song Resource*.

"Wide Wide World." Miss Amy, *Wide Wide World*.

"World Citizen." Pease, Tom, *Boogie! Boogie! Boogie!*; Stotts, Stuart, *One Big Dance*.

"The World Is a Rainbow." Greg and Steve, *We All Live Together*, vol. 2.

"A World United." Vitamin L, *Swingin' in the Key of L*.

Bubbles

"Bubbles." Parachute Express, *Feel the Music*.

"Bubbles." Strausman, Paul, *Blue Jay, Blue Jay!*

"I Am a Bubble." Diamond, Charlotte, *Charlotte Diamond's World*.

"In That Bubble." Crow, Dan, *Oops!*

"Squeaky Song." Walker, Graham, *Fiddlesticks*.

Bullying

"Big Bad Bully Boy." Del Bianco, Lou, *Lost in School*.

"Billy the Bully." Roberts, Justin, *Not Naptime*.

"The Bully." Sprout, Jonathan, *Dr. Music*.

"I'm Just a Kid like You." Kinnoin, Dave, *Daring Dewey*.

"Listen to Me." Harley, Bill, *Big Big World*.

Burping

"Eat, Repeat." Yosi, *What's Eatin' Yosi?*

"Nonsense for Breakfast." Kinnoin, Dave, *Dunce Cap Kelly.*

"Somebody Burped." Paxton, Tom, *Your Shoes, My Shoes.*

"Wyatt Burp." Sprout, Jonathan, *Dr. Music.*

Celebration

"All Things Bright and Beautiful." Moo, Anna, *Anna Moo Crackers.*

"Amazing." Palmer, Hap, *Turn On the Music.*

"Beat of My Heart." Grunsky, Jack, *Jack in the Box 2.*

"A Beautiful Day." Marxer, Marcy, *Jump Children*; Rosen, Gary, *Teddy Bears' Picnic*; Rosenshontz, *Tickles You!* (Same song as "It's a Beautiful Day.")

"Beauty." Banana Slug String Band, *Wings of Slumber.*

"Beauty Is Everything." Harper, Jessica, *Hey, Picasso.*

"Blue Sky Sparklin' Day." McMahon, Elizabeth, *Blue Sky Sparklin' Day.*

"Celebrate!" LaFond, Lois, *Turning It Upside Down.*

"Celebrate." Stotts, Stuart, and Tom Pease, *Celebrate: A Song Resource.*

"Come Blow Your Horn." Chapin, Tom, *This Pretty Planet.*

"Country Life." Zanes, Dan, *Catch That Train!*

"The Crow's Toes." Paxton, Tom, *I've Got a Yo-Yo.*

"Daydream." Grunsky, Jack, *Like a Flower to the Sun.*

"Don't Blink." Parachute Express, *Don't Blink.*

"Get Up and Get Going." Moo, Anna, *Making Moosic.*

"Happy Day." Grunsky, Jack, *Sing and Dance.*

"Harvest Blessing." Tickle Tune Typhoon, *Hearts and Hands.*

"I Love the Morning." McMahon, Elizabeth, *Waltzing with Fireflies.*

"In My Bones." Gemini, *The Best of Gemini*, vol. 2.

"It's a Beautiful Day." Fink, Cathy, and Marcy Marxer, *A Cathy & Marcy Collection for Kids.* (Same song as "A Beautiful Day.")

"It's a Beautiful Day." Greg and Steve, *We All Live Together*, vol. 4.

"It's a Kids' World." Daddy A Go Go, *Eat Every Bean and Pea on Your Plate.*

"It's A Wonderful Life." Harper, Jessica, *A Wonderful Life.*

"Joy, Joy, Joy." Vitamin L, *Walk a Mile.*

"Just like the Sun." Raffi, *Evergreen, Everblue*; Raffi, *Everything Grows.*

"Let's Go." Parachute Express, *Don't Blink.*

"Life Is Good." Kinder, Brian, *Again.*

"A Light That Always Shines." Harley, Bill, *There's a Pea on My Plate.*

"Like a Flower to the Sun." Grunsky, Jack, *Like a Flower to the Sun*.

"Marvelous Day." SteveSongs, *Marvelous Day*.

"My Day." Lonnquist, Ken, *Welcome 2 Kenland*.

"On the Day That You Were Born." Allard, Peter and Ellen, *Sing It! Say It! Stamp It! Sway It!* vol. 2.

"On the Day You Were Born." Fink, Cathy, and Marcy Marxer, *All Wound Up!*; Grammer, Red, *Hello World*.

"One Light, One Sun." Barchas, Sarah, *Bridges across the World*; Raffi, *Evergreen, Everblue*; Raffi, *One Light One Sun*.

"One Step, One Mile." Ode, Eric, *Grandpa's Truck*.

"Ordinary-Extraordinary." Moo, Anna, *Moochas Gracias*.

"Peanut Butter Sandwich." McMahon, Elizabeth, *Tea Party Shuffle*.

"Rhythm of the Land." Grunsky, Jack, *Like a Flower to the Sun*.

"Say Hey." Stotts, Stuart, *One Big Dance*.

"Seven Wonders." Craig n Co., *Rock n Together*.

"Shout Hooray!" Cosgrove, Jim, *Pick Me! Pick Me!*

"Shout the Happiness." Harper, Jessica, *Inside Out*.

"Simple Gifts." Grammer, Red, *Red Grammer's Favorite Sing Along Songs*; Raffi, *Bananaphone*.

"Simple Pleasures." Vitamin L, *Swingin' in the Key of L*.

"So Glad I'm Here." Mitchell, Elizabeth, *You Are My Sunshine*; Sweet Honey in the Rock, *All for Freedom*.

"Song for You." Roberts, Justin, *Meltdown!*

"A Song of One." Chapin, Tom, *Mother Earth*.

"Sun in My Eyes." Ralph's World, *The Amazing Adventures of Kid Astro*.

"Take Time to Wonder." Banana Slug String Band, *Singing in Our Garden*.

"There's Something Wonderful." Moo, Anna, *Anna Moo Crackers*.

"This Shall Forever Be." Lonnquist, Ken, *Earthy Songs*.

"Turn the World Around." Allard, Peter and Ellen, *Raise the Children*; Fink, Cathy, and Marcy Marxer, *All Wound Up!*; Harley, Bill, *Big Big World*; Miss Amy, *Wide Wide World*; Pease, Tom, *Daddy Starts to Dance*; Rymer, Brady, *I Found It!*; Various Artists, *Peace Is the World Smiling*.

"Wave after Wave." Grunsky, Jack, *Jack in the Box 1*.

"We're Gonna Shine." Penner, Fred, *Fred's Favourites*; Penner, Fred, *Sing with Fred*.

"What a Day!" Penner, Fred, *Fred's Favourites*; Penner, Fred, *Sing with Fred*; Penner, Fred, *What a Day!*

"When You Were Born." Milkshake, *Happy Songs*.

"Where I Live." Raffi, *Evergreen, Everblue*.

"With People I Like." Banana Slug String Band, *Dirt Made My Lunch*.

"Wonders of the World." Vitamin L, *Swingin' in the Key of L*.

"Yonder Come Day/Shining over China." Harper, Jessica, *Inside Out*.

"You Should Have Been There." Harley, Bill, *One More Time*; Harley, Bill, *There's a Pea on My Plate*.

Childhood

"Boy Girl Boy Girl." Harper, Jessica, *Rhythm in My Shoes*.

"Cada Niño: Every Child." Hinojosa, Tish, *Cada Niño: Every Child*.

"Child." Kaye, Mary, *Spin Your Web*.

"Children of the Future." Sprout, Jonathan, *On the Radio*.

"Do That Again." Troubadour, *On the Trail*.

"11 East Steps." Trout Fishing in America, *Family Music Party*.

"Every Child." Raffi, *Raffi Radio*.

"Everybody Once Was a Kid." Gemini, *The Best of Gemini*.

"Googleheads." Berkner, Laurie, *Victor Vito*.

"I Like Being a Kid." Kinder, Brian, *A Kid like You*.

"If I Ran the World." McCutcheon, John, *Family Garden*.

"I'm a Kid." Frezza, Rebecca, *Tall and Small*.

"It Takes a Village." Raffi, *Let's Play*.

"It's a Kids' World." Daddy A Go Go, *Eat Every Bean and Pea on Your Plate*.

"It's Hard to Be a Kid." Daddy A Go Go, *Monkey in the Middle*.

"Just Kidding." Various Artists, *Folk Playground*.

"Katy." Paxton, Tom, *Goin' to the Zoo*.

"Kids Are Kids." Gemini, *The Best of Gemini*, vol. 2.

"Kids on Strike." McCutcheon, John, *Bigger Than Yourself*.

"Little Children." Silberg, "Miss Jackie," *Lollipops and Spaghetti*; Silberg, "Miss Jackie," *Sing It Again Please*.

"Marching Shoulder to Shoulder." Polisar, Barry Louis, *Naughty Songs for Boys and Girls*.

"On Children." Various Artists, *Peace Is the World Smiling*.

"Princess Katie." SteveSongs, *Little Superman*.

"Raise the Children." Allard, Peter and Ellen, *Raise the Children*.

"Red Balloon." Harper, Jessica, *40 Winks*.

"Rock My Baby." Frezza, Rebecca, *Road Trip*.

"Something to Share (Song for UNICEF)." Grunsky, Jack, *Sing and Dance*.

"Sweet as a Swing Set." Harper, Jessica, *Nora's Room*.

"Tickle My Heart." Green Chili Jam Band, *Starfishing*.
"Under the Rainbow." Alsop, Peter, *Pluggin' Away*.
"We the Children." Parachute Express, *Doctor Looney's Remedy*.
"When I Was a Child." Moos, Anna, *When I Was a Child*.
"You Can Make a Miracle." Diamond, Charlotte, *Diamonds and Dragons*.

Circus

"At the Circus." Barchas, Sarah, *If I Had a Pony*.
"Circus Boy." Foote, Norman, *1000 Pennies*.
"The Circus Is Near." Rosenshontz, *Rock 'n Roll Teddy Bear*.
"The Circus Leaves Town." Lonnquist, Ken, *The Circus Kenlando*; Lonnquist, Ken, *The Switcher-On of Stars*.
"Circus Lullaby." Arnold, Linda, *Circus Magic*.
"Circus of the World." Arnold, Linda, *Circus Magic*.
"Circus Parade." Arnold, Linda, *Circus Magic*.
"Circus Poodles." Arnold, Linda, *Circus Magic*.
"The Circus Song." Muldaur, Maria, *On the Sunny Side*.
"Circus Train." Arnold, Linda, *Circus Magic*.
"The Circus Train." Roth, Kevin, *Train Songs and Other Tracks*.
"Clover the Clown." Arnold, Linda, *Circus Magic*.
"Clown Song." Palmer, Hap, *Turn On the Music*.
"Harry's Haunted Halloween Circus." Ralph's World, *At the Bottom of the Sea*.
"How I Became a Clown." Chapin, Tom, *Some Assembly Required*.
"I Love a Circus." Crow, Dan, *Dan Crow Live*; Crow, Dan, *A Friend, a Laugh, a Walk in the Woods*.
"I'm a Clown." Beall, Pamela, and Susan Nipp, *Wee Sing and Pretend*.
"King of the Flying Trapeze." Arnold, Linda, *Circus Magic*.
"Rumble to the Bottom." Colleen and Uncle Squaty, *Rumble to the Bottom*.
"The Singing Ringmaster." Arnold, Linda, *Circus Magic*.
"Under the Big Top." Arnold, Linda, *Circus Magic*.
"Water for the Elephants." Zanes, Dan, *Family Dance*.

Cities/Neighborhoods/Towns

"All over My Home Town." Strausman, Paul, *Rainbows, Stones, and Dinosaur Bones*.
"Around the Block." Parachute Express, *Sunny Side Up*.
"Hometown." Chapin, Tom, *In My Hometown*.

"The House I Live In." Raven, Nancy, *The House We Live In*, vols. 1 and 2.

"I Live in a City." Raven, Nancy, *Singing, Prancing, and Dancing*.

"It Takes a Village." Raffi, *Let's Play*.

"Linger for Awhile." Zanes, Dan, *Night Time!*

"My Town Is a Salad Bowl." Chapin, Tom, *In My Hometown*.

"Walkin' Home." Del Bianco, Lou, *A Little Bit Clumsy*.

"Wander in the Summer Wind." Zanes, Dan, *Catch That Train!*

"We All Live in a Neighborhood." Coffey, James, *Come Ride Along with Me*.

"Welcome." Vitamin L, *Everyone's Invited!*

Cleverness

"The Brainiacs." Harper, Monty, *Imagine That*.

"My Baby Is a Genius." Harper, Jessica, *Rhythm in My Shoes*.

Clocks/Time

"All Is Well." Big Jeff, *Big Jeff and His Middle-Sized Band*.

"The Cuckoo Clock." Fink, Cathy, *Grandma Slid down the Mountain*.

"Five More Minootsa." Pullara, Steve, *A Big Bowl of Musicroni*.

"Grandfather Clock." Foote, Norman, *If the Shoe Fits*.

"Grandfather's Clock." Grammer, Red, *Down the Do-Re-Mi*; Penner, Fred, *Storytime*; Staines, Bill, *One More River*; Various Artists, *A Child's Celebration of Folk Music*.

"Hickory Dickory Dock." Barchas, Sarah, *Get Ready, Get Set, Sing!*; Beall, Pamela, and Susan Nipp, *Wee Sing Children's Songs and Fingerplays*; Beall, Pamela, and Susan Nipp, *Wee Sing for Baby*; Beall, Pamela, and Susan Nipp, *Wee Sing Nursery Rhymes and Lullabies*; Feldman, Jean, *Nursery Rhymes and Good Ol' Times*.

"Hickory Dickory Dock." Palmer, Hap, *Two Little Sounds*.

"Hickory Dickory Dock." SteveSongs, *On a Flying Guitar*.

"Jolly Clock." Palmer, Hap, *Can Cockatoos Count by Twos?*

"Learning How to Tell Time." Mr. Al, *Put Your Groove On*.

"More Than Just a Minute." Roberts, Justin, *Meltdown!*; Various Artists, *Hear and Gone in 60 Seconds*.

"The Mouse and the Clock." Colleen and Uncle Squaty, *Fingerplays, Movement and Story Songs*.

"My Grandfather Clock." McGrath, Bob, and Katherine Smithrim, *Songs and Games for Toddlers*; Peterson, Carole, *Sticky Bubble Gum*.

"'Round the Clock." Beall, Pamela, and Susan Nipp, *Wee Sing Children's Songs and Fingerplays.*
"Stepping Out on the Town." Palmer, Hap, *Can a Cherry Pie Wave Goodbye?*
"Tick Tock." Arnold, Linda, *Make Believe.*
"Time." Sweet Honey in the Rock, *Still the Same Me.*
"Time." Tickle Tune Typhoon, *Singing Science.*
"Time for Bed." Allard, Peter and Ellen, *Pizza Pizzaz.*
"A Tiny Little Gear." Various Artists, *Hear and Gone in 60 Seconds.*
"Wrist Watch." Mayer, Hans, *Just a Little Hug.*

Clothing

"All Dressed Up." Allard, Peter and Ellen, *Good Kid.*
"All Week Long." Barchas, Sarah, *Get Ready, Get Set, Sing!*
"Baby's Clothes." Beall, Pamela, and Susan Nipp, *Wee Sing for Baby.*
"Bring Your Clothes." Berkner, Laurie, *Whaddaya Think of That?*
"Clothes Encounter." Simmons, Al, *The Celery Stalks at Midnight.*
"Clothesline Hop." Atkinson, Lisa, *The One and Only Me.*
"Dirty Laundry Boogie." Knight, Tom, *Don't Kiss a Codfish.*
"Dress Up Queen." Parachute Express, *Don't Blink.*
"500 Tee Shirts." Charette, Rick, *King Kong Chair.*
"Green Dress Song." Raven, Nancy, *You Gotta Juba.*
"Hand-Me-Down Blues." Various Artists, *Hear and Gone in 60 Seconds.*
"Hats on Bees." Tucker, Nancy, *Escape of the Slinkys.*
"I Can Put My Clothes On by Myself." Palmer, Hap, *Peek-a-Boo.*
"I Had an Old Coat." Allard, Peter and Ellen, *Good Kid.*
"I Had an Old Overcoat." The Learning Station, *Literacy in Motion.*
"I Want to Wear." Buchman, Rachel, *Hello Everybody!*
"If You're Wearing Colors." The Learning Station, *Get Funky and Musical Fun.*
"Jenny Jenkins." Beall, Pamela, and Susan Nipp, *Wee Sing Fun 'n' Folk*; Garcia, Jerry, and David Grisman, *Not for Kids Only*; Raven, Nancy, *Hop, Skip, and Sing*; Sharon, Lois, and Bram, *Great Big Hits*; Sharon, Lois, and Bram, *School Days.*
"The Laundry." Diamond, Charlotte, *Diamond in the Rough.*
"Laundry Bag." Kaldor, Connie, *A Duck in New York City.*
"Let's Get Dressed." Kaye, Mary, *Spin Your Web.*
"Mary Wore Her Red Dress (Mary Was a Bird)." Raffi, *Everything Grows*; Raffi, *Quiet Time*; Raven, Nancy, *People and Animal Songs.*
"Old Man Noah's Raincoat." Ode, Eric, *Trash Can.*

"Rubber Boots and Raincoats." Kaldor, Connie, *A Poodle in Paris*.

"The Washing Machine." The Chenille Sisters, *The Big Picture and Other Songs for Kids*.

"What Are You Wearing?" Beall, Pamela, and Susan Nipp, *Wee Sing Children's Songs and Fingerplays*.

"What Are You Wearing?" Palmer, Hap, *Two Little Sounds*.

"What You Gonna Wear?" Fink, Cathy, and Marcy Marxer, *Help Yourself*.

"When My Shoes Are Loose." Fink, Cathy, and Marcy Marxer, *Help Yourself*.

"Who's Wearing Yellow?" Barchas, Sarah, *Get Ready, Get Set, Sing!*

Hats

"Goofy Hat Dance." Greg and Steve, *Fun and Games*.

"Grampa's Hat." Kinnoin, Dave, *Getting Bigger*.

"I Got a Hat." The Learning Station, *Seasonal Songs in Motion*.

"I Like My Hat." Peterson, Carole, *Stinky Cake*.

"I Love My Little Hat." Old Town School of Folk Music, *Wiggleworms Love You*.

"My Hat It Has Three Corners." Beall, Pamela, and Susan Nipp, *Wee Sing Silly Songs*.

"Pancake Hat." Pirtle, Sarah, *The Wind Is Telling Secrets*.

"Tall Silk Hat." Magical Music Express, *Music Is Magic*; Sharon, Lois, and Bram, *School Days*.

"Where Did You Get That Hat?" Simmons, Al, *The Celery Stalks at Midnight*.

Mittens

"The Mitten." McMahon, Elizabeth, *Blue Sky Sparklin' Day*.

"The Mitten Song." Buchman, Rachel, *Sing a Song of Seasons*.

"The Mitten Song." Peterson, Carole, *H.U.M.—All Year Long*.

"The Mitten Song." Walker, Mary Lu, *The Frog's Party*.

"Three Little Kittens." Feldman, Jean, *Nursery Rhymes and Good Ol' Times*.

Pajamas

"I Can't Find My Pyjamas." Simmons, Al, *Something Fishy at Camp Wiganishie*.

"I Got Pajamas." Fink, Cathy, and Marcy Marxer, *Pocket Full of Stardust*.

"In My Pajamas." Kinder, Brian, *One More Time*.

"Old Pajamas." Roberts, Justin, *Great Big Sun*.

"Pajama Time." Boynton, Sandra, *Philadelphia Chickens*.

"Pyjamarama." Grunsky, Jack, *Dancing Feet*; Grunsky, Jack, *Jack in the Box 1*.

Pants

"Bouncin' Baby." Roberts, Justin, *Great Big Sun*.

"Fancy Pants Dance." Cosgrove, Jim, *Pick Me! Pick Me!*

"I Lost My Pants." Polisar, Barry Louis, *Teacher's Favorites*.

"My Pants Fell Down." Trout Fishing in America, *My Best Day*.

"Sam's Mens Wear/Sam, You Made the Pants Too Long." Simmons, Al, *The Celery Stalks at Midnight*.

Shoes

"Barefoot Blues." Harper, Jessica, *Nora's Room*.

"Barefoot Blues." Lonnquist, Ken, *The Lost Songs of Kenland*.

"Boots." Berkner, Laurie, *Victor Vito*.

"Brand New Shoes." Foote, Norman, *Shake a Leg*.

"I Can't Find My Shoes." Daddy A Go Go, *Big Rock Rooster*.

"I Can't Tie My Shoe." Polisar, Barry Louis, *Old Enough to Know Better*.

"I Lost My Shoes." LaFond, Lois, *One World*.

"I Love My Shoes." Ode, Eric, *I Love My Shoes*.

"Late Last Night." Scruggs, Joe, *Late Last Night*.

"A Little Brown Dog Named Joe." Harper, Jessica, *Inside Out*.

"Little Spot." Kinnoin, Dave, *Getting Bigger*.

"Monkey's New Shoes." Mayer, Hans, *Just a Little Hug*.

"My Cool Shoes." Various Artists, *Hear and Gone in 60 Seconds*.

"New Boots." McCutcheon, John, *Wintersongs*.

"New Shoes." Allard, Peter and Ellen, *Good Kid*.

"One Shoe Bear." Rosenshontz, *Rosenshontz Greatest Hits*.

"Only One Shoe." Chapin, Tom, *Some Assembly Required*.

"The Other Shoe." Scruggs, Joe, *Late Last Night*.

"School Shoes." Kinder, Brian, *A Kid like You*.

"Shoe Tyin' Blues." Dana, *Dana's Best Sing and Play-a-Long Tunes*.

"Show Me Your Shoes." Mr. Al, *Mr. Al Concert Live*; Mr. Al, *Rockin' the Alphabet*.

"Sneakers." Boynton, Sandra, *Dog Train*.

"Sneakers." Tickle Tune Typhoon, *Circle Around*.

"Something in My Shoe." Raffi, *Rise and Shine*; Simmons, Al, *Something Fishy at Camp Wiganishie*.

"Sticky Shoe." Lonnquist, Ken, *Sci-Fi Hi-Fi*.

"Stinky Blues." Yosi, *Under a Big Bright Yellow Umbrella*.

"This Hat." Berkner, Laurie, *Under a Shady Tree*.

"Tie Your Shoe." Roberts, Justin, *Yellow Bus*.

"Walkin' Shoes." Rymer, Brady, *Look at My Belly*.

"Where Do My Sneakers Go at Night?" Charette, Rick, *Where Do My Sneakers Go at Night?*

"Your Shoes, My Shoes." Paxton, Tom, *Your Shoes, My Shoes*.

Socks

"Black Socks." Fink, Cathy, and Marcy Marxer, *Scat like That*; Harley, Bill, *Monsters in the Bathroom*; Harley, Bill, *Play It Again*.

"Gypsy Socks." Simmons, Al, *The Truck I Bought from Moe*.

"Missing Sock." Charette, Rick, *Where Do My Sneakers Go at Night?*

"Old Sock Stew." Gill, Jim, *Jim Gill Sings the Sneezing Song and Other Contagious Tunes*.

Underwear

"Big Underwear." Scruggs, Joe, *Ants*.

"God Bless My Underwear." Mayer, Hans, *See You Later, Alligator*.

"I Have Lost My Underwear." McGrath, Bob, *Sing Along with Bob #2*.

"Pink Polka Dot Underwear." Lonnquist, Ken, *Welcome 2 Kenland*.

"A Thousand Little Stickers in His Underwear." Kinnoin, Dave, *Daring Dewey*.

"Underwear." Polisar, Barry Louis, *Family Concert*; Polisar, Barry Louis, *Teacher's Favorites*.

Clumsiness

"A Little Bit Clumsy." Del Bianco, Lou, *A Little Bit Clumsy*.

"Oops!" Gemini, *The Best of Gemini*.

"Oops Oops Bang Bang." Kaldor, Connie, *A Poodle in Paris*.

Collecting Things

"Bottle Caps." Berkner, Laurie, *Victor Vito*.

"Counting Feathers." Simmons, Al, *Something Fishy at Camp Wiganishie*.

"I Collect Rocks." Simmons, Al, *Something Fishy at Camp Wiganishie*.

Colors

"All My Colors." Ralph's World, *Ralph's World*.

"All the Colors." Barchas, Sarah, *Bridges across the World*; Barchas, Sarah, *¡Piñata! and More*.

"All Week Long." Barchas, Sarah, *Get Ready, Get Set, Sing!*

"As Pretty as Pink." Mr. Al, *Sing Me a Color.*

"Balloons, Balloons." Barchas, Sarah, *Get Ready, Get Set, Sing!*

"Big Truck." Frezza, Rebecca, *Music in My Head.*

"Black Is Beautiful." Mr. Al, *Sing Me a Color.*

"Blue Is a Color." Mr. Al, *Sing Me a Color.*

"Brown Is the Coolest Color Around." Mr. Al, *Sing Me a Color.*

"Color Game." Gill, Jim, *Jim Gill Sings Do Re Mi on His Toe Leg Knee.*

"The Color Rap." Mr. Al, *Sing Me a Color.*

"Color Song." Parachute Express, *Feel the Music.*

"De Colores." Pirtle, Sarah, *Two Hands Hold the Earth*; Raven, Nancy, *You Gotta Juba.*

"Colors." Beall, Pamela, and Susan Nipp, *Wee Sing Games, Games, Games.*

"Colors." Frezza, Rebecca, *Tall and Small.*

"Colors." Kaye, Mary, *I Sang It Just for You.*

"Colors in Motion." Palmer, Hap, *Can Cockatoos Count by Twos?*

"The Colors of the Earth." Pirtle, Sarah, *The Wind Is Telling Secrets.*

"Colors of the Rainbow." Allard, Peter and Ellen, *Pizza Pizzaz.*

"Everything Has a Color." The Learning Station, *Children Love to Sing and Dance.*

"Green Dress Song." Raven, Nancy, *You Gotta Juba.*

"Gummy Bears." Feldman, Jean, *Is Everybody Happy?*

"I Can Make a Snowman." Peterson, Carole, *H.U.M.—All Year Long.*

"I Can Sing a Rainbow." Penner, Fred, *Sing with Fred.*

"I Have a Horse." Barchas, Sarah, *Get Ready, Get Set, Sing!*

"I Like Silver, I Like Gold." Rudnick, Ben, *Emily Songs.*

"I Like the Color Red." Mr. Al, *Mr. Al a Carte*; Mr. Al, *Sing Me a Color.*

"If We Didn't Have Colors." Fite, Stephen, *Monkey Business.*

"If You're Wearing Colors." The Learning Station, *Get Funky and Musical Fun.*

"I've Got the Blues, Greens and Reds." Chapin, Tom, *Billy the Squid.*

"Jenny Jenkins." Beall, Pamela, and Susan Nipp, *Wee Sing Fun 'n' Folk*; Garcia, Jerry, and David Grisman, *Not for Kids Only*; Raven, Nancy, *Hop, Skip, and Sing*; Sharon, Lois, and Bram, *Great Big Hits*; Sharon, Lois, and Bram, *School Days.*

"Kaleidoscope Blues." Tucker, Nancy, *Escape of the Slinkys.*

"Lavender's Blue." Sharon, Lois, and Bram, *Mainly Mother Goose.*

"Let's Paint a Picture." Grunsky, Jack, *Follow the Leader*; Grunsky, Jack, *Playground.*

"Little Bird." Raven, Nancy, *Hop, Skip, and Sing.*

"Little Old Wagon." Peterson, Carole, *Sticky Bubble Gum.*

"Little Red Caboose." Berkner, Laurie, *Buzz Buzz.*

"Mariposa." Barchas, Sarah, *¡Piñata! and More.*

"Mary Wore Her Red Dress (Mary Was a Bird)." Raffi, *Everything Grows*; Raffi, *Quiet Time*; Raven, Nancy, *People and Animal Songs.*

"Mixing Colors." Rosen, Gary, *Tot Rock.*

"Orange, Orange, Orange." Mr. Al, *Sing Me a Color.*

"The Orange Song." Big Jeff, *Big Jeff.*

"Parade of Colors." Palmer, Hap, *Can a Cherry Pie Wave Goodbye?*

"Pick Out the Purple." Mr. Al, *Sing Me a Color.*

"Please Stand Up." Mr. Al, *Mr. Al a Carte.*

"Put a Little Color on You." Palmer, Hap, *Can a Cherry Pie Wave Goodbye?*

"Rainbow Island." Dana, *Dana's Best Travelin' Tunes.*

"Rainbow of Colors." Greg and Steve, *We All Live Together*, vol. 5.

"Rainbow of Feelings." Strausman, Paul, *Blue Jay, Blue Jay!*

"Rainbow 'round Me." Pelham, Ruth, *Under One Sky*; Stotts, Stuart, and Tom Pease, *Celebrate: A Song Resource.*

"Red Banana." Ralph's World, *Green Gorilla, Monster, and Me.*

"Red Bird." Barchas, Sarah, *Get Ready, Get Set, Sing!*; Barchas, Sarah, *¡Piñata! and More.*

"Red Brontosaurus." Kimmy Schwimmy, *Kimmy Schwimmy Music*, vol. 1.

"Show Me Green." Mr. Al, *Sing Me a Color.*

"Show Me Your Shoes." Mr. Al, *Mr. Al Concert Live*; Mr. Al, *Rockin' the Alphabet.*

"Stand Up." Fite, Stephen, *Havin' Fun and Feelin' Groovy.*

"They Call the Color Yellow." Mr. Al, *Sing Me a Color.*

"Wave White Ribbons." Mr. Al, *Sing Me a Color.*

"We've Got a Rainbow." Kimmy Schwimmy, *Kimmy Schwimmy Music*, vol. 1.

"Who's Wearing Yellow?" Barchas, Sarah, *Get Ready, Get Set, Sing!*

"A World of Colors." Barchas, Sarah, *If I Had a Pony.*

"Yellow Crayon." Guthrie, Woody, *Nursery Days.*

Continents (see also Countries; Languages)

"Song of the Seven Continents." Jenkins, Ella, *Sharing Cultures with Ella Jenkins.*

Africa

"Deepest Africa." The Chenille Sisters, *Teaching Hippopotami to Fly!*; Pease, Tom, *Wobbi-Do-Wop!*

"Jane Jane." Raffi, *Let's Play.*

"Mysteries of the Nile." Moo, Anna, *Anna Moo Crackers.*

"The Nile Is Wild." Lonnquist, Ken, *Earthy Songs*; Lonnquist, Ken, *Sci-Fi Hi-Fi*.
"Shango." Barchas, Sarah, *Bridges across the World*.

Australia

"Animals Down Under." Tickle Tune Typhoon, *Singing Science*.
"Bush Lullaby." Herdman, Priscilla, *Stardreamer*.
"Didgeridoo." Shontz, Bill, *The Day I Read a Book*.
"Kookaburra." Barchas, Sarah, *Bridges across the World*; Beall, Pamela, and Susan
    Nipp, *Wee Sing Animals, Animals, Animals*; Beall, Pamela, and Susan Nipp,
    Wee Sing around the World; Beall, Pamela, and Susan Nipp, *Wee Sing Sing-
    Alongs*; Staines, Bill, *The Happy Wanderer*; Walker, Graham, *Jumpety Jump*.
"Nyanpi Matilda (Waltzing Matilda)." Various Artists, *World Playground*.
"Waltzing Matilda." Zanes, Dan, *House Party*.
"Yi-Rrana." Various Artists, *Dreamland*.

Computers

"Get off the Computer." Daddy A Go Go, *Big Rock Rooster*.

Consumerism

"All I Need." Nagler, Eric, *Eric's World Record*.
"Buy Me This and Buy Me That." Fink, Cathy, and Marcy Marxer, *Changing Channels*.
"Everybody Wants One." Harper, Monty, *Imagine That*.
"Everywhere You Go." Polisar, Barry Louis, *Old Enough to Know Better*.

Cooking/Baking

"Betty Batter." Ralph's World, *Happy Lemon*.
"Birthday Cake." Parachute Express, *Sunny Side Up*.
"Come and Get It." Riders in the Sky, *Harmony Ranch*.
"The Cookie Bakers of the Night." Berkner, Laurie, *Buzz Buzz*.
"Cookin' in the Kitchen." Chapin, Tom, *Making Good Noise*.
"Cookin' Saturday." Rymer, Brady, *I Found It!*
"Cooking Breakfast for the One I Love." Muldaur, Maria, *On
    the Sunny Side*.
"Helping Mommy in the Kitchen." Palmer, Hap, *Turn On the Music*.
"I'm Making Breakfast." Parachute Express, *Don't Blink*.
"Kitchen Sing Sing." Raffi, *Raffi Radio*.

"Let's Get Cookin'." Yosi, *What's Eatin' Yosi?*

"Mother's Day." Chapin, Tom, *Moonboat.*

"Nuke It." Scruggs, Joe, *Even Trolls Have Moms.*

"Pat-a-Cake." Scruggs, Joe, *Traffic Jams.*

Cooperation/Sportsmanship

"All Work Together." Guthrie, Woody, *Woody's 20 Grow Big Songs*; Guthrie, Woody and Arlo, *This Land Is Your Land.*

"Co-operation." Diamond, Charlotte, *Diamonds and Dragons.*

"Cooperation." Mr. Al and Stephen Fite, *Back to School Again.*

"Do It Together." Harley, Bill, *Big Big World.*

"Everybody Pitchin' In." Foote, Norman, *Pictures on the Fridge.*

"Fairness." Grammer, Red, *Be Bop Your Best!*

"I Wanna Play." Harley, Bill, *I Wanna Play.*

"It Takes Each One to Make This World a Little Bit Better." Barchas, Sarah, *Bridges across the World.*

"London Bridge." Dana, *Dana's Best Travelin' Tunes.*

"Look to the People." Pelham, Ruth, *Under One Sky.*

"Most Valuable Player." Harley, Bill, *Down in the Backpack*; Tucker, Nancy, *Escape of the Slinkys.*

"New Games." Alsop, Peter, *Pluggin' Away.*

"Play Fair." McCutcheon, John, *Bigger Than Yourself.*

"The Principle." McCutcheon, John, *Bigger Than Yourself.*

"Respect." Grammer, Red, *Be Bop Your Best!*

"Some Assembly Required." Chapin, Tom, *Some Assembly Required.*

"Sore Loser." Chapin, Tom, *Billy the Squid.*

"Teamwork." Vitamin L, *Everyone's Invited!*

"That's How You Play the Game." Vitamin L, *Every Moment!*

"The Union Team." Various Artists, *cELLAbration! A Tribute to Ella Jenkins.*

"United We Stand." Greg and Steve, *Ready, Set, Move!*

"Use a Word." Grammer, Red, *Teaching Peace.*

"We Gotta Work It Out." Stotts, Stuart, and Tom Pease, *Celebrate: A Song Resource.*

"We Shall Not Be Moved." Zanes, Dan, *House Party.*

"Winners." Kaldor, Connie, *A Poodle in Paris.*

"With Two Wings." Grammer, Red, *Teaching Peace.*

"Working Together." Craig n Co., *Rock n Together.*

"Working Together." Parachute Express, *Doctor Looney's Remedy*.

"Write It Down." McCutcheon, John, *Bigger Than Yourself*.

Counting/Numbers

"African Numbers." Sweet Honey in the Rock, *I Got Shoes*.

"Alice the Camel." The Learning Station, *All-Time Children's Favorites*.

"Alligator in the Elevator." Charette, Rick, *Alligator in the Elevator*.

"The Ants Go Marching." Beall, Pamela, and Susan Nipp, *Wee Sing Animals, Animals, Animals*; Beall, Pamela, and Susan Nipp, *Wee Sing Silly Songs*; Colleen and Uncle Squaty, *Rumble to the Bottom*; The Learning Station, *Get Funky and Musical Fun*; Sharon, Lois, and Bram, *Everybody Sing!*; Strausman, Paul, *Camels, Cats, and Rainbows*.

"The Beaver Call." Feldman, Jean, *Dr. Jean Sings Silly Songs*.

"Betty Beep." Palmer, Hap, *Can Cockatoos Count by Twos?*

"A Bowl of Cherries." Allard, Peter and Ellen, *Sing It! Say It! Stamp It! Sway It!* vol. 3.

"Buzzing in the Garden." Allard, Peter and Ellen, *Pizza Pizzaz*.

"By 'n By." Buchman, Rachel, *Sing a Song of Seasons*; Roth, Kevin, *Travel Song Sing Alongs*; Sharon, Lois, and Bram, *One Elephant, Deux Éléphants*.

"Chay Chay Koolay." Barchas, Sarah, *Bridges across the World*.

"Count Bounce." Greg and Steve, *Kids in Motion*.

"Count Ten." Raven, Nancy, *Singing, Prancing, and Dancing*.

"Count to Ten and Try Again." Fink, Cathy, and Marcy Marxer, *Changing Channels*.

"The Countdown." Fite, Stephen, *Havin' Fun and Feelin' Groovy*.

"Counting Cows." Cosgrove, Jim, *Mr. Stinky Feet's Road Trip*.

"Counting Song." Grammer, Red, *Can You Sound Just like Me?*

"The Counting Song." Mayer, Hans, *Stars of the Swing Set*.

"The Counting Song." Mr. Al, *Rockin' the Alphabet*.

"Counting Those Railroad Cars." Coffey, James, *My Mama Was a Train*.

"Counting Together." The Learning Station, *Children Love to Sing and Dance*.

"Cow in the Car." Dana, *Dana's Best Travelin' Tunes*.

"18 Wheels on a Big Rig." Ralph's World, *At the Bottom of the Sea*; Trout Fishing in America, *Family Music Party*; Trout Fishing in America, *Mine!*

"Every Little Star." Fink, Cathy, and Marcy Marxer, *Pocket Full of Stardust*.

"Everyone Counts." Moo, Anna, *Anna Moo Crackers*.

"Farmer Brown Had Ten Green Apples." Jenkins, Ella, *Growing Up with Ella Jenkins*. (Same song as "Five Green Apples.")

"Fingers and Toes." Milkshake, *Happy Songs.*

"Five Big Dump Trucks." Beall, Pamela, and Susan Nipp, *Wee Sing in the Car.*

"Five Brown Buns." Sharon, Lois, and Bram, *Great Big Hits.*

"Five Fish Swimming in the Sea." Feldman, Jean, *Dr. Jean Sings Silly Songs.*

"Five Frogs." Moo, Anna, *Anna Moo Crackers.*

"Five Green Apples." Allard, Peter and Ellen, *Sing It! Say It! Stamp It! Sway It!* vol. 1; Sharon, Lois, and Bram, *Mainly Mother Goose*; Sharon, Lois, and Bram, *School Days.* (Same song as "Farmer Brown Had Ten Green Apples.")

"Five Little Cats." Barchas, Sarah, *Get Ready, Get Set, Sing!*

"Five Little Chickadees." Allard, Peter and Ellen, *Sing It! Say It! Stamp It! Sway It!* vol. 2.

"Five Little Ducks." Barchas, Sarah, *Get Ready, Get Set, Sing!*; Beall, Pamela, and Susan Nipp, *Wee Sing Animals, Animals, Animals*; Buchman, Rachel, *Hello Everybody!*; McGrath, Bob, and Katherine Smithrim, *Songs and Games for Toddlers*; Raffi, *Raffi in Concert*; Raffi, *Rise and Shine*; Trout Fishing in America, *Mine!*

"Five Little Frogs." Raffi, *Singable Songs for the Very Young.*

"Five Little Hotdogs." Feldman, Jean, *Just for Fun!*

"Five Little Leaves." Avni, Fran, *Tuning into Nature*; Buchman, Rachel, *Sing a Song of Seasons.*

"Five Little Monkeys." Barchas, Sarah, *If I Had a Pony*; Greg and Steve, *Ready, Set, Move!*; The Learning Station, *Literacy in Motion*; The Learning Station, *Tony Chestnut and Fun Time Action Songs*; McGrath, Bob, *Sing Along with Bob #1*; Palmer, Hap, *So Big*; Yosi, *Monkey Business.* (Similar to "No More Monkeys" and "Ten Little Monkeys.")

"Five Little Pumpkins." Raffi, *Singable Songs for the Very Young.*

"Five Little Sparrows." Diamond, Charlotte, *My Bear Gruff.*

"Five Miles from Home." Beall, Pamela, and Susan Nipp, *Wee Sing in the Car.*

"Five Shiny Pennies." Allard, Peter and Ellen, *Raise the Children.*

"Four Little Duckies." Ralph's World, *Ralph's World.*

"Go Down Emmanuel Road." Zanes, Dan, *Rocket Ship Beach.*

"Going over the Sea." Allard, Peter and Ellen, *Sing It! Say It! Stamp It! Sway It!* vol. 2; Beall, Pamela, and Susan Nipp, *Wee Sing around the World*; Feldman, Jean, *Just for Fun!*

"Goodnight, Goodnight." Fink, Cathy, and Marcy Marxer, *Blanket Full of Dreams.*

"Gummy Bears." Feldman, Jean, *Is Everybody Happy?*

"Hundredth Day of School." Fite, Stephen, *Monkey Business.*

"I Can Work with One Hammer." Greg and Steve, *Fun and Games.*

"If You Got 1." Roberts, Justin, *Great Big Sun.*

"Let's Do the Numbers Rumba." Raffi, *Rise and Shine.*

"Mama Crow." Pirtle, Sarah, *The Wind Is Telling Secrets.*

"Monkeys and the Alligator." Feldman, Jean, *Dr. Jean and Friends.*

"My Tooth It Is Wiggling." Allard, Peter and Ellen, *Pizza Pizzaz.*

"Nine Little Reindeer." Silberg, "Miss Jackie," *The Complete Sniggles, Squirrels, and Chicken Pox.*

"Ninety-nine Bottles of Pop." Beall, Pamela, and Susan Nipp, *Wee Sing Silly Songs.*

"No More Monkeys." Mr. Al, *Mr. Al Concert Live*; Mr. Al, *Put Your Groove On.* (Similar to "Five Little Monkeys" and "Ten Little Monkeys.")

"The Number Game." Greg and Steve, *We All Live Together*, vol. 5.

"The Number Rock." Greg and Steve, *We All Live Together*, vol. 2.

"Numbers All Around." LaFond, Lois, *Turning It Upside Down.*

"Numbers Can Tell about You." Palmer, Hap, *Can Cockatoos Count by Twos?*

"Old John Braddelum." Allard, Peter and Ellen, *Sing It! Say It! Stamp It! Sway It!* vol. 2; Sharon, Lois, and Bram, *One Elephant, Deux Éléphants.*

"One More River." Beall, Pamela, and Susan Nipp, *Wee Sing Sing-Alongs.*

"One, Two, Buckle My Shoe." Beall, Pamela, and Susan Nipp, *Wee Sing Children's Songs and Fingerplays*; The Learning Station, *Tony Chestnut and Fun Time Action Songs.*

"One Two Three." Barchas, Sarah, *Bridges across the World.*

"Over in the Meadow." Feldman, Jean, *Dr. Jean Sings Silly Songs*; McCutcheon, John, *Mail Myself to You*; Old Town School of Folk Music, *Wiggleworms Love You.*

"Rockin' to One Hundred." Fite, Stephen, *Cool to Be in School.*

"Roll Over." Barchas, Sarah, *Get Ready, Get Set, Sing!* (Same song as "Six on the Bed" and "Ten in the Bed.")

"Safe at Home." Banana Slug String Band, *Penguin Parade.*

"Say the Number." Fite, Stephen, *Havin' Fun and Feelin' Groovy.*

"Seven Silly Squirrels." Avni, Fran, *Little Ears: Songs for Reading Readiness*; Avni, Fran, *Tuning into Nature.*

"Six Little Monkeys." Yosi, *Under a Big Bright Yellow Umbrella.*

"Six on the Bed." The Learning Station, *Here We Go Loopty Loo.* (Same song as "Roll Over" and "Ten in the Bed.")

"Skip Counting." Fite, Stephen, *Cool to Be in School.*

"A Song of One." Chapin, Tom, *Mother Earth.*

"Speckled Frogs." Old Town School of Folk Music, *Wiggleworms Love You.*

"Stop at the Petshop." Barchas, Sarah, *If I Had a Pony.*

"Strings on My Banjo." Gill, Jim, *Jim Gill Makes It Noisy in Boise, Idaho.*

"Swahili Counting Song." The Learning Station, *Literacy in Motion.*

"10 Cats Counting." Marxer, Marcy, *Jump Children.*

"Ten Fingers." Moo, Anna, *Making Moosic.*

"Ten Green Bottles." Jenkins, Ella, *Growing Up with Ella Jenkins*; Jenkins, Ella, *Songs Children Love to Sing.*

"Ten in the Bed." Allard, Peter and Ellen, *Sing It! Say It! Stamp It! Sway It!* vol. 3; Arnold, Linda, *Sing Along Stew*; Beall, Pamela, and Susan Nipp, *Wee Sing Silly Songs*; Penner, Fred, *Rhyme a Word or Two*; Sharon, Lois, and Bram, *Great Big Hits 2*; Sharon, Lois, and Bram, *Sleepytime.* (Same song as "Roll Over" and "Six on the Bed.")

"Ten Little Kittens/Witches/Turkeys/Snowmen." Barchas, Sarah, *Get Ready, Get Set, Sing!*

"Ten Little Monkeys." Palmer, Hap, *Two Little Sounds.* (Similar to "Five Little Monkeys" and "No More Monkeys.")

"Ten Sleepy Sheep." Harper, Jessica, *40 Winks.*

"This Old Man." Avni, Fran, *Artichokes and Brussel Sprouts*; Barchas, Sarah, *Get Ready, Get Set, Sing!*; Bartels, Joanie, *Sillytime Magic*; Beall, Pamela, and Susan Nipp, *Wee Sing Children's Songs and Fingerplays*; Beall, Pamela, and Susan Nipp, *Wee Sing Nursery Rhymes and Lullabies*; Cassidy, Nancy, *Nancy Cassidy's KidsSongs*; Dana, *Dana's Best Sing and Play-a-Long Tunes*; Greg and Steve, *Playing Favorites*; Jenkins, Ella, *Songs Children Love to Sing*; The Learning Station, *All-Time Children's Favorites*; McGrath, Bob, and Katherine Smithrim, *Songs and Games for Toddlers*; Penner, Fred, *Rhyme a Word or Two*; Raffi, *Baby Beluga*; Rosenthal, Phil, *The Paw Paw Patch*; Various Artists, *A Child's Celebration of Song*; Various Artists, *Folk Playground.*

"Three Blue Pigeons." Beall, Pamela, and Susan Nipp, *Wee Sing Animals, Animals, Animals*; Beall, Pamela, and Susan Nipp, *Wee Sing Children's Songs and Fingerplays.*

"3 Is the Magic Number." Mitchell, Elizabeth, *You Are My Sunshine.*

"Three Little Angels." Byers, Kathy, *'Round the Campfire.*

"Time for Bed." Allard, Peter and Ellen, *Pizza Pizzaz.*

"Tug-a-Tug to Twenty-Two." Palmer, Hap, *Can a Jumbo Jet Sing the Alphabet?*

"Turning and Turning." Frezza, Rebecca, *Tall and Small.*

"Twenty Pumpkins." Barchas, Sarah, *Get Ready, Get Set, Sing!*

"Ukulele Blue Yodel." Colleen and Uncle Squaty, *Sing-a-Move-a-Dance.*

"Uno Uno, Dos Dos." Silberg, "Miss Jackie," *Joining Hands with Other Lands.*

"West Indian Counting Song." Zanes, Dan, *House Party.*

"What's on the List?" Fite, Stephen, *Gobs of Fun.*

"When You Are One." McGrath, Bob, and Katherine Smithrim, *Songs and Games for Toddlers.*

"Who Built the Ark?" Raffi, *More Singable Songs.*

"Whole Bed." Scruggs, Joe, *Bahamas Pajamas.*

"Zero the Hero Number Stomp." Feldman, Jean, *Just for Fun!*

Countries (see also Continents; Languages; United States)

"The Alphabet of Nations." They Might Be Giants, *Here Come the ABCs.*

"Around the World and Back Again." Chapin, Tom, *Around the World and Back Again.*

"Birthdays around the World." Silberg, "Miss Jackie," *Joining Hands with Other Lands.*

"Dance, Dance, Dance." Chapin, Tom, *Around the World and Back Again.*

"Friends around the World." Yosi, *Under a Big Bright Yellow Umbrella.*

"I Hate My Name." Charette, Rick, *Where Do My Sneakers Go at Night?*

"Joining Hands with Other Lands." Silberg, "Miss Jackie," *Joining Hands with Other Lands.*

"Let's Have a Party." Silberg, "Miss Jackie," *Joining Hands with Other Lands.*

"Like Me and You." Raffi, *Quiet Time*; Raffi, *One Light One Sun*; Raffi, *Raffi in Concert*; Various Artists, *A Child's Celebration of the World.*

"Magical Madcap Tour." Harper, Monty, *Take Me to Your Library.*

"Meet My Travelin' Friends." Palmer, Hap, *Two Little Sounds.*

"My Aunt Came Back." Beall, Pamela, and Susan Nipp, *Wee Sing in the Car.*

"On a Vacation." The Chenille Sisters, *Teaching Hippopotami to Fly!*

"The Picnic of the World." Chapin, Tom, *Mother Earth.*

"Places in the World." Grammer, Red, *Teaching Peace.*

"Rock around the World." Pease, Tom, *I'm Gonna Reach!*; Stotts, Stuart, *Are We There Yet?*

"So Long My Mom." Harley, Bill, *Play It Again.*

Algeria

"Berceuse." Various Artists, *The Planet Sleeps.*

"Nezha." Various Artists, *World Playground 2.*

Argentina

"Canción Para Dormir a Uno Niño." Various Artists, *Dreamland.*

"Mi Chacra (My Farm)." Beall, Pamela, and Susan Nipp, *Wee Sing around the World.*

Austria

"Cuckoo." Barchas, Sarah, *Bridges across the World*.
"Peter's Brook (Peter's Brünnele)." Magical Music Express, *Friendship Stew*.

Benin

"Battú." Various Artists, *African Playground*.
"Naïma." Various Artists, *Dreamland*.

Bolivia

"La Mariposa." Various Artists, *World Playground*.

Bosnia and Herzegovina

"Oj Talasi." Various Artists, *The Planet Sleeps*.

Brazil

"Bonjour Pra Você (Good Morning to You)." Various Artists, *World Playground*.
"Ciranda (The Circle Game)." Beall, Pamela, and Susan Nipp, *Wee Sing around the World*.
"Nega de Cabello Duro." Raven, Nancy, *Friends and Family*.
"Rodopiou." Various Artists, *Latin Playground*.
"Sambalele." Raven, Nancy, *The House We Live In*, vols. 1 and 2.
"Lá Vai Alguém." Various Artists, *Dreamland*.

Cambodia

"Phnom Penh Lullaby." Various Artists, *The Planet Sleeps*.

Cameroon

"Rainbow Day." Moo, Anna, *Making Moosic*.
"Sweet Bitowo." Various Artists, *The Planet Sleeps*.

Canada

"Alberta Postcard." Trout Fishing in America, *My Best Day*.
"C-A-N-A-D-A." Raffi, *Bananaphone*.
"Chi Mi Na Morbheanna." Various Artists, *The Planet Sleeps*.
"Down in Manitoba." Foote, Norman, *1000 Pennies*.
"Going over the Sea." Beall, Pamela, and Susan Nipp, *Wee Sing around the World*.

"Home by Barna." Various Artists, *World Playground*.

"A Lullaby." Various Artists, *Dreamland*.

"La Marmotteuse." Various Artists, *World Playground 2*.

"Mr. P.G." Simmons, Al, *The Truck I Bought from Moe*.

"Skookumchuck, Sechelt, Sasquatch, Sicamous." Diamond, Charlotte, *Charlotte Diamond's World*.

"The Trans Canadian Super Continental Special Express." Penner, Fred, *Fred's Favourites*; Penner, Fred, *Storytime*.

Chile

"Hoce Tuto Guagua." Various Artists, *The Planet Sleeps*.

"El Hombre Primitivo." Raven, Nancy, *Friends and Family*.

China

"Bamboo Flute." Grunsky, Jack, *Playground*.

"Flute Song." Raven, Nancy, *Friends and Family*.

"Fung Swei (After School)." Beall, Pamela, and Susan Nipp, *Wee Sing around the World*.

"Lullaby." Various Artists, *Asian Dreamland*.

Colombia

"La Arāna Picua." Various Artists, *Latin Playground*.

"A Mover La Colita." Various Artists, *World Playground 2*.

Congo

"Hello Hello." Various Artists, *African Playground*.

Cuba

"Chopping the Cane." Raven, Nancy, *Jambalaya!*

"Duerme Negrito." Raven, Nancy, *Friends and Family*.

"Guantanamera." Seeger, Pete, *Pete Seeger's Family Concert*; Various Artists, *Latin Playground*.

Denmark

"En Enebær Busk (The Mulberry Bush)." Beall, Pamela, and Susan Nipp, *Wee Sing around the World*.

Ecuador

"Chocolate." Various Artists, *Latin Playground*.

England

"Lavender's Blue." Beall, Pamela, and Susan Nipp, *Wee Sing around the World*; Cassidy, Nancy, *Nancy Cassidy's KidsSongs*; Sharon, Lois, and Bram, *Mainly Mother Goose*.

"The Noble Duke of York." Beall, Pamela, and Susan Nipp, *Wee Sing and Play*.

"Old King Cole." Beall, Pamela, and Susan Nipp, *Wee Sing Nursery Rhymes and Lullabies*; McGrath, Bob, *Sing Along with Bob #2*; Sharon, Lois, and Bram, *Name Games*.

"Ten Green Bottles." Jenkins, Ella, *Growing Up with Ella Jenkins*; Jenkins, Ella, *Songs Children Love to Sing*.

"This Old Man." Avni, Fran, *Artichokes and Brussel Sprouts*; Barchas, Sarah, *Get Ready, Get Set, Sing!*; Bartels, Joanie, *Sillytime Magic*; Beall, Pamela, and Susan Nipp, *Wee Sing Children's Songs and Fingerplays*; Beall, Pamela, and Susan Nipp, *Wee Sing Nursery Rhymes and Lullabies*; Cassidy, Nancy, *Nancy Cassidy's KidsSongs*; Dana, *Dana's Best Sing and Play-a-Long Tunes*; Greg and Steve, *Playing Favorites*; Jenkins, Ella, *Songs Children Love to Sing*; The Learning Station, *All-Time Children's Favorites*; McGrath, Bob, and Katherine Smithrim, *Songs and Games for Toddlers*; Penner, Fred, *Rhyme a Word or Two*; Raffi, *Baby Beluga*; Rosenthal, Phil, *The Paw Paw Patch*; Various Artists, *A Child's Celebration of Song*; Various Artists, *Folk Playground*.

Ethiopia

"Hoya Hoye." Various Artists, *African Playground*.

"Zichronot M'Africa (Memories of Africa)." Various Artists, *World Playground*.

Finland

"Piri Pieni Pyörii (The Circle Goes Around)." Beall, Pamela, and Susan Nipp, *Wee Sing around the World*.

France (see also Languages—French)

"Bongo Bong." Various Artists, *World Playground*.

"Frère Jacques." Barchas, Sarah, *Bridges across the World*; Beall, Pamela, and Susan Nipp, *Wee Sing around the World*; Jenkins, Ella, *Sharing Cultures with Ella Jenkins*; McGrath, Bob, *Sing Along with Bob #2*; McGrath, Bob, and Katherine Smithrim, *Songs and Games for Toddlers*; Walker, Graham, *Knobbledee Knees.*

"A Poodle in Paris." Kaldor, Connie, *A Poodle in Paris.*

Germany

"Alle Meine Entchen (All My Little Ducklings)." Beall, Pamela, and Susan Nipp, *Wee Sing around the World.*

"Oh How Lovely Is the Evening." Barchas, Sarah, *Bridges across the World.*

"Schlafe Mein Prinzchen, Schlaf Ein." Various Artists, *The Planet Sleeps.*

Ghana

"Chay Chay Koolay." Barchas, Sarah, *Bridges across the World.* (Same song as "Che Che Koolay," "Je Je Kule," and "Kye Kye Kule.")

"Che Che Koolay." Colleen and Uncle Squaty, *Movin' Party.* (Same song as "Chay Chay Koolay," "Je Je Kule," and "Kye Kye Kule.")

"Je Je Kule." Gemini, *The Best of Gemini*, vol. 2; Parachute Express, *Doctor Looney's Remedy.* (Same song as "Chay Chay Koolay," "Che Che Koolay," and "Kye Kye Kule.")

"Kye Kye Kule." Fink, Cathy, and Marcy Marxer, *Nobody Else like Me.* (Same song as "Chay Chay Koolay," "Che Che Koolay," and "Je Je Kule.")

"Tue Tue (Clapping Game)." Beall, Pamela, and Susan Nipp, *Wee Sing around the World.*

Greece

"Pou'n-do To Dachtilidi (Where Is the Ring)." Beall, Pamela, and Susan Nipp, *Wee Sing around the World.*

"Tik Tik Tak." Various Artists, *World Playground.*

Guyana

"Brown Girl in the Ring." Beall, Pamela, and Susan Nipp, *Wee Sing around the World*; Raffi, *Everything Grows*; Zanes, Dan, *Rocket Ship Beach.*

Haiti

"Mayi A Gaye." Various Artists, *The Planet Sleeps.*

"Pa 'Piye Sou Do M'." Various Artists, *Caribbean Playground.*

"Panama." Various Artists, *Caribbean Playground.*

India

"Anilae, Anilae (Chipmunk, Chipmunk)." Beall, Pamela, and Susan Nipp, *Wee Sing around the World.*

"Gup!" Raven, Nancy, *The House We Live In*, vols. 1 and 2.

"Lullaby." Various Artists, *Asian Dreamland.*

"Monkeys in the Trees in India." Kaldor, Connie, *A Poodle in Paris.*

"Sleep, Queen of the Dolls." Various Artists, *The Planet Sleeps.*

"Teri Yaadein." Various Artists, *World Playground 2.*

Indonesia

"Pat Gulipat." Various Artists, *Reggae Playground.*

Iran

"Attal, Mattal." Beall, Pamela, and Susan Nipp, *Wee Sing around the World.*

Ireland

"Ag Criost An Síol." Various Artists, *The Planet Sleeps.*

"In Dublin's Fair City." Jenkins, Ella, *Sharing Cultures with Ella Jenkins.* (Same song as "Molly Malone.")

"Molly Malone." Raven, Nancy, *The House We Live In*, vols. 1 and 2. (Same song as "In Dublin's Fair City.")

"Praties Song." Raven, Nancy, *The House We Live In*, vols. 1 and 2.

"St. Patrick Saves the Day." Cosgrove, Jim, *Bop Bop Dinosaur.*

"Thingamajig." Bartles, Joanie, *Put On Your Dancing Shoes.*

"Top of the Morning." Moo, Anna, *Making Moosic.*

"Wee Falorie Man." Beall, Pamela, and Susan Nipp, *Wee Sing around the World.*

Israel

"Mayim, Mayim (Water, Water)." Fink, Cathy, and Marcy Marxer, *All Wound Up!*

"Noomey." Various Artists, *The Planet Sleeps.*

"Zichronot M'Africa (Memories of Africa)." Various Artists, *World Playground.*

"Zum Gali Gali." Beall, Pamela, and Susan Nipp, *Wee Sing around the World.*

Italy (see also Languages—Italian)

"Eh Cumpari." Pullara, Steve, *A Big Bowl of Musicroni*; Pullara, Steve, *Hop like a Frog.*

"Mio Galletto (My Little Rooster)." Beall, Pamela, and Susan Nipp, *Wee Sing around the World*.

Jamaica

"Chi Chi Bud (Chi Chi Bird)." Beall, Pamela, and Susan Nipp, *Wee Sing around the World*.

"Freedom Train." Various Artists, *World Playground 2*.

"Jamaica Farewell." Cassidy, Nancy, *Nancy Cassidy's KidsSongs*; Various Artists, *Caribbean Playground*; Zanes, Dan, *House Party*.

"Reggae Dancin'." Various Artists, *Caribbean Playground*.

"Three Little Birds." Mitchell, Elizabeth, *You Are My Little Bird*; Various Artists, *Caribbean Playground*; Various Artists, *World Playground*.

Japan (see also Languages—Japanese)

"Aka Tonbo." Various Artists, *Asian Dreamland*.

"Amami No Komori Uta." Various Artists, *Asian Dreamland*.

"Ame, Ame (Rain Song)." Beall, Pamela, and Susan Nipp, *Wee Sing around the World*.

"Asadoya Yunta." Various Artists, *Asian Dreamland*.

"Cradle Song." Various Artists, *Dreamland*.

"Dokokade Yoruga Naita." Various Artists, *Asian Dreamland*.

"Goldfish." Raven, Nancy, *The House We Live In*, vols. 1 and 2.

"Itsuki No Komoriuta." Various Artists, *The Planet Sleeps*.

"Japanese Rain Song." Barchas, Sarah, *Bridges across the World*.

"Kokoro Ni Dakarete." Various Artists, *Asian Dreamland*.

"Moon Boat." Various Artists, *Asian Dreamland*.

Kenya

"Jambo Bwana." Various Artists, *African Playground*.

"Kanyoni Kanja (Little Bird Outside)." Beall, Pamela, and Susan Nipp, *Wee Sing around the World*.

Korea

"Arirang." Beall, Pamela, and Susan Nipp, *Wee Sing around the World*; Raven, Nancy, *Friends and Family*.

"Pom Na Tu Ri (Springtime Outing)." Mitchell, Elizabeth, *You Are My Little Bird*.

Madagascar

"Hendry." Various Artists, *African Playground*.
"Ny Fitiavako An'I Mama." Various Artists, *Dreamland*.

Malaysia

"Pok Amai, Amai (Clap Together)." Beall, Pamela, and Susan Nipp, *Wee Sing around the World*.

Martinique

"Votek Zouk." Various Artists, *Caribbean Playground*.

Mexico

"Arriba Del Cielo." Various Artists, *Dreamland*.
"Chocolate." Raven, Nancy, *The House We Live In*, vols. 1 and 2.
"Cinco de Mayo." Barchas, Sarah, *¡Piñata! and More*.
"Cinco de Mayo." Kinder, Brian, *Special Days*.
"De Bolón Pin Pon." Various Artists, *Latin Playground*.
"Las Fronterizas/The Frontier Women." Hinojosa, Tish, *Cada Niño: Every Child*.
"El Gatito." Jenkins, Ella, *Sharing Cultures with Ella Jenkins*.
"Hanal Weech." Various Artists, *Latin Playground*.
"Hasta Los Muertos Salen a Bailar: Even the Dead Are Rising Up to Dance." Hinojosa, Tish, *Cada Niño: Every Child*.
"Little Blue Chevy." Various Artists, *Hear and Gone in 60 Seconds*.
"Lluvia De Estrellas." Various Artists, *Latin Playground*.
"The Mexican Hat Dance." Bartles, Joanie, *Put On Your Dancing Shoes*.
"Nichim Uvil." Various Artists, *World Playground 2*.
"Pin Pón." Beall, Pamela, and Susan Nipp, *Wee Sing around the World*.
"The 16th of September." Barchas, Sarah, *¡Piñata! and More*.

The Netherlands

"Alle Eendjes." Beall, Pamela, and Susan Nipp, *Wee Sing around the World*.

New Zealand

"Epo I Tai Tai E (I Will Be Happy)." Beall, Pamela, and Susan Nipp, *Wee Sing around the World*.
"Moe Moe." Various Artists, *The Planet Sleeps*.

Nigeria

"Akwa Nwa Nere Nnwa (The Little Nanny Story)." Beall, Pamela, and Susan Nipp, *Wee Sing around the World.*

"Funga Alafia." Barchas, Sarah, *Bridges across the World.*

"Laba Laba." Various Artists, *African Playground.*

Norway

"Ro, Ro Til Fiskeskjaer (Row, Row to the Fishing Spot)." Beall, Pamela, and Susan Nipp, *Wee Sing around the World.*

Peru

"La Luna Subio." Lonnquist, Ken, *The Switcher-On of Stars.*

The Philippines

"Planting Rice." Raven, Nancy, *The House We Live In*, vols. 1 and 2.

Puerto Rico

"Bomba Le Le." Various Artists, *Latin Playground.*

"Bomba Te Traigo Yo." Various Artists, *Caribbean Playground.*

"El Coquí (The Frog)." Beall, Pamela, and Susan Nipp, *Wee Sing around the World.*

"Dolores." Raven, Nancy, *Friends and Family.*

"Que Bonita Bandera." Jenkins, Ella, *Sharing Cultures with Ella Jenkins.*

The Republic of Cape Verde

"Barco di Papel." Various Artists, *African Playground.*

Russia

"The Birch Tree." Raven, Nancy, *Friends and Family.*

"Cradle Song." Various Artists, *Asian Dreamland.*

"Lullaby." Various Artists, *Dreamland.*

"May There Always Be Sunshine." Allard, Peter and Ellen, *Raise the Children*; Charette, Rick, *King Kong Chair*; Diamond, Charlotte, *10 Carrot Diamond*; Feldman, Jean, *Keep On Singing and Dancing with Dr. Jean*; Fink, Cathy, and Marcy Marxer, *Nobody Else like Me*; Gemini, *The Best of Gemini*, vol. 2; Gill, Jim, *Jim Gill Sings the Sneezing Song and Other Contagious Tunes*; Gill,

Jim, *Jim Gill's Irrational Anthem*; Pease, Tom, *Boogie! Boogie! Boogie!*; Pirtle, Sarah, *Two Hands Hold the Earth*; Raffi, *Let's Play*; Raven, Nancy, *The House We Live In*, vols. 1 and 2.

"Red-Haired Family." Raven, Nancy, *The House We Live In*, vols. 1 and 2.

"Rushing around Russia." Various Artists, *cELLAbration! A Tribute to Ella Jenkins*.

"Sleigh Bells." Barchas, Sarah, *Bridges across the World*.

Scotland

"Coulter's Candy." Beall, Pamela, and Susan Nipp, *Wee Sing around the World*.

"Cradle Spell of Dunvegan." Various Artists, *Dreamland*.

"Loch Lomond." Zanes, Dan, *Catch That Train!*

"Mingulay Boat Song." Grammer, Red, *Red Grammer's Favorite Sing Along Songs*.

"Rat-Tat-Tat-Tat-Tattoo." Parachute Express, *Doctor Looney's Remedy*.

Senegal

"Fatou Yo." Various Artists, *World Playground*.

"Sing Lo-Lo." Various Artists, *African Playground*.

South Africa

"Kalimba." Various Artists, *African Playground*.

"Langa Mo." Various Artists, *African Playground*.

"Mbube." Various Artists, *African Playground*.

"Pata Pata 2000." Various Artists, *World Playground 2*.

"Sangoma." Various Artists, *African Playground*.

"Smile Smile Smile." Zanes, Dan, *Night Time!*

"Thula Mama." Various Artists, *Dreamland*.

"Tsenzenina." Various Artists, *I'm Gonna Let It Shine*.

Spain

"Mi Burro (My Burro)." Beall, Pamela, and Susan Nipp, *Wee Sing around the World*.

"Zuhaitzarena." Various Artists, *World Playground 2*.

Sweden

"Små Grodorna (Little Frogs)." Beall, Pamela, and Susan Nipp, *Wee Sing around the World*.

Switzerland

"Weggis Zue (Swiss Hiking Song)." Beall, Pamela, and Susan Nipp, *Wee Sing around the World.*

Tatarstan

"Lullaby." Various Artists, *Dreamland.*

Tibet

"Om Ma Nye Bhe Mae Hum." Various Artists, *Asian Dreamland.*

Tonga

"Ana Latu." Various Artists, *The Planet Sleeps.*

Trinidad and Tobago

"All Aboard." Various Artists, *Caribbean Playground.*
"Music Farm." Various Artists, *World Playground 2.*

Turkey

"Ali Baba'nin Çiftliği (Ali Baba's Farm)." Beall, Pamela, and Susan Nipp, *Wee Sing around the World.*
"Üsküdara." Jenkins, Ella, *Sharing Cultures with Ella Jenkins.*

Uganda

"Munomuno." Various Artists, *African Playground.*

Ukraine

"Veselee Husi (Jolly, Happy Ganders)." Beall, Pamela, and Susan Nipp, *Wee Sing around the World.*

Uruguay

"Yo Quiero." Various Artists, *Latin Playground.*

Venezuela

"América Baila." Various Artists, *Latin Playground.*
"Los Chimi-Chimitos." Raven, Nancy, *Friends and Family.*

Vietnam

"Rice Harvest Song." Raven, Nancy, *The House We Live In*, vols. 1 and 2.

Yugoslavia

"Ringe, Ringe Raja (Ring around Raja)." Beall, Pamela, and Susan Nipp, *Wee Sing around the World*.

Zaire

"Bebe Moke (Baby So Small)." Beall, Pamela, and Susan Nipp, *Wee Sing around the World*.

Cowboys/Cowgirls

"Almost Home." Howdy, Buck, *Giddyup!*
"Ballad of the Lonesome Rider." Madsen, Gunnar, *Ants in My Pants!*
"Bicycle Cowboy." Tickle Tune Typhoon, *All of Us Will Shine*.
"The Big Corral." Riders in the Sky, *Harmony Ranch*.
"Big Husky Brute." Raven, Nancy, *Hop, Skip, and Sing*.
"Born to Ride." Howdy, Buck, *Skidaddle!*
"Buckaroo." Howdy, Buck, *Skidaddle!*
"Buffalo Boys." Bartles, Joanie, *Put On Your Dancing Shoes*.
"Chester the Donkey." Walker, Graham, *Cats' Night Out*.
"Country Kid." Dana, *Dana's Best Sing and Play-a-Long Tunes*.
"Cowboy Song." Kinder, Brian, *One More Time*.
"The Cowboy Song." Parachute Express, *Friends, Forever Friends*.
"The Cowboy's ABC." Riders in the Sky, *Saddle Pals*.
"Cowboy's Lament." Penner, Fred, *Sing with Fred*.
"A Cowboy's Life." Harley, Bill, *There's a Pea on My Plate*.
"Cowgirl Song." Rudnick, Ben, *Emily Songs*.
"Cowgirl's Lullaby." Fink, Cathy, and Marcy Marxer, *Blanket Full of Dreams*.
"The Desperado." Cassidy, Nancy, *Nancy Cassidy's KidsSongs*.
"Don't Fence Me In." Howdy, Buck, *Skidaddle!*
"Down the Lullaby Trail." Riders in the Sky, *Saddle Pals*.
"Get Along Little Dogies." Riders in the Sky, *Saddle Pals*.
"(Ghost) Riders in the Sky." Cassidy, Nancy, *Nancy Cassidy's KidsSongs*; Howdy, Buck, *Skidaddle!*

"Goodbye Old Paint." Zanes, Dan, *Rocket Ship Beach*.

"Goodnight Serenade." Fink, Cathy, and Marcy Marxer, *Pocket Full of Stardust*.

"Harmony Ranch." Riders in the Sky, *Harmony Ranch*.

"Hawaiian Cowboy Song." Raven, Nancy, *The House We Live In*, vols. 1 and 2.

"Home on the Range." Greg and Steve, *Rockin' down the Road*; Madsen, Gunnar, *Ants in My Pants!*; McGrath, Bob, *Sing Along with Bob #1*; Staines, Bill, *The Happy Wanderer*.

"Home on the Range." Milkshake, *Play!*

"I Got a Horse." Simmons, Al, *Something Fishy at Camp Wiganishie*.

"I'd Like to Be a Cowgirl." Fink, Cathy, *Grandma Slid down the Mountain*.

"I'm an Old Cowhand." Kirk, John, and Trish Miller, *The Big Rock Candy Mountain*.

"I'm Going to Leave Old Texas Now." Riders in the Sky, *Saddle Pals*. (Same song as "Old Texas.")

"Little Pony Hoo." Green Chili Jam Band, *Starfishing*.

"Long Tall Texan." Greg and Steve, *Rockin' down the Road*.

"Neighborhood Cowboy." Mayer, Hans, *See You Later, Alligator*.

"Night Herding Song." Raven, Nancy, *People and Animal Songs*.

"The Old Chisholm Trail." Beall, Pamela, and Susan Nipp, *Wee Sing and Pretend*; Cassidy, Nancy, *Nancy Cassidy's KidsSongs*; Penner, Fred, *Storytime*; Riders in the Sky, *Saddle Pals*.

"Old Texas." Beall, Pamela, and Susan Nipp, *Wee Sing and Pretend*; Cassidy, Nancy, *Nancy Cassidy's KidsSongs*; Raven, Nancy, *The House We Live In*, vols. 1 and 2. (Same song as "I'm Going to Leave Old Texas Now.")

"Pecos Bill." Howdy, Buck, *Giddyup!*; Riders in the Sky, *Harmony Ranch*.

"Ragtime Cowboy Joe." Ralph's World, *Ralph's World*.

"Ride, Cowboy, Ride." Howdy, Buck, *Giddyup!*

"Ride 'Em High/The Cowpoke Dance." Marxer, Marcy, *Jump Children*.

"Rockabye Ranch." Atkinson, Lisa, *The One and Only Me*.

"Sammy the Snail." Cosgrove, Jim, *Pick Me! Pick Me!*

"Scaredy Cat Cowboy." Daddy A Go Go, *Mojo A Go Go*.

"Sleepy Joe." Knight, Tom, *Don't Kiss a Codfish*.

"There's a Great Big Candy Roundup." Riders in the Sky, *Saddle Pals*.

"Whoa Nellie." Arnold, Linda, *Favorites in the Key of Fun*.

"Whoopie Ti Yi Yo." Raven, Nancy, *Hop, Skip, and Sing*.

"Windy Bill." Lonnquist, Ken, *The Circus Kenlando*.

"Wyatt Burp." Sprout, Jonathan, *Dr. Music*.

"Yee Haw." SteveSongs, *Morning til Night*.

"Yipee-I-Oh Boy Life." Howdy, Buck, *Skidaddle!*

"Yippie-Yi-Yo and Away We Go." Riders in the Sky, *Saddle Pals*.

"Young Buckaroo." Knight, Tom, *Easy as Pie*.

Days of the Week

"All Week Long." Barchas, Sarah, *Get Ready, Get Set, Sing!*

"Bulbe." Raven, Nancy, *Jambalaya!*

"Days of the Week." Beall, Pamela, and Susan Nipp, *Wee Sing Children's Songs and Fingerplays*.

"The Days of the Week." Diamond, Charlotte, *Diamond in the Rough*.

"Days of the Week." Feldman, Jean, *Dr. Jean and Friends*.

"Days of the Week." Greg and Steve, *We All Live Together*, vol. 4.

"Days of the Week." SteveSongs, *Morning til Night*.

"Eating Every Day." Allard, Peter and Ellen, *Pizza Pizzaz*.

"En Enebær Busk (The Mulberry Bush)." Beall, Pamela, and Susan Nipp, *Wee Sing around the World*.

"Everybody Happy?" Sharon, Lois, and Bram, *Great Big Hits 2*; Sharon, Lois, and Bram, *School Days*.

"Everybody Loves Saturday Night." Gemini, *The Best of Gemini*, vol. 2; McGrath, Bob, *Sing Along with Bob #1*; Silberg, "Miss Jackie," *Sing It Again Please*.

"How Many Days." Nagler, Eric, *Improvise with Eric Nagler*.

"I'm a Big Old Train." Big Jeff, *Big Jeff*.

"I'm Gonna Catch You." Berkner, Laurie, *Under a Shady Tree*.

"It's a Shame." Fink, Cathy, *Grandma Slid down the Mountain*.

"Monday Again." Kinnoin, Dave, *Getting Bigger*.

"My Week." Lonnquist, Ken, *The Circus Kenlando*.

"One Wet Windy Wednesday." Avni, Fran, *I'm All Ears: Sing into Reading*.

"Saturday." Frezza, Rebecca, *Road Trip*.

"Seven Days a Week." Dana, *Dana's Best Travelin' Tunes*.

"Seven Days a Week." Fite, Stephen, *Havin' Fun and Feelin' Groovy*.

"Seven Days in a Week." Mr. Al and Stephen Fite, *Back to School Again*.

"Seven Days to Rock." Fink, Cathy, *When the Rain Comes Down*.

"Seven Nights to Read." Stotts, Stuart, *Are We There Yet?*

"This Little Light of Mine." Magical Music Express, *Music Is Magic*.

"Today Is Monday." Beall, Pamela, and Susan Nipp, *Wee Sing Sing-Alongs*; Feldman, Jean, *Dr. Jean and Friends*.

"Weekdays Go 'Round." Allard, Peter and Ellen, *Pizza Pizzaz.*

"Weekly Rap." Palmer, Hap, *Can a Cherry Pie Wave Goodbye?*

"What a Week It's Been." Hullabaloo, *Sing Along with Sam.*

Death

"Go Tell Aunt Rhody." Abell, Timmy, *I Know an Old Lady*; Raven, Nancy, *People and Animal Songs.*

"Gonna Keep a Place." Raven, Nancy, *Nancy Raven Sings Her Favorites.*

"Goodbye Little Birdie." Lonnquist, Ken, *The Circus Kenlando.*

"Grandfather's Clock." Penner, Fred, *Storytime*; Staines, Bill, *One More River*; Various Artists, *A Child's Celebration of Folk Music.*

"Little Old Woman All Skin and Bone." Hinton, Sam, *Whoever Shall Have Some Good Peanuts.*

"Little Rabbit, Where's Your Mammy?" Fink, Cathy, *Grandma Slid down the Mountain.*

"My Dog Sam." Harley, Bill, *50 Ways to Fool Your Mother*; Harley, Bill, *One More Time.*

"Old Bastun Was Dead." Hinton, Sam, *Whoever Shall Have Some Good Peanuts.*

"Old Blue." Hinton, Sam, *Whoever Shall Have Some Good Peanuts.*

"Where Will I Go?" Alsop, Peter, *Stayin' Over.*

Differences

"Everyone's a Little Bit Different." Harley, Bill, *One More Time.*

"I'm Me and You're You." Berkner, Laurie, *Under a Shady Tree.*

"A Little like You and a Little like Me." Fink, Cathy, and Marcy Marxer, *Nobody Else like Me.*

"The Mighty Worm." Ralph's World, *Peggy's Pie Parlor.*

"My Friend Jake." Polisar, Barry Louis, *Teacher's Favorites.*

"My Very Own Frame." Vitamin L, *Swingin' in the Key of L.*

"No One's Normal." Alsop, Peter, *Pluggin' Away.*

"Okay to Be Different." Milkshake, *Play!*

"Rapp Song." Grammer, Red, *Teaching Peace.*

"That's What Makes the World 'Round." Polisar, Barry Louis, *Old Enough to Know Better.*

"There's a Light in You." Harley, Bill, *Down in the Backpack.*

"Us Kids Brush Our Teeth." Alsop, Peter, *Stayin' Over.*

"We've All Got Differences." Fite, Stephen, *We're Just like Crayons.*

"What's the Situation with You?" LaFond, Lois, *Turning It Upside Down*.

"You Are You." Roth, Kevin, *Travel Song Sing Alongs*; Roth, Kevin, *Unbearable Bears*.

Digging

"Diga Biga." Green Chili Jam Band, *Magic Bike*.

"Digging." Kaye, Mary, *Mouse Jamboree*.

"Don't Play with Bruno." Chapin, Tom, *Moonboat*.

"Dumptruck." Ralph's World, *The Amazing Adventures of Kid Astro*.

"There's a Hole in My Back Yard." Various Artists, *Grandma's Patchwork Quilt*.

Dinosaurs

"At the Dinosaur Baseball Game." Arnold, Linda, *Favorites in the Key of Fun*; Arnold, Linda, *Peppermint Wings*.

"Big Pterodactyl in the Sky." Big Jeff, *Big Jeff*.

"Born to Chew (We Eat Meat)." Madsen, Gunnar, *Old Mr. Mackle Hackle*.

"Brontosaurus." Beall, Pamela, and Susan Nipp, *Wee Sing and Pretend*.

"Brontosaurus Got a Sweet Tooth." Roberts, Justin, *Not Naptime*.

"A Brontosaurus with Bronchitis." Polisar, Barry Louis, *Naughty Songs for Boys and Girls*.

"Dan's Dinosaur Galore." Roth, Kevin, *Dinosaurs and Dragons*.

"Dinosaur and the Progress of Man." Foote, Norman, *Foote Prints*.

"Dinosaur Boogie." Feldman, Jean, *Just for Fun!*

"Dinosaur Rap." Roth, Kevin, *Dinosaurs and Dragons*.

"Dinosaur Round." Boynton, Sandra, *Rhinoceros Tap*.

"Dinosaur Rumble." Ralph's World, *Happy Lemon*.

"The Dinosaur Song." Knight, Tom, *Don't Kiss a Codfish*.

"The Dinosaur Song." Madsen, Gunnar, *Old Mr. Mackle Hackle*.

"The Dinosaur Song." Polisar, Barry Louis, *Old Enough to Know Better*.

"Dinosaurs." LaFond, Lois, *I Am Who I Am*.

"Dinosaurs." Tickle Tune Typhoon, *Circle Around*.

"Dinosaurs at Play." Paxton, Tom, *I've Got a Yo-Yo*.

"Dinosaur's Revenge." Coffey, James, *Come Ride Along with Me*.

"Dinosaurumpus." Thaddeus Rex, *We Wanna Rock*.

"Do the Dino Rap." Grunsky, Jack, *Dancing Feet*; Grunsky, Jack, *Playground*.

"The Great Green Squishy Mean Bibliovore." Harper, Monty, *The Great Green Squishy Mean Concert CD*.

"I Am a Dinosaur." Kimmy Schwimmy, *Kimmy Schwimmy Music*, vol. 1.

"If I Had a Dinosaur." Raffi, *More Singable Songs*.

"I'm a Three-Toed, Triple-Eyed, Double-Jointed Dinosaur." Polisar, Barry Louis, *Family Concert*; Polisar, Barry Louis, *Old Dog, New Tricks*; Thaddeus Rex, *Martian Television Invasion*.

"It Must Be a Dinosaur." Raven, Nancy, *Nancy Raven Sings Her Favorites*; Raven, Nancy, *You Gotta Juba*.

"Millions and Millions of Years Ago." Barchas, Sarah, *If I Had a Pony*.

"My Pet Dinosaur." Peterson, Carole, *Sticky Bubble Gum*.

"Ornithomimus." Beall, Pamela, and Susan Nipp, *Wee Sing and Pretend*.

"Please Don't Bring a Tyrannosaurus to Show and Tell." Scruggs, Joe, *Late Last Night*.

"Prehistoric Mystery." Lonnquist, Ken, *Sci-Fi Hi-Fi*.

"The Professor." Roth, Kevin, *Dinosaurs and Dragons*; Roth, Kevin, *Travel Song Sing Alongs*.

"Pteranodon." Beall, Pamela, and Susan Nipp, *Wee Sing and Pretend*.

"Red Brontosaurus." Kimmy Schwimmy, *Kimmy Schwimmy Music*, vol. 1.

"Rinkydinkosaurus." Lonnquist, Ken, *Welcome 2 Kenland*.

"There's a Dinosaur." Kimmy Schwimmy, *Kimmy Schwimmy Music*, vol. 1.

"There's a Dinosaur Knocking at My Door." Arnold, Linda, *Favorites in the Key of Fun*; Arnold, Linda, *Happiness Cake*.

"This Old Bone." Tickle Tune Typhoon, *Singing Science*.

"Those Dinosaur Blues." Boynton, Sandra, *Philadelphia Chickens*.

"We Are the Dinosaurs." Berkner, Laurie, *Whaddaya Think of That?*

"We Are the Dinosaurs." Trout Fishing in America, *Big Trouble*.

"What Happened to the Dinosaurs?" Barchas, Sarah, *If I Had a Pony*.

"What Happened to the Dinosaurs?" Strausman, Paul, *Rainbows, Stones, and Dinosaur Bones*.

"When I Was a Dinosaur." The Chenille Sisters, *1, 2, 3 for Kids*; Trout Fishing in America, *Big Trouble*.

"You're a Dinosaur." Harper, Monty, *The Great Green Squishy Mean Concert CD*.

Disabilities

"The Best That I Can." Rosen, Gary, *Pet Sounds*; Rosenshontz, *Rock 'n Roll Teddy Bear*; Rosenshontz, *Rosenshontz Greatest Hits*.

"Everyone Is Differently Abled." Tickle Tune Typhoon, *All of Us Will Shine*; Tickle Tune Typhoon, *Healthy Beginnings*.

"I Can Talk with You." Charette, Rick, *Chickens on Vacation*.

"I'm a Little Cookie." Alsop, Peter, *Take Me with You*; McCutcheon, John, *Mail Myself to You*; Pease, Tom, *Boogie! Boogie! Boogie!*; Raven, Nancy, *The House We Live In*, vols. 1 and 2; Various Artists, *Grandma's Patchwork Quilt*.

"Jenifer Montgomery." Stotts, Stuart, *Are We There Yet?*

"My Special Friend." Fite, Stephen, *We're Just like Crayons*.

"Walkin' on My Wheels." Crow, Dan, *A Friend, a Laugh, a Walk in the Woods*; Fink, Cathy, and Marcy Marxer, *Nobody Else like Me*.

Divorce

"Daddy Is Moving Away." Fite, Stephen, *We're Just like Crayons*.

"Dear Diary." Rosenshontz, *Family Vacation*.

"I Cried." Alsop, Peter, *Stayin' Over*; Pelham, Ruth, *Under One Sky*.

"Little Squirrel Came Home." Knight, Tom, *The Library Boogie*.

"Tommy Says." Harley, Bill, *Big Big World*.

"Two Moms." Knight, Tom, *The Library Boogie*.

Dolls

"Barbie's Head Is Missing." Harley, Bill, *I Wanna Play*.

"Dolly Ball." Kaye, Mary, *I Sang It Just for You*.

"My Dolly." Beall, Pamela, and Susan Nipp, *Wee Sing Nursery Rhymes and Lullabies*.

"My Dolly." Guthrie, Woody, *Nursery Days*; Guthrie, Woody, *Woody's 20 Grow Big Songs*.

"Pin Pón." Beall, Pamela, and Susan Nipp, *Wee Sing around the World*.

"Raggedy Rag Doll Friend." Palmer, Hap, *Peek-a-Boo*.

"Rock-A My Dolly." Beall, Pamela, and Susan Nipp, *Wee Sing for Baby*.

"Talking Toy Box." Scruggs, Joe, *Even Trolls Have Moms*.

Drawing/Painting

"The Big Picture." The Chenille Sisters, *The Big Picture and Other Songs for Kids*.

"Chalk." Roberts, Justin, *Meltdown!*

"Dragons and Dinosaurs." Diamond, Charlotte, *Diamonds and Dragons*.

"Drawing on the Sidewalk." Rymer, Brady, *I Found It!*

"Hey, Picasso." Harper, Jessica, *Hey, Picasso*; Various Artists, *Hear and Gone in 60 Seconds*.

"I'll Write and I'll Draw." Guthrie, Woody, *Songs to Grow On for Mother and Child*.

"Let's Paint a Picture." Grunsky, Jack, *Follow the Leader*; Grunsky, Jack, *Playground*.

"Magical Art Room." Lonnquist, Ken, *Sci-Fi Hi-Fi*.

"Oodles of Doodles." Foote, Norman, *Shake a Leg*.

"Refrigerator Picture." Scruggs, Joe, *Deep in the Jungle*.

Dreams (see also Bedtime; Wishes)

"The Bandshell Right Next to the Zoo." Lithgow, John, *Farkle and Friends*.

"Book of Dreams." Milkshake, *Bottle of Sunshine*.

"By the Light of the Moon." Grunsky, Jack, *Jack in the Box 2*.

"Coconut Moon." Green Chili Jam Band, *Coconut Moon*.

"Dads in the Sky." Daddy A Go Go, *Cool Songs for Cool Kids*.

"Dream a Little Dream." Muldaur, Maria, *On the Sunny Side*.

"Dream about Dreams." Kinnoin, Dave, *Daring Dewey*.

"Dream Catcher." Grunsky, Jack, *Jack in the Box 2*; Grunsky, Jack, *World Safari*.

"Dream Song." Harper, Jessica, *40 Winks*.

"Dream Time." Green Chili Jam Band, *Coconut Moon*.

"Dreamcatcher." Herdman, Priscilla, *Daydreamer*.

"I Had a Dream." Scruggs, Joe, *Abracadabra*.

"Jennifer's Rabbit." Paxton, Tom, *Goin' to the Zoo*.

"Just a Dream." Sprout, Jonathan, *On the Radio*.

"Last Night I Had a Dream." Berkner, Laurie, *Whaddaya Think of That?*

"A Little Dreamin'." Lonnquist, Ken, *The Lost Songs of Kenland*.

"Moon, My Dad, and Me." Fink, Cathy, and Marcy Marxer, *Blanket Full of Dreams*.

"Movie in My Pillow." Frezza, Rebecca, *Road Trip*.

"Peppermint Wings." Arnold, Linda, *Peppermint Wings*.

"Planet Bruno." Chapin, Tom, *Some Assembly Required*.

"Sail Away Tonight." Fink, Cathy, and Marcy Marxer, *Pocket Full of Stardust*.

"Sailing." Parachute Express, *Don't Blink*.

"The Silliest Dream." Fink, Cathy, and Marcy Marxer, *Pocket Full of Stardust*.

"Someone like Me." Harper, Jessica, *40 Winks*.

"The Strangest Dream." Nagler, Eric, *Improvise with Eric Nagler*.

"Visiting Cinderella." Harper, Jessica, *40 Winks*.

"When I Climb the Tallest Tree." Charette, Rick, *A Little Peace and Quiet*.

"When You Are Sleeping." Milkshake, *Happy Songs*.

"Wings of Slumber." Banana Slug String Band, *Wings of Slumber*.

Earth

"Beautiful Planet." Frezza, Rebecca, *Road Trip*.

"Big Beautiful Planet." Raffi, *Evergreen, Everblue*; Raffi, *Rise and Shine*.

"Big Big World." Harley, Bill, *Big Big World*; Harley, Bill, *Play It Again*.

"Big World after All." Harper, Monty, *Take Me to Your Library*.

"Care for the World." Avni, Fran, *Tuning into Nature*.

"Earth Is Our Home." Kinnoin, Dave, *Daring Dewey*.

"The Earth Is Still Sleeping." McMahon, Elizabeth, *Waltzing with Fireflies*.

"Earth, My Body." Pirtle, Sarah, *Heart of the World*.

"The Earth, My Home." Tucker, Nancy, *Escape of the Slinkys*.

"Earth's Family." Atkinson, Lisa, *The Elephant in Aisle Four*.

"Evergreen, Everblue." Raffi, *Evergreen, Everblue*.

"Happy Earth Day." Chapin, Tom, *Billy the Squid*; Chapin, Tom, *This Pretty Planet*.

"Heart of the World." Pirtle, Sarah, *Heart of the World*.

"Hooray for the World." Grammer, Red, *Teaching Peace*.

"Hug the Earth." Various Artists, *Peace Is the World Smiling*.

"Island of Life." Lonnquist, Ken, *Earthy Songs*; Stotts, Stuart, *Are We There Yet?*

"The Little Blue Dot." Pullara, Steve, *Spinning Tails*.

"Living Together." Kinnoin, Dave, *Getting Bigger*.

"Looking for a Planet." Green Chili Jam Band, *Coconut Moon*.

"Magical Earth." Pirtle, Sarah, *Magical Earth*.

"Mother Earth's Routine." Chapin, Tom, *Mother Earth*.

"On This Big Green Earth." Stotts, Stuart, *One Big Dance*.

"One Earth." Arnold, Linda, *Happiness Cake*.

"One Earth." Rosenshontz, *Rosenshontz Greatest Hits*; Shontz, Bill, *Animal Tales*.

"Our Dear, Dear Mother." Raffi, *Evergreen, Everblue*.

"The Rhythm of the World." Fink, Cathy, and Marcy Marxer, *Pocket Full of Stardust*.

"Song of the Earth." Chapin, Tom, *Around the World and Back Again*; Chapin, Tom, *This Pretty Planet*.

"This Pretty Planet." Chapin, Tom, *Family Tree*; Chapin, Tom, *This Pretty Planet*.

"This Pretty Planet II." Chapin, Tom, *This Pretty Planet*.

"Up in Space." Walker, Mary Lu, *The Frog's Party*.

"Walk the World Now, Children." Chapin, Tom, *Some Assembly Required*.

"Walkin' around the Sun." Pease, Tom, *Wobbi-Do-Wop!*

"We've Got the Whole World." Greg and Steve, *Playing Favorites*.

"What a Wonderful World." Dana, *Dana's Best Sing and Swing-a-Long Tunes*; Feldman, Jean, *Just for Fun!*; Grunsky, Jack, *Jack in the Box 2*; Herdman, Priscilla, *Daydreamer*; Raffi, *Let's Play*; Rosenshontz, *Uh-Oh!*; Zanes, Dan, *Night Time!*

"The Whole Earth Anthem." Fink, Cathy, and Marcy Marxer, *Air Guitar*.

"The World Is Big, the World Is Small." Various Artists, *cELLAbration! A Tribute to Ella Jenkins*.

"The World We Love." Raffi, *Bananaphone*; Various Artists, *A Child's Celebration of Folk Music*.

"The World's Big Family." Strausman, Paul, *The World's Big Family*.

Earthquakes

"Shake, Shake, Shake (The Earthquake Song)." Knight, Tom, *The Classroom Boogie*.

"We're Talkin' Earthquake!" Raven, Nancy, *Jambalaya!*

Ecology/Nature (see also Animals; Plants; Pollution; Recycling)

"Air Cycle Swing." Banana Slug String Band, *Adventures on the Air Cycle*; Banana Slug String Band, *Singing in Our Garden*.

"All My Friends Live in the Woods." Zanes, Dan, *Rocket Ship Beach*.

"Biodiversity." SteveSongs, *Little Superman*.

"The Cells Start Moving." Pirtle, Sarah, *Heart of the World*.

"Decomposition." Banana Slug String Band, *Dirt Made My Lunch*; Banana Slug String Band, *Singing in Our Garden*.

"Earth, Wind, Air, and Fire." Diamond, Charlotte, *Diamonds and Dragons*.

"Ecology." Banana Slug String Band, *Singing in Our Garden*.

"Ecology." Tickle Tune Typhoon, *Singing Science*.

"Everybody's Got to Have a Home." Shontz, Bill, *Animal Tales*.

"FBI (Fungus, Bacteria and Invertebrates)." Banana Slug String Band, *Singing in Our Garden*.

"The Forest Is Calling." Diamond, Charlotte, *My Bear Gruff*.

"The Green Grass Grows All Around." Beall, Pamela, and Susan Nipp, *Wee Sing Silly Songs*; Buchman, Rachel, *Sing a Song of Seasons*; Greg and Steve, *Rockin' down the Road*; Hinton, Sam, *Whoever Shall Have Some Good Peanuts*; The Learning Station, *Seasonal Songs in Motion*; Rosenthal, Phil, *The Green Grass Grew All Around*; Roth, Kevin, *Travel Song Sing Alongs*. (Same song as "In the Woods There Was a Tree.")

"Habitat." Tucker, Nancy, *Glad That You Asked*.

"In the Great Outdoors." Charette, Rick, *Toad Motel.*

"In the Woods There Was a Tree." Feldman, Jean, *Just for Fun!* (Same song as "The Green Grass Grows All Around.")

"Lambeth Children." Raven, Nancy, *Singing, Prancing, and Dancing.*

"Land of the Silver Birch." Grammer, Red, *Down the Do-Re-Mi.*

"Moose and Caribou." Grunsky, Jack, *Jack in the Box 1*; Grunsky, Jack, *World Safari.*

"Mother Nature." Allard, Peter and Ellen, *Raise the Children.*

"Mother Nature's Lullaby." Banana Slug String Band, *Wings of Slumber.*

"Nature Song." Sweet Honey in the Rock, *Still the Same Me.*

"Nature's ABC's." Haynes, Sammie, *Nature's ABCs.*

"Nature's All around Us." Haynes, Sammie, *Nature's ABCs.*

"A Place at the Fire." Lonnquist, Ken, *Earthy Songs*; Lonnquist, Ken, *The Switcher-On of Stars.*

"Rattlin' Bog." Allard, Peter and Ellen, *Good Kid*; Beall, Pamela, and Susan Nipp, *Wee Sing Fun 'n' Folk*; Grammer, Red, *Down the Do-Re-Mi*; Sharon, Lois, and Bram, *School Days*; Zanes, Dan, *Night Time!*

"Singing to the Moon." Banana Slug String Band, *Wings of Slumber.*

"Spin Spider Spin." Knight, Tom, *The Classroom Boogie.*

"Sun, Soil, Water and Air." Banana Slug String Band, *Dirt Made My Lunch*; Banana Slug String Band, *Singing in Our Garden.*

"Surrounded by Friendship." Zanes, Dan, *House Party.*

"That's a Habitat." Arnold, Linda, *Splash Zone.*

"There's a Hole in the Middle of the Tree." Avni, Fran, *Tuning into Nature.*

"Touch the Sky." Pirtle, Sarah, *The Wind Is Telling Secrets.*

"A Tree Is Just a Tree." Kaldor, Connie, *A Poodle in Paris.*

"Walking in the Woods." Barchas, Sarah, *If I Had a Pony.*

"What Do Animals Need?" Banana Slug String Band, *Penguin Parade.*

Emotions

"Aaargh!" Alsop, Peter, *Stayin' Over.*

"Baa, Neigh, Cock-a-Doodle-Doo." Howdy, Buck, *Giddyup!*

"A Blue Recipe." Various Artists, *Hear and Gone in 60 Seconds.*

"Communication." Ode, Eric, *Trash Can.*

"Count to Ten and Try Again." Fink, Cathy, and Marcy Marxer, *Changing Channels.*

"Dance." Harper, Jessica, *Hey, Picasso.*

"Everyone Has Feelings." Barchas, Sarah, *Bridges across the World*.

"EWOP (Everything Works Out Perfectly)." Magical Music Express, *Friendship Stew*.

"Hi, Hi, I Love You." Chapin, Tom, *Zag Zig*.

"I Don't Like It." Mr. Al, *Put Your Groove On*.

"If You're Happy and You Know It." Barchas, Sarah, *Get Ready, Get Set, Sing!*; The Learning Station, *All-Time Children's Favorites*; Raffi, *Let's Play*.

"I'm So Mad . . ." Gill, Jim, *Jim Gill Sings the Sneezing Song and Other Contagious Tunes*.

"I'm So Mad I Could Scream." Silberg, "Miss Jackie," *Peanut Butter, Tarzan, and Roosters*; Silberg, "Miss Jackie," *Sing It Again Please*.

"In My Heart." The Chenille Sisters, *The Big Picture and Other Songs for Kids*.

"I've Got the Blues, Greens and Reds." Chapin, Tom, *Billy the Squid*.

"Joy and Sorrow." The Dream Project, *We've All Got Stories*.

"Jumping to Conclusions." Vitamin L, *Everyone's Invited!*

"Kaleidoscope Blues." Tucker, Nancy, *Escape of the Slinkys*.

"A Little Polka." Bartles, Joanie, *Put On Your Dancing Shoes*.

"No More Cryin' Tonight." Cosgrove, Jim, *Stinky Feet*.

"One Hug." Mayer, Hans, *See You Later, Alligator*.

"Rainbow of Feelings." Strausman, Paul, *Blue Jay, Blue Jay!*

"Sad, Bad, Terrible Day." The Learning Station, *Get Funky and Musical Fun*.

"Say When." Magical Music Express, *Music Is Magic*.

"Show Me What You Feel." Greg and Steve, *Kids in Motion*.

"Some Days." LaFond, Lois, *One World*.

"The Story of My Feelings." Berkner, Laurie, *Victor Vito*.

"Sunny Side Up." Parachute Express, *Sunny Side Up*.

"Talk to Me." Fink, Cathy, and Marcy Marxer, *Changing Channels*.

"There Is Always Something You Can Do." Pirtle, Sarah, *Two Hands Hold the Earth*.

"Tommy Says." Harley, Bill, *Big Big World*.

"Treasure Every Step." Haynes, Sammie, *Nature's ABCs*.

"Use a Word." Fink, Cathy, and Marcy Marxer, *Changing Channels*.

"What Do I Do?" Pelham, Ruth, *Under One Sky*.

"When I Get a Feeling." Grammer, Red, *Hello World*.

"Where Are My Feelings?" Fink, Cathy, and Marcy Marxer, *Help Yourself*.

"Your Face Will Surely Show It." Gill, Jim, *Jim Gill Makes It Noisy in Boise, Idaho*.

Anger

"The Anger Bug." Cosgrove, Jim, *Stinky Feet*.

"Angry." The Learning Station, *Literacy in Motion*.

"Awfullish Day." Mayer, Hans, *Just a Little Hug*.

"Feelings—Angry." The Learning Station, *Seasonal Songs in Motion*.

"Meltdown." Roberts, Justin, *Meltdown!*

"Not Fair." Scruggs, Joe, *Ants*.

"Something I Ate." Harper, Monty, *Jungle Junk!*

"Sore Loser." Chapin, Tom, *Billy the Squid*.

"Talk It Out." Pirtle, Sarah, *Magical Earth*.

"When Things Don't Go Your Way." Palmer, Hap, *Turn On the Music*.

"Who's the Winner?" Ralph's World, *The Amazing Adventures of Kid Astro*.

Embarrassment

"I Can't Tie My Shoe." Polisar, Barry Louis, *Old Enough to Know Better*.

"I Might Die of Embarrassment." Troubadour, *On the Trail*.

Fear

"Big Kids." Lithgow, John, *Singin' in the Bathtub*.

"Boogedy Blues." Lonnquist, Ken, *The Lost Songs of Kenland*.

"Boogie! Boogie! Boogie!" Pease, Tom, *Boogie! Boogie! Boogie!*

"The Boogieman." Pullara, Steve, *Hop like a Frog*.

"Don't Leave Me in the House Alone." Polisar, Barry Louis, *Old Enough to Know Better*.

"Feelings—Scared." The Learning Station, *Seasonal Songs in Motion*.

"Frank Stein." Tucker, Nancy, *Escape of the Slinkys*.

"Goodnight." Foote, Norman, *Pictures on the Fridge*.

"Hall of a Hundred Doors." Trout Fishing in America, *Mine!*

"I Don't Believe It." Harley, Bill, *You're in Trouble*.

"I Thought It Was a Monster." Roberts, Justin, *Yellow Bus*.

"I Wouldn't Be Scared, Not Me." Stotts, Stuart, *One Big Dance*.

"I'm Not Afraid of the Dark." Charette, Rick, *A Little Peace and Quiet*.

"In Control." LaFond, Lois, *One World*.

"It's All Right." Del Bianco, Lou, *When I Was a Kid*.

"It's OK." Rosen, Gary, *Cookin'*.

"A Little Night Light." Parachute Express, *Doctor Looney's Remedy*.

"Monster in My Room." Frezza, Rebecca, *Music in My Head*.

"Monsters." Mayer, Hans, *See You Later, Alligator*.

"Monsters and Giants." Brown, Greg, *Bathtub Blues*.

"Monsters in the Bathroom." Harley, Bill, *Monsters in the Bathroom*; Harley, Bill, *Play It Again*.

"Mouse in the House." Various Artists, *Reggae Playground*.

"Phobias." McCutcheon, John, *Family Garden*.

"Scared." Milkshake, *Happy Songs*.

"Scaredy Cat Cowboy." Daddy A Go Go, *Mojo A Go Go*.

"Scary Things." Raven, Nancy, *Nancy Raven Sings Her Favorites*; Raven, Nancy, *You Gotta Juba*.

"Spook Spooked!" Strausman, Paul, *The World's Big Family*.

"Talking Toy Box." Scruggs, Joe, *Even Trolls Have Moms*.

"There's a Werewolf under My Bed." Troubadour, *On the Trail*.

"Thump Thump Thump." Polisar, Barry Louis, *Naughty Songs for Boys and Girls*.

"Under Your Bed." Scruggs, Joe, *Traffic Jams*.

"Watch Out." Harley, Bill, *You're in Trouble*.

"What Do They Do with the Children?" Scruggs, Joe, *Late Last Night*.

"What If?" Alsop, Peter, *Pluggin' Away*.

"When You Don't Know What It Is." Harley, Bill, *You're in Trouble*.

"Wild Things." Mayer, Hans, *Stars of the Swing Set*.

Happiness

"Epo I Tai Tai E (I Will Be Happy)." Beall, Pamela, and Susan Nipp, *Wee Sing around the World*.

"Feelin' Good Inside." Charette, Rick, *Bubble Gum*.

"Feelings—Happy." The Learning Station, *Seasonal Songs in Motion*.

"The Happiest Song I Know." Chapin, Tom, *Some Assembly Required*.

"Happiness Cake." Arnold, Linda, *Happiness Cake*.

"Happy Feet." Penner, Fred, *Fred's Favourites*.

"A Happy Party." Thaddeus Rex, *Martian Television Invasion*.

"Happy Song." Milkshake, *Happy Songs*.

"Happy Talk." Arnold, Linda, *Favorites in the Key of Fun*.

"Happy That You're Here." Trout Fishing in America, *InFINity*.

"I Love to Laugh." Sweet Honey in the Rock, *Still the Same Me*.

"If You're Happy and You Know It." Arnold, Linda, *Happiness Cake*; Beall, Pamela, and Susan Nipp, *Wee Sing Children's Songs and Fingerplays*; Dana, *Dana's Best Sing and Play-a-Long Tunes*; Feldman, Jean, *Is Everybody Happy?*; Greg and Steve, *We All Live Together*, vol. 3; Marxer, Marcy, *Jump Children*; McGrath, Bob, *Sing Along with Bob #1*; Miss Amy, *Wide Wide World*.

"I'm Happy." Mr. Al, *Mr. Al a Carte*.

"Land of Laughter." Arnold, Linda, *Favorites in the Key of Fun*.

"A Laugh Can Turn It Around." The Chenille Sisters, *1, 2, 3 for Kids*.

"Laughter." Vitamin L, *Everyone's Invited!*

"The More We Get Together." Berkner, Laurie, *Buzz Buzz*; Feldman, Jean, *Is Everybody Happy?*; Grunsky, Jack, *Jack in the Box 2*; Raffi, *Raffi in Concert*; Raffi, *Singable Songs for the Very Young.*

"Put On a Happy Face." Bartels, Joanie, *Morning Magic*; Muldaur, Maria, *On the Sunny Side.*

"Roller in the Coaster." Roberts, Justin, *Way Out.*

"Sing a Happy Song." Rosenshontz, *Tickles You!*

"Smile." Beall, Pamela, and Susan Nipp, *Wee Sing Sing-Alongs.*

"S-M-I-L-E." Dana, *Dana's Best Sing and Swing-a-Long Tunes.*

"Smile." LaFond, Lois, *One World.*

"Smile." Milkshake, *Bottle of Sunshine.*

"Smile Smile Smile." Zanes, Dan, *Night Time!*

"So Happy You're Here." Palmer, Hap, *So Big.*

"Something in My Pocket." McGrath, Bob, and Katherine Smithrim, *Songs and Games for Toddlers.*

"Start Your Day with a Smile." Yosi, *Monkey Business.*

"Things Are Coming My Way." Pease, Tom, *I'm Gonna Reach!*

"This Happy Hour." Harper, Jessica, *Rhythm in My Shoes.*

"Too Happy to Sit." Parachute Express, *Who's Got a Hug?*

"When You Look That Way at Me." Cosgrove, Jim, *Bop Bop Dinosaur.*

"You Make Me So Happy." LaFond, Lois, *Lois LaFond and the Rockadiles.*

"You've Got to Laugh a Little." Cosgrove, Jim, *Bop Bop Dinosaur.*

Love

"All I Want Is You." Polisar, Barry Louis, *Old Dog, New Tricks.*

"All My Life." Kinder, Brian, *Again.*

"Appearances." Lonnquist, Ken, *The Switcher-On of Stars.*

"Being Here with You." Lonnquist, Ken, *The Switcher-On of Stars.*

"Bushel and a Peck." Muldaur, Maria, *Swingin' in the Rain*; Various Artists, *Sing Along with Putumayo*; Zanes, Dan, *Rocket Ship Beach.*

"Count on Me." Lonnquist, Ken, *Welcome 2 Kenland.*

"Deeper Than the Deep Blue." Foote, Norman, *1000 Pennies.*

"Evermore." Boynton, Sandra, *Dog Train.*

"Fly Me to the Moon." Ralph's World, *At the Bottom of the Sea.*

"For Who I Am." Lonnquist, Ken, *Sci-Fi Hi-Fi.*

"The Frog Song." Harper, Monty, *The Great Green Squishy Mean Concert CD.*

"Give a Little Love Away." Fink, Cathy, and Marcy Marxer, *Blanket Full of Dreams*.

"The Gorilla Song." Raffi, *Bananaphone*.

"Gotta Be Mine." Various Artists, *Hear and Gone in 60 Seconds*.

"Gotta Lotta Love." Parachute Express, *Don't Blink*.

"Hey, We'll Fill the World with Love." Rosenshontz, *Tickles You!*

"How Do You Say . . ." McMahon, Elizabeth, *Tea Party Shuffle*.

"I Just Love You." Yosi, *What's Eatin' Yosi?*

"I Love You." Abell, Timmy, *The Farmer's Market*.

"I Love You More Than Cheese." Boynton, Sandra, *Rhinoceros Tap*.

"I Need You like a Donut Needs a Hole." Polisar, Barry Louis, *Old Dog, New Tricks*.

"If You Love Me." Raven, Nancy, *Singing, Prancing, and Dancing*.

"It Only Takes a Minute." Fink, Cathy, and Marcy Marxer, *Scat like That*; Various Artists, *Hear and Gone in 60 Seconds*.

"Joy Ride." Harper, Jessica, *Hey, Picasso*.

"Ki Ku." Tickle Tune Typhoon, *Patty-Cakes and Peek-a-Boos*.

"Like Love." Abell, Timmy, *Little Red Wagon*.

"L.O.V.E." Arnold, Linda, *Happiness Cake*.

"Love Changes Everything." Moo, Anna, *Making Moosic*.

"Love Grows One by One." Herdman, Priscilla, *Daydreamer*; McMahon, Elizabeth, *Blue Sky Sparklin' Day*; Ode, Eric, *Grandpa's Truck*; Pease, Tom, *I'm Gonna Reach!*; Peterson, Carole, *H.U.M.—All Year Long*; Stotts, Stuart, and Tom Pease, *Celebrate: A Song Resource*.

"Love in Your Pocket." Harper, Jessica, *Rhythm in My Shoes*.

"Love Is a Little Word." Foote, Norman, *If the Shoe Fits*.

"Love Is a Special Way of Feeling." Avni, Fran, *Artichokes and Brussel Sprouts*.

"Love Makes a Family." Fink, Cathy, and Marcy Marxer, *Blanket Full of Dreams*.

"Love Round." Tickle Tune Typhoon, *Patty-Cakes and Peek-a-Boos*.

"Love This Baby." Harper, Monty, *The Great Green Squishy Mean Concert CD*.

"Love You a Million." Kaye, Mary, *Mouse Jamboree*.

"Magic Penny." Fink, Cathy, *When the Rain Comes Down*; Fink, Cathy, and Marcy Marxer, *A Cathy & Marcy Collection for Kids*; Foote, Norman, *Pictures on the Fridge*; Silberg, "Miss Jackie," *Lollipops and Spaghetti*; Tickle Tune Typhoon, *Circle Around*.

"Many Things to Know." Ralph's World, *At the Bottom of the Sea*.

"My Hat's on the Side of My Head." Simmons, Al, *The Celery Stalks at Midnight*.

"My Heart (Does a Little Dance)." Bartles, Joanie, *Put On Your Dancing Shoes*.

"No Matter What Goes Right." Trout Fishing in America, *Family Music Party*.

"Offer of Love." Kinnoin, Dave, *Dunce Cap Kelly*.

"1, 2, 3, Four-Ever Friends." Colleen and Uncle Squaty, *1, 2, 3, Four-Ever Friends*.

"Pluckin' the Petals." Harper, Jessica, *A Wonderful Life*.

"Put On Love." Walker, Mary Lu, *The Frog's Party*.

"Silver and Gold." Harper, Jessica, *Hey, Picasso*.

"Simplemente Por Amor: Simply for Love." Hinojosa, Tish, *Cada Niño: Every Child*.

"Skidamarink." Beall, Pamela, and Susan Nipp, *Wee Sing Children's Songs and Fingerplays*; Old Town School of Folk Music, *Wiggleworms Love You*. (Same song as "Skinnamarink.")

"Skinnamarink." Marxer, Marcy, *Jump Children*; McGrath, Bob, *Sing Along with Bob #1*; Peterson, Carole, *Stinky Cake*; Sharon, Lois, and Bram, *Great Big Hits 2*; Sharon, Lois, and Bram, *One Elephant, Deux Éléphants*. (Same song as "Skidamarink.")

"Sucking Cider from a Straw." Ralph's World, *The Amazing Adventures of Kid Astro*.

"Wherever You Go (I Love You)." Fink, Cathy, and Marcy Marxer, *Air Guitar*.

"Why Do I Love You?" Polisar, Barry Louis, *Juggling Babies*.

"Wild Mountain Thyme." Zanes, Dan, *Night Time!*

"With a Giggle and a Hug and a Tickle and a Kiss." Polisar, Barry Louis, *Naughty Songs for Boys and Girls*.

"You Are My Sunshine." Dana, *Dana's Best Travelin' Tunes*; Fite, Stephen, *Havin' Fun and Feelin' Groovy*; McGrath, Bob, *Sing Along with Bob #2*; Mitchell, Elizabeth, *You Are My Sunshine*; Old Town School of Folk Music, *Wiggleworms Love You*; Penner, Fred, *Sing with Fred*; Strausman, Paul, *Camels, Cats, and Rainbows*; Various Artists, *Sing Along with Putumayo*.

"You're as Sweet as Sugar on a Stick." Polisar, Barry Louis, *Naughty Songs for Boys and Girls*.

Sadness

"Au Revoir." Alsop, Peter, *Uh-Oh!*

"Baby (Why Are You Crying So?)." Simmons, Al, *The Celery Stalks at Midnight*.

"Boo Hoo." LaFond, Lois, *I Am Who I Am*.

"Cheer Up." Penner, Fred, *What a Day!*

"Color It In." Big Jeff, *Big Jeff*.

"Cryin' in the Dugout." Daddy A Go Go, *Eat Every Bean and Pea on Your Plate*.

"Do You Mind If I Cry?" Fite, Stephen, *We're Just like Crayons*.

"Don't You Cry, Now Don't You Fuss." Polisar, Barry Louis, *Juggling Babies*.

"Feelings—Sad." The Learning Station, *Seasonal Songs in Motion*.

"A Friend like You." Penner, Fred, *What a Day!*

"Heartache to Happy." Chapin, Tom, *Around the World and Back Again*.

"I Cried." Alsop, Peter, *Stayin' Over*; Pelham, Ruth, *Under One Sky*.

"I Need to Say I'm Sorry." Walker, Mary Lu, *The Frog's Party*.

"Just a Matter of Time." Vitamin L, *Swingin' in the Key of L*.

"Mama Is Sad." Roberts, Justin, *Yellow Bus*.

"Monday Again." Kinnoin, Dave, *Getting Bigger*.

"Sad, Bad, Terrible Day." The Learning Station, *Literacy in Motion*.

"There's a Lot of Magic in Tears." Arnold, Linda, *Happiness Cake*.

"When I'm Down I Get Up and Dance." Palmer, Hap, *So Big*.

"You Never Praise Me Enough." Diamond, Charlotte, *Diamond in the Rough*.

Family (see also Babies)

"Dad Says That I Look like Him." Polisar, Barry Louis, *Naughty Songs for Boys and Girls*.

"Family." Allard, Peter and Ellen, *Good Kid*.

"The Family." Beall, Pamela, and Susan Nipp, *Wee Sing for Baby*.

"Family." Craig n Co., *Rock n Together*.

"Family." Harley, Bill, *You're in Trouble*.

"Family of Friends." Alsop, Peter, *Uh-Oh!*

"Family Revival." McCutcheon, John, *Family Garden*.

"The Family Song." Tickle Tune Typhoon, *Healthy Beginnings*.

"Family Tree." Chapin, Tom, *Family Tree*.

"Forever and Ever." Various Artists, *Hear and Gone in 60 Seconds*.

"Gotta Lotta Love." Parachute Express, *Don't Blink*.

"Grandma's Pond." Thaddeus Rex, *We Wanna Rock*.

"Happy Adoption Day." McCutcheon, John, *Family Garden*; Various Artists, *A Child's Celebration of Family*.

"How Many People." McCutcheon, John, *Family Garden*.

"I Never See Maggie Alone." Ralph's World, *Peggy's Pie Parlor*.

"I Sneaked into the Kitchen in the Middle of the Night." Polisar, Barry Louis, *Family Concert*; Polisar, Barry Louis, *Family Trip*.

"I'm My Own Grandpa." Abell, Timmy, *Little Red Wagon*; Kirk, John, and Trish Miller, *The Big Rock Candy Mountain*; Ralph's World, *Peggy's Pie Parlor*; Various Artists, *A Child's Celebration of Silliest Songs*.

"Is My Family." McCutcheon, John, *Family Garden*.

"It Takes Two to Make One." Rosen, Gary, *Pet Sounds*; Rosenshontz, *Tickles You!*

"It's My Mother and My Father and My Sister and the Dog." Polisar, Barry Louis, *Family Trip*.

"My Mother Is a Baker." Feldman, Jean, *Dr. Jean and Friends*.

"One Big Happy Family." Polisar, Barry Louis, *Old Enough to Know Better*.

"Our Family." Arnold, Linda, *Happiness Cake*.

"The Ragtime Dance." Chapin, Tom, *Zag Zig*.

"Red-Haired Family." Raven, Nancy, *The House We Live In*, vols. 1 and 2.

"Still the Ones for Me." McCutcheon, John, *Bigger Than Yourself*.

"Suppertime." Roberts, Justin, *Way Out*.

"When I Was a Little Girl." Buchman, Rachel, *Hello Everybody!*

"When Parents Were Young." Lonnquist, Ken, *Sci-Fi Hi-Fi*.

"Who Are the People in My Family?" Barchas, Sarah, *Get Ready, Get Set, Sing!*

Aunts

"Aunt Anna Came to Our House." Polisar, Barry Louis, *Family Trip*.

"My Aunt Came Back." Beall, Pamela, and Susan Nipp, *Wee Sing Games, Games, Games*; Beall, Pamela, and Susan Nipp, *Wee Sing in the Car*.

Brothers

"Brothers and Sisters." Rosenshontz, *Uh-Oh!*

"But They'll Never Have a Baby as Nice as Me." Polisar, Barry Louis, *Juggling Babies*.

"Give Him Back." Rosen, Gary, *Tot Rock*.

"I Love My Brother (Sometimes)." Various Artists, *Hear and Gone in 60 Seconds*.

"Irritation Man." Daddy A Go Go, *Eat Every Bean and Pea on Your Plate*.

"A Mind of His Own." Parachute Express, *Friends, Forever Friends*.

"My Brother Did It." Roberts, Justin, *Meltdown!*

"My Brother Eats Bugs." Mayer, Hans, *See You Later, Alligator*.

"My Brother Thinks He's a Banana." Polisar, Barry Louis, *Family Concert*; Polisar, Barry Louis, *Old Dog, New Tricks*.

"My Brother Threw Up on My Stuffed Toy Bunny." Alsop, Peter, *Wha' D'Ya Wanna Do?*; Polisar, Barry Louis, *Family Concert*; Polisar, Barry Louis, *Family Trip*.

"My Sister's a Monkey." Pullara, Steve, *One Potato, Two Potato*.

"She's My Sister, He's My Brother." Kaldor, Connie, *A Poodle in Paris*.

"Sister My Brother." Foote, Norman, *Pictures on the Fridge*.

"Sleep the Whole Day Through." Harley, Bill, *I Wanna Play*.

"There Goes My Brother Again." Harley, Bill, *50 Ways to Fool Your Mother*; Harley, Bill, *One More Time*; Harley, Bill, *Play It Again*.

"A Thousand Little Stickers in His Underwear." Kinnoin, Dave, *Daring Dewey*.

"Tommy Don't Lick That Pipe." McCutcheon, John, *Wintersongs*.

"What Can You Do with Your Baby Brother?" Ralph's World, *At the Bottom of the Sea*.
"Yesterday I Gave Away My Brother (Not Really)." Charette, Rick, *Bubble Gum*.

Cousins

"Cousins." Chapin, Tom, *Mother Earth*.
"Lot'sa Cousins." Pullara, Steve, *A Big Bowl of Musicroni*.

Fathers (see also Family—Parents)

"Come and Play Catch with Me." Paxton, Tom, *I've Got a Yo-Yo*.
"Dad and Me." McCutcheon, John, *Summersongs*.
"Dad Caught Stars." Roberts, Justin, *Not Naptime*.
"Dad Threw the TV out the Window." Fink, Cathy, and Marcy Marxer, *Changing Channels*; Harley, Bill, *Play It Again*; Harley, Bill, *You're in Trouble*.
"Daddy Be a Horsie." Palmer, Hap, *Peek-a-Boo*.
"Daddy Does the Dishes." Rosenshontz, *Family Vacation*; Rosenshontz, *Rosenshontz Greatest Hits*.
"Dads Can Dance." Rudnick, Ben, *Blast Off!*
"Dad's Got That Look." McCutcheon, John, *Family Garden*.
"Dads in the Sky." Daddy A Go Go, *Cool Songs for Cool Kids*.
"Dads Who Rock." Daddy A Go Go, *Eat Every Bean and Pea on Your Plate*.
"Don't Trick Your Dad." Alsop, Peter, *Wha' D'Ya Wanna Do?*
"High Standards." Alsop, Peter, *Pluggin' Away*.
"I Caught Daddy Watching Cartoons." Daddy A Go Go, *Big Rock Rooster*.
"Moon, My Dad and Me." Fink, Cathy, and Marcy Marxer, *Blanket Full of Dreams*.
"Mr. Mom." Rosen, Gary, *Cookin'*.
"My Dad's a Jungle Gym." Alsop, Peter, *Uh-Oh!*
"My Dad's the Greatest." Allard, Peter and Ellen, *Good Kid*.
"When Daddy Starts to Dance." Pease, Tom, *Daddy Starts to Dance*; Stotts, Stuart, *One Big Dance*.
"When Daddy Was a Little Boy." Palmer, Hap, *Turn On the Music*.
"When I'm with My Dad." Charette, Rick, *Where Do My Sneakers Go at Night?*
"Yea Daddy." Crow, Dan, *A Friend, a Laugh, a Walk in the Woods*.

Grandfathers (see also Family—Grandparents)

"Grampa's Hat." Kinnoin, Dave, *Getting Bigger*.
"Grandfather's Clock." Grammer, Red, *Down the Do-Re-Mi*; Penner, Fred, *Storytime*; Staines, Bill, *One More River*; Various Artists, *A Child's Celebration of Folk Music*.

"Grandpa Says." Daddy A Go Go, *Mojo A Go Go*.

"Grandpa's Laugh." Vitamin L, *Every Moment!*

"Grandpa's Riding Lawn Mower." Charette, Rick, *Popcorn and Other Songs to Munch On*.

"Silver Dollar." Pease, Tom, *Daddy Starts to Dance*.

Grandmothers (see also Family—Grandparents)

"Going to Grandma's." Abell, Timmy, *Little Red Wagon*.

"Grandma." Pelham, Ruth, *Under One Sky*.

"Grandma Slid down the Mountain." Fink, Cathy, *Grandma Slid down the Mountain*; Fink, Cathy, and Marcy Marxer, *A Cathy & Marcy Collection for Kids*.

"Grandma (Tell Me a Story)." Moos, Anna, *When I Was a Child*.

"Grandma's Eyes." Diamond, Charlotte, *Diamonds and Daydreams*.

"Grandma's House Tonight." Harper, Monty, *Take Me to Your Library*.

"Grandma's Sleeping in My Bed Tonight." Scruggs, Joe, *Late Last Night*.

"Grandma's Video Camera." Pullara, Steve, *Spinning Tails*.

"I Miss Grandma." Polisar, Barry Louis, *Family Trip*.

"My Grandma and Me." Grunsky, Jack, *Sing and Dance*.

"On My Grandma's Patchwork Quilt." Various Artists, *Grandma's Patchwork Quilt*.

"Señora Santa Ana." Hinojosa, Tish, *Cada Niño: Every Child*.

"Siempre Abuelita: Always Grandma." Hinojosa, Tish, *Cada Niño: Every Child*.

Grandparents (see also Family—Grandfathers; Family—Grandmothers)

"Goin' to Gramma and Grampa's House." Kinnoin, Dave, *Daring Dewey*.

"Grandma Grandpa Song." Kinder, Brian, *A Kid like You*.

"Grandmas and Grandpas." Scruggs, Joe, *Deep in the Jungle*.

"I Can Do Anything." Polisar, Barry Louis, *Family Concert*; Polisar, Barry Louis, *Juggling Babies*.

"Pen Pals." Gemini, *The Best of Gemini*.

"Water from Another Time." Herdman, Priscilla, *Daydreamer*.

Mothers (see also Family—Parents)

"Electrician's Daughter." Lonnquist, Ken, *Welcome 2 Kenland*.

"Even Trolls Have Moms." Scruggs, Joe, *Even Trolls Have Moms*.

"50 Ways to Fool Your Mother." Harley, Bill, *50 Ways to Fool Your Mother*; Harley, Bill, *Play It Again*.

"Hurricane Mom." Lonnquist, Ken, *Sci-Fi Hi-Fi*.

"I Drive My Mommy Crazy." Rosen, Gary, *Tot Rock*; Rosenshontz, *Rosenshontz Greatest Hits*.

"Mama Hug." Rymer, Brady, *Every Day Is a Birthday*.

"Mama Is Sad." Roberts, Justin, *Yellow Bus*.

"Mommy's Lips." Daddy A Go Go, *Monkey in the Middle*.

"A Mother Is Forever." Diamond, Charlotte, *Diamonds and Daydreams*.

"Mother Is You." Del Bianco, Lou, *When I Was a Kid*.

"Mother's Day." Chapin, Tom, *Moonboat*.

"Music in My Mother's House." Stotts, Stuart, *One Big Dance*.

"My Awesome Mom." Thaddeus Rex, *Martian Television Invasion*.

"My Mommy Comes Back." Palmer, Hap, *Peek-a-Boo*.

"My Mother and I." Pirtle, Sarah, *Heart of the World*.

"My Mother Ran Away Today." Polisar, Barry Louis, *Family Concert*; Polisar, Barry Louis, *Naughty Songs for Boys and Girls*.

"My Mother's Snoring." Lonnquist, Ken, *The Lost Songs of Kenland*.

"No One Loves You More Than Your M-O-Double-M-Y." Lithgow, John, *Singin' in the Bathtub*.

"Skateboard." Scruggs, Joe, *Deep in the Jungle*.

"Super Mom." Nagler, Eric, *Improvise with Eric Nagler*.

"That's What My Mama Says." Del Bianco, Lou, *A Little Bit Clumsy*.

"What Does Your Mama Do?" Fink, Cathy, *Grandma Slid down the Mountain*; Pease, Tom, *Boogie! Boogie! Boogie!*

Parents (see also Family—Fathers; Family—Mothers)

"Be Kind to Your Parents." Arnold, Linda, *Make Believe*.

"Get off the Computer." Daddy A Go Go, *Big Rock Rooster*.

"Keep Up with You." Rymer, Brady, *Every Day Is a Birthday*.

"Mom and Dad Are Always Right." Polisar, Barry Louis, *Naughty Songs for Boys and Girls*.

"Mom Said, 'No,' I Said 'Why?'" Polisar, Barry Louis, *Family Concert*; Polisar, Barry Louis, *Family Trip*.

"Pat Your Daddy." Alsop, Peter, *Uh-Oh!*

Sisters

"Big Sister." Miss Amy, *Underwater*.

"Brothers and Sisters." Rosenshontz, *Uh-Oh!*

"Cartwheels and Somersaults." Roberts, Justin, *Meltdown!*

"Footprints." McCutcheon, John, *Wintersongs*.

"Give Him Back." Rosen, Gary, *Tot Rock*.

"Going to the Prom." McCutcheon, John, *Springsongs*.

"I Have Six Sisters." Del Bianco, Lou, *A Little Bit Clumsy*.

"I Used to Have a Sister." Polisar, Barry Louis, *Old Enough to Know Better*.

"My Sister's a Monkey." Pullara, Steve, *One Potato, Two Potato*.

"Natural Disaster." McCutcheon, John, *Autumnsongs*.

"Never Cook Your Sister in a Frying Pan." Polisar, Barry Louis, *Naughty Songs for Boys and Girls*.

"Oh No, I Like My Sister." Polisar, Barry Louis, *Family Trip*.

"Safari into My Sister's Nose." Alsop, Peter, *Pluggin' Away*.

"She's My Sister, He's My Brother." Kaldor, Connie, *A Poodle in Paris*.

"Sister My Brother." Foote, Norman, *Pictures on the Fridge*.

"Why Did I Have to Have a Sister?" Diamond, Charlotte, *10 Carrot Diamond*.

Uncles

"Waltzing with Bears." Herdman, Priscilla, *Stardreamer*; Knight, Tom, *Don't Kiss a Codfish*; Rosen, Gary, *Teddy Bears' Picnic*.

"We're on Our Way." SteveSongs, *Marvelous Day!*

Farms

"Ali Baba'nin Çiftliği (Ali Baba's Farm)." Beall, Pamela, and Susan Nipp, *Wee Sing around the World*.

"Ali Baba's Farm." Beall, Pamela, and Susan Nipp, *Wee Sing in the Car*.

"Barnyard Blues." Ralph's World, *Happy Lemon*.

"Barnyard Boogie." Colleen and Uncle Squaty, *Sing-a-Move-a-Dance*.

"Barnyard Boogie." Grammer, Red, *Teaching Peace*.

"Barnyard Dance." Boynton, Sandra, *Rhinoceros Tap*.

"Barnyard Talk." Arnold, Linda, *Happiness Cake*.

"Barnyard Talkin'." Tickle Tune Typhoon, *Patty-Cakes and Peek-a-Boos*.

"Black Bat Farm." Peterson, Carole, *H.U.M.—All Year Long*.

"Cows in the Kitchen." Avni, Fran, *Little Ears: Songs for Reading Readiness*.

"Down by the Barnyard." Allard, Peter and Ellen, *Sing It! Say It! Stamp It! Sway It!* vol. 3.

"Down on Grandpa's Farm." Raffi, *One Light One Sun*. (Same song as "Grandpa's Farm.")

"Down to the Farm." Greg and Steve, *We All Live Together*, vol. 5.

"Farmer Brown Had Ten Green Apples." Jenkins, Ella, *Growing Up with Ella Jenkins*. (Same song as "Five Green Apples.")

"The Farmer in the Dell." Beall, Pamela, and Susan Nipp, *Wee Sing and Play*; Feldman, Jean, *Nursery Rhymes and Good Ol' Times*; The Learning Station, *All-Time Children's Favorites*; McGrath, Bob, *Sing Along with Bob #1*; Sharon, Lois, and Bram, *Everybody Sing!*

"The Farmer's Son." Harper, Jessica, *40 Winks*.

"Father Grumble." Beall, Pamela, and Susan Nipp, *Wee Sing Fun 'n' Folk*; McCutcheon, John, *Howjadoo*.

"Five Green Apples." Allard, Peter and Ellen, *Sing It! Say It! Stamp It! Sway It!* vol. 1; Sharon, Lois, and Bram, *Mainly Mother Goose*; Sharon, Lois, and Bram, *School Days*. (Same song as "Farmer Brown Had Ten Green Apples.")

"Goofy Old MacDonald." Peterson, Carole, *H.U.M.—All Year Long*.

"Grandpa's Farm." Fink, Cathy, and Marcy Marxer, *A Cathy & Marcy Collection for Kids*; Marxer, Marcy, *Jump Children*; Sharon, Lois, and Bram, *Everybody Sing!*; Sharon, Lois, and Bram, *Great Big Hits*; Sharon, Lois, and Bram, *Sing A to Z*. (Same song as "Down on Grandpa's Farm.")

"La Grunja." Magical Music Express, *Friendship Stew*.

"Hard Scrabble Harvest." Herdman, Priscilla, *Daydreamer*.

"Hay!" Allard, Peter and Ellen, *Sing It! Say It! Stamp It! Sway It!* vol. 2.

"Headin' on Down to the Barn." Grammer, Red, *Down the Do-Re-Mi*.

"Heavenly Music." Greg and Steve, *Playing Favorites*.

"Hinky Dinky 'Double D' Farm." Beall, Pamela, and Susan Nipp, *Wee Sing Silly Songs*.

"In the Moo." Knight, Tom, *Easy as Pie*.

"Mi Chacra (My Farm)." Beall, Pamela, and Susan Nipp, *Wee Sing around the World*.

"Mi Granja/My Farm." Barchas, Sarah, *¡Piñata! and More*.

"Music Farm." Various Artists, *World Playground 2*.

"My Farm." Barchas, Sarah, *If I Had a Pony*.

"My Mother's Snoring." Lonnquist, Ken, *The Lost Songs of Kenland*.

"Naturally." Raffi, *Bananaphone*.

"Oats and Beans and Barley." Raffi, *Baby Beluga*. (Same song as "Oats, Peas, Beans.")

"Oats, Peas, Beans." Beall, Pamela, and Susan Nipp, *Wee Sing and Play*; Buchman, Rachel, *Sing a Song of Seasons*; Raven, Nancy, *Jambalaya!*; Raven, Nancy, *Nancy Raven Sings Her Favorites*. (Same song as "Oats and Beans and Barley.")

"Oh My!" Ode, Eric, *Grandpa's Truck*.

"Old MacDonald." Barchas, Sarah, *Get Ready, Get Set, Sing!*; Beall, Pamela, and Susan Nipp, *Wee Sing Animals, Animals, Animals*; Beall, Pamela, and Susan Nipp, *Wee Sing Children's Songs and Fingerplays*; The Dream Project, *We've All Got Stories*; Feldman, Jean, *Nursery Rhymes and Good Ol' Times*; McGrath, Bob, *Sing Along with Bob #2*; Various Artists, *Sing Along with Putumayo*.

"Old MacDonald Had a 'Whzz.'" Silberg, "Miss Jackie," *Peanut Butter, Tarzan, and Roosters*.

"Old Pool Farm." Pullara, Steve, *One Potato, Two Potato*. (Same song as "Grandpa's Farm.")

"On the Funny Farm." Rosen, Gary, *Pet Sounds*; Rosenshontz, *Uh-Oh!*

"Pig Latin Polka Dance." Fink, Cathy, and Marcy Marxer, *Scat like That*.

"Robot Farm." Big Jeff, *Big Jeff and His Middle-Sized Band*.

"The Seed Cycle." Beall, Pamela, and Susan Nipp, *Wee Sing and Play*.

"Thank the Farmer." Daddy A Go Go, *Monkey in the Middle*.

"Welcome to the Farm." Ode, Eric, *Grandpa's Truck*.

"We're Going to the Country." Colleen and Uncle Squaty, *Rumble to the Bottom*.

"When I First Came to This Land." Colleen and Uncle Squaty, *1, 2, 3, Four-Ever Friends*; Diamond, Charlotte, *Diamond in the Rough*; Harley, Bill, *50 Ways to Fool Your Mother*; Rosenthal, Phil, *The Paw Paw Patch*.

"Wild Dog on the Farm." Pease, Tom, *Boogie! Boogie! Boogie!*

Fish (see also Recreation/Sports—Fishing)

"All the Fish." Silberg, "Miss Jackie," *Sing It Again Please*.

"The Aquarium." McMahon, Elizabeth, *Tea Party Shuffle*.

"At the Codfish Ball." The Chenille Sisters, *1, 2, 3 for Kids*; Lithgow, John, *Singin' in the Bathtub*; Muldaur, Maria, *Animal Crackers in My Soup*.

"At the 'Quarium." Paxton, Tom, *Goin' to the Zoo*.

"Baby Fish." Feldman, Jean, *Dr. Jean Sings Silly Songs*.

"Billy the Squid." Chapin, Tom, *Billy the Squid*.

"Fish Tank Full of Guppies." Pullara, Steve, *Spinning Tails*.

"Fishies." Banana Slug String Band, *Penguin Parade*.

"Fishy Doo-Ah." Tucker, Nancy, *Glad That You Asked*.

"Five Fish Swimming in the Sea." Feldman, Jean, *Dr. Jean Sings Silly Songs*.

"Genie Fish." Lonnquist, Ken, *Sci-Fi Hi-Fi*.

"The Goldfish." Berkner, Laurie, *Victor Vito*.

"Ichthyology." Tickle Tune Typhoon, *Singing Science*.

"Jaws." Colleen and Uncle Squaty, *Fingerplays, Movement and Story Songs*.

"Jump Again Salmon." Pirtle, Sarah, *Heart of the World*.

"Jump Salmon Jump." Pirtle, Sarah, *Two Hands Hold the Earth*.

"Let's Be Friends." Arnold, Linda, *Splash Zone*.

"Lillyfish." SteveSongs, *On a Flying Guitar*.

"Little Fish." Walker, Graham, *Fiddlesticks*.

"Lulu." Big Jeff, *Big Jeff*.

"Nibble, Bite, Gulp or Crunch." Arnold, Linda, *Splash Zone*.

"Octopus." Diamond, Charlotte, *10 Carrot Diamond*.

"Les Petits Poissons." Sharon, Lois, and Bram, *Sing A to Z*; Sharon, Lois, and Bram, *Sleepytime*.

"That's a Moray." Arnold, Linda, *Splash Zone*.

"Three Little Fishies." Bartels, Joanie, *Bathtime Magic*; Muldaur, Maria, *Swingin' in the Rain*; Various Artists, *A Child's Celebration of Silliest Songs*.

"Uncle Junie and the Shark." Pirtle, Sarah, *Heart of the World*.

"Wishy the Fish/The Shark Song." Kimmy Schwimmy, *Kimmy Schwimmy Music*, vol. 1.

Flying

"Back When I Could Fly." Trout Fishing in America, *Family Music Party*; Trout Fishing in America, *My World*.

"Big Balloon." Pullara, Steve, *Spinning Tails*.

"Bird's Eye View." Lonnquist, Ken, *Sci-Fi Hi-Fi*.

"Do You Wish You Could Fly?" Byers, Kathy, *Do You Wish You Could Fly?*

"Fly Fly Fly." Mayer, Hans, *See You Later, Alligator*.

"Flying." Dana, *Dana's Best Travelin' Tunes*.

"Flying, Flying." Madsen, Gunnar, *Old Mr. Mackle Hackle*.

"Flying Lesson." Various Artists, *A Child's Celebration of Song 2*.

"Flying 'round the Mountain." Scruggs, Joe, *Even Trolls Have Moms*.

"I Wanna Fly." Coffey, James, *Animal Groove*.

"I Wish I Could Fly." Kimmy Schwimmy, *Kimmy Schwimmy Music*, vol. 1.

"If I Had Wings." Palmer, Hap, *Turn On the Music*.

"If I Were a Kite." Frezza, Rebecca, *Music in My Head*.

"If You Want to Fly." SteveSongs, *Marvelous Day!*

"Junior Birdmen." Feldman, Jean, *Is Everybody Happy?* (Same song as "Up in the Air, Junior Birdmen.")

"Peppermint Wings." Arnold, Linda, *Peppermint Wings*.

"Superman." Frezza, Rebecca, *Music in My Head*.

"Up in the Air, Junior Birdmen." Sharon, Lois, and Bram, *Everybody Sing!*;
    Sharon, Lois, and Bram, *Sing A to Z*. (Same song as "Junior Birdmen.")

"We're Flying." Bartels, Joanie, *Travelin' Magic*.

"The Wings." Harper, Jessica, *A Wonderful Life*.

Food

"Aiken Drum." Gemini, *The Best of Gemini*, vol. 2; McGrath, Bob, *Sing Along with Bob #1*; Old Town School of Folk Music, *Wiggleworms Love You*; Raffi, *Singable Songs for the Very Young*; Rosenthal, Phil, *Folksongs and Bluegrass for Children*; Rosenthal, Phil, *Turkey in the Straw*; Silberg, "Miss Jackie," *Sing It Again Please*.

"All Filled Up." Gill, Jim, *Jim Gill Makes It Noisy in Boise, Idaho*.

"Alligator Pie." Magical Music Express, *Music Is Magic*; Peterson, Carole, *H.U.M.—All Year Long*.

"Apple Juice." Alsop, Peter, *Uh-Oh!*

"Baked Beans." Howdy, Buck, *Giddyup!*

"Bean Soup and Rice." Ralph's World, *At the Bottom of the Sea*.

"Bon Appétit." Fink, Cathy, and Marcy Marxer, *Bon Appétit!*

"Breakfast Time." Milkshake, *Happy Songs*.

"Buono Appetito." Grammer, Red, *Hello World*.

"Campfire." McCutcheon, John, *Autumnsongs*.

"Catches." Chapin, Tom, *Moonboat*.

"Chemistry." Walker, Mary Lu, *The Frog's Party*.

"Cherries." McMahon, Elizabeth, *Tea Party Shuffle*.

"Chicken Gizzards and Collard Greens." Yosi, *What's Eatin' Yosi?*

"Chicken Lips and Lizard Hips." Cassidy, Nancy, *Nancy Cassidy's KidsSongs*.

"Chilly Chili." Yosi, *What's Eatin' Yosi?*

"Corner Grocery Store." Raffi, *Corner Grocery Store*.

"Don't Eat the Food That Is Sitting on Your Plate." Polisar, Barry Louis, *Teacher's Favorites*.

"Don't Think about Food." Kinder, Brian, *A Kid like You*.

"E Eats Everything." They Might Be Giants, *Here Come the ABCs*.

"Eat Every Bean and Pea on Your Plate." Daddy A Go Go, *Eat Every Bean and Pea on Your Plate*.

"Eat It Up." Rosenshontz, *Share It*.

"Eat Your Food, Don't Wear It." Rosen, Gary, *Cookin'*.

"Eating Every Day." Allard, Peter and Ellen, *Pizza Pizzaz*.

"Everybody Eats When They Come to My House." Lithgow, John, *Singin' in the Bathtub*; Pease, Tom, *Daddy Starts to Dance*; Sharon, Lois, and Bram, *Great Big Hits 2*.

"Fancy Dinner." Foote, Norman, *Foote Prints*.

"Filling Up a Shopping Cart." Charette, Rick, *King Kong Chair*.

"Food Jokes." Fink, Cathy, and Marcy Marxer, *Bon Appétit!*

"The Food Pyramid." Fink, Cathy, and Marcy Marxer, *Bon Appétit!*

"Food Song." Silberg, "Miss Jackie," *Joining Hands with Other Lands*; Silberg, "Miss Jackie," *Touched by a Song*.

"Fresh Brown Eggs." Yosi, *What's Eatin' Yosi?*

"Gobble across the USA." Cosgrove, Jim, *Mr. Stinky Feet's Road Trip*.

"Green Eggs and Ham." The Learning Station, *Literacy in Motion*; The Learning Station, *Rock n' Roll Songs That Teach*.

"Hinky Dinky 'Double D' Farm." Beall, Pamela, and Susan Nipp, *Wee Sing Silly Songs*.

"Home Dairy Bakery." McMahon, Elizabeth, *Blue Sky Sparklin' Day*.

"I Like to Eat Sweets." Kaye, Mary, *I Sang It Just for You*.

"I Love You More Than Cheese." Boynton, Sandra, *Rhinoceros Tap*.

"I Talk to My Food." Pirtle, Sarah, *Two Hands Hold the Earth*.

"I'm a Little Cookie." Alsop, Peter, *Take Me with You*; McCutcheon, John, *Mail Myself to You*; Pease, Tom, *Boogie! Boogie! Boogie!*; Raven, Nancy, *The House We Live In*, vols. 1 and 2; Various Artists, *Grandma's Patchwork Quilt*.

"I'm a Raisin in a Bowl of Raisin Bran." Paxton, Tom, *Your Shoes, My Shoes*.

"I'm Too Full for Broccoli." Scruggs, Joe, *Abracadabra*.

"It's Gonna Be Dinner Soon." Chapin, Tom, *Around the World and Back Again*.

"Jelly, Jelly in My Belly." Sharon, Lois, and Bram, *Everybody Sing!*

"Junk Food Jump." Trout Fishing in America, *InFINity*.

"Just Desserts." Yosi, *What's Eatin' Yosi?*

"Ketchup." Paxton, Tom, *Goin' to the Zoo*.

"Late at Night When I'm Hungry." Charette, Rick, *Bubble Gum*.

"Let's Eat." Kaye, Mary, *Mouse Jamboree*.

"Let's Go to the Market." Greg and Steve, *We All Live Together*, vol. 5.

"Let's Make Some Lemonade." Charette, Rick, *Bubble Gum*.

"A Little Taste of This, A Little Taste of That." Fink, Cathy, and Marcy Marxer, *Bon Appétit!*

"Lunch." Gemini, *The Best of Gemini.*

"Lunch Box Rock." Parachute Express, *Friends, Forever Friends.*

"Midnight Snack." Walker, Graham, *Cats' Night Out.*

"Mrs. Murphy's Chowder." Cassidy, Nancy, *Nancy Cassidy's KidsSongs.*

"My Favorite Food." Dana, *Dana's Best Sing and Play-a-Long Tunes.*

"My Town Is a Salad Bowl." Chapin, Tom, *In My Hometown.*

"Naturally." Raffi, *Bananaphone.*

"Oh How Delicious Are Hot Tamales." Barchas, Sarah, *¡Piñata! and More.*

"Pineapple Pickles." Walker, Graham, *Cats' Night Out.*

"The Pretzel Store." Berkner, Laurie, *Buzz Buzz.*

"Raindrops and Lemon Drops." Scruggs, Joe, *Traffic Jams.*

"Sally Eats Shoelaces, Straw, and String." Polisar, Barry Louis, *Old Enough to Know Better.*

"Separate on the Plate." Del Bianco, Lou, *A Little Bit Clumsy.*

"S'mores." Howdy, Buck, *Giddyup!*

"S'mores." Parachute Express, *Doctor Looney's Remedy.*

"The Sneezing Song." Gill, Jim, *Jim Gill Sings the Sneezing Song and Other Contagious Tunes.*

"Strange Food." Tickle Tune Typhoon, *Singing Science.*

"Supermarket Tango." Grunsky, Jack, *Dancing Feet*; Grunsky, Jack, *Jack in the Box 1.*

"Suppertime." Roberts, Justin, *Way Out.*

"They Said 'Eat the Broccoli.'" Polisar, Barry Louis, *Naughty Songs for Boys and Girls.*

"Today Is Sunday." Feldman, Jean, *Dr. Jean and Friends.*

"Try Just a Little." Knight, Tom, *Don't Kiss a Codfish.*

"Tummy Tango." Greg and Steve, *Kids in Motion.*

"Victor Vito." Berkner, Laurie, *Victor Vito.*

"Vitamin Si." Chapin, Tom, *Zag Zig.*

"We're Going on a Picnic." Haynes, Sammie, *Nature's ABCs.*

"When I Pack My Lunch." Trout Fishing in America, *It's a Puzzle.*

"Whoever Shall Have Some Good Peanuts." Fink, Cathy, *When the Rain Comes Down*; Hinton, Sam, *Whoever Shall Have Some Good Peanuts.*

"You Are What You Eat." Shontz, Bill, *Animal Tales.*

Beverages

"Apple Juice." Beall, Pamela, and Susan Nipp, *Wee Sing in the Car.*

"The Coffee Song." Ralph's World, *At the Bottom of the Sea.*

"Get Your Ice Cold Lemonade." Charette, Rick, *Chickens on Vacation.*

"Happy Lemons." Ralph's World, *Happy Lemon*.

"Homemade Lemonade." Chapin, Tom, *In My Hometown*.

"Hot Chocolate." McCutcheon, John, *Wintersongs*.

"I Spilled My Juice." Charette, Rick, *Chickens on Vacation*.

"Juice." Alsop, Peter, *Stayin' Over*.

"Sucking Cider from a Straw." Ralph's World, *The Amazing Adventures of Kid Astro*.

"The Tea Tale." Ralph's World, *The Amazing Adventures of Kid Astro*.

"What I Want Is a Proper Cup of Coffee." Trout Fishing in America, *Big Trouble*; Trout Fishing in America, *Family Music Party*.

Bread/Buns/Sandwiches

"African Bread Song." Raven, Nancy, *Jambalaya!*; Raven, Nancy, *Nancy Raven Sings Her Favorites*.

"Biscuit Blues." Riders in the Sky, *Saddle Pals*.

"Biscuits in the Oven." Raffi, *Baby Beluga*.

"Deli." Gemini, *The Best of Gemini*.

"Exceptional Piece of Toast." Tucker, Nancy, *Escape of the Slinkys*.

"Five Brown Buns." Sharon, Lois, and Bram, *Great Big Hits*.

"I Always Leave the Crust." Charette, Rick, *Alligator in the Elevator*.

"Sandwiches." Alsop, Peter, *Wha' D'Ya Wanna Do?*; Cassidy, Nancy, *Nancy Cassidy's KidsSongs*; Penner, Fred, *Sing with Fred*; Penner, Fred, *Storytime*.

"Shortnin' Bread." Berkner, Laurie, *Under a Shady Tree*; McGrath, Bob, *Sing Along with Bob #2*.

Cakes/Donuts

"Birthday Cake." Parachute Express, *Sunny Side Up*.

"Broken Donuts." Charette, Rick, *Where Do My Sneakers Go at Night?*

"Donut Man Blues." Pullara, Steve, *Spinning Tails*.

"I Sneaked into the Kitchen in the Middle of the Night." Polisar, Barry Louis, *Family Concert*; Polisar, Barry Louis, *Family Trip*.

"If I Knew You Were Comin' I'd've Baked a Cake." Muldaur, Maria, *Swingin' in the Rain*.

"Pat-a-Cake." Scruggs, Joe, *Traffic Jams*.

"Stinky Cake!" Peterson, Carole, *Stinky Cake*.

Candy

"The Big Rock Candy Mountain." Beall, Pamela, and Susan Nipp, *Wee Sing in the Car*; Beall, Pamela, and Susan Nipp, *Wee Sing Fun 'n' Folk*; Chapin, Tom,

Family Tree; Chapin, Tom, *Great Big Fun for the Very Little One*; Grammer, Red, *Red Grammer's Favorite Sing Along Songs*; Kirk, John, and Trish Miller, *The Big Rock Candy Mountain*.

"Chocolate." Rosen, Gary, *Cookin'*.

"Gummy Bears." Feldman, Jean, *Is Everybody Happy?*

"The Lollipop Tree." Silberg, "Miss Jackie," *Lollipops and Spaghetti*; Silberg, "Miss Jackie," *Sing It Again Please*.

"The Magic Garden." The Chenille Sisters, *The Big Picture and Other Songs for Kids*.

"On the Good Ship Lollipop." Muldaur, Maria, *Animal Crackers in My Soup*.

"Six Licorice Sticks." Harper, Jessica, *Rhythm in My Shoes*.

"There's a Great Big Candy Roundup." Riders in the Sky, *Saddle Pals*.

Cookies

"The Cookie Bakers of the Night." Berkner, Laurie, *Buzz Buzz*.

"Cookies." Fink, Cathy, *When the Rain Comes Down*.

"Faraway Cookies." Boynton, Sandra, *Philadelphia Chickens*.

"Momma Makes Cookies." Kinder, Brian, *Again*.

"One Last Cookie." Del Bianco, Lou, *A Little Bit Clumsy*.

"One Little Cookie." Roberts, Justin, *Yellow Bus*.

"Who Stole the Cookies?" The Learning Station, *Here We Go Loopty Loo*.

Crackers

"Animal Crackers." Alsop, Peter, *Take Me with You*.

"Animal Crackers in My Soup." Bartels, Joanie, *Sillytime Magic*; Lithgow, John, *Farkle and Friends*.

"Eatin' Animal Crackers." Rymer, Brady, *I Found It!*

Fruit

"All the Nations Like Bananas." Diamond, Charlotte, *My Bear Gruff*.

"Apple Picker's Reel." Herdman, Priscilla, *Daydreamer*; Staines, Bill, *The Happy Wanderer*.

"Apple Pickin' Time." Pease, Tom, *I'm Gonna Reach!*

"The Apple Seed." Silberg, "Miss Jackie," *Touched by a Song*.

"The Apple Tree." Peterson, Carole, *H.U.M.—All Year Long*.

"Apple Tree." Roberts, Justin, *Great Big Sun*.

"Apples and Bananas." Cassidy, Nancy, *Nancy Cassidy's KidsSongs*; Crow, Dan, *Dan Crow Live*; Crow, Dan, *Oops!*; Pease, Tom, *Boogie! Boogie! Boogie!*;

Raffi, *One Light One Sun*; Raffi, *Raffi in Concert*; Various Artists, *A Child's Celebration of Silliest Songs*. (Similar to "Pepperoni Pizza.")

"Apples, Bananas, Peaches, Tomatoes." Palmer, Hap, *Two Little Sounds*.

"Baby Prune." McGrath, Bob, *Sing Along with Bob #1*.

"Banana!" Fink, Cathy, and Marcy Marxer, *Bon Appétit!*; Raven, Nancy, *Jambalaya!*

"The Banana Boat Song." Various Artists, *A Child's Celebration of Song*; Various Artists, *A Child's Celebration of the World*. (Same song as "Day-O.")

"The Banana Song." Gill, Jim, *Jim Gill Sings the Sneezing Song and Other Contagious Tunes*.

"The Banana Wish Song." Fink, Cathy, and Marcy Marxer, *Pillow Full of Wishes*.

"Bananaphone." Raffi, *Bananaphone*; Various Artists, *A Child's Celebration of Song 2*; Various Artists, *Sing Along with Putumayo*.

"Bananas." Knight, Tom, *Don't Kiss a Codfish*.

"Bananas." Paxton, Tom, *I've Got a Yo-Yo*.

"B-Bananas/Monkey See, Monkey Do!" Peterson, Carole, *Stinky Cake*.

"Blackberry Pickin'." Rosen, Gary, *Cookin'*.

"Blueberry Dreams." Kaye, Mary, *Spin Your Web*.

"Broadway Banana." Arnold, Linda, *Favorites in the Key of Fun*.

"The Caribbean Mango Song." Silberg, "Miss Jackie," *Joining Hands with Other Lands*; Silberg, "Miss Jackie," *Touched by a Song*.

"Criss Cross Applesauce." Yosi, *Monkey Business*.

"Day-O." Arnold, Linda, *Sing Along Stew*; Cassidy, Nancy, *Nancy Cassidy's KidsSongs*; Grammer, Red, *Red Grammer's Favorite Sing Along Songs*; Jenkins, Ella, *Sharing Cultures with Ella Jenkins*; Magical Music Express, *Friendship Stew*; Raffi, *Baby Beluga*; Raffi, *Raffi in Concert*. (Same song as "The Banana Boat Song.")

"Farmer Brown Had Ten Green Apples." Jenkins, Ella, *Growing Up with Ella Jenkins*. (Same song as "Five Green Apples.")

"Five a Day." Fink, Cathy, and Marcy Marxer, *Bon Appétit!*

"Five Green Apples." Allard, Peter and Ellen, *Sing It! Say It! Stamp It! Sway It!* vol. 1; Sharon, Lois, and Bram, *Mainly Mother Goose*; Sharon, Lois, and Bram, *School Days*. (Same song as "Farmer Brown Had Ten Green Apples.")

"Fruit and Vegetable." Silberg, "Miss Jackie," *Touched by a Song*.

"Fruit Salad." Grunsky, Jack, *Sing and Dance*.

"Fruit Salad Salsa." Berkner, Laurie, *Victor Vito*.

"The Fruit Song." The Chenille Sisters, *The Big Picture and Other Songs for Kids*.

"Fruits and Vegetables." Barchas, Sarah, *Get Ready, Get Set, Sing!*

"I Like Bananas Because They Have No Bones." Bartels, Joanie, *Sillytime Magic.*

"My Brother Thinks He's a Banana." Polisar, Barry Louis, *Family Concert*; Polisar, Barry Louis, *Old Dog, New Tricks.*

"Pineapple." Avni, Fran, *I'm All Ears: Sing into Reading.*

"Pop, Pop, Pop." Haynes, Sammie, *Nature's ABCs.*

"Too Much Mango." Hullabaloo, *Sing Along with Sam.*

"Watermelon." Jonas, Billy, *What Kind of Cat Are You?!*; McCutcheon, John, *Family Garden.*

"Watermelon." Tucker, Nancy, *Glad That You Asked.*

"What Do You Do With a Fruit?" Rosen, Gary, *Tot Rock.*

"Where the Blackberries Grow." Foote, Norman, *1000 Pennies.*

Gum

"American Gum." Crow, Dan, *Oops!*

"Bubble Gum." Charette, Rick, *Bubble Gum.*

"Bubble Gum." Guthrie, Woody, *Nursery Days.*

"Bubble Gum." McGrath, Bob, and Katherine Smithrim, *Songs and Games for Toddlers.*

"Bubble Gum." Scruggs, Joe, *Abracadabra.*

"Bubblegum." Feldman, Jean, *Dr. Jean Sings Silly Songs.*

"Chomping Gum." Palmer, Hap, *Turn On the Music.*

"Choo'n Gum." Muldaur, Maria, *Swingin' in the Rain.*

"Fly Fly Fly." Mayer, Hans, *See You Later, Alligator.*

"Jenny the Bubble Gum Queen." Rosenshontz, *Rosenshontz Greatest Hits*; Rosenshontz, *Uh-Oh.*

"Ooey Gooey." Cosgrove, Jim, *Ooey Gooey.*

"Sticky Bubble Gum." Peterson, Carole, *Sticky Bubble Gum.*

Honey

"Honey for the Bears." Ralph's World, *At the Bottom of the Sea.*

"Honey, Honey, Honey." Kaldor, Connie, *A Duck in New York City.*

Ice Cream

"Dreamin' on a Giant Ice Cream Sundae." Pullara, Steve, *One Potato, Two Potato.*

"I Like Chocolate Ice Cream." Charette, Rick, *King Kong Chair.*

"Ice Cream Cone." Berkner, Laurie, *Buzz Buzz*.
"Ice Cream Man." McCutcheon, John, *Summersongs*.
"Slurp It Up!" Pullara, Steve, *One Potato, Two Potato*.

Jam/Jelly (see also Food—Peanut Butter)

"Blackberry Jam." Ode, Eric, *Trash Can*.
"Green Chili Jam." Green Chili Jam Band, *Magic Bike*.
"Jelly Man Kelly." Various Artists, *A Child's Celebration of Song*.

Macaroni and Cheese

"Macaroni and Cheese." Charette, Rick, *Chickens on Vacation*.
"Macaroni and Cheese." Rudnick, Ben, *Fun and Games*.

Meat

"Angie's Meatballs." Del Bianco, Lou, *Lost in School*.
"Five Little Hotdogs." Feldman, Jean, *Just for Fun!*
"Hotdog." Kinder, Brian, *One More Time*.
"I Had Ham." Crow, Dan, *Dan Crow Live*; Crow, Dan, *Oops!*
"Old Baloney." Madsen, Gunnar, *Ants in My Pants!*
"One Meatball." Strausman, Paul, *Camels, Cats, and Rainbows*; Tucker, Nancy,
    Happy as a Clam.

Pancakes

"I Want a Pancake." Simmons, Al, *Something Fishy at Camp Wiganishie*.
"Pancakes." Charette, Rick, *Alligator in the Elevator*.
"Pancakes." Knight, Tom, *Easy as Pie*.
"Pancakes." Pease, Tom, *Wobbi-Do-Wop!*

Pasta/Spaghetti

"Lasagna." McMahon, Elizabeth, *Blue Sky Sparklin' Day*.
"Noodles." The Chenille Sisters, *Teaching Hippopotami to Fly!*
"On Top of Spaghetti." McGrath, Bob, *Sing Along with Bob #1*; Silberg, "Miss
    Jackie," *Lollipops and Spaghetti*; Silberg, "Miss Jackie," *Sing It Again Please*;
    Strausman, Paul, *Rainbows, Stones, and Dinosaur Bones*; Various Artists, *A
    Child's Celebration of Silliest Songs*; Yosi, *What's Eatin' Yosi?*
"Pass the Purple Pesto Pasta Please." Yosi, *What's Eatin' Yosi?*
"Pasta." Arnold, Linda, *Peppermint Wings*.

"Pasta Pasta Pasta." Pullara, Steve, *A Big Bowl of Musicroni.*
"Spaghetti (Twist and Twirl)." Fink, Cathy, and Marcy Marxer, *All Wound Up!*

Peanut Butter

"Peanut Butter." Arnold, Linda, *Happiness Cake.*
"Peanut Butter." Cosgrove, Jim, *Mr. Stinky Feet's Road Trip.*
"Peanut Butter." Feldman, Jean, *Keep On Singing and Dancing with Dr. Jean.*
"Peanut Butter." McCutcheon, John, *Howjadoo.*
"Peanut Butter." Scruggs, Joe, *Late Last Night.*

"Peanut Butter." Walker, Mary Lu, *The Frog's Party.*
"Peanut Butter and Jelly." Fink, Cathy, *Grandma Slid down the Mountain*; Fink, Cathy, and Marcy Marxer, *A Cathy & Marcy Collection for Kids*; Greg and Steve, *Fun and Games*; Magical Music Express, *Music Is Magic*; Sharon, Lois, and Bram, *Great Big Hits*; Sharon, Lois, and Bram, *School Days*; Strausman, Paul, *Camels, Cats, and Rainbows.*
"Peanut Butter and Jelly." Knight, Tom, *Don't Kiss a Codfish.*
"Peanut Butter Blues." Moo, Anna, *Moochas Gracias.*
"Peanut Butter Blues." Rosenshontz, *Family Vacation.*
"Peanut Butter Jambalaya." Dana, *Dana's Best Sing and Play-a-Long Tunes.*
"Peanut Butter Pie." Paxton, Tom, *Goin' to the Zoo.*
"Peanut Butter Sandwich." Raffi, *Singable Songs for the Very Young.*

Peanuts

"Bag of Peanuts." Simmons, Al, *The Truck I Bought from Moe.*
"Found a Peanut." Beall, Pamela, and Susan Nipp, *Wee Sing Silly Songs.*
"Goober Peas." Cosgrove, Jim, *Stinky Feet.*
"A Peanut Sat on the Railroad Track." Various Artists, *A Child's Celebration of Silliest Songs.*

Pickles

"Pickle Bicycle." Kinder, Brian, *A Kid like You.*
"The Pickle Song." Cosgrove, Jim, *Stinky Feet.*

Pie

"Apple Pie Time." McMahon, Elizabeth, *Magic Parade.*
"Bananas." SteveSongs, *On a Flying Guitar.*
"I Love Pie." Fink, Cathy, and Marcy Marxer, *Scat like That.*

"Peanut Butter Pie." Paxton, Tom, *Goin' to the Zoo*.

"Peggy's Pie Parlor." Ralph's World, *Peggy's Pie Parlor*.

"Purple Pumpkin Pie." Knight, Tom, *Easy as Pie*.

"Rhubarb Pie." Berkner, Laurie, *Under a Shady Tree*.

"Sillie Pie." Bartels, Joanie, *Sillytime Magic*.

"Voo Doo." Lonnquist, Ken, *Welcome 2 Kenland*; Lonnquist, Ken, *The Switcher-On of Stars*.

Pizza

"I Am a Pizza." Alsop, Peter, *Wha' D'Ya Wanna Do?*; Arnold, Linda, *Peppermint Wings*; Diamond, Charlotte, *10 Carrot Diamond*.

"I Like to Eat Pepperoni Pizza." Fite, Stephen, *Gobs of Fun*. (Same song as "Pepperoni Pizza"; similar to "Apples and Bananas.")

"It's a Pizza." Fite, Stephen, *Cool to Be in School*.

"It's a Pizza." Yosi, *What's Eatin' Yosi?*

"Maria and Don Cheech's Pizzaria." Pullara, Steve, *A Big Bowl of Musicroni*.

"Pepperoni Pizza." Feldman, Jean, *Dr. Jean Sings Silly Songs*. (Same song as "I Like to Eat Pepperoni Pizza"; similar to "Apples and Bananas.")

"Pizza." Gemini, *The Best of Gemini*.

"Pizza." Rosenshontz, *Family Vacation*.

"Pizza Pie." McMahon, Elizabeth, *Tea Party Shuffle*.

"Pizza Pizzaz." Allard, Peter and Ellen, *Pizza Pizzaz*.

"Pizza Rules." Mr. Al, *Mr. Al a Carte*.

"Pizza Shake." Harley, Bill, *Big Big World*; Harley, Bill, *One More Time*.

"The Pizza That Ate Chicago." Paxton, Tom, *Your Shoes, My Shoes*.

Popcorn

"Popcorn." Arnold, Linda, *Make Believe*.

"Popcorn." Charette, Rick, *Popcorn and Other Songs to Munch On*.

"Popcorn." Gemini, *The Best of Gemini*, vol. 2.

"Popcorn." Greg and Steve, *We All Live Together*, vol. 2.

"Popcorn Calling Me." Berkner, Laurie, *Buzz Buzz*.

"The Popcorn Pop." Rosen, Gary, *Tot Rock*.

Soup/Stew

"Alphabet Soup." Chapin, Tom, *Moonboat*.

"Alphabet Soup." Various Artists, *Hear and Gone in 60 Seconds*.

"Animal Crackers in My Soup." Bartels, Joanie, *Sillytime Magic*; Lithgow, John, *Farkle and Friends*; Muldaur, Maria, *Animal Crackers in My Soup*.

"Chicken Noodle Soup." Yosi, *What's Eatin' Yosi?*

"Chicken Soup with Rice." Rosen, Gary, *Cookin'*.

"I Feel Crazy, So I Jump in the Soup." Berkner, Laurie, *Victor Vito*.

"Ode to Soup." Gemini, *The Best of Gemini*, vol. 2.

"Sitting in the Soup." Pirtle, Sarah, *The Wind Is Telling Secrets*.

"Soup." Kaye, Mary, *Spin Your Web*.

"Soup." McCutcheon, John, *Wintersongs*.

"The Stew Song." Simmons, Al, *Something Fishy at Camp Wiganishie*.

"Stone Soup." Arnold, Linda, *Make Believe*.

"Stone Soup." Chapin, Tom, *Mother Earth*.

"Stone Soup." Knight, Tom, *Don't Kiss a Codfish*.

"Stone Soup." McMahon, Elizabeth, *Magic Parade*.

Vegetables

"Alfredo Potato." Charette, Rick, *Popcorn and Other Songs to Munch On*.

"Artichokes and Brussel Sprouts." Avni, Fran, *Artichokes and Brussel Sprouts*.

"The Barnyard Dance." McCutcheon, John, *Mail Myself to You*.

"The Barnyard Dance: El Baile Vegetal." Hinojosa, Tish, *Cada Niño: Every Child*.

"Boiled Okra and Spinach." Trout Fishing in America, *Mine!*

"Bud the Spud." Simmons, Al, *The Truck I Bought from Moe*.

"Bulbes (Potatoes)." Yosi, *What's Eatin' Yosi?*

"(Don't Give Me That) Broccoli." Boynton, Sandra, *Dog Train*.

"Five a Day." Fink, Cathy, and Marcy Marxer, *Bon Appétit!*

"Fruit and Vegetable." Silberg, "Miss Jackie," *Touched by a Song*.

"Fruits and Vegetables." Barchas, Sarah, *Get Ready, Get Set, Sing!*

"Green Food." Miss Amy, *Underwater*.

"Greens 'n Beans." Raven, Nancy, *Jambalaya!*; Raven, Nancy, *Nancy Raven Sings Her Favorites*.

"Hot Potato." The Learning Station, *Here We Go Loopty Loo*.

"I Like Potatoes." Greg and Steve, *We All Live Together*, vol. 5.

"I Love Tomatoes." Kaldor, Connie, *A Duck in New York City*.

"It's No Fun When Ya Gotta Eat an Onion." Alsop, Peter, *Take Me with You*.

"Little Holly Ho-Hum." The Chenille Sisters, *1, 2, 3 for Kids*.

"Mashed Potatoes." Gill, Jim, *Jim Gill Sings Do Re Mi on His Toe Leg Knee*.

"Mashed Potatoes." Paxton, Tom, *Goin' to the Zoo.*
"New Potato Polka." Diamond, Charlotte, *Charlotte Diamond's World.*
"O, Lonely Peas." Boynton, Sandra, *Rhinoceros Tap.*
"One Potato, Two Potato." Pullara, Steve, *One Potato, Two Potato.*
"Pea Pickers Reel." Pease, Tom, *Boogie! Boogie! Boogie!*
"Potato." Fink, Cathy, and Marcy Marxer, *Bon Appétit!*
"The Potato Goat." Crow, Dan, *Oops!*
"Praties Song." Raven, Nancy, *The House We Live In*, vols. 1 and 2.
"Sweet Potato Round." Raven, Nancy, *Jambalaya!*
"Sweet Potatoes." Raven, Nancy, *The House We Live In*, vols. 1 and 2; Staines, Bill,
    The Happy Wanderer.
"There's a Pea on My Plate." Harley, Bill, *One More Time*; Harley, Bill, *There's a
    Pea on My Plate.*
"The Valley of the Vegetables." Berkner, Laurie, *Buzz Buzz.*
"Vegaboogie." Tickle Tune Typhoon, *Circle Around.*
"The Vegetable Lament." Arnold, Linda, *Favorites in the Key of Fun*; Arnold,
    Linda, *Make Believe.*
"Vegetation Migration/Celery Stalks at Midnight." Simmons, Al, *The Celery
    Stalks at Midnight.*
"The Veggie Song (Go, Go, Go)." SteveSongs, *Marvelous Day!*
"When the Peas Went Pop!" Buchman, Rachel, *Sing a Song of Seasons.*
"Yam Jam." Arnold, Linda, *Peppermint Wings.*
"Yambo." Crow, Dan, *Oops!*
"You've Gotta Eat Your Spinach." Muldaur, Maria, *Animal Crackers in My Soup.*
"The Zucchini Song." Crow, Dan, *A Friend, a Laugh, a Walk in the Woods.*

Forgetfulness

"Barefoot Blues." Harper, Jessica, *Nora's Room.*
"By the Way." Scruggs, Joe, *Deep in the Jungle.*
"I Forgot." Allard, Peter and Ellen, *Raise the Children.*
"I Forgot." Polisar, Barry Louis, *Old Enough to Know Better.*
"We're on Our Way." SteveSongs, *Marvelous Day!*

Freedom

"All for Freedom." Sweet Honey in the Rock, *All for Freedom.*
"Calypso Freedom." Sweet Honey in the Rock, *All for Freedom*; Various Artists,
    I'm Gonna Let It Shine.

"Everybody Ought to Know." Sweet Honey in the Rock, *All for Freedom*.

"Everybody Says Freedom." Various Artists, *I'm Gonna Let It Shine*.

"Freedom Now." Sweet Honey in the Rock, *I Got Shoes*.

"Freedom Train." Coffey, James, *I Love Toy Trains*; Sweet Honey in the Rock, *I Got Shoes*; Various Artists, *World Playground 2*.

"Harriet Tubman." Fink, Cathy, and Marcy Marxer, *Air Guitar*.

"I'm on My Way." Byers, Kathy, *'Round the Campfire*; Harley, Bill, *50 Ways to Fool Your Mother*; Various Artists, *I'm Gonna Let It Shine*.

"Lady of the Night." Silberg, "Miss Jackie," *Joining Hands with Other Lands*; Silberg, "Miss Jackie," *Touched by a Song*.

"Oh Freedom." Various Artists, *I'm Gonna Let It Shine*.

"One Little Step towards Freedom." Various Artists, *I'm Gonna Let It Shine*.

"Sing Mandela Free." Various Artists, *I'm Gonna Let It Shine*.

"Some Rights in the World." Vitamin L, *Every Moment!*

"The Thought That Stayed Free." Paxton, Tom, *I've Got a Yo-Yo*.

"Up over My Head." Various Artists, *I'm Gonna Let It Shine*.

"We Shall Not Be Moved." Sweet Honey in the Rock, *Still the Same Me*.

"Without Freedom." The Dream Project, *We've All Got Stories*.

"Woke Up This Morning with My Mind on Freedom." Various Artists, *I'm Gonna Let It Shine*.

Friendship (see also Imaginary Friends)

"ABRA-CA-DABRA." Atkinson, Lisa, *I Wanna Tickle the Fish*.

"All of My Friends." Chapin, Tom, *Billy the Squid*.

"Best Friend." Roberts, Justin, *Way Out*.

"Best Friends." Gemini, *The Best of Gemini*, vol. 2.

"Best Friends." SteveSongs, *On a Flying Guitar*.

"Count on Me." Trout Fishing in America, *Family Music Party*; Trout Fishing in America, *Mine!*

"Family of Friends." Alsop, Peter, *Uh-Oh!*

"A Friend, a Laugh, a Walk in the Woods." Crow, Dan, *A Friend, a Laugh, a Walk in the Woods*.

"The Friend I'm Looking For." Ode, Eric, *Trash Can*.

"A Friend in You." Mr. Al and Stephen Fite, *Back to School Again*.

"A Friend like You." Penner, Fred, *What a Day!*

"Friends." The Chenille Sisters, *Teaching Hippopotami to Fly!*

"Friends." Frezza, Rebecca, *Road Trip*.

"Friends." Livingston, Bob, *Open the Window*.

"Friends Are Better Than Crocodiles." Walker, Graham, *Cats' Night Out*.

"Friends Forever." Greg and Steve, *We All Live Together*, vol. 5.

"Friends, Forever Friends." Parachute Express, *Friends, Forever Friends*.

"Friendship." Harper, Jessica, *Hey, Picasso*.

"Friendship." McCutcheon, John, *Bigger Than Yourself*.

"The Friendship Song." Fite, Stephen, *We're Just like Crayons*.

"Friendship Stew." Magical Music Express, *Friendship Stew*.

"Hey Little Friend." Allard, Peter and Ellen, *Sing It! Say It! Stamp It! Sway It!* vol. 3.

"Hi Hi, I Love You." Chapin, Tom, *Zag Zig*.

"Hold On to Your Friends." Thaddeus Rex, *Martian Television Invasion*.

"I Made a New Friend." Vitamin L, *Swingin' in the Key of L*.

"I Really Want to Be Your Friend." Kinder, Brian, *A Kid like You*.

"I Want to Get to Know You." Vitamin L, *Walk a Mile*.

"I Will Be Your Friend." Various Artists, *Sing Along with Putumayo*.

"If You Will Be My Friend." Barchas, Sarah, *Bridges across the World*.

"I've Got a Friend (And He Won't Be Quiet)." Trout Fishing in America, *My Best Day*.

"Let Me Be Your Friend." The Dream Project, *We've All Got Stories*.

"Let's Be Friends." Tickle Tune Typhoon, *All of Us Will Shine*.

"Linger." Byers, Kathy, *'Round the Campfire*.

"Make New Friends." Beall, Pamela, and Susan Nipp, *Wee Sing Sing-Alongs*; Fink, Cathy, and Marcy Marxer, *Air Guitar*; Sweet Honey in the Rock, *All for Freedom*.

"The More We Get Together." Barchas, Sarah, *Get Ready, Get Set, Sing!*; Beall, Pamela, and Susan Nipp, *Wee Sing Sing-Alongs*; Berkner, Laurie, *Buzz Buzz*; Feldman, Jean, *Is Everybody Happy?*; Grunsky, Jack, *Jack in the Box 2*; McGrath, Bob, *Sing Along with Bob #1*; Raffi, *Raffi in Concert*; Raffi, *Singable Songs for the Very Young*.

"My Best Friend." Milkshake, *Play!*

"My Friend Juan." Yosi, *Under a Big Bright Yellow Umbrella*.

"My Special Friend." Fite, Stephen, *We're Just like Crayons*.

"My Special Friend." Vitamin L, *Everyone's Invited!*

"One Little Song." Stotts, Stuart, and Tom Pease, *Celebrate: A Song Resource*.

"Quite a Combination." Arnold, Linda, *Favorites in the Key of Fun*.

"Shake a Friend's Hand." Peterson, Carole, *Stinky Cake*.

"Shakin' Hands." Fink, Cathy, *When the Rain Comes Down*; Fink, Cathy, and Marcy Marxer, *A Cathy & Marcy Collection for Kids*.

"Shining Star." Zanes, Dan, *House Party*.

"So Nice to Be Here." Allard, Peter and Ellen, *Sing It! Say It! Stamp It! Sway It!* vol. 1.

"Special Friends." The Learning Station, *Children Love to Sing and Dance*; The Learning Station, *Literacy in Motion*.

"Stick Together." McCutcheon, John, *Bigger Than Yourself*.

"Take Good Care of Each Other." Fink, Cathy, and Marcy Marxer, *Air Guitar*.

"That's What Friends Are For." Harley, Bill, *Monsters in the Bathroom*.

"That's What I Like about You." Fink, Cathy, and Marcy Marxer, *Changing Channels*.

"Twogether." Avni, Fran, *Artichokes and Brussel Sprouts*.

"Visualize Friendship." Lonnquist, Ken, *The Circus Kenlando*.

"Welcome." Vitamin L, *Everyone's Invited!*

"What Are Friends For." Silberg, "Miss Jackie," *Touched by a Song*.

"What I Like about You." Stotts, Stuart, and Tom Pease, *Celebrate: A Song Resource*.

"Who Will Be My Friend?" Peterson, Carole, *Tiny Tunes*.

"Wonderful Pals." Foote, Norman, *Shake a Leg*.

"Won't You Be My Partner?" Stotts, Stuart, and Tom Pease, *Celebrate: A Song Resource*.

"You Are My Friend." Magical Music Express, *Friendship Stew*.

"You Are My Friend." Moo, Anna, *Making Moosic*.

"You're Never Alone." Grunsky, Jack, *Sing and Dance*.

Furniture

"Able the Table." Foote, Norman, *Shake a Leg*.

"King Kong Chair." Charette, Rick, *King Kong Chair*.

"Musical Chairs." Beall, Pamela, and Susan Nipp, *Wee Sing Games, Games, Games*.

"My Big Bed." Rymer, Brady, *Look at My Belly*.

"The Rocking Chair." Scruggs, Joe, *Abracadabra*.

"Under the Bed." Rymer, Brady, *I Found It!*

"Waterbed Afternoons." Charette, Rick, *Where Do My Sneakers Go at Night?*

Gardens

"Another Garden Song." Tucker, Nancy, *Happy as a Clam*.

"Brown Gold." Chapin, Tom, *Some Assembly Required*.

"The Changing Garden of Mr. Bell." Raffi, *Bananaphone*.

"Emma Lou." Raven, Nancy, *Jambalaya!*; Raven, Nancy, *Nancy Raven Sings Her Favorites*.

"Family Garden." McCutcheon, John, *Family Garden*.

"The Garden." Roth, Kevin, *Unbearable Bears*.

"The Garden Song." Diamond, Charlotte, *10 Carrot Diamond*; Fink, Cathy, and Marcy Marxer, *Bon Appétit!*; Penner, Fred, *Sing with Fred*; Peter, Paul, and Mary, *Peter, Paul, and Mommy, Too*; Rosenshontz, *Tickles You!*; Tucker, Nancy, *Happy as a Clam*; Various Artists, *A Child's Celebration of Folk Music*; Various Artists, *A Child's Celebration of Song*.

"$H_2O + O_2$ + Sun." Frezza, Rebecca, *Road Trip*.

"In My Garden." Raffi, *One Light One Sun*.

"In Our Garden." Allard, Peter and Ellen, *Sing It! Say It! Stamp It! Sway It!* vol. 1.

"Little Raindrop." Roberts, Justin, *Great Big Sun*.

"The Magic Garden." The Chenille Sisters, *The Big Picture and Other Songs for Kids*.

"Move with the Moon." Pirtle, Sarah, *Heart of the World*.

"Plant a Garden." Milkshake, *Play!*

"The Pumpkin Man." McCutcheon, John, *Autumnsongs*; Various Artists, *Grandma's Patchwork Quilt*.

"Seeds for My Garden." Grunsky, Jack, *Like a Flower to the Sun*.

"Tulips and Daisies." Avni, Fran, *Tuning into Nature*.

"Vegetation Migration/Celery Stalks at Midnight." Simmons, Al, *The Celery Stalks at Midnight*.

"The Zucchini Song." Crow, Dan, *A Friend, a Laugh, a Walk in the Woods*.

Gluttony

"Cindy's Absent (I Am Very Sad to Say That Cindy Won't Be Out to Play)." Polisar, Barry Louis, *Teacher's Favorites*.

"I Sold My Cat." Lonnquist, Ken, *Welcome 2 Kenland*.

"Mary Kate's Birthday Cake." Cosgrove, Jim, *Pick Me! Pick Me!*

Good-bye Songs

"Aloha." Silberg, "Miss Jackie," *The Complete Sniggles, Squirrels, and Chicken Pox*.

"Arrivederci Nonna." Pullara, Steve, *A Big Bowl of Musicroni*.

"Au Revoir." Alsop, Peter, *Uh-Oh!*

"Blow a Kiss." Berkner, Laurie, *Under a Shady Tree*.

"Bye Bye." Gemini, *The Best of Gemini*.

"Bye-Bye Pizza Pie." Parachute Express, *Sunny Side Up*.

"Bye Bye Song." Lonnquist, Ken, *Welcome 2 Kenland*.

"Can It Be Over?" Harper, Monty, *The Great Green Squishy Mean Concert CD*.

"Cataplin." Various Artists, *Hear and Gone in 60 Seconds*.

"Family Goodbyes." Gill, Jim, *Moving Rhymes for Modern Times*.

"Give Me a Hug." Kimmy Schwimmy, *Kimmy Schwimmy Music*, vol. 1.

"Good-bye." Greg and Steve, *We All Live Together*, vol. 1.

"Goodbye." Magical Music Express, *Friendship Stew*.

"Goodbye." SteveSongs, *On a Flying Guitar*.

"Goodbye." Yosi, *Monkey Business*.

"Goodbye Medley." Peterson, Carole, *Sticky Bubble Gum*.

"Goodbye, My Friend." Pirtle, Sarah, *The Wind Is Telling Secrets*.

"Good-bye My Friends." Palmer, Hap, *Can a Jumbo Jet Sing the Alphabet?*

"Good-bye, So Long, Farewell, Toodle-oo." Palmer, Hap, *Two Little Sounds*.

"A Goodbye Song." Allard, Peter and Ellen, *Sing It! Say It! Stamp It! Sway It!* vol. 2.

"Good-bye Song." Grunsky, Jack, *Follow the Leader*; Grunsky, Jack, *Playground*.

"Greeting and Farewell Song." Jenkins, Ella, *Growing Up with Ella Jenkins*.

"Happy Trails." Fink, Cathy, *When the Rain Comes Down*; Howdy, Buck, *Giddyup!*

"Hello, I Must Be Going." Gill, Jim, *Moving Rhymes for Modern Times*.

"I Had a Friend." Berkner, Laurie, *Buzz Buzz*.

"It Is Time to Say Good-bye." Feldman, Jean, *Dr. Jean Sings Silly Songs*.

"It's Time to Go." Palmer, Hap, *Can Cockatoos Count by Twos?*

"Now It's Time to Say Goodbye." Ralph's World, *Ralph's World*.

"One Day Soon." Howdy, Buck, *Skidaddle!*

"Peace Be with You." Ladysmith Black Mambazo, *Gift of the Tortoise*.

"Remember." Lonnquist, Ken, *The Switcher-On of Stars*.

"Say Goodbye!" Peterson, Carole, *Tiny Tunes*.

"See You Later Alligator." Fite, Stephen, *Havin' Fun and Feelin' Groovy*.

"See-You-Later Song." Parachute Express, *Who's Got a Hug?*

"Shake Hands with Friends." Jenkins, Ella, *Growing Up with Ella Jenkins*.

"So Long." Cosgrove, Jim, *Pick Me! Pick Me!*

"So Long." Fite, Stephen, *Monkey Business*.

"So Long." Grunsky, Jack, *Like a Flower to the Sun*.

"So Long Children." Allard, Peter and Ellen, *Sing It! Say It! Stamp It! Sway It!* vol. 1.

"So Long It's Been Good to Know You." Guthrie, Woody and Arlo, *This Land Is Your Land*; Zanes, Dan, *Night Time!*

"Sobonana Kusasa." Old Town School of Folk Music, *Wiggleworms Love You*; Pease, Tom, *Boogie! Boogie! Boogie!*

"Time to Say Goodbye." Barchas, Sarah, *Bridges across the World*.

"Together Tomorrow." Chapin, Tom, *Family Tree*; Chapin, Tom, *Great Big Fun for the Very Little One*.

"Tomorrow's a New Day." Mr. Al and Stephen Fite, *Back to School Again*.

"Wave Bye-Bye." Boynton, Sandra, *Dog Train.*
"Wave Goodbye." Colleen and Uncle Squaty, *Rumble to the Bottom.*

Growing

"Apple Tree." Roberts, Justin, *Great Big Sun.*
"As You Sleep So Peacefully (A Father's Day Nightmare)." Polisar, Barry Louis, *Juggling Babies.*
"Bigger." Roberts, Justin, *Way Out.*
"Can't Rock the Baby." Scruggs, Joe, *Ants.*
"Couldn't Do It a Year Ago." LaFond, Lois, *I Am Who I Am.*
"Everything Grows." Raffi, *Everything Grows*; Raffi, *Raffi in Concert.*
"Everything Grows." Tickle Tune Typhoon, *Singing Science.*
"Footprints." McCutcheon, John, *Wintersongs.*
"For Those about to Walk, We Salute You." Daddy A Go Go, *Eat Every Bean and Pea on Your Plate.*
"Getting Bigger." Kinnoin, Dave, *Getting Bigger.*
"The Growing." Atkinson, Lisa, *I Wanna Tickle the Fish.*
"Growing." Kimmy Schwimmy, *Kimmy Schwimmy Music*, vol. 1.
"Growing." Palmer, Hap, *So Big.*
"I Can Do It Myself." Miss Amy, *Underwater.*
"I Know I'm Gonna Drive a Car." Frezza, Rebecca, *Road Trip.*
"I Wonder If I'm Growing." Raffi, *Singable Songs for the Very Young.*
"I'm a Toddler." Tickle Tune Typhoon, *Patty-Cakes and Peek-a-Boos.*
"I'm Too Old for That." Daddy A Go Go, *Mojo A Go Go.*
"It's Better Than That." Trout Fishing in America, *InFINity.*
"A Kid like You." Kinder, Brian, *A Kid like You.*
"A Little Acorn." The Chenille Sisters, *The Big Picture and Other Songs for Kids.*
"Little Kid." Alsop, Peter, *Uh-Oh!*
"Rhythm in Her Shoes." Harper, Jessica, *Rhythm in My Shoes.*
"Riding with No Hands." Ralph's World, *Happy Lemon.*
"Right Foot, Left Foot." Parachute Express, *Don't Blink.*
"Stay There." Harper, Jessica, *Hey, Picasso.*
"Taking Off My Training Wheels." Roberts, Justin, *Meltdown!*
"There's More to a Seed." Ode, Eric, *Grandpa's Truck.*
"Turn Around." McCutcheon, John, *Mail Myself to You.*
"What'cha Gonna Be." Kinder, Brian, *Again.*
"When I Grow Up." The Chenille Sisters, *The Big Picture and Other Songs for Kids.*

"When I Grow Up." Crow, Dan, *Dan Crow Live*.

"When I Grow Up." Foote, Norman, *1000 Pennies*.

"When I Grow Up." Frezza, Rebecca, *Music in My Head*.

"When I Grow Up." Harley, Bill, *Monsters in the Bathroom*.

"When I Grow Up." Knight, Tom, *Don't Kiss a Codfish*.

"When I Grow Up." Stotts, Stuart, and Tom Pease, *Celebrate: A Song Resource*.

"When My Shoes Are Loose." Fink, Cathy, and Marcy Marxer, *Help Yourself*.

Hair

"Afro." Lonnquist, Ken, *Sci-Fi Hi-Fi*.

"Daddy's Whiskers." Nagler, Eric, *Improvise with Eric Nagler*. (Same song as "Father's Old Grey Whiskers" and "Father's Whiskers.")

"Father's Old Grey Whiskers." Cassidy, Nancy, *Nancy Cassidy's KidsSongs*. (Same song as "Daddy's Whiskers" and "Father's Whiskers.")

"Father's Whiskers." Beall, Pamela, and Susan Nipp, *Wee Sing Silly Songs*. (Same song as "Daddy's Whiskers" and "Father's Old Grey Whiskers.")

"Haircut." Craig n Co., *Rock n Together*.

"Haircut." McCutcheon, John, *Summersongs*.

"I'm Not Bald." Harper, Monty, *Imagine That*.

"Michael Finnegan." Beall, Pamela, and Susan Nipp, *Wee Sing Silly Songs*; Hinton, Sam, *Whoever Shall Have Some Good Peanuts*; Sharon, Lois, and Bram, *Name Games*.

"My Hair Had a Party Last Night." Trout Fishing in America, *Family Music Party*; Trout Fishing in America, *My Best Day*; Trout Fishing in America, *My World*.

Health/Nutrition

"Aerobics." Fink, Cathy, and Marcy Marxer, *Bon Appétit!*

"Big Strong Muscles." Fink, Cathy, and Marcy Marxer, *Bon Appétit!*

"Breakfast Power." Fink, Cathy, and Marcy Marxer, *Bon Appétit!*

"Chew Chew Cha Cha." Tickle Tune Typhoon, *Healthy Beginnings*.

"Eat Every Bean and Pea on Your Plate." Daddy A Go Go, *Eat Every Bean and Pea on Your Plate*.

"Eat It Up." Rosenshontz, *Share It*.

"Exercise Time." Mr. Al, *Dance like This*; Mr. Al, *Mr. Al Concert Live*.

"The Food Pyramid." Fink, Cathy, and Marcy Marxer, *Bon Appétit!*

"Getting Our Exercise." Kinder, Brian, *One More Time*.

"Have a Little Smoke?" Polisar, Barry Louis, *Juggling Babies*.

"Hygiene Olympics." Tickle Tune Typhoon, *Healthy Beginnings*.

"Junk Food Jump." Trout Fishing in America, *InFINity*.

"March of the Germs." Tickle Tune Typhoon, *Healthy Beginnings*.

"Muscle Music." Tickle Tune Typhoon, *Circle Around*; Tickle Tune Typhoon, *Healthy Beginnings*.

"No Excuse t' Use Booze." Alsop, Peter, *Stayin' Over*.

"No Tobacco." Tickle Tune Typhoon, *Healthy Beginnings*.

"Nutrition Song." The Learning Station, *Children Love to Sing and Dance*.

"Pump, Pump Shuffle." The Learning Station, *Tony Chestnut and Fun Time Action Songs*.

"Star Sun." Scruggs, Joe, *Bahamas Pajamas*.

"Take Care of Your Body." Stotts, Stuart, and Tom Pease, *Celebrate: A Song Resource*.

"Tobacco." Lonnquist, Ken, *The Circus Kenlando*.

"Vitamin Si." Chapin, Tom, *Zag Zig*.

"Water." Fink, Cathy, and Marcy Marxer, *Bon Appétit!*

"You Are What You Eat." Fink, Cathy, and Marcy Marxer, *Help Yourself*.

Hello Songs

"Aloha." Silberg, "Miss Jackie," *The Complete Sniggles, Squirrels, and Chicken Pox*.

"Bluebird." Milkshake, *Bottle of Sunshine*.

"Bon Jour." Various Artists, *A Child's Celebration of the World*.

"The Children of the World Say Hello." Barchas, Sarah, *Bridges across the World*.

"Glad to See You." Allard, Peter and Ellen, *Sing It! Say It! Stamp It! Sway It!* vol. 2.

"Greeting and Farewell Song." Jenkins, Ella, *Growing Up with Ella Jenkins*.

"Greetings." Green Chili Jam Band, *Coconut Moon*.

"Hello!" Alsop, Peter, *Uh-Oh!*

"Hello." Arnold, Linda, *Peppermint Wings*.

"Hello." Gemini, *The Best of Gemini*.

"Hello." Silberg, "Miss Jackie," *Peanut Butter, Tarzan, and Roosters*.

"Hello." Zanes, Dan, *Rocket Ship Beach*.

"Hello and How Are You?" Old Town School of Folk Music, *Wiggleworms Love You*.

"Hello Everybody." Allard, Peter and Ellen, *Sing It! Say It! Stamp It! Sway It!* vol. 1.

"Hello Everybody." Mr. Al, *Mr. Al a Carte*; Mr. Al, *Mr. Al Concert Live*.

"Hello Everybody." Peterson, Carole, *Sticky Bubble Gum*.

"Hello Ev'rybody!" Buchman, Rachel, *Hello Everybody!*; Peterson, Carole, *H.U.M.—All Year Long*.

"Hello, Hello." Fite, Stephen, *Monkey Business*.

"Hello, Hello." Pelham, Ruth, *Under One Sky*.

"Hello, Hello, Hello." Fink, Cathy, and Marcy Marxer, *Nobody Else like Me.*

"Hello, How Are You." Feldman, Jean, *Dr. Jean Sings Silly Songs.*

"Hello, Neighbor." Feldman, Jean, *Keep On Singing and Dancing with Dr. Jean.*

"Hello There, Hello There." Allard, Peter and Ellen, *Sing It! Say It! Stamp It! Sway It!* vol. 1.

"Hello to the Children of the World." Beall, Pamela, and Susan Nipp, *Wee Sing around the World.*

"Hello World." Grammer, Red, *Hello World.*

"Hello World." Greg and Steve, *Fun and Games.*

"How Do You Do?" Zanes, Dan, *House Party.*

"Howdido." Guthrie, Woody, *Nursery Days.* (Same song as "Howdy Do," "Howjadoo," and "How'ji Do.")

"Howdy Do." Guthrie, Woody, *Woody's 20 Grow Big Songs*; Guthrie, Woody and Arlo, *This Land Is Your Land.* (Same song as "Howdido," "Howjadoo," and "How'ji Do.")

"Howdy Song." Harper, Monty, *Take Me to Your Library.*

"Howjadoo." McCutcheon, John, *Howjadoo*; Nagler, Eric, *Improvise with Eric Nagler*; Raven, Nancy, *Singing, Prancing, and Dancing.* (Same song as "Howdido," "Howdy Do," and "How'ji Do.")

"How'ji Do." Kirk, John, and Trish Miller, *The Big Rock Candy Mountain.* (Same song as "Howdido," "Howdy Do," and "Howjadoo.")

"I Know Your Face." Pelham, Ruth, *Under One Sky.*

"Jambo." Various Artists, *cELLAbration! A Tribute to Ella Jenkins.*

"Konnichi-wa." Moo, Anna, *Moochas Gracias.*

"Many Ways to Say Hello." Silberg, "Miss Jackie," *Joining Hands with Other Lands.*

"A New Way to Say Hello." Big Jeff, *Big Jeff.*

"Oh Hey Oh Hi Hello." Gill, Jim, *Jim Gill Makes It Noisy in Boise, Idaho.*

"Rapp Song." Grammer, Red, *Teaching Peace.*

"'Round the World with Ways to Say Hello." Palmer, Hap, *Can a Jumbo Jet Sing the Alphabet?*

"Say Hello." Greg and Steve, *Kidding Around.*

"Say Hi!" Grammer, Red, *Teaching Peace.*

"Say Hi to the Animals." Ralph's World, *Happy Lemon.*

"Siyanibingalela." Grunsky, Jack, *Jack in the Box 1*; Grunsky, Jack, *World Safari.*

"Something 'bout a Circle." Parachute Express, *Don't Blink.*

"Special Friends." The Learning Station, *Literacy in Motion.*

"Time to Sing." Raffi, *One Light One Sun.*

"Way over There." Colleen and Uncle Squaty, *1, 2, 3, Four-Ever Friends.*

Heroes/Superheroes

"Here's to the Hero." Vitamin L, *Walk a Mile*.

"I Wanna Be an Action Figure." Daddy A Go Go, *Big Rock Rooster*.

"I Wish I Could Fly." Kimmy Schwimmy, *Kimmy Schwimmy Music*, vol. 1.

"Superhero." Milkshake, *Play!*

"Superman." Frezza, Rebecca, *Music in My Head*.

Hiccupping

"A Happy Horse." Crow, Dan, *A Friend, a Laugh, a Walk in the Woods*.

"Hiccups." Big Jeff, *Big Jeff and His Middle-Sized Band*.

"Pickup Hiccup Truck." Cosgrove, Jim, *Bop Bop Dinosaur*.

"Princess Di's Distress." Chapin, Tom, *Moonboat*.

Home/Houses

"Almost Home." Howdy, Buck, *Giddyup!*

"Almost Home." Scruggs, Joe, *Bahamas Pajamas*.

"Everybody's Got to Have a Home." Shontz, Bill, *Animal Tales*.

"Follow the Voice." Pirtle, Sarah, *Magical Earth*.

"Home." Fink, Cathy, and Marcy Marxer, *All Wound Up!*

"Home Is a Welcoming Sound." Chapin, Tom, *Some Assembly Required*.

"A House Is a House for Me." Penner, Fred, *Rhyme a Word or Two*.

"In My Backyard." Penner, Fred, *Sing with Fred*; Penner, Fred, *What a Day!*

"It Feels like Home." Chapin, Tom, *In My Hometown*.

"Let's Live Peacefully." Arnold, Linda, *Favorites in the Key of Fun*.

"Milky Way." Harley, Bill, *Down in the Backpack*.

"My House." Grammer, Red, *Can You Sound Just like Me?*

"100 Year Old House." McMahon, Elizabeth, *Waltzing with Fireflies*.

"Place to Be." Raven, Nancy, *Singing, Prancing, and Dancing*.

"Some Houses." Jonas, Billy, *What Kind of Cat Are You?!*

"Way Back Home." Simmons, Al, *The Truck I Bought from Moe*.

Hugs

"Four Hugs a Day." Diamond, Charlotte, *10 Carrot Diamond*.

"Give Me a Hug." Kimmy Schwimmy, *Kimmy Schwimmy Music*, vol. 1.

"The Hug Bug." Diamond, Charlotte, *Diamond in the Rough*.

"Hug Bug." Tickle Tune Typhoon, *Circle Around*.

"Hugga Hugga." Rosen, Gary, *Teddy Bears' Picnic*; Rosenshontz, *Rosenshontz Greatest Hits*.

"The Hugging Song." Greg and Steve, *Kidding Around*.

"I Need a Hug." Alsop, Peter, *Uh-Oh!*

"Just a Little Hug." Mayer, Hans, *Just a Little Hug*.

"Mama Hug." Rymer, Brady, *Every Day Is a Birthday*.

"Sharing a Hug and a Squeeze." Charette, Rick, *A Little Peace and Quiet*.

"Who's Got a Hug." Parachute Express, *Who's Got a Hug?*

"You Gotta Have Hugs." Mr. Al, *Mr. Al a Carte*; Mr. Al, *Mr. Al Concert Live*.

Hurrying

"Another Busy Day." Chapin, Tom, *Around the World and Back Again*.

"Busy Busy Busy." Boynton, Sandra, *Philadelphia Chickens*.

"A Day in the Life of Elizabeth." Harper, Jessica, *Rhythm in My Shoes*.

"Hey Tom, Take Your Time." Vitamin L, *Swingin' in the Key of L*.

"Hurry Up Blues." Palmer, Hap, *Turn On the Music*.

"Slow Down." Roth, Kevin, *Train Songs and Other Tracks*.

Illness

"Achoo!" Lonnquist, Ken, *Sci-Fi Hi-Fi*.

"Alien in My Lungs." Jonas, Billy, *What Kind of Cat Are You?!*

"Baby Bear's Chicken Pox." Avni, Fran, *Artichokes and Brussel Sprouts*; Silberg, "Miss Jackie," *The Complete Sniggles, Squirrels, and Chicken Pox*.

"A Brontosaurus with Bronchitis." Polisar, Barry Louis, *Naughty Songs for Boys and Girls*.

"Cheerio." Sharon, Lois, and Bram, *Everybody Sing!*; Sharon, Lois, and Bram, *Great Big Hits 2*.

"Chicken Pox." Troubadour, *On the Trail*.

"Chicken Pox (Oh No, They're Here)." Charette, Rick, *Popcorn and Other Songs to Munch On*.

"Chicken Pox Party." Parachute Express, *Don't Blink*.

"A Cold for Sale." Lonnquist, Ken, *The Circus Kenlando*.

"Ebeneezer Sneezer." Penner, Fred, *Rhyme a Word or Two*.

"The Flu." Craig n Co., *Rock n Together*.

"The Flu." McCutcheon, John, *Wintersongs*.

"Gotta Lotta Livin' to Do." Alsop, Peter, *Pluggin' Away*.

"I've Got the Measles." Paxton, Tom, *I've Got a Yo-Yo*.

"Miss Lucy." Sharon, Lois, and Bram, *Great Big Hits 2*; Sharon, Lois, and Bram, *Name Games*.

"My Brother Threw Up on My Stuffed Toy Bunny." Alsop, Peter, *Wha' D'Ya Wanna Do?*; Polisar, Barry Louis, *Family Concert*; Polisar, Barry Louis, *Family Trip*.

"98.8." Roberts, Justin, *Not Naptime*.

"Poison Ivy." Gill, Jim, *Jim Gill Sings the Sneezing Song and Other Contagious Tunes*.

"A Sick Song." Polisar, Barry Louis, *Juggling Babies*.

"The Sneezing Song." Gill, Jim, *Jim Gill Sings the Sneezing Song and Other Contagious Tunes*.

Imaginary Characters/Creatures

Aliens

"Alien Babies (Revisited)." Pullara, Steve, *Spinning Tails*.

"Alien in My Nose." Trout Fishing in America, *It's a Puzzle*; Trout Fishing in America, *My Best Day*.

"Greetings Earthlings." Lonnquist, Ken, *Sci-Fi Hi-Fi*.

"Heck, I'd Go!" Muldaur, Maria, *Swingin' in the Rain*; Various Artists, *A Child's Celebration of Silliest Songs*.

"I Got a New Friend." Rudnick, Ben, *Blast Off!*

"Just a Dream." Sprout, Jonathan, *On the Radio*.

"Little Green Man." Walker, Graham, *Knobbledee Knees*.

"Martian Welcome." SteveSongs, *On a Flying Guitar*.

"Planet Bruno." Chapin, Tom, *Some Assembly Required*.

"Schlurpknopf." Yosi, *What's Eatin' Yosi?*

"Sci Fi Hi Fi Twist." Lonnquist, Ken, *Sci-Fi Hi-Fi*.

"Take Me to Your Leader." Coffey, James, *I Love Toy Trains*.

"Take Me to Your Library." Harper, Monty, *Take Me to Your Library*.

"UFO Man." Cosgrove, Jim, *Ooey Gooey*.

"Ziddle Zoom." Walker, Graham, *Jumpety Jump*.

Dragons

"Delilah the Dragon." Walker, Graham, *Jumpety Jump*.

"Do the Dragon." Berkner, Laurie, *Under a Shady Tree*.

"Dragon, Dragon." Roth, Kevin, *Dinosaurs and Dragons*.

"Dragonfire." Boynton, Sandra, *Dog Train*.

"The Giggling Dragon." Crow, Dan, *The Giggling Dragon.*

"Mostly Sam." Rosen, Gary, *Cookin'.*

"Nine-Foot Dragon and Four-Foot Boy." Jonas, Billy, *What Kind of Cat Are You?!*

"Puff (The Magic Dragon)." Arnold, Linda, *Happiness Cake*; Cassidy, Nancy,
    Nancy Cassidy's KidsSongs; Penner, Fred, *Sing with Fred*; Peter, Paul, and
    Mary, *Peter, Paul, and Mommy*; Peter, Paul, and Mary, *Peter, Paul, and
    Mommy, Too*; Roth, Kevin, *Dinosaurs and Dragons*; Roth,
    Kevin, *Travel Song Sing Alongs*; Various Artists, *A Child's
    Celebration of Song.*

"Sally and the Dragon." Knight, Tom, *The Library Boogie.*

"The Singing Dragon." Roth, Kevin, *Dinosaurs and Dragons*;
    Roth, Kevin, *Travel Song Sing Alongs.*

Elves/Fairies/Leprechauns

"Fairy House." Kaye, Mary, *I Sang It Just for You.*

"A Fairy Went A-Marketing." Herdman, Priscilla, *Daydreamer.*

"Keemo Kimo." Penner, Fred, *Rhyme a Word or Two.*

"The King of Elves." Kaye, Mary, *Mouse Jamboree.*

"Kitchen Elf." Walker, Graham, *Fiddlesticks.*

"The Leprechaun Song." Walker, Graham, *Cats' Night Out.*

"Little Pixies." Crow, Dan, *The Giggling Dragon.*

"Make Believe." Arnold, Linda, *Favorites in the Key of Fun.*

"Mist in the Jar." Lonnquist, Ken, *The Circus Kenlando.*

"Mr. Tillywinkle." Walker, Graham, *Knobbledee Knees.*

"Paddy's Hat." Walker, Graham, *Knobbledee Knees.*

"Thingamajig." Bartles, Joanie, *Put On Your Dancing Shoes.*

"Tooth Fairy Song." Troubadour, *On the Trail.*

Ghosts

"Ghost." Kinder, Brian, *Again.*

"The Ghost of Bleak House." Chapin, Tom, *Billy the Squid.*

"(Ghost) Riders in the Sky." Cassidy, Nancy, *Nancy Cassidy's KidsSongs*; Howdy,
    Buck, *Skidaddle!*

"John Russell Watkins." Penner, Fred, *Storytime.*

"Mr. Hoover's Ghost." Stotts, Stuart, *Are We There Yet?*

"Old Bastun Was Dead." Hinton, Sam, *Whoever Shall Have Some Good Peanuts*;
    Raven, Nancy, *People and Animal Songs.*

"Skin and Bones." Raffi, *More Singable Songs.*

Giants

"Climb That Beanstalk." Knight, Tom, *The Classroom Boogie.*
"Giant in Little Bitty Town." Kimmy Schwimmy, *Kimmy Schwimmy Music*, vol. 1.
"Jack and the Beanstalk." Dana, *Dana's Best Rock and Roll Fairy Tales.*
"Jack the Giant." Crow, Dan, *Dan Crow Live*; Crow, Dan, *The Giggling Dragon.*

Mermaids

"The Dolphins and the Mermaid." Lonnquist, Ken, *The Lost Songs of Kenland*; Lonnquist, Ken, *The Switcher-On of Stars.*
"The Eddystone." Peter, Paul, and Mary, *Peter, Paul, and Mommy, Too.*

Monsters

"The Apple of My Eye." Polisar, Barry Louis, *Old Dog, New Tricks.*
"Boo Boo Boogie." Tickle Tune Typhoon, *Hearts and Hands.*
"The Boogieman." Pullara, Steve, *Hop like a Frog.*
"Frank Stein." Tucker, Nancy, *Escape of the Slinkys.*
"Fred." Polisar, Barry Louis, *Old Enough to Know Better.*
"I'm Playing with a Monster." Avni, Fran, *I'm All Ears: Sing into Reading.*
"I'm Wild." The Learning Station, *Literacy in Motion.*
"Maybe the Monster." Roberts, Justin, *Meltdown!*
"Monster Boogie." Berkner, Laurie, *Buzz Buzz.*
"Monster Day." Arnold, Linda, *Peppermint Wings.*
"Monster in My Room." Frezza, Rebecca, *Music in My Head.*
"The Monster Song." Tickle Tune Typhoon, *Circle Around.*
"Monsters." Grammer, Red, *Can You Sound Just like Me?*
"Monsters and Giants." Brown, Greg, *Bathtub Blues.*
"Monsters in the Bathroom." Harley, Bill, *Monsters in the Bathroom*; Harley, Bill, *Play It Again.*
"Monsters Never Comb Their Hair." Atkinson, Lisa, *The One and Only Me.*
"There's a Werewolf under My Bed." Troubadour, *On the Trail.*
"Werewolf." SteveSongs, *On a Flying Guitar.*

Ogres/Trolls

"Billy Goat Walk." Kimmy Schwimmy, *Kimmy Schwimmy Music*, vol. 1.
"Billy Goats Gruff." McMahon, Elizabeth, *Magic Parade.*
"Even Trolls Have Moms." Scruggs, Joe, *Even Trolls Have Moms.*

"John Russell Watkins." Penner, Fred, *Storytime.*
"Mean Ogres." Kaye, Mary, *I Sang It Just for You.*
"Mighty Big Plans." Scruggs, Joe, *Bahamas Pajamas.*
"Rockabilly Goats Gruff." Knight, Tom, *The Classroom Boogie.*
"Three Billy Goats Groove." Dana, *Dana's Best Rock and Roll Fairy Tales.*
"Three Billy Goats Gruff." Greg and Steve, *Rockin' down the Road.*
"The Trouble with Trolls." Crow, Dan, *The Giggling Dragon.*

Sasquatch

"Sasquatch." Diamond, Charlotte, *10 Carrot Diamond.*

Unicorns

"Fly High Unicorn." Diamond, Charlotte, *Diamonds and Dragons.*
"The Unicorn." Tucker, Nancy, *Happy as a Clam.*
"The Unicorn Song." Abell, Timmy, *The Farmer's Market*; Cosgrove, Jim, *Stinky Feet*; Howdy, Buck, *Skidaddle!*; Various Artists, *A Child's Celebration of the World.*

Vampires

"Dracula Came to Our School." Avni, Fran, *I'm All Ears: Sing into Reading.*

Witches

"Baba Yaga." Kaye, Mary, *I Sang It Just for You.*
"John Russell Watkins." Penner, Fred, *Storytime.*
"Old Witch." Lonnquist, Ken, *Welcome 2 Kenland.*
"Voo Doo." Lonnquist, Ken, *Welcome 2 Kenland*; Lonnquist, Ken, *The Switcher-On of Stars.*
"Which Witch." Crow, Dan, *Dan Crow Live.*
"The Witch." Polisar, Barry Louis, *Old Enough to Know Better.*

Wizards

"Mr. Wizard Lizard." Arnold, Linda, *Peppermint Wings.*

Imaginary Friends

"Humpty Dumpty." Kaye, Mary, *I Sang It Just for You.*
"Imaginary Friend." McCutcheon, John, *Family Garden.*
"Me and My Invisible Friend." Ralph's World, *Green Gorilla, Monster, and Me.*

"Nobody." Trout Fishing in America, *Big Trouble*.
"Our Imaginary Rhino." Roberts, Justin, *Meltdown!*
"Zuppie Mashon." LaFond, Lois, *Turning It Upside Down*.

Imaginary Places

"Backwards Land." Palmer, Hap, *Turn On the Music*.
"Bally Roo." Knight, Tom, *The Library Boogie*.
"The Big Rock Candy Mountain." Beall, Pamela, and Susan Nipp, *Wee Sing in the Car*; Beall, Pamela, and Susan Nipp, *Wee Sing Fun 'n' Folk*; Chapin, Tom, *Family Tree*; Chapin, Tom, *Great Big Fun for the Very Little One*; Grammer, Red, *Red Grammer's Favorite Sing Along Songs*; Kirk, John, and Trish Miller, *The Big Rock Candy Mountain*.
"La La Land." Lonnquist, Ken, *Sci-Fi Hi-Fi*.
"La La Land." Trout Fishing in America, *It's a Puzzle*.
"Land of Laughter." Arnold, Linda, *Favorites in the Key of Fun*.
"Make-Believe Town." Peter, Paul, and Mary, *Peter, Paul, and Mommy*.
"Shaboozle." Knight, Tom, *Don't Kiss a Codfish*.
"Village of Gold." Green Chili Jam Band, *Coconut Moon*.

Imagination

"Back When I Could Fly." Trout Fishing in America, *Family Music Party*; Trout Fishing in America, *My World*.
"Backyard Spaceship." Roberts, Justin, *Way Out*.
"Columbus Said." McMahon, Elizabeth, *Waltzing with Fireflies*.
"Do You Wish You Could Fly?" Byers, Kathy, *Do You Wish You Could Fly?*
"Dragons and Dinosaurs." Diamond, Charlotte, *Diamonds and Dragons*.
"Dragons and Dreams and Daring Deeds." Ode, Eric, *I Love My Shoes*.
"The Gorilla Song." Raffi, *Bananaphone*.
"Hey Daddy." Various Artists, *A Child's Celebration of Song*.
"How Would You Feel If You Were a Wheel?" Penner, Fred, *Fred's Favourites*; Penner, Fred, *Sing with Fred*.
"I Believe in Make Believe." Crow, Dan, *The Giggling Dragon*.
"I Like It." Craig n Co., *Rock n Together*.
"I Think I'll Try Some." Buchman, Rachel, *Hello Everybody!*
"I Wish I Could Fly." Kimmy Schwimmy, *Kimmy Schwimmy Music*, vol. 1.
"I Wish I Were." Feldman, Jean, *Dr. Jean Sings Silly Songs*.
"I'd Like to Be." Banana Slug String Band, *Wings of Slumber*.

"I'd Love to Be . . ." Tucker, Nancy, *Glad That You Asked*.

"If I Could Be Anything." Pelham, Ruth, *Under One Sky*.

"If I Had Wings." Palmer, Hap, *Turn On the Music*.

"If I Ran the World." McCutcheon, John, *Family Garden*.

"If I Was a Bird." Old Town School of Folk Music, *Wiggleworms Love You*.

"If I Were." Abell, Timmy, *The Farmer's Market*.

"If I Were a Dog." Cosgrove, Jim, *Pick Me! Pick Me!*

"Imagination." Crow, Dan, *The Giggling Dragon*.

"Imagination." Fite, Stephen, *Gobs of Fun*.

"Imagination." Penner, Fred, *Fred's Favourites*; Penner, Fred, *Sing with Fred*; Penner, Fred, *What a Day!*

"Imagination." Rosenshontz, *Rosenshontz Greatest Hits*; Rosenshontz, *Tickles You!*

"Imagination Nation." Milkshake, *Play!*

"Imagine That." Harper, Monty, *Imagine That*.

"Imagine That!" Shontz, Bill, *The Day I Read a Book*.

"It's All How You Look at It." Rymer, Brady, *Look at My Belly*; Various Artists, *Folk Playground*.

"Jump like a Kangaroo." Barchas, Sarah, *If I Had a Pony*.

"Just Kidding." Various Artists, *Folk Playground*.

"Let's Play." Arnold, Linda, *Peppermint Wings*.

"Live in Your Imagination." Grunsky, Jack, *Jack in the Box 2*.

"Look in Your Pocket." Rymer, Brady, *Every Day Is a Birthday*.

"Magic Bike." Green Chili Jam Band, *Magic Bike*.

"Magic Scarf." Palmer, Hap, *Can Cockatoos Count by Twos?*

"Make Believe." Arnold, Linda, *Favorites in the Key of Fun*.

"My World." Trout Fishing in America, *Family Music Party*; Trout Fishing in America, *My World*.

"Open the Window." Livingston, Bob, *Open the Window*.

"Planet Mirth." Lonnquist, Ken, *The Circus Kenlando*.

"Rainbow without End." Strausman, Paul, *The World's Big Family*.

"Ruler of the Woods." Livingston, Bob, *Open the Window*.

"Superman." Kinder, Brian, *One More Time*.

"Surfin' in My Imagination." Ralph's World, *At the Bottom of the Sea*.

"Swing and Sway." Scruggs, Joe, *Even Trolls Have Moms*.

"Swinging on a Star." Bartels, Joanie, *Sillytime Magic*; Lithgow, John, *Singin' in the Bathtub*; Pease, Tom, *Boogie! Boogie! Boogie!*; Rudnick, Ben, *Fun and Games*. (Same song as "Would You Like to Swing on a Star?")

"Tower of Blocks." Ralph's World, *Green Gorilla, Monster, and Me*.

"Using Your Imagination." Harper, Monty, *Imagine That.*

"Where Do You Go." Livingston, Bob, *Open the Window.*

"Where Have You Been?" Herdman, Priscilla, *Daydreamer.*

"The Wings." Harper, Jessica, *A Wonderful Life.*

"World of Make Believe." Parachute Express, *Feel the Music.*

"Would You Like to Swing on a Star?" Muldaur, Maria, *On the Sunny Side;*
    Various Artists, *A Child's Celebration of Folk Music.* (Same song as
    "Swinging on a Star.")

Insects

"B3 (Bee Boppin' Boogie)." Frezza, Rebecca, *Road Trip.*

"Bugs." Beall, Pamela, and Susan Nipp, *Wee Sing and Pretend.*

"Bugs." Rosenshontz, *Uh-Oh!*

"The Bugs Are A-Comin'." Beall, Pamela, and Susan Nipp, *Wee Sing in the Car.*

"Escape of the Bugs." Harper, Monty, *Jungle Junk!*

"Flea Fly." Allard, Peter and Ellen, *Sing It! Say It! Stamp It! Sway It!* vol. 2;
    Sharon, Lois, and Bram, *One Elephant, Deux Éléphants.*

"I Am an Insect." Tickle Tune Typhoon, *Singing Science.*

"The Kid Who Ate a Bug." Harper, Monty, *Jungle Junk!*

"My Brother Eats Bugs." Mayer, Hans, *See You Later, Alligator.*

"My Favorite Kind of Bugs." Howdy, Buck, *Giddyup!*

"Never Swat a Fly." Muldaur, Maria, *On the Sunny Side.*

"No Bones Within." Banana Slug String Band, *Adventures on the Air Cycle;*
    Banana Slug String Band, *Singing in Our Garden.*

"Poor Little Bug." Walker, Graham, *Jumpety Jump.*

"The Terrible Bug." Pirtle, Sarah, *The Wind Is Telling Secrets.*

"There Ain't No Bugs on Me." Garcia, Jerry, and David Grisman, *Not for Kids
    Only;* Various Artists, *A Child's Celebration of Folk Music.*

Ants

"Ants." Avni, Fran, *Tuning into Nature.*

"Ants." Banana Slug String Band, *Penguin Parade.*

"The Ants Go Marching." Beall, Pamela, and Susan Nipp, *Wee Sing Animals,
    Animals, Animals;* Beall, Pamela, and Susan Nipp, *Wee Sing Silly Songs;*
    Colleen and Uncle Squaty, *Rumble to the Bottom;* The Learning Station,
    Get Funky and Musical Fun; Sharon, Lois, and Bram, *Everybody Sing!;*
    Strausman, Paul, *Camels, Cats, and Rainbows.*

"The Ants' Great Escape." Mayer, Hans, *See You Later, Alligator*.

"The Ants in Your Pants Dance." The Chenille Sisters, *Teaching Hippopotami to Fly!*

"The Ants' Picnic." Mayer, Hans, *Just a Little Hug*.

"The Farm." Scruggs, Joe, *Ants*.

"The Parade." Scruggs, Joe, *Ants*.

"We Are Ants." Ralph's World, *The Amazing Adventures of Kid Astro*.

Bees

"Baby Bumblebee." Beall, Pamela, and Susan Nipp, *Wee Sing Animals, Animals, Animals*; Beall, Pamela, and Susan Nipp, *Wee Sing Silly Songs*. (Same song as "Bringing Home a Baby Bumble Bee" and "Gifts for Mommy.")

"Be the Best Bee." Tucker, Nancy, *Escape of the Slinkys*.

"The Bee and the Pup." Beall, Pamela, and Susan Nipp, *Wee Sing Fun 'n' Folk*.

"Bee Song." Raven, Nancy, *You Gotta Juba*.

"Bee-I-Ee." Walker, Graham, *Fiddlesticks*.

"Boogie Woogie Dancin' Bear." Coffey, James, *Animal Groove*.

"Bringing Home a Baby Bumble Bee." Feldman, Jean, *Dr. Jean Sings Silly Songs*. (Same song as "Baby Bumblebee" and "Gifts for Mommy.")

"Bumble Bee Boogie." Arnold, Linda, *Happiness Cake*.

"Bumblebee (Buzz Buzz)." Berkner, Laurie, *Buzz Buzz*.

"The Bumblebee Song." Polisar, Barry Louis, *Old Dog, New Tricks*.

"Busy Little Honey Bee." Strausman, Paul, *Blue Jay, Blue Jay!*

"Buzzing in the Garden." Allard, Peter and Ellen, *Pizza Pizzaz*.

"Fiddle Dee Dee." Beall, Pamela, and Susan Nipp, *Wee Sing Nursery Rhymes and Lullabies*; Raven, Nancy, *People and Animal Songs*.

"Gifts for Mommy." Peterson, Carole, *Sticky Bubble Gum*. (Same song as "Baby Bumblebee" and "Bringing Home a Baby Bumble Bee.")

"Honey, Honey, Honey." Kaldor, Connie, *A Duck in New York City*.

"Honeybee." Knight, Tom, *The Library Boogie*.

"I Hear a Bee." Moo, Anna, *Making Moosic*.

"Says the Bee." Ungar, Jay, and Lyn Hardy, *A Place to Be*.

"What Do You Suppose?" McGrath, Bob, and Katherine Smithrim, *Songs and Games for Toddlers*.

Beetles

"Alexander Beetle." Abell, Timmy, *I Know an Old Lady*.

Boll Weevils

"The Boll Weevil." Beall, Pamela, and Susan Nipp, *Wee Sing Animals, Animals, Animals.*

Butterflies/Moths/Caterpillars

"Arabella Miller." Beall, Pamela, and Susan Nipp, *Wee Sing in the Car*; Sharon, Lois, and Bram, *Mainly Mother Goose*; Sharon, Lois, and Bram, *Name Games.* (Same song as "Little Arabella Miller.")

"Butterflies Fly." Charette, Rick, *A Little Peace and Quiet.*

"Butterfly." Arnold, Linda, *Favorites in the Key of Fun.*

"Butterfly." Atkinson, Lisa, *The Elephant in Aisle Four.*

"The Butterfly." Feldman, Jean, *Dr. Jean Sings Silly Songs.*

"Butterfly." Magical Music Express, *Friendship Stew.*

"Butterfly." McMahon, Elizabeth, *Waltzing with Fireflies.*

"The Butterfly Waltz." Big Jeff, *Big Jeff.*

"Butterfly Wishes." Pirtle, Sarah, *Heart of the World.*

"Caterpillar." Moos, Anna, *When I Was a Child.*

"Caterpillar Dance." Knight, Tom, *Don't Kiss a Codfish.*

"Friends." Walker, Mary Lu, *The Frog's Party.*

"Hey Caterpillar." Avni, Fran, *I'm All Ears: Sing into Reading.*

"Hungry Caterpillar." The Learning Station, *Literacy in Motion*; The Learning Station, *Seasonal Songs in Motion.*

"The Inchworm." Lithgow, John, *Singin' in the Bathtub*; Raven, Nancy, *Friends and Family.*

"Kelly the Caterpillar." Rosen, Gary, *Cookin'*; Rosen, Gary, *Pet Sounds.*

"Little Arabella Miller." Allard, Peter and Ellen, *Sing It! Say It! Stamp It! Sway It!* vol. 2; Colleen and Uncle Squaty, *Rumble to the Bottom.* (Same song as "Arabella Miller.")

"The Little Caterpillar." Beall, Pamela, and Susan Nipp, *Wee Sing and Pretend.*

"Mariposa." Barchas, Sarah, *¡Piñata! and More.*

"Metamorphosis." Lonnquist, Ken, *Earthy Songs.*

"The Wooly Booger." Paxton, Tom, *I've Got a Yo-Yo.*

Cockroaches

"Cockroach Conga." Pullara, Steve, *Spinning Tails.*

"Las Cucarachas." Moos, Anna, *When I Was a Child.*

Crickets

"The Cricket Song." Walker, Mary Lu, *The Frog's Party*.

Fireflies

"Dad Caught Stars." Roberts, Justin, *Not Naptime*.

"Fireflies." Harley, Bill, *I Wanna Play*.

"Fireflies." Moo, Anna, *Anna Moo Crackers*.

"Firefly." Zanes, Dan, *Night Time!*

"Firefly Time." Pease, Tom, *Daddy Starts to Dance*.

"Flickerbug." Lonnquist, Ken, *Earthy Songs*; Lonnquist, Ken, *The Switcher-On of Stars*.

"The Lightning Bug Song." The Chenille Sisters, *Teaching Hippopotami to Fly!*

"Little Light of Mine." Rosenshontz, *Rock 'n Roll Teddy Bear*.

"Waltzing with Fireflies." McMahon, Elizabeth, *Waltzing with Fireflies*.

Flies/Fleas

"Baby Bye." Beall, Pamela, and Susan Nipp, *Wee Sing for Baby*.

"Fiddle Dee Dee." Beall, Pamela, and Susan Nipp, *Wee Sing Nursery Rhymes and Lullabies*; Raven, Nancy, *People and Animal Songs*.

"A Flea and a Fly in a Flue." Fink, Cathy, *Grandma Slid down the Mountain*; Fink, Cathy, and Marcy Marxer, *A Cathy & Marcy Collection for Kids*.

"Fleas." Colleen and Uncle Squaty, *Rumble to the Bottom*.

"Juicy Black Fly." Rudnick, Ben, *Blast Off!*

"Little Flea." Beall, Pamela, and Susan Nipp, *Wee Sing for Baby*.

"Shoo Fly." Beall, Pamela, and Susan Nipp, *Wee Sing Fun 'n' Folk*; Mitchell, Elizabeth, *You Are My Flower*; Raven, Nancy, *Hop, Skip, and Sing*; Sweet Honey in the Rock, *I Got Shoes*.

"Spider and the Fly." Lonnquist, Ken, *Sci-Fi Hi-Fi*.

"Spider and the Fly." Tucker, Nancy, *Escape of the Slinkys*.

Grasshoppers

"Grasshopper." Beall, Pamela, and Susan Nipp, *Wee Sing Animals, Animals, Animals*; Beall, Pamela, and Susan Nipp, *Wee Sing Silly Songs*.

"Grasshopper." Grunsky, Jack, *Follow the Leader*; Grunsky, Jack, *Sing and Dance*.

"Grasshoppers Three." Beall, Pamela, and Susan Nipp, *Wee Sing Fun 'n' Folk*.

Ladybugs

"The Best Bugs of All Bugs." Crow, Dan, *Oops!*
"Ladybug." Beall, Pamela, and Susan Nipp, *Wee Sing Animals, Animals, Animals.*
"The Ladybug and the Moon." Roth, Kevin, *Travel Song Sing Alongs.*
"Ladybug Picnic." Mitchell, Elizabeth, *You Are My Sunshine.*

Mosquitoes

"The Mosquito." Beall, Pamela, and Susan Nipp, *Wee Sing Animals, Animals, Animals.*
"Mosquito." Simmons, Al, *The Celery Stalks at Midnight.*
"Pesky Mosquitoes." Charette, Rick, *Toad Motel.*
"Tiny Mosquito." Madsen, Gunnar, *Old Mr. Mackle Hackle.*

Islands

"Island Rock." Banana Slug String Band, *Slugs at Sea.*
"Lazy Island Melody." Grunsky, Jack, *Like a Flower to the Sun.*
"Pig Island." Boynton, Sandra, *Philadelphia Chickens.*
"Rainbow Island." Dana, *Dana's Best Travelin' Tunes.*
"Stuck on a Rock." Lonnquist, Ken, *The Switcher-On of Stars.*
"Swing and Sway." Scruggs, Joe, *Even Trolls Have Moms.*
"This Little Island." Banana Slug String Band, *Wings of Slumber.*
"Tiger Island." Knight, Tom, *Easy as Pie.*
"Twisting Low." Rudnick, Ben, *Fun and Games.*

Jokes and Riddles

"Animal Quiz." Palmer, Hap, *Can a Cherry Pie Wave Goodbye?*
"Eye Spy." Foote, Norman, *Shake a Leg.*
"Food Jokes." Fink, Cathy, and Marcy Marxer, *Bon Appétit!*
"Knock Knock." Mayer, Hans, *Stars of the Swing Set.*
"The Limerick Song." Fink, Cathy, and Marcy Marxer, *Scat like That.*
"Noses." Banana Slug String Band, *Penguin Parade.*
"A Riddle in the Middle." Fink, Cathy, and Marcy Marxer, *Scat like That.*
"The Riddle Song." Beall, Pamela, and Susan Nipp, *Wee Sing Sing-Alongs*; Greg and Steve, *Fun and Games*; Staines, Bill, *One More River.*
"The Riddle Song." Various Artists, *A Child's Celebration of Silliest Songs.*
"Who Am I?" Parachute Express, *Feel the Music.*
"Why'd the Chicken Cross the Road." Rudnick, Ben, *Blast Off!*

Jungles/Rainforests

"A Forest in the Rain." Chapin, Tom, *Around the World and Back Again.*

"In the Jungle." Rosenthal, Phil, *Animal Songs*; Rosenthal, Phil, *Folksongs and Bluegrass for Children.*

"Jungle Junk." Harper, Monty, *Jungle Junk!*

"On into the Amazon." Tickle Tune Typhoon, *Singing Science.*

"Out in the Jungle." Cosgrove, Jim, *Bop Bop Dinosaur*; Cosgrove, Jim, *Stinky Feet.*

"Rumble in the Jungle." Kimmy Schwimmy, *Kimmy Schwimmy Music*, vol. 1.

"Toucan." Lonnquist, Ken, *Earthy Songs*; Lonnquist, Ken, *Sci-Fi Hi-Fi.*

Kindness

"A Beautiful Way." Vitamin L, *Everyone's Invited!*

"Bon Jour!" Various Artists, *A Child's Celebration of the World.*

"Caring and Compassion." Grammer, Red, *Be Bop Your Best!*

"Do Be Do Good." Rosenshontz, *Rock 'n Roll Teddy Bear.*

"Everyday Angel." Diamond, Charlotte, *Diamonds and Daydreams.*

"Helping Hand." Gemini, *The Best of Gemini*, vol. 2.

"Hero." SteveSongs, *Marvelous Day!*

"If We Care." Gemini, *The Best of Gemini*, vol. 2.

"Kindness." Grammer, Red, *Be Bop Your Best!*

"Kindness." SteveSongs, *Little Superman.*

"Less of Me." Staines, Bill, *One More River.*

"Simple Act of Kindness." Kinnoin, Dave, *Getting Bigger.*

"That Is a Mighty Power." Vitamin L, *Everyone's Invited!*

"Try to Be Nice to Everybody." Mr. Al, *Put Your Groove On.*

"You Made Me a Pallet on the Floor." Sharon, Lois, and Bram, *Sleepytime.*

"You're Never Alone." Grunsky, Jack, *Sing and Dance.*

Kisses

"Blow a Kiss." Berkner, Laurie, *Under a Shady Tree.*

"Kiss a Cow." Crow, Dan, *Oops!*

"Puppy Kisses." Atkinson, Lisa, *The Elephant in Aisle Four.*

"The Sloppy Kiss." Rosen, Gary, *Teddy Bears' Picnic.*

Kites

"If I Were a Kite." Frezza, Rebecca, *Music in My Head.*
"If I Were a Kite." Moo, Anna, *Making Moosic.*
"The Tea Tale." Ralph's World, *The Amazing Adventures of Kid Astro.*

Languages

"All around the World." Fink, Cathy, and Marcy Marxer, *Pillow Full of Wishes.*
"Aloha." Silberg, "Miss Jackie," *The Complete Sniggles, Squirrels, and Chicken Pox.*
"Cataplin." Various Artists, *Hear and Gone in 60 Seconds.*
"The Children of the World Say Hello." Barchas, Sarah, *Bridges across the World.*
"The Days of the Week." Diamond, Charlotte, *Diamond in the Rough.*
"Dreams of Harmony." Pease, Tom, *Daddy Starts to Dance*; Various Artists, *A Child's Celebration of the World.*
"Everybody Loves Saturday Night." Gemini, *The Best of Gemini*, vol. 2.
"Everyone Counts." Moo, Anna, *Anna Moo Crackers.*
"Four Little Duckies." Ralph's World, *Ralph's World.*
"Frère Jacques." Barchas, Sarah, *Bridges across the World.*
"Goodbye." Yosi, *Monkey Business.*
"Good-bye My Friends." Palmer, Hap, *Can a Jumbo Jet Sing the Alphabet?*
"Happy Birthday around the World." Barchas, Sarah, *Bridges across the World.*
"'Happy Birthday' around the World." Rymer, Brady, *Every Day Is a Birthday.*
"Hello." Arnold, Linda, *Peppermint Wings.*
"Hello." Gemini, *The Best of Gemini.*
"Hello." Zanes, Dan, *Rocket Ship Beach.*
"Hello and How Are You?" Old Town School of Folk Music, *Wiggleworms Love You.*
"Hello, Hello, Hello." Fink, Cathy, and Marcy Marxer, *Nobody Else like Me.*
"Hello to the Children of the World." Beall, Pamela, and Susan Nipp, *Wee Sing around the World.*
"How Do You Say Yes?" Silberg, "Miss Jackie," *Joining Hands with Other Lands.*
"Howdy Song." Harper, Monty, *Take Me to Your Library.*
"If You Will Be My Friend." Barchas, Sarah, *Bridges across the World.*
"It Only Takes a Minute." Fink, Cathy, and Marcy Marxer, *Scat like That*; Various Artists, *Hear and Gone in 60 Seconds.*
"Languages We Speak." Barchas, Sarah, *¡Piñata! and More.*
"Learning Languages." Magical Music Express, *Friendship Stew.*
"Look through the Kaleidoscope." Diamond, Charlotte, *Charlotte Diamond's World.*

"Many Ways to Say Hello." Silberg, "Miss Jackie," *Joining Hands with Other Lands*.

"Numbers All Around." LaFond, Lois, *Turning It Upside Down*.

"On a Vacation." The Chenille Sisters, *Teaching Hippopotami to Fly!*; Various Artists, *A Child's Celebration of the World*.

"One Two Three." Barchas, Sarah, *Bridges across the World*.

"One World." LaFond, Lois, *One World*.

"Part of the Family." LaFond, Lois, *Lois LaFond and the Rockadiles*; LaFond, Lois, *One World*.

"Peace." Barchas, Sarah, *Bridges across the World*.

"Peace in Twelve Languages." Knight, Tom, *The Classroom Boogie*.

"Please." Barchas, Sarah, *Bridges across the World*.

"Please Is a Pleasant Expression." Jenkins, Ella, *Songs Children Love to Sing*; Various Artists, *cELLAbration! A Tribute to Ella Jenkins*.

"Rapp Song." Grammer, Red, *Teaching Peace*.

"'Round the World with Ways to Say Hello." Palmer, Hap, *Can a Jumbo Jet Sing the Alphabet?*

"Siyanibingelela." Grunsky, Jack, *Jack in the Box 1*; Grunsky, Jack, *World Safari*.

"Thank You." Barchas, Sarah, *Bridges across the World*.

"Time to Say Goodbye." Barchas, Sarah, *Bridges across the World*.

"Way over There." Colleen and Uncle Squaty, *1, 2, 3, Four-Ever Friends*.

"The Wonderful World of Yes." Chapin, Tom, *Around the World and Back Again*.

"Yes/No." Barchas, Sarah, *Bridges across the World*.

"Yes to the World." Tickle Tune Typhoon, *Singing Science*.

African Languages

"Adukbe." Various Artists, *World Playground 2*. (Baka)

"African Numbers 8." Sweet Honey in the Rock, *I Got Shoes*. (Swahili)

"Akwa Nwa Nere Nnwa." Beall, Pamela, and Susan Nipp, *Wee Sing around the World*. (Ibo)

"Barco di Papel." Various Artists, *African Playground*. (Crioulo)

"Battú." Various Artists, *African Playground*. (Yoruba)

"Bebe Moke (Baby So Small)." Beall, Pamela, and Susan Nipp, *Wee Sing around the World*. (Lingala)

"Chay Chay Koolay." Barchas, Sarah, *Bridges across the World*. (Same song as "Che Che Koolay," "Je Je Kule," and "Kye Kye Kule.")

"Che Che Koolay." Colleen and Uncle Squaty, *Movin' Party*. (Same song as "Chay Chay Koolay," "Je Je Kule," and "Kye Kye Kule.")

"Fatou Yo (I Am Fatou)." Various Artists, *World Playground*. (Mandingo)

"Finger Dance." Ladysmith Black Mambazo, *Gift of the Tortoise*. (Zulu)

"Funga Alafia." Barchas, Sarah, *Bridges across the World*; Magical Music Express, *Friendship Stew*. (Liberian/Yoruba)

"Harambe." Various Artists, *Reggae Playground*. (Swahili)

"Hoya Hoye." Various Artists, *African Playground*. (Amharic)

"Hendry." Various Artists, *African Playground*. (Malagasy)

"Ise Oluwa." Sweet Honey in the Rock, *All for Freedom*. (Yoruba)

"Jambo." Various Artists, *cELLAbration! A Tribute to Ella Jenkins*. (Zulu)

"Jambo Bwana." Various Artists, *African Playground*. (Zulu)

"Je Je Kule." Gemini, *The Best of Gemini*, vol. 2; Parachute Express, *Doctor Looney's Remedy*. (Same song as "Chay Chay Koolay," "Che Che Koolay," and "Kye Kye Kule.")

"Kanje Kanje." Ladysmith Black Mambazo, *Gift of the Tortoise*. (Zulu)

"Kanyoni Kanja (Little Bird Outside)." Beall, Pamela, and Susan Nipp, *Wee Sing around the World*. (Kikuyu)

"Kwanzaa." The Learning Station, *Literacy in Motion*; The Learning Station, *Seasonal Songs in Motion*. (Swahili)

"Kye Kye Kule." Fink, Cathy, and Marcy Marxer, *Nobody Else like Me*. (Same song as "Chay Chay Koolay," "Che Che Koolay," and "Je Je Kule.")

"Laba Laba." Various Artists, *African Playground*. (Yoruba)

"Langa Mo." Various Artists, *African Playground*. (Zulu)

"Mbube." Various Artists, *African Playground*. (Zulu)

"Munomuno." Various Artists, *African Playground*. (Luganda)

"Nezha." Various Artists, *World Playground 2*. (Tamazight)

"Nomyekelo." Ladysmith Black Mambazo, *Gift of the Tortoise*. (Zulu)

"Paparam Vingo." Ladysmith Black Mambazo, *Gift of the Tortoise*. (Zulu)

"Pata Pata." Various Artists, *A Child's Celebration of the World*.

"Pata Pata 2000." Various Artists, *World Playground 2*. (Xhosa)

"Peace Be with You." Ladysmith Black Mambazo, *Gift of the Tortoise*. (Zulu)

"Pigogo." Zanes, Dan, *Catch That Train!* (Zulu)

"Rain Chant." Ladysmith Black Mambazo, *Gift of the Tortoise*. (Zulu)

"Shabalala." Ladysmith Black Mambazo, *Gift of the Tortoise*. (Zulu)

"Shango." Barchas, Sarah, *Bridges across the World*.

"Sangoma." Various Artists, *African Playground*. (Zulu)

"She She Ko Le." Pirtle, Sarah, *The Wind Is Telling Secrets*. (Hausa)

"Siyahamba." Zanes, Dan, *Night Time!* (South Africa)

"Sobonana Kusasa." Old Town School of Folk Music, *Wiggleworms Love You*;
Pease, Tom, *Boogie! Boogie! Boogie!* (Zulu)

"Somagwaza." Sweet Honey in the Rock, *I Got Shoes*. (Bantu)

"Somagwaza/Hey, Motswala." Peter, Paul, and Mary, *Peter, Paul, and Mommy,
Too*. (Bantu)

"Swahili Counting Song." The Learning Station, *Literacy in Motion*. (Swahili)

"Tama Tama Tamali." Sweet Honey in the Rock, *I Got Shoes*.

"Thekwane." Ladysmith Black Mambazo, *Gift of the Tortoise*. (Zulu)

"There Come Our Mothers." Ladysmith Black Mambazo, *Gift of the Tortoise*;
Various Artists, *A Child's Celebration of the World*. (Zulu)

"Thula Mama." Various Artists, *Dreamland*. (Xhosa)

"Tsenzenina." Various Artists, *I'm Gonna Let It Shine*.

"Tue Tue." Beall, Pamela, and Susan Nipp, *Wee Sing around the World*; Harley,
Bill, *There's a Pea on My Plate*.

"Tuwe Tuwe." Sweet Honey in the Rock, *Still the Same Me*. (Ghana)

"Two Shelleni." Ladysmith Black Mambazo, *Gift of the Tortoise*. (Zulu)

"Le Vieil Elephant." Various Artists, *Reggae Playground*. (Pulaar)

"Vulani Ring! Ring." Ladysmith Black Mambazo, *Gift of the Tortoise*. (Zulu)

"Zaminamina." Pease, Tom, *Daddy Starts to Dance*. (Senegal)

American Indian

"Anishanabe." Various Artists, *A Child's Celebration of the World*.

"Mother Earth." Pirtle, Sarah, *Magical Earth*. (Navajo)

"Uhé Basho Sho." Beall, Pamela, and Susan Nipp, *Wee Sing around the World*.
(Omaha)

"Wosho Paiute Bannock Lullaby." Barchas, Sarah, *Bridges across the World*.

"Yhanawy Hay Yowna." Various Artists, *The Planet Sleeps*. (Iroquois)

Arabic

"Clam Fishing." Raven, Nancy, *The House We Live In*, vols. 1 and 2.

"Saba Il Xheer." Stotts, Stuart, *Are We There Yet?*

Bahasa Indonesia

"Pat Gulipat." Various Artists, *Reggae Playground*.

Bararra

"Yi-Rrana." Various Artists, *Dreamland*.

Basque

"Zuhaitzarena." Various Artists, *World Playground 2.*

Cantonese

"The Bamboo Flute." Grunsky, Jack, *Playground.*
"May There Always Be Sunshine." Diamond, Charlotte, *10 Carrot Diamond.*

Creole

"Ying Yang." Various Artists, *Reggae Playground.*

Danish

"En Enebær Busk (The Mulberry Bush)." Beall, Pamela, and Susan Nipp, *Wee Sing around the World.*

Dutch

"Alle Eendjes." Beall, Pamela, and Susan Nipp, *Wee Sing around the World.*

Finnish

"Piri Pieni Pyörii (The Circle Goes Around)." Beall, Pamela, and Susan Nipp, *Wee Sing around the World.*

French

"African Numbers 10." Sweet Honey in the Rock, *I Got Shoes.*
"Allons Danser, Colinda." Grunsky, Jack, *Sing and Dance.*
"Alouette." Penner, Fred, *Sing with Fred*; Silberg, "Miss Jackie," *Sing It Again Please.*
"La Bastringue." Diamond, Charlotte, *Diamond in the Rough.*
"Bats ta pâte (Making Bread)." Diamond, Charlotte, *My Bear Gruff.*
"A Beautiful Day." Rosen, Gary, *Teddy Bears' Picnic.*
"Bon Jour." Various Artists, *A Child's Celebration of the World.*
"Bon Soir Mes Amis." Penner, Fred, *Rhyme a Word or Two.*
"Bonjour, Bonjour." Various Artists, *French Playground.*
"Bonjour, Mes Amis." Pirtle, Sarah, *Heart of the World.*
"Chatouiller le Ciel Avec Toi." Various Artists, *French Playground.*
"Clam Fishing." Raven, Nancy, *The House We Live In*, vols. 1 and 2.
"Clic-Clac Oh C'est Beau!" Various Artists, *French Playground.*
"Collinda." Diamond, Charlotte, *Diamond in the Rough.*

"Croque." Various Artists, *French Playground*.

"Donne-Moi la Main (Give Me Your Hand)." Diamond, Charlotte, *Diamond in the Rough*.

"Embrasse Quatre Fois." Diamond, Charlotte, *10 Carrot Diamond*.

"Everybody Loves Saturday Night." Silberg, "Miss Jackie," *Sing It Again Please*.

"Fais Do Do." Raffi, *Quiet Time*; Raffi, *One Light One Sun*; Various Artists, *The Planet Sleeps*.

"Fais Do Do/Rock-a-Bye Baby." Sharon, Lois, and Bram, *Mainly Mother Goose*.

"First Lullaby." Herdman, Priscilla, *Stardreamer*; Staines, Bill, *The Happy Wanderer*.

"Frère Jacques." Beall, Pamela, and Susan Nipp, *Wee Sing around the World*; Jenkins, Ella, *Sharing Cultures with Ella Jenkins*; McGrath, Bob, *Sing Along with Bob #2*; Raffi, *Corner Grocery Store*; Walker, Graham, *Knobbledee Knees*.

"Frère Jacques/This Is the Way." Tickle Tune Typhoon, *Patty-Cakes and Peek-a-Boos*.

"Good Morning Sunshine." Grunsky, Jack, *Follow the Leader*; Grunsky, Jack, *Jack in the Box 2*.

"I Am a Pizza." Diamond, Charlotte, *10 Carrot Diamond*.

"J'ai Perdu le 'Do' de Ma Clarinette." Diamond, Charlotte, *10 Carrot Diamond*.

"Jamais on n'a Vu." Sharon, Lois, and Bram, *Sleepytime*.

"L'île Maurice." Various Artists, *French Playground*.

"Lutece." Various Artists, *French Playground*.

"Le Martin en Patins." Various Artists, *French Playground*.

"May There Always Be Sunshine." Diamond, Charlotte, *10 Carrot Diamond*.

"Michaud." Raffi, *Rise and Shine*; Sharon, Lois, and Bram, *One Elephant, Deux Éléphants*.

"Mon Corps." Old Town School of Folk Music, *Wiggleworms Love You*.

"Mon Petit Bonhomme." Various Artists, *Reggae Playground*.

"Monsieur Bibendum." Various Artists, *French Playground*.

"One Elephant." Sharon, Lois, and Bram, *Great Big Hits*; Sharon, Lois, and Bram, *One Elephant, Deux Éléphants*; Sharon, Lois, and Bram, *School Days*.

"Petit Français." Various Artists, *French Playground*.

"Les Petites Marionnettes." Grunsky, Jack, *Jack in the Box 2*; Raffi, *More Singable Songs*.

"Les Petits Poissons." Sharon, Lois, and Bram, *Sleepytime*; Sharon, Lois, and Bram, *Sing A to Z*.

"La P'tite Monnaie." Various Artists, *French Playground*.

"Rainbows." LaFond, Lois, *I Am Who I Am*; LaFond, Lois, *Turning It Upside Down*.

"Savez-Vous Planter les Choux?" Raffi, *Everything Grows*; Raven, Nancy, *Jambalaya!*; Sharon, Lois, and Bram, *Great Big Hits*; Sharon, Lois, and Bram, *Mainly Mother Goose*.

"Sensation (Bidi Bom Bom)." Various Artists, *French Playground*.

"Tete, Epaules." Raffi, *Rise and Shine*.

"To Everyone in All the World." Raffi, *Baby Beluga*.

"The Train of Beauty (Le Train de Beauté)." Roth, Kevin, *Train Songs and Other Tracks*.

"Tu Cantarás, Yo Cantaré." Jenkins, Ella, *Songs Children Love to Sing*.

"La Vie en Rose." Simmons, Al, *The Celery Stalks at Midnight*.

"Le Vieil Eléphant." Various Artists, *Reggae Playground*.

"Votek Zouk." Various Artists, *Caribbean Playground*.

"We're Gonna Shine." Penner, Fred, *Fred's Favourites*; Penner, Fred, *Sing with Fred*.

"Wonderful." Various Artists, *French Playground*.

"Y'a un Chat (The Cat at the Door)." Diamond, Charlotte, *My Bear Gruff*.

"Y'a un Rat—Sur le Pont D'Avignon." Raffi, *Corner Grocery Store*.

"Les Zombies et les Loups-Garou." Raffi, *Corner Grocery Store*.

German

"Alle Meine Entchen (All My Little Darlings)." Beall, Pamela, and Susan Nipp, *Wee Sing around the World*.

"May There Always Be Sunshine." Diamond, Charlotte, *10 Carrot Diamond*.

"Oh How Lovely Is the Evening." Barchas, Sarah, *Bridges across the World*.

"Schlafe Mein Prinzchen, Schlaf Ein." Various Artists, *The Planet Sleeps*.

Greek

"Pou'n-do To Dachtilidi (Where Is the Ring)." Beall, Pamela, and Susan Nipp, *Wee Sing around the World*.

"Tik Tik Tak." Various Artists, *World Playground*.

Hawaiian

"Haleakala." Crow, Dan, *A Friend, a Laugh, a Walk in the Woods*.

"Nani Wale Na Hala (Pretty Hala Trees)." Beall, Pamela, and Susan Nipp, *Wee Sing around the World*.

"This Little Island." Banana Slug String Band, *Wings of Slumber*.

Hebrew

"Celtic Hinei Mah Tov." Allard, Peter and Ellen, *Pizza Pizzaz*.

"Hava Nagila." Barchas, Sarah, *Bridges across the World*.

"Mayim, Mayim (Water, Water)." Fink, Cathy, and Marcy Marxer, *All Wound Up!*

"Noomey." Various Artists, *The Planet Sleeps.*
"Numi Numi." Various Artists, *Dreamland.*
"Tzena Tzena." Sharon, Lois, and Bram, *Sing A to Z.*
"Zichronot M'Africa (Memories of Africa)." Various Artists, *World Playground.*
"Zum Gali Gali." Beall, Pamela, and Susan Nipp, *Wee Sing around the World.*

Hindi

"Teri Yaadein." Various Artists, *World Playground 2.*

Icelandic

"Sofdu Unga Astin Min." Miss Amy, *Wide, Wide World.*

Italian

"Bada Bing, Buon Natale." Pullara, Steve, *A Big Bowl of Musicroni.*
"Eh Cumpari." Pullara, Steve, *A Big Bowl of Musicroni*; Pullara, Steve, *Hop like a Frog.*
"Fala Nina, Fala Nana." Various Artists, *A Child's Celebration of the World.*
"The Flood." Pirtle, Sarah, *Magical Earth.*
"I Papaveri (The Poppy Song)." Chapin, Tom, *Around the World and Back Again.*
"Italian Rhyme." Various Artists, *A Child's Celebration of the World.*
"Mio Galletto (My Little Rooster)." Beall, Pamela, and Susan Nipp, *Wee Sing around the World.*
"Say It Right." Pullara, Steve, *A Big Bowl of Musicroni.*

Japanese

"African Numbers 12." Sweet Honey in the Rock, *I Got Shoes.*
"Aka Tonbo." Various Artists, *Asian Dreamland.*
"Amami No Komori Uta." Various Artists, *Asian Dreamland.*
"Ame, Ame (Rain Song)." Beall, Pamela, and Susan Nipp, *Wee Sing around the World.*
"Bento Uri." Raven, Nancy, *Jambalaya!*
"Dokokade Yoruga Naita." Various Artists, *Asian Dreamland.*
"The Frog's Story." Magical Music Express, *Friendship Stew.*
"Goldfish." Raven, Nancy, *The House We Live In,* vols. 1 and 2.
"Haru Ga Kita." Raffi, *Everything Grows*; Raffi, *Quiet Time.*
"Itsuki No Komoriuta." Various Artists, *The Planet Sleeps.*
"Japanese Rain Song." Barchas, Sarah, *Bridges across the World.*
"Konnichi-wa." Moo, Anna, *Moochas Gracias.*

"Moon Boat." Various Artists, *Asian Dreamland.*
"One Crane." Pease, Tom, *Wobbi-Do-Wop!*
"Zousan (Little Elephant)." Mitchell, Elizabeth, *You Are My Little Bird.*

Korean

"Arirang." Beall, Pamela, and Susan Nipp, *Wee Sing around the World*; Raven, Nancy, *Friends and Family.*
"Pom Na Tu Ri (Springtime Outing)." Mitchell, Elizabeth, *You Are My Little Bird.*

Ladino

"Durme Durme." Various Artists, *Dreamland.*

Malagasy

"Ny Fitiavako An'I Mama." Various Artists, *Dreamland.*

Malaysian

"Pok Amai Amai." Beall, Pamela, and Susan Nipp, *Wee Sing around the World.*

Mandarin

"Fong Swei." Beall, Pamela, and Susan Nipp, *Wee Sing around the World.*

Maori

"Epo I Tai Tai E (I Will Be Happy)." Beall, Pamela, and Susan Nipp, *Wee Sing around the World.*
"Moe Moe." Various Artists, *The Planet Sleeps.*

Maya

"Hanal Weech." Various Artists, *Latin Playground.*

Norwegian

"Ro, Ro Til Fiskeskjaer (Row, Row to the Fishing Spot)." Beall, Pamela, and Susan Nipp, *Wee Sing around the World.*

Patua (Brazil and French Guiana)

"Nazaré Pereira." Various Artists, *World Playground.*

Pitjantjatjara (Australian Aboriginal)

"Nyanpi Matilda (Waltzing Matilda)." Various Artists, *World Playground*.

Portuguese

"As Meninas dos Meus Olhos." Various Artists, *Reggae Playground*.

"Bonjour Pra Você (Good Morning to You)." Various Artists, *World Playground*.

"Ciranda (Circle Game)." Beall, Pamela, and Susan Nipp, *Wee Sing around the World*.

"Let's Go." Parachute Express, *Don't Blink*.

"Rodopiou." Various Artists, *Latin Playground*.

"Lá Vai Alguém." Various Artists, *Dreamland*.

Russian

"By-ush Ki By-u." Chapin, Tom, *Around the World and Back Again*.

"Lullaby." Various Artists, *Dreamland*.

"May There Always Be Sunshine." Diamond, Charlotte, *10 Carrot Diamond*; Fink, Cathy, and Marcy Marxer, *Nobody Else like Me*; Gemini, *The Best of Gemini*, vol. 2; Pease, Tom, *Boogie! Boogie! Boogie!*; Pirtle, Sarah, *Two Hands Hold the Earth*; Raffi, *Let's Play*; Raven, Nancy, *The House We Live In*, vols. 1 and 2.

"Rushing around Russia." Various Artists, *cELLAbration! A Tribute to Ella Jenkins*.

Spanish

"African Numbers 16." Sweet Honey in the Rock, *I Got Shoes*.

"Al Tambor." Raven, Nancy, *The House We Live In*, vols. 1 and 2.

"América Baila." Various Artists, *Latin Playground*.

"La Arāna Picua." Various Artists, *Latin Playground*.

"Arco Iris." Barchas, Sarah, *¡Piñata! and More*.

"Arriba Del Cielo." Various Artists, *Dreamland*.

"Arroz Con Leche." Raven, Nancy, *People and Animal Songs*.

"La Bamba." Diamond, Charlotte, *10 Carrot Diamond*; Grammer, Red, *Red Grammer's Favorite Sing Along Songs*; Grunsky, Jack, *Dancing Feet*; Grunsky, Jack, *Playground*.

"The Barnyard Dance: El Baile Vegetal." Hinojosa, Tish, *Cada Niño: Every Child*.

"Bella Hortelana." Raven, Nancy, *The House We Live In*, vols. 1 and 2.

"Bomba Le Le." Various Artists, *Latin Playground*.

"Bomba Te Traigo Yo." Various Artists, *Caribbean Playground*.

"Boom Boom Tarara." Various Artists, *World Playground.*

"Brilla, Brilla, Estrellita." Old Town School of Folk Music, *Wiggleworms Love You.*

"Caballito Blanco." Sharon, Lois, and Bram, *Great Big Hits*; Sharon, Lois, and Bram, *Sing A to Z.*

"Cada Niño: Every Child." Hinojosa, Tish, *Cada Niño: Every Child.*

"Los Chimi-Chimitos." Raven, Nancy, *Friends and Family*; Raven, Nancy, *Nancy Raven Sings Her Favorites.*

"Chocolate." Raven, Nancy, *The House We Live In*, vols. 1 and 2; Various Artists, *Latin Playground.*

"Chopping the Cane." Raven, Nancy, *Jambalaya!*; Raven, Nancy, *Nancy Raven Sings Her Favorites.*

"Cinco de Mayo." Barchas, Sarah, *¡Piñata! and More.*

"Come My Little Donkey." Moo, Anna, *Anna Moo Crackers.*

"Conejito En Mi Hombro." Alsop, Peter, *Uh-Oh!*

"El Coquí (The Frog)." Beall, Pamela, and Susan Nipp, *Wee Sing around the World.*

"Days of the Week." Greg and Steve, *We All Live Together*, vol. 4.

"De Bolón Pin Pon." Various Artists, *Latin Playground.*

"De Colores." Arnold, Linda, *Sing Along Stew*; Barchas, Sarah, *Bridges across the World*; Barchas, Sarah, *¡Piñata! and More*; Fink, Cathy, and Marcy Marxer, *All Wound Up!*; Penner, Fred, *Rhyme a Word or Two*; Penner, Fred, *Sing with Fred*; Pirtle, Sarah, *Two Hands Hold the Earth*; Raffi, *One Light One Sun*; Raffi, *Raffi in Concert*; Raven, Nancy, *You Gotta Juba*; Tickle Tune Typhoon, *Hearts and Hands.*

"Dolores." Raven, Nancy, *Friends and Family.*

"Duerme Negrito." Raven, Nancy, *Friends and Family.*

"Dulce, Dulce." Jenkins, Ella, *Songs Children Love to Sing*; Various Artists, *cELLAbration! A Tribute to Ella Jenkins.*

"Los Elefantes." Old Town School of Folk Music, *Wiggleworms Love You.*

"Es el día de Dar Gracias." Barchas, Sarah, *¡Piñata! and More.*

"Escala Musical: Music Scale." Hinojosa, Tish, *Cada Niño: Every Child.*

"Everybody Loves Saturday Night." Silberg, "Miss Jackie," *Sing It Again Please.*

"Fiesta Musical." Various Artists, *A Child's Celebration of the World.*

"El Gatito." Jenkins, Ella, *Sharing Cultures with Ella Jenkins.*

"La Granja." Magical Music Express, *Friendship Stew.*

"Grillo Julián." Raven, Nancy, *Nancy Raven Sings Her Favorites*; Raven, Nancy, *You Gotta Juba.*

"Guantanamera." Seeger, Pete, *Pete Seeger's Family Concert*; Various Artists, *Latin Playground.*

"Hasta Los Muertos Salena Bailar: Even the Dead Are Rising Up to Dance." Hinojosa, Tish, *Cada Niño: Every Child*.

"Head, Shoulders, Knees, and Toes." Magical Music Express, *Music Is Magic*.

"Hide and Seek/Las Escondidas." Arnold, Linda, *Splash Zone*.

"El Hombre Primitivo." Raven, Nancy, *Friends and Family*; Raven, Nancy, *Nancy Raven Sings Her Favorites*.

"The House We Live In." Raven, Nancy, *The House We Live In*, vols. 1 and 2.

"I Love Pie." Fink, Cathy, and Marcy Marxer, *Scat like That*.

"In Spanish, en Español." Barchas, Sarah, *¡Piñata! and More*.

"It's a Penguin Party/A La Fiesta De Pingüinos." Arnold, Linda, *Splash Zone*.

"It's Fun to Be Bilingual." Barchas, Sarah, *¡Piñata! and More*.

"¡Leamos! (Let's Read!)" Barchas, Sarah, *¡Piñata! and More*.

"A Little Night Light." Parachute Express, *Doctor Looney's Remedy*.

"Lluvia De Estrellas." Various Artists, *Latin Playground*.

"La Luna Subio." Lonnquist, Ken, *The Switcher-On of Stars*.

"Magnolia." Hinojosa, Tish, *Cada Niño: Every Child*.

"Malti." Zanes, Dan, *Family Dance*.

"Las Mañanitas." Barchas, Sarah, *¡Piñata! and More*.

"María Isabel." Old Town School of Folk Music, *Wiggleworms Love You*.

"Mariposa." Barchas, Sarah, *¡Piñata! and More*.

"La Mariposa (The Butterfly)." Various Artists, *World Playground*.

"Mariposa Olé." Zanes, Dan, *Catch That Train!*

"May There Always Be Sunshine." Diamond, Charlotte, *10 Carrot Diamond*; Fink, Cathy, and Marcy Marxer, *Nobody Else like Me*; Pease, Tom, *Boogie! Boogie! Boogie!*; Raven, Nancy, *The House We Live In*, vols. 1 and 2.

"The Mexican Hat Dance." Bartles, Joanie, *Put On Your Dancing Shoes*.

"Mi Burro." Beall, Pamela, and Susan Nipp, *Wee Sing around the World*.

"Mi Carmelita." Diamond, Charlotte, *Diamonds and Daydreams*.

"Mi Casa, My House." Silberg, "Miss Jackie," *Joining Hands with Other Lands*; Silberg, "Miss Jackie," *Touched by a Song*.

"Mi Chacra (My Farm)." Beall, Pamela, and Susan Nipp, *Wee Sing around the World*.

"Mi Cuerpo." Stotts, Stuart, and Tom Pease, *Celebrate: A Song Resource*.

"Mi Cuerpo Hace Musica." Pirtle, Sarah, *The Wind Is Telling Secrets*.

"Mi Granja/My Farm." Barchas, Sarah, *¡Piñata! and More*.

"Months of the Year." Greg and Steve, *We All Live Together*, vol. 2.

"A Mover La Colita." Various Artists, *World Playground 2*.

"My Friend Juan." Yosi, *Under a Big Bright Yellow Umbrella*.

"My Hands on My Head." Feldman, Jean, *Dr. Jean and Friends*.

"Oh How Delicious Are Hot Tamales." Barchas, Sarah, *¡Piñata! and More*.

"One Elephant/Un Elefante." Raven, Nancy, *Nancy Raven Sings Her Favorites*; Raven, Nancy, *You Gotta Juba*.

"Pajarito Canta." Cosgrove, Jim, *Ooey Gooey*.

"Pájaro Rojo." Barchas, Sarah, *¡Piñata! and More*.

"Paz y Libertad." Pirtle, Sarah, *Magical Earth*.

"Pin Pón." Beall, Pamela, and Susan Nipp, *Wee Sing around the World*.

"¡Piñata!" Barchas, Sarah, *¡Piñata! and More*.

"Los Pollitos (The Little Chicks)." Barchas, Sarah, *¡Piñata! and More*; Beall, Pamela, and Susan Nipp, *Wee Sing around the World*; Mitchell, Elizabeth, *You Are My Little Bird*; Old Town School of Folk Music, *Wiggleworms Love You*.

"Que Bonita Bandera." Jenkins, Ella, *Sharing Cultures with Ella Jenkins*.

"Qué Fortunidad!" Zanes, Dan, *Night Time!*

"Queremos Bailer." Zanes, Dan, *House Party*.

"Quien: Who." Hinojosa, Tish, *Cada Niño: Every Child*.

"Quiéreme Mucho (Cuando Se Quiere De Veras)." Jenkins, Ella, *Sharing Cultures with Ella Jenkins*.

"Quiero Caña." Raven, Nancy, *Friends and Family*.

"La Raspa/Fiesta de Niños." Various Artists, *cELLAbration! A Tribute to Ella Jenkins*.

"Señora Santa Ana." Hinojosa, Tish, *Cada Niño: Every Child*.

"El Sereno." Sharon, Lois, and Bram, *Mainly Mother Goose*.

"Sí Se Puede." McCutcheon, John, *Autumnsongs*.

"Siempre Abuelita: Always Grandma." Hinojosa, Tish, *Cada Niño: Every Child*.

"Simplemente Por Amor: Simply for Love." Hinojosa, Tish, *Cada Niño: Every Child*.

"The 16th of September." Barchas, Sarah, *¡Piñata! and More*.

"Somos El Barco." Harley, Bill, *50 Ways to Fool Your Mother*; McCutcheon, John, *Mail Myself to You*; Pease, Tom, *I'm Gonna Reach!*; Peter, Paul, and Mary, *Peter, Paul, and Mommy, Too*; Seeger, Pete, *Pete Seeger's Family Concert*; Tucker, Nancy, *Happy as a Clam*.

"Sun Sun." Raven, Nancy, *Friends and Family*.

"Try to Be Nice to Everybody." Mr. Al, *Put Your Groove On*.

"Tumbalele." Harley, Bill, *You're in Trouble*.

"Turn Around and Dance." Mr. Al, *Put Your Groove On*.

"Twelve Months in a Year." Fite, Stephen, *Havin' Fun and Feelin' Groovy*.

"Uno Uno, Dos Dos." Silberg, "Miss Jackie," *Joining Hands with Other Lands*.

"Walkin' the Dog." Zanes, Dan, *Catch That Train!*

"We're Gonna Shine." Penner, Fred, *Fred's Favourites*; Penner, Fred, *Sing with Fred*.

"Where Is Mary?" Jenkins, Ella, *Sharing Cultures with Ella Jenkins*.

"Ya Se Van Los Pastores." Jenkins, Ella, *Sharing Cultures with Ella Jenkins*.

"Yo Quiero." Various Artists, *Latin Playground*.

"Yo Yo Sweet Yo Yo." Zanes, Dan, *Family Dance*.

Swedish

"Små Grodorna (Little Frogs)." Beall, Pamela, and Susan Nipp, *Wee Sing around the World*.

Swiss German

"Weggis Zue (Swiss Hiking Song)." Beall, Pamela, and Susan Nipp, *Wee Sing around the World*.

Tamil (India)

"Anilae, Anilae (Chipmunk, Chipmunk)." Beall, Pamela, and Susan Nipp, *Wee Sing around the World*.

Tatar

"Cradle Song." Various Artists, *Asian Dreamland*.

"Lullaby." Various Artists, *Dreamland*.

Tibetan

"Om Ma Mye Bhe Mae Hum." Various Artists, *Asian Dreamland*.

"Tsetang Gangla (On the Playground)." Raffi, *Let's Play*.

Turkish

"Ali Baba'nin Çiftliği (Ali Baba's Farm)." Beall, Pamela, and Susan Nipp, *Wee Sing around the World*.

Tzotzil (Mexico)

"Nichim Uvil." Various Artists, *World Playground 2*.

Laziness

"Free Ride In." Pease, Tom, *I'm Gonna Reach!*

"Lazy Bones." Tucker, Nancy, *Glad That You Asked*.

"Lazy Mary, Will You Get Up?" Bartels, Joanie, *Morning Magic*; Beall, Pamela, and Susan Nipp, *Wee Sing Nursery Rhymes and Lullabies*.

"Leroy Is a Late Bloomer." Polisar, Barry Louis, *Naughty Songs for Boys and Girls*.

"Wake Up, You Lazybones!" Peterson, Carole, *Tiny Tunes*.

Libraries (see also Books/Reading)

"At the Library." Ode, Eric, *Trash Can*.

"At Your Library." Harley, Bill, *I Wanna Play*.

"Dewey's Decimals." Shontz, Bill, *The Day I Read a Book*.

"The Great Green Squishy Mean Bibliovore." Harper, Monty, *The Great Green Squishy Mean Concert CD*.

"Hanging Out with Heroes at the Library." Harper, Monty, *The Great Green Squishy Mean Concert CD*.

"I Like to Go to the Library." Allard, Peter and Ellen, *Pizza Pizzaz*.

"Kazooey Decimal." Thaddeus Rex, *We Wanna Rock*.

"The Library." Haynes, Sammie, *Nature's ABCs*.

"Library." SteveSongs, *Little Superman*.

"The Library Boogie." Knight, Tom, *The Library Boogie*.

"The Library Book." Kaye, Mary, *Mouse Jamboree*.

"The Library Cat." Charette, Rick, *King Kong Chair*.

"Library Song." Chapin, Tom, *Moonboat*.

"The Library Song." Knight, Tom, *The Library Boogie*.

"Shut Up in the Library." Polisar, Barry Louis, *Old Enough to Know Better*.

"Take Me to Your Library." Harper, Monty, *Take Me to Your Library*.

Literary/Folklore Characters (see also Books/Reading)

"Anansi." Raffi, *Corner Grocery Store*.

"Baba Yaga." Kaye, Mary, *I Sang It Just for You*.

"Big Bad Wolf." Kaye, Mary, *I Sang It Just for You*.

"Billy Goat Walk." Kimmy Schwimmy, *Kimmy Schwimmy Music*, vol. 1.

"Billy Goats Gruff." McMahon, Elizabeth, *Magic Parade*.

"Brown Bear, Brown Bear, What Do You See?" Greg and Steve, *Playing Favorites*.

"Casey Jones." Coffey, James, *My Mama Was a Train*.

"Chicken Soup with Rice." Rosen, Gary, *Cookin'*.

"Climb That Beanstalk." Knight, Tom, *The Classroom Boogie*.

"Country Mouse and the City Mouse." McMahon, Elizabeth, *Magic Parade*.

"Do You Wish You Could Fly?" Byers, Kathy, *Do You Wish You Could Fly?*

"The Garden." Roth, Kevin, *Unbearable Bears*.

"The Gingerbread Man." Dana, *Dana's Best Rock and Roll Fairy Tales*; Stotts, Stuart, and Tom Pease, *Celebrate: A Song Resource*.

"The Gingerbread Man." McMahon, Elizabeth, *Tea Party Shuffle*.

"Gingerbread Man." Scruggs, Joe, *Bahamas Pajamas*.

"Goldilocks and the 3 Bears." The Learning Station, *La Di Da La Di Di Dance with Me*; The Learning Station, *Literacy in Motion*.

"Goldilocks Rap." Shontz, Bill, *Teddy Bear's Greatest Hits*.

"The Goldilocks Rock." Dana, *Dana's Best Rock and Roll Fairy Tales*.

"Goodnight Story Time." Palmer, Hap, *Peek-a-Boo*.

"Green Eggs and Ham." The Learning Station, *Literacy in Motion*; The Learning Station, *Rock n' Roll Songs That Teach*.

"House at Pooh Corner." Shontz, Bill, *Teddy Bear's Greatest Hits*; Various Artists, *A Child's Celebration of Song*.

"Hungry Caterpillar." The Learning Station, *Literacy in Motion*; The Learning Station, *Seasonal Songs in Motion*.

"I Could Spend a Happy Moment." Rosen, Gary, *Teddy Bears' Picnic*.

"I'm a Book." Foote, Norman, *Foote Prints*.

"Jack and the Beanstalk." Dana, *Dana's Best Rock and Roll Fairy Tales*.

"John Henry." McCutcheon, John, *Howjadoo*.

"Just Right." Knight, Tom, *The Library Boogie*.

"King Midas." Kaye, Mary, *I Sang It Just for You*.

"The Library Boogie." Knight, Tom, *The Library Boogie*.

"Library Song." Chapin, Tom, *Moonboat*.

"Lines Written by a Bear of Very Little Brain." Rosen, Gary, *Teddy Bears' Picnic*.

"Little Anancy." Various Artists, *Caribbean Playground*.

"Little Blue Engine." Beall, Pamela, and Susan Nipp, *Wee Sing and Pretend*.

"The Little Engine That Could." Ives, Burl, *Burl Ives Sings Little White Duck*.

"The Little Red Hen." Avni, Fran, *Artichokes and Brussel Sprouts*; Avni, Fran, *Tuning into Nature*.

"The Little Red Hen." Greg and Steve, *Fun and Games*.

"The Little Red Hen." McMahon, Elizabeth, *Blue Sky Sparklin' Day*.

"Little Red Hen." Stotts, Stuart, and Tom Pease, *Celebrate: A Song Resource*.

"Lots of Little Pigs." Berkner, Laurie, *Buzz Buzz*.

"The Mitten." McMahon, Elizabeth, *Blue Sky Sparklin' Day*.

"The Night the Froggies Flew." Colleen and Uncle Squaty, *Fingerplays, Movement and Story Songs*.

"No Good Toys (Harry Potter)." SteveSongs, *Little Superman*.

"Oh Fiddlesticks." Thaddeus Rex, *We Wanna Rock*.

"Oh the Butterflies Are Flying." Rosen, Gary, *Teddy Bears' Picnic*.

"Oh Yes, He Did It." Shontz, Bill, *Animal Tales*.

"Pecos Bill." Howdy, Buck, *Giddyup!*; Riders in the Sky, *Harmony Ranch*.

"Princess and the Pea." Lonnquist, Ken, *The Lost Songs of Kenland*.

"Princess Power." Miss Amy, *Wide, Wide World*.

"Rapunzel Got a Mohawk." Scruggs, Joe, *Ants*.

"Read a Book." Shontz, Bill, *The Day I Read a Book*.

"Reading Books." Thaddeus Rex, *Martian Television Invasion*.

"Robin Hood." Kirk, John, and Trish Miller, *The Big Rock Candy Mountain*.

"Rockabilly Goats Gruff." Knight, Tom, *The Classroom Boogie*.

"Sing Ho! for the Life of a Bear/Teddy Bears' Picnic." Rosen, Gary, *Teddy Bears' Picnic*.

"Sneezles." Rosen, Gary, *Teddy Bears' Picnic*.

"Stone Soup." Arnold, Linda, *Make Believe*.

"Stone Soup." Chapin, Tom, *Mother Earth*.

"Stone Soup." Knight, Tom, *Don't Kiss a Codfish*.

"Stone Soup." McMahon, Elizabeth, *Magic Parade*.

"Superman." Frezza, Rebecca, *Music in My Head*.

"Tarzan." Feldman, Jean, *Dr. Jean and Friends*.

"Tarzan of the Apes." Silberg, "Miss Jackie," *Peanut Butter, Tarzan, and Roosters*; Silberg, "Miss Jackie," *Sing It Again Please*.

"The Three Bears." Rosen, Gary, *Teddy Bears' Picnic*.

"Three Billy Goats Groove." Dana, *Dana's Best Rock and Roll Fairy Tales*.

"Three Billy Goats Gruff." Greg and Steve, *Rockin' down the Road*.

"The Three Boppin Bears Rap." Feldman, Jean, *Dr. Jean Sings Silly Songs*.

"3 Cheers for Pooh." Rosen, Gary, *Teddy Bears' Picnic*.

"Three Lil Pigs." Roberts, Justin, *Great Big Sun*.

"The Three Little Pig Blues." Greg and Steve, *Playing Favorites*.

"3 Little Piggies." Miss Amy, *Underwater*.

"Three Little Piggies." Strausman, Paul, *Blue Jay, Blue Jay!*

"Too Much Noise." McMahon, Elizabeth, *Magic Parade*.

"The Ugly Duckling." Greg and Steve, *We All Live Together*, vol. 4; Various Artists, *A Child's Celebration of Song*.

"Visiting Cinderella." Harper, Jessica, *40 Winks*.

"Who's Afraid of the Big Bad Wolf?" Rosenshontz, *Share It*; Shontz, Bill, *The Day I Read a Book*.

"Wild Things." The Learning Station, *Literacy in Motion*.

"Winnie the Pooh/The Wonderful Thing about Tiggers." Ralph's World, *Ralph's World*.

"Yertle the Turtle." Various Artists, *A Child's Celebration of Song 2*.

Losing Things

"Baby's Got the Car Keys." Trout Fishing in America, *Family Music Party*; Trout Fishing in America, *My World*.

"Daddy's Song." Haynes, Sammie, *Nature's ABCs*.

"Down in the Backpack." Harley, Bill, *Down in the Backpack*.

"Go and Hush the Baby." Polisar, Barry Louis, *Family Trip*.

"I Can't Find My Pyjamas." Simmons, Al, *Something Fishy at Camp Wiganishie*.

"I Can't Find My Shoes." Daddy A Go Go, *Big Rock Rooster*.

"I Found It!" Rymer, Brady, *I Found It!*

"I Lost My Pants." Polisar, Barry Louis, *Teacher's Favorites*.

"I Lost My Shoes." LaFond, Lois, *One World*.

"I Lost the Tooth." Roberts, Justin, *Way Out*.

"It's Gone." Trout Fishing in America, *It's a Puzzle*.

"Only One Shoe." Chapin, Tom, *Some Assembly Required*.

"The Other Shoe." Scruggs, Joe, *Late Last Night*.

"Twilight Zone Home." Scruggs, Joe, *Even Trolls Have Moms*.

"We Lost Our Car . . . in the Parking Lot." Pullara, Steve, *Hop like a Frog*.

Luck

"I'm Lucky." Grammer, Red, *Can You Sound Just like Me?*

"Lucky Girl." Fink, Cathy, and Marcy Marxer, *Blanket Full of Dreams*.

"Lucky Streak." Diamond, Charlotte, *Diamonds and Dragons*.

Lullabies

"All Eyes on You." Roberts, Justin, *Yellow Bus*.

"All Is Well." Abell, Timmy, *Little Red Wagon*.

"All Night, All Day." Beall, Pamela, and Susan Nipp, *Wee Sing Children's Songs and Fingerplays*; Beall, Pamela, and Susan Nipp, *Wee Sing Nursery Rhymes and Lullabies*.

"All the Pretty Horses." Beall, Pamela, and Susan Nipp, *Wee Sing Children's Songs and Fingerplays*; Beall, Pamela, and Susan Nipp, *Wee Sing Nursery Rhymes and Lullabies*; Berkner, Laurie, *Whaddaya Think of That?*; Various Artists, *A Child's Celebration of Song 2.*

"All Through the Night." Beall, Pamela, and Susan Nipp, *Wee Sing Nursery Rhymes and Lullabies*; Chapin, Tom, *Mother Earth*; Diamond, Charlotte, *Diamonds and Daydreams*; Peter, Paul, and Mary, *Peter, Paul, and Mommy.*

"Armenian Lullaby." Beall, Pamela, and Susan Nipp, *Wee Sing Nursery Rhymes and Lullabies.*

"Baby Bye Oh." Tickle Tune Typhoon, *Patty-Cakes and Peek-a-Boos.*

"Bedtime Girl." Ralph's World, *Ralph's World.*

"Billy Don't You Cry Now." Rosenshontz, *Rock 'n Roll Teddy Bear.*

"Blessed Be." Raffi, *Let's Play*; Raffi, *Quiet Time.*

"Brahm's Lullaby." Beall, Pamela, and Susan Nipp, *Wee Sing Nursery Rhymes and Lullabies.*

"Bush Lullaby." Herdman, Priscilla, *Stardreamer.*

"Bye, Baby Bunting." Beall, Pamela, and Susan Nipp, *Wee Sing Nursery Rhymes and Lullabies.*

"Bye, Bye, Baby." Beall, Pamela, and Susan Nipp, *Wee Sing Nursery Rhymes and Lullabies.*

"By-ush Ki By-u." Chapin, Tom, *Around the World and Back Again.*

"Captain of the Moon." Green Chili Jam Band, *Starfishing.*

"City Lullaby." Chapin, Tom, *Billy the Squid.*

"Close Your Eyes." Diamond, Charlotte, *Diamond in the Rough.*

"Close Your Eyes." Herdman, Priscilla, *Stardreamer.*

"Cowgirl's Lullaby." Fink, Cathy, and Marcy Marxer, *Blanket Full of Dreams.*

"Cradle Spell of Dunvegan." Various Artists, *Dreamland.*

"Don't Fall Asleep." Buchman, Rachel, *Baby and Me.*

"Dream a Little Dream." Muldaur, Maria, *On the Sunny Side.*

"The Eagle's Lullaby." Hinton, Sam, *Whoever Shall Have Some Good Peanuts.*

"Evening Breeze Lullaby." Scruggs, Joe, *Traffic Jams.*

"Everything Is Alright." Rudnick, Ben, *Fun and Games.*

"Fais Do Do/Rock-a-Bye-Baby." Sharon, Lois, and Bram, *Mainly Mother Goose.*

"Fala Nina, Fala Nana." Various Artists, *A Child's Celebration of the World.*

"First Lullaby." Herdman, Priscilla, *Stardreamer*; Staines, Bill, *The Happy Wanderer.*

"The First Star Lullaby." Herdman, Priscilla, *Stardreamer.*

"German Cradle Song." Beall, Pamela, and Susan Nipp, *Wee Sing for Baby.*

"Go to Sleep." Miss Amy, *Underwater.*

"Go to Sleep." Rosenthal, Phil, *Animal Songs.*

"Golden Slumbers." Beall, Pamela, and Susan Nipp, *Wee Sing Nursery Rhymes and Lullabies.*

"Good Night." Beall, Pamela, and Susan Nipp, *Wee Sing Children's Songs and Fingerplays.*

"Good Night." Cosgrove, Jim, *Stinky Feet.*

"Good Night." Kinder, Brian, *Again.*

"Good Night to You All." Beall, Pamela, and Susan Nipp, *Wee Sing Nursery Rhymes and Lullabies.*

"Goodnight." Roberts, Justin, *Great Big Sun.*

"Goodnight." Sweet Honey in the Rock, *Still the Same Me.*

"Goodnight Barnyard." SteveSongs, *Morning til Night.*

"Goodnight Little Darling." Guthrie, Woody, *Songs to Grow On for Mother and Child.*

"Goodnight, Little Max." Kinnoin, Dave, *Dunce Cap Kelly.*

"Goodnight, My Love." Muldaur, Maria, *Animal Crackers in My Soup.*

"Goodnight Sweetheart." Miss Amy, *Underwater.*

"Goodnight Waltz." Fink, Cathy, and Marcy Marxer, *Pillow Full of Wishes.*

"Hobo's Lullaby." Seeger, Pete, *For Kids and Just Plain Folks.*

"Hoosh-Ta, Bay-Bah." Colleen and Uncle Squaty, *Rumble to the Bottom.*

"Hush." Fink, Cathy, and Marcy Marxer, *Pillow Full of Wishes.*

"Hush-A-Bye, Baby Bye." Beall, Pamela, and Susan Nipp, *Wee Sing for Baby.*

"Hush Little Baby." Beall, Pamela, and Susan Nipp, *Wee Sing Children's Songs and Fingerplays*; Beall, Pamela, and Susan Nipp, *Wee Sing for Baby*; Beall, Pamela, and Susan Nipp, *Wee Sing Nursery Rhymes and Lullabies*; Buchman, Rachel, *Baby and Me*; Marxer, Marcy, *Jump Children*; McGrath, Bob, *Sing Along with Bob #2*; Old Town School of Folk Music, *Wiggleworms Love You*; Rosenthal, Phil, *The Green Grass Grew All Around*; Rosenthal, Phil, *The Paw Paw Patch*; Sharon, Lois, and Bram, *Great Big Hits 2*; Sharon, Lois, and Bram, *Sing A to Z*; Silberg, "Miss Jackie," *Lollipops and Spaghetti*; Silberg, "Miss Jackie," *Sing It Again Please.*

"Hush, My Child." Beall, Pamela, and Susan Nipp, *Wee Sing Nursery Rhymes and Lullabies.*

"Hush Now, My Baby." Beall, Pamela, and Susan Nipp, *Wee Sing for Baby.*

"In This Room." Harper, Jessica, *40 Winks.*

"It's Nighttime." Fink, Cathy, and Marcy Marxer, *Blanket Full of Dreams.*

"It's Time to Go to Sleep." Buchman, Rachel, *Baby and Me.*

"Jack's Lullaby." SteveSongs, *Marvelous Day!*

"The King's Lullaby." SteveSongs, *Morning til Night.*

"Kristen's Song." Walker, Mary Lu, *The Frog's Party.*

"Little Brother's Lullaby." Beall, Pamela, and Susan Nipp, *Wee Sing for Baby.*

"Little Fishies." Simmons, Al, *Something Fishy at Camp Wiganishie*.

"Little One." Boynton, Sandra, *Rhinoceros Tap*.

"Lovely Lullaby." McMahon, Elizabeth, *Magic Parade*.

"Lula Lullaby." Nagler, Eric, *Improvise with Eric Nagler*.

"Lullaby." The Chenille Sisters, *The Big Picture and Other Songs for Kids*.

"Lullaby." McMahon, Elizabeth, *Tea Party Shuffle*.

"Lullaby." Trout Fishing in America, *Big Trouble*; Trout Fishing in America, *Family Music Party*.

"A Lullaby." Various Artists, *Dreamland*.

"Lullaby Bear." Roth, Kevin, *Unbearable Bears*.

"Lullaby for a Crying Baby (A Parent's Lament)." Polisar, Barry Louis, *Juggling Babies*.

"Lullaby for Teddy-O." Herdman, Priscilla, *Stardreamer*.

"Lullaby of the Moon." Knight, Tom, *Don't Kiss a Codfish*.

"Lullaby to a Doll." Muldaur, Maria, *Animal Crackers in My Soup*.

"Me and My Balloon." Yosi, *Under a Big Bright Yellow Umbrella*.

"Mockingbird." Peter, Paul, and Mary, *Peter, Paul, and Mommy*; Raven, Nancy, *People and Animal Songs*.

"Mommie's Lullaby." Arnold, Linda, *Make Believe*.

"Moonlight." Fink, Cathy, and Marcy Marxer, *Pillow Full of Wishes*.

"Moonlight Express." Penner, Fred, *Fred's Favourites*.

"Mozart's Lullaby." Beall, Pamela, and Susan Nipp, *Wee Sing Nursery Rhymes and Lullabies*.

"Night Is Near." Beall, Pamela, and Susan Nipp, *Wee Sing for Baby*.

"The Night Rides in on Ships." LaFond, Lois, *One World*.

"Nighty Noodles." Harley, Bill, *One More Time*; Harley, Bill, *The Town around the Bend*.

"One Sweet Song." Rosen, Gary, *Pet Sounds*; Rosenshontz, *Tickles You!*

"Prairie Lullaby." Muldaur, Maria, *On the Sunny Side*; Riders in the Sky, *Harmony Ranch*.

"Quiet Time." Rosenshontz, *Rock 'n Roll Teddy Bear*.

"The Quiet Time." Roth, Kevin, *Travel Song Sing Alongs*.

"Raisins and Almonds." Beall, Pamela, and Susan Nipp, *Wee Sing for Baby*; Raven, Nancy, *People and Animal Songs*.

"Reggae Lullaby." Various Artists, *Reggae Playground*.

"Rock to Sleep." Boynton, Sandra, *Dog Train*.

"Rock-a-Bye Baby." Beall, Pamela, and Susan Nipp, *Wee Sing for Baby*; Beall, Pamela, and Susan Nipp, *Wee Sing Nursery Rhymes and Lullabies*.

"Rockabye Ranch." Atkinson, Lisa, *The One and Only Me*.

"Rockin' to a Lullaby." The Learning Station, *Rock n' Roll Songs That Teach*.

"Rocky, Rocky." Buchman, Rachel, *Hello Everybody!*

"Rosy, My Posy." Beall, Pamela, and Susan Nipp, *Wee Sing for Baby*.

"Russian Lullaby." The Chenille Sisters, *1, 2, 3 for Kids*.

"The Sandman." Knight, Tom, *Easy as Pie*.

"The Sandman." Walker, Graham, *Cats' Night Out*.

"Señora Santa Ana." Hinojosa, Tish, *Cada Niño: Every Child*.

"Shadowtown." Strausman, Paul, *Rainbows, Stones, and Dinosaur Bones*.

"Silly Lullaby." Boynton, Sandra, *Philadelphia Chickens*.

"Sleep, Baby, Sleep." Beall, Pamela, and Susan Nipp, *Wee Sing Children's Songs and Fingerplays*; Beall, Pamela, and Susan Nipp, *Wee Sing for Baby*; Beall, Pamela, and Susan Nipp, *Wee Sing Nursery Rhymes and Lullabies*.

"Sleep Eye." Guthrie, Woody, *Nursery Days*; Guthrie, Woody, *Woody's 20 Grow Big Songs*.

"Sleep like a Little Pea." Fink, Cathy, and Marcy Marxer, *Blanket Full of Dreams*.

"Sleep Little Devil." Harper, Monty, *Jungle Junk!*

"Sleep My Little One." Grunsky, Jack, *Jack in the Box 2*.

"Slow Down Lizzie." Harper, Jessica, *40 Winks*.

"Slumber Song." Beall, Pamela, and Susan Nipp, *Wee Sing for Baby*.

"Sofdu Unga Astin Min." Miss Amy, *Wide, Wide World*.

"Spirit Lullaby." Sweet Honey in the Rock, *I Got Shoes*.

"Suo-Gan." Diamond, Charlotte, *Diamonds and Daydreams*.

"Sweet Dreamer's Serenade." Atkinson, Lisa, *I Wanna Tickle the Fish*.

"Swingtime Lullaby." Fink, Cathy, and Marcy Marxer, *Blanket Full of Dreams*.

"Tender Shepherd." McCutcheon, John, *Howjadoo*.

"A Tinker, A Tailor." Harper, Jessica, *40 Winks*.

"Upon My Violin." Kinnoin, Dave, *Getting Bigger*.

"Wake You Up in the Morning." Pelham, Ruth, *Under One Sky*.

"Winkum, Winkum." Beall, Pamela, and Susan Nipp, *Wee Sing for Baby*.

"Wosho Paiute Bannock Lullaby." Barchas, Sarah, *Bridges across the World*.

"Wynken, Blynken, and Nod." Various Artists, *A Child's Celebration of Song*.

"You Might as Well Go to Sleep." Brown, Greg, *Bathtub Blues*.

Mail

"Junk Mail." McCutcheon, John, *Springsongs*.

"Mail Myself to You." Abell, Timmy, *The Farmer's Market*; Cassidy, Nancy, *Nancy Cassidy's KidSongs*; Guthrie, Woody and Arlo, *This Land Is Your Land*;

McCutcheon, John, *Mail Myself to You*; Raven, Nancy, *Nancy Raven Sings Her Favorites*; Raven, Nancy, *Singing, Prancing, and Dancing.*

"Mailman." Guthrie, Woody, *Woody's 20 Grow Big Songs.*

"Pen Pals." Gemini, *The Best of Gemini.*

Making Things

"Beautiful Things." Avni, Fran, *Tuning into Nature.*

"Build a Fort." Penner, Fred, *Sing with Fred.*

"Build That Clubhouse." Del Bianco, Lou, *When I Was a Kid.*

"Castillo de Arena." Frezza, Rebecca, *Music in My Head.*

"Everyone's an Artist." Knight, Tom, *The Classroom Boogie.*

"School Glue." Scruggs, Joe, *Abracadabra.*

"Treehouse." Arnold, Linda, *Peppermint Wings.*

"Water, Sand, Blocks, and Clay." Rymer, Brady, *Look at My Belly.*

"With My Own Hands." Grunsky, Jack, *Jack in the Box 1.*

Manners

"Abracadabra." Scruggs, Joe, *Abracadabra.*

"Don't Put Your Finger up Your Nose." Polisar, Barry Louis, *Family Concert*; Polisar, Barry Louis, *Naughty Songs for Boys and Girls.*

"The Goops." Trout Fishing in America, *It's a Puzzle.*

"The Magic Word." Sprout, Jonathan, *Dr. Music.*

"Manners Make a Princess Shine." Parachute Express, *Friends, Forever Friends.*

"Mind Your Manners." Mr. Al, *Put Your Groove On.*

"Never Speak with Your Mouth Full." Alsop, Peter, *Uh-Oh!*

"Please." Barchas, Sarah, *Bridges across the World.*

"Please Is a Pleasant Expression." Jenkins, Ella, *Songs Children Love to Sing*; Various Artists, *cELLAbration! A Tribute to Ella Jenkins.*

"Please Pass the Peas." Peterson, Carole, *H.U.M.—All Year Long.*

"Thank You." Barchas, Sarah, *Bridges across the World.*

"Three Little Words." Fite, Stephen, *Gobs of Fun.*

Messiness

"Amanda Schlupp." Palmer, Hap, *Turn On the Music.*

"American Gum." Crow, Dan, *Oops!*

"But I'm Just Thirteen." Polisar, Barry Louis, *Family Trip.*

"Clean My Room." Ralph's World, *At the Bottom of the Sea*.
"Covered in Glue." Ralph's World, *Peggy's Pie Parlor*.
"Dust Bunny." Coffey, James, *Animal Groove*.
"Girlquake." Harper, Jessica, *Rhythm in My Shoes*.
"Hurricane Mom." Lonnquist, Ken, *Sci-Fi Hi-Fi*.
"I Drive My Mommy Crazy." Rosenshontz, *Rosenshontz Greatest Hits*.
"I Hate to Clean My Room." Charette, Rick, *Alligator in the Elevator*.
"I Love Mud." Charette, Rick, *Alligator in the Elevator*.
"I Stepped in Dog Doo." Thaddeus Rex, *We Wanna Rock*.
"I Will Never Clean Up My Room." Fink, Cathy, and Marcy Marxer, *All Wound Up!*
"Lard (A Tragedy)." Green Chili Jam Band, *Coconut Moon*.
"Mud." McCutcheon, John, *Summersongs*.
"Neat Mess." Chapin, Tom, *Moonboat*.
"Oh My Goodness, Look at This Mess!" Sweet Honey in the Rock, *Still the Same Me*.
"Uh-Oh!" Alsop, Peter, *Uh-Oh!*
"Under My Bed." Rymer, Brady, *I Found It!*
"Who Made This Mess?" Harley, Bill, *Big Big World*; Pease, Tom, *Wobbi-Do-Wop!*
"Yecch!" Alsop, Peter, *Wha' D'Ya Wanna Do?*

Misbehavior

"Another Time Out." Pease, Tom, *Daddy Starts to Dance*.
"Bad Day Today." Del Bianco, Lou, *Lost in School*.
"Barbie's Head Is Missing." Harley, Bill, *I Wanna Play*.
"Big Trouble." Trout Fishing in America, *Big Trouble*.
"Dagnabbit!" Fink, Cathy, and Marcy Marxer, *Scat like That*.
"Dunce Cap Kelly." Kinnoin, Dave, *Dunce Cap Kelly*.
"Grounded." McCutcheon, John, *Springsongs*.
"He Eats Asparagus, Why Can't You Be That Way." Alsop, Peter, *Take Me with You*; Polisar, Barry Louis, *Family Trip*.
"I Didn't Mean To." Polisar, Barry Louis, *Teacher's Favorites*.
"I Don't Wanna." Ralph's World, *Green Gorilla, Monster, and Me*.
"I Like to Fuss." Boynton, Sandra, *Philadelphia Chickens*.
"The 'I Never Did Like You Anyhow' Stomp." Polisar, Barry Louis, *Old Enough to Know Better*.
"I Would If I Could." Chapin, Tom, *Great Big Fun for the Very Little One*.
"If You Have a Kid Who Complains All the Time." Polisar, Barry Louis, *Old Enough to Know Better*.

"I'm a Little Twerp." Madsen, Gunnar, *Old Mr. Mackle Hackle.*
"It Did It All by Itself." Trout Fishing in America, *InFINity.*
"It Wasn't Me." Frezza, Rebecca, *Tall and Small.*
"It's Time-Out Time Again." Paxton, Tom, *Your Shoes, My Shoes.*
"Mikey Won't." Chapin, Tom, *Zag Zig.*
"Mr. Nobody." Walker, Mary Lu, *The Frog's Party.*
"No Whine Zone." Pease, Tom, *Daddy Starts to Dance*; Stotts, Stuart, *One Big Dance.*
"Nobody." Trout Fishing in America, *Big Trouble.*
"One Big Happy Family." Polisar, Barry Louis, *Old Enough to Know Better.*
"Stanley Stole My Shoelaces and Rubbed It in His Armpit." Polisar, Barry Louis, *Old Enough to Know Better.*
"Tantrum." Boynton, Sandra, *Dog Train.*
"To the South Pole." Harley, Bill, *I Wanna Play.*
"When the House Is Dark and Quiet." Polisar, Barry Louis, *Family Concert*; Polisar, Barry Louis, *Family Trip.*
"The Witch." Polisar, Barry Louis, *Old Enough to Know Better.*
"Wrong Right." Trout Fishing in America, *It's a Puzzle.*
"You Can't Go." Trout Fishing in America, *InFINity.*
"You're in Trouble." Harley, Bill, *Play It Again*; Harley, Bill, *You're in Trouble.*

Money

"Ayee I Owe You." Palmer, Hap, *One Little Sound.*
"Five Pennies Make a Nickel." Palmer, Hap, *Two Little Sounds.*
"Five Shiny Pennies." Allard, Peter and Ellen, *Raise the Children.*
"Heads or Tails." Rosen, Gary, *Teddy Bears' Picnic.*
"I Got a Dime." McCutcheon, John, *Bigger Than Yourself.*
"Looking for Pennies." Kaye, Mary, *I Sang It Just for You.*
"Money Song." Feldman, Jean, *Is Everybody Happy?*
"Pay Me My Money Down." Zanes, Dan, *Night Time!*
"Piggy Bank." Greg and Steve, *We All Live Together*, vol. 3.
"Seven Days a Week." Dana, *Dana's Best Travelin' Tunes.*
"Silver Dollar." Pease, Tom, *Daddy Starts to Dance.*
"Thousand Pennies." Foote, Norman, *1000 Pennies.*

Months of the Year

"January, February, March." Fink, Cathy, and Marcy Marxer, *A Cathy & Marcy Collection for Kids*; Marxer, Marcy, *Jump Children.*

"Chicken Soup with Rice." Rosen, Gary, *Cookin'*.

"Macarena Months." Feldman, Jean, *Dr. Jean and Friends*.

"Months of the Year." Charette, Rick, *King Kong Chair*.

"Months of the Year." Greg and Steve, *We All Live Together*, vol. 2.

"Months of the Year." Mr. Al and Stephen Fite, *Back to School Again*.

"Months on the Move." Palmer, Hap, *Can Cockatoos Count by Twos?*

"Sing a Song of September." Silberg, "Miss Jackie," *The Complete Sniggles, Squirrels, and Chicken Pox*; Silberg, "Miss Jackie," *Sing about Martin*.

"Twelve Months." Barchas, Sarah, *Get Ready, Get Set, Sing!*

"Twelve Months in a Year." Fite, Stephen, *Havin' Fun and Feelin' Groovy*.

Morningtime

"Are You Sleeping?" Beall, Pamela, and Susan Nipp, *Wee Sing Sing-Alongs*; Rosenthal, Phil, *The Paw Paw Patch*. (Same song as "Frère Jacques.")

"Children of the Morning." Grunsky, Jack, *Playground*.

"Early Bird." Muldaur, Maria, *Animal Crackers in My Soup*.

"Five Minutes More." Various Artists, *Hear and Gone in 60 Seconds*.

"Frère Jacques." Barchas, Sarah, *Bridges across the World*; Beall, Pamela, and Susan Nipp, *Wee Sing around the World*; Jenkins, Ella, *Sharing Cultures with Ella Jenkins*; McGrath, Bob, *Sing Along with Bob #2*; McGrath, Bob, and Katherine Smithrim, *Songs and Games for Toddlers*; Walker, Graham, *Knobbledee Knees*. (Same song as "Are You Sleeping?")

"Frère Jacques/This Is the Way." Tickle Tune Typhoon, *Patty-Cakes and Peek-a-Boos*.

"Get Up." Foote, Norman, *Pictures on the Fridge*.

"Getting Up Time." Palmer, Hap, *Peek-a-Boo*.

"Good Morning!" Barchas, Sarah, *Get Ready, Get Set, Sing!*

"Good Morning." Beall, Pamela, and Susan Nipp, *Wee Sing Children's Songs and Fingerplays*.

"Good Morning." Greg and Steve, *We All Live Together*, vol. 2.

"Good Morning." Kinder, Brian, *Again*.

"Good Morning Sunshine." Grunsky, Jack, *Follow the Leader*; Grunsky, Jack, *Jack in the Box 2*.

"Great Big Sun." Roberts, Justin, *Great Big Sun*.

"I Brush My Teeth." Silberg, "Miss Jackie," *Sing It Again Please*.

"I Hate Getting Up in the Morning." Charette, Rick, *Chickens on Vacation*.

"I'm Up." Strausman, Paul, *Blue Jay, Blue Jay!*

"Me and the Morning." Grammer, Red, *Down the Do-Re-Mi*.

"Morning Time Blues." Fite, Stephen, *We're Just like Crayons*.

"Rise and Shine." Bartels, Joanie, *Morning Magic*; Raffi, *Raffi in Concert*.

"Rise and Shine." Knight, Tom, *Easy as Pie*; McMahon, Elizabeth, *Tea Party Shuffle*.

"Rock 'round the Mulberry Bush." Greg and Steve, *We All Live Together*, vol. 3.

"Say Good Day!" Peterson, Carole, *Tiny Tunes*. (Same song as "When Cats Get Up in the Morning.")

"Shake Your Bootie Wootie." Moo, Anna, *Making Moosic*.

"Sleeping Beauty." Kaye, Mary, *I Sang It Just for You*.

"Sleepy Eye." Rosenthal, Phil, *The Green Grass Grew All Around*.

"Start the Day Off Right." Rosen, Gary, *Cookin'*.

"Start Your Day with a Smile." Yosi, *Monkey Business*.

"Still Gotta Get Up in the Morning." Sweet Honey in the Rock, *Still the Same Me*.

"Sunday Morning." Rosenshontz, *Uh-Oh!*

"Sunny Side Up." Lonnquist, Ken, *The Lost Songs of Kenland*.

"Time to Get Ready to Go." Parachute Express, *Feel the Music*.

"Wake Up!" Cosgrove, Jim, *Ooey Gooey*.

"Wake Up." Guthrie, Woody, *Nursery Days*; Guthrie, Woody, *Woody's 20 Grow Big Songs*.

"Wake Up Jacob." Pease, Tom, *Boogie! Boogie! Boogie!*; Raven, Nancy, *Jambalaya!*

"Wake Up Sleepyhead." Mayer, Hans, *Just a Little Hug*.

"Wake Up Toes." Bartels, Joanie, *Morning Magic*.

"Wake Up You Sleepy-Head." Allard, Peter and Ellen, *Sing It! Say It! Stamp It! Sway It!* vol. 1.

"Waking Up." Pirtle, Sarah, *The Wind Is Telling Secrets*.

"When Cats Get Up in the Morning." Old Town School of Folk Music, *Wiggleworms Love You*. (Same song as "Say Good Day!")

Mountains

"The Bear Went over the Mountain." Beall, Pamela, and Susan Nipp, *Wee Sing Animals, Animals, Animals*; Beall, Pamela, and Susan Nipp, *Wee Sing Silly Songs*; Feldman, Jean, *Dr. Jean Sings Silly Songs*; Greg and Steve, *Ready, Set, Move!*; McGrath, Bob, *Sing Along with Bob #1*.

"The Big Rock Candy Mountain." Beall, Pamela, and Susan Nipp, *Wee Sing in the Car*; Kirk, John, and Trish Miller, *The Big Rock Candy Mountain*.

"Douglas Mountain." Herdman, Priscilla, *Stardreamer*; Raffi, *More Singable Songs*; Raffi, *Quiet Time*.

"Down the Mountainside We Go." Various Artists, *Grandma's Patchwork Quilt*.

"Grandma Slid down the Mountain." Fink, Cathy, *Grandma Slid down the Mountain*; Fink, Cathy, and Marcy Marxer, *A Cathy & Marcy Collection for Kids*.

"I Love the Mountains." Beall, Pamela, and Susan Nipp, *Wee Sing in the Car*; Byers, Kathy, *'Round the Campfire*.

"Walking in the Tetons." Banana Slug String Band, *Goin' Wild*.

"Whisperville Mountain." Atkinson, Lisa, *The Elephant in Aisle Four*.

Movement

"All around the Circle." Allard, Peter and Ellen, *Sing It! Say It! Stamp It! Sway It!* vol. 2.

"All around the Kitchen." Zanes, Dan, *Family Dance*.

"Ants in My Pants." Allard, Peter and Ellen, *Pizza Pizzaz*.

"Baby 1, 2, 3." Allard, Peter and Ellen, *Sing It! Say It! Stamp It! Sway It!* vol. 3.

"The Balancing Act." Greg and Steve, *Kids in Motion*.

"The Bean Bag." Palmer, Hap, *Can a Jumbo Jet Sing the Alphabet?*

"Beanbag Boogie." Greg and Steve, *Kids in Motion*.

"The Beat." LaFond, Lois, *I Am Who I Am*.

"Bodies 1-2-3." Allard, Peter and Ellen, *Sing It! Say It! Stamp It! Sway It!* vol. 2.

"Body Boogie." The Learning Station, *Get Funky and Musical Fun*.

"Body Bop." The Learning Station, *Seasonal Songs in Motion*.

"The Body Rock." Greg and Steve, *Kidding Around*; Greg and Steve, *Kids in Motion*.

"The Boogie Walk." Greg and Steve, *We All Live Together*, vol. 2.

"Bop 'til You Drop." Mr. Al, *Mr. Al a Carte*; Mr. Al, *Mr. Al Concert Live*.

"A Bowl of Cherries." Allard, Peter and Ellen, *Sing It! Say It! Stamp It! Sway It!* vol. 3.

"Button Factory." The Learning Station, *Rock n' Roll Songs That Teach*.

"Can't Wait to Celebrate." Gill, Jim, *Jim Gill's Irrational Anthem*.

"Circle of Friends." Colleen and Uncle Squaty, *Movin' Party*.

"Clap My Hands." Milkshake, *Happy Songs*.

"Clap Your Hands." Old Town School of Folk Music, *Wiggleworms Love You*.

"Clap Your Hands." Peterson, Carole, *Sticky Bubble Gum*; Raven, Nancy, *Hop, Skip, and Sing*.

"Clap Your Hands." Tickle Tune Typhoon, *Circle Around*.

"Cock-a-Doodle Doo." The Learning Station, *Here We Go Loopty Loo*.

"Copy Cat." Greg and Steve, *Kidding Around*.

"Copycat." Rosen, Gary, *Cookin'*.

"Couch Potato Pokey." Feldman, Jean, *Is Everybody Happy?*

"Crab Walking." The Learning Station, *Get Funky and Musical Fun*.

"Dance and Boogie." Mr. Al, *Mr. Al Concert Live*; Mr. Al, *Put Your Groove On.*

"Down the Sidewalk." Big Jeff, *Big Jeff.*

"Everybody Clap Your Hands." Peterson, Carole, *Stinky Cake.*

"Everybody Dance." Palmer, Hap, *Can a Jumbo Jet Sing the Alphabet?*

"Eyebrows Touch the Moon." The Learning Station, *Literacy in Motion.*

"Family Goodbyes." Gill, Jim, *Moving Rhymes for Modern Times.*

"Fancy Dancing." Mr. Al, *Rockin' the Alphabet.*

"Fast Boogie." Mr. Al, *Put Your Groove On.*

"Feel the Music." Parachute Express, *Feel the Music.*

"Follow Along." Palmer, Hap, *One Little Sound.*

"Follow Directions." SteveSongs, *Little Superman.*

"Follow Me, I Am the Leader." The Learning Station, *Get Funky and Musical Fun.*

"Follow the Leader." Jenkins, Ella, *Songs Children Love to Sing.*

"Following You." Palmer, Hap, *Can a Cherry Pie Wave Goodbye?*

"The Freeze." Greg and Steve, *Kids in Motion*; Greg and Steve, *We All Live Together*, vol. 2.

"From Your Seat." The Learning Station, *Get Funky and Musical Fun.*

"Fun with the Rhyme Time Band." Palmer, Hap, *Can a Jumbo Jet Sing the Alphabet?*

"Get Ready, Get Set, Sing!" Barchas, Sarah, *Get Ready, Get Set, Sing!*

"Get Up and Go." Greg and Steve, *We All Live Together*, vol. 5.

"Giggle Tickle Fiddle Little Wiggle Around." Polisar, Barry Louis, *Old Dog, New Tricks.*

"Glad to See You." Allard, Peter and Ellen, *Sing It! Say It! Stamp It! Sway It!* vol. 2.

"Groove and Boogie." Mr. Al, *Dance like This.*

"Hand Jive." Greg and Steve, *We All Live Together*, vol. 4.

"Hands Are for Clapping." Gill, Jim, *Jim Gill Sings the Sneezing Song and Other Contagious Tunes.*

"Head, Shoulders, Baby." Dana, *Dana's Best Sing and Play-a-Long Tunes*; Sharon, Lois, and Bram, *School Days.*

"Head, Shoulders, Knees, and Toes." Bartels, Joanie, *Bathtime Magic*; Beall, Pamela, and Susan Nipp, *Wee Sing Children's Songs and Fingerplays*; Cassidy, Nancy, *Nancy Cassidy's KidsSongs*; The Learning Station, *Here We Go Loopty Loo*; Magical Music Express, *Music Is Magic*; McGrath, Bob, *Sing Along with Bob #1.*

"Head to Toe Dance." The Learning Station, *Literacy in Motion.*

"Heel, Toe." The Learning Station, *Here We Go Loopty Loo.*

"Here We Go Loopty Loo." The Learning Station, *Here We Go Loopty Loo.* (Same song as "Loop 'd Loo" and "Looby Loo.")

"Hey, Betty Martin." Buchman, Rachel, *Hello Everybody!*; Raven, Nancy, *Hop, Skip, and Sing.*

"Hippity-Hop." Avni, Fran, *Artichokes and Brussel Sprouts.*

"The Hokey Pokey." Beall, Pamela, and Susan Nipp, *Wee Sing and Play*; The Chenille Sisters, *1, 2, 3 for Kids*; Dana, *Dana's Best Sing and Play-a-Long Tunes*; Greg and Steve, *Kidding Around*; Howdy, Buck, *Giddyup!*; The Learning Station, *All-Time Children's Favorites*; McGrath, Bob, *Sing Along with Bob #2*; Peterson, Carole, *Sticky Bubble Gum*; Sharon, Lois, and Bram, *Great Big Hits 2*; Tickle Tune Typhoon, *All of Us Will Shine*; Zanes, Dan, *Family Dance.*

"Hop Along Hop." Walker, Graham, *Cats' Night Out.*

"Hop Scotch Polka." McGrath, Bob, and Katherine Smithrim, *Songs and Games for Toddlers.*

"Hula Hoop." Fink, Cathy, and Marcy Marxer, *Bon Appétit!*

"I Am Here and You Are Here." Allard, Peter and Ellen, *Sing It! Say It! Stamp It! Sway It!* vol. 3.

"I Can't Sit Still." Mr. Al, *Dance like This.*

"I Got a Wiggle." Colleen and Uncle Squaty, *1, 2, 3, Four-Ever Friends.*

"I Move My Feet." Charette, Rick, *King Kong Chair.*

"I Went to School One Morning." Sharon, Lois, and Bram, *School Days.*

"If You Got 1." Roberts, Justin, *Great Big Sun.*

"If You're Happy and You Know It." Arnold, Linda, *Happiness Cake*; Beall, Pamela, and Susan Nipp, *Wee Sing Children's Songs and Fingerplays*; Dana, *Dana's Best Sing and Play-a-Long Tunes*; Feldman, Jean, *Is Everybody Happy?*; Greg and Steve, *We All Live Together*, vol. 3; The Learning Station, *All-Time Children's Favorites*; Marxer, Marcy, *Jump Children.*

"I'm a Pretzel." Palmer, Hap, *So Big.*

"The Irrational Anthem." Gill, Jim, *Jim Gill's Irrational Anthem.*

"It Makes Me Jump." Fite, Stephen, *Cool to Be in School.*

"I've Got Music in Me." Greg and Steve, *Fun and Games.*

"I've Got Two Hands." Allard, Peter and Ellen, *Sing It! Say It! Stamp It! Sway It!* vol. 3.

"Jim Along Josie." Beall, Pamela, and Susan Nipp, *Wee Sing Games, Games, Games*; Greg and Steve, *Ready, Set, Move!*; Penner, Fred, *Rhyme a Word or Two*; Raven, Nancy, *Hop, Skip, and Sing.*

"Jump." Avni, Fran, *Artichokes and Brussel Sprouts.*

"Jump." Milkshake, *Bottle of Sunshine.*

"Jump Children." Fink, Cathy, and Marcy Marxer, *A Cathy & Marcy Collection for Kids*; Marxer, Marcy, *Jump Children.*

"Jump Down, Turn Around." Greg and Steve, *Ready, Set, Move!*

"Jump Up, Turn Around." Gill, Jim, *Moving Rhymes for Modern Times.*

"Jumpalong Jake." Chapin, Tom, *Great Big Fun for the Very Little One.*

"Jumpin' Beans." Grunsky, Jack, *Follow the Leader*; Grunsky, Jack, *Sing and Dance.*

"Junior's Hand Jive." Mr. Al, *Put Your Groove On.*

"Keep Moving." The Learning Station, *Here We Go Loopty Loo.* (Same song as "One Finger, One Thumb.")

"Keep On Dancing." Avni, Fran, *Artichokes and Brussel Sprouts.*

"Let's Clap Our Hands Together." Colleen and Uncle Squaty, *Fingerplays, Movement and Story Songs.*

"Let's Get Started." Mr. Al, *Mr. Al a Carte*; Mr. Al, *Mr. Al Concert Live.*

"Let's Party." Mr. Al, *Dance like This.*

"London Bridge (Bouncing Down)." The Learning Station, *Seasonal Songs in Motion.*

"Looby Loo." Beall, Pamela, and Susan Nipp, *Wee Sing Children's Songs and Fingerplays*; Beall, Pamela, and Susan Nipp, *Wee Sing Games, Games, Games*; McGrath, Bob, *Sing Along with Bob #1*; Old Town School of Folk Music, *Wiggleworms Love You*; Peterson, Carole, *Tiny Tunes*; Rosenthal, Phil, *The Paw Paw Patch*; Sharon, Lois, and Bram, *One Elephant, Deux Éléphants.* (Same song as "Here We Go Loopty Loo" and "Loop 'd Loo.")

"Loop 'd Loo." Greg and Steve, *We All Live Together*, vol. 1. (Same song as "Here We Go Loopty Loo" and "Looby Loo.")

"Lost in the Zoo." Dana, *Dana's Best Sing and Play-a-Long Tunes.*

"Me-tronome." Allard, Peter and Ellen, *Good Kid.*

"Monkey See, Monkey Do." Mr. Al, *Mr. Al a Carte.*

"Mother Gooney Bird." Feldman, Jean, *Dr. Jean and Friends.*

"Move-A-Roni." Colleen and Uncle Squaty, *Movin' Party.*

"Move Over." Sharon, Lois, and Bram, *Mainly Mother Goose.*

"Move with Me." The Learning Station, *Children Love to Sing and Dance.*

"Move Your Body." Mr. Al, *Mr. Al Concert Live.*

"Movin' Party." Colleen and Uncle Squaty, *Movin' Party.*

"Movin' round the Room." Colleen and Uncle Squaty, *Sing-a-Move-a-Dance.*

"Mr. Knickerbocker." Greg and Steve, *Fun and Games.*

"Mr. Robot." Kimmy Schwimmy, *Kimmy Schwimmy Music*, vol. 1.

"Must Be Working." Kinder, Brian, *A Kid like You.*

"My Bonnie." Gill, Jim, *Jim Gill Sings Do Re Mi on His Toe Leg Knee.*

"The Nothing Wrong Song." Gill, Jim, *Jim Gill Sings Do Re Mi on His Toe Leg Knee.*

"On My Way to School." Chapin, Tom, *Mother Earth.*

"On the Move." Crow, Dan, *A Friend, a Laugh, a Walk in the Woods.*

"One Finger, One Thumb." Allard, Peter and Ellen, *Sing It! Say It! Stamp It! Sway It!* vol. 1; Beall, Pamela, and Susan Nipp, *Wee Sing Children's Songs and Fingerplays*; McGrath, Bob, *Sing Along with Bob #2.* (Same song as "Keep Moving.")

"Palmas." LaFond, Lois, *Turning It Upside Down.*

"Peaceful Feet." Various Artists, *Hear and Gone in 60 Seconds.*

"Peter Hammers." Beall, Pamela, and Susan Nipp, *Wee Sing Children's Songs and Fingerplays.*

"The Pinky Dance." Mr. Al, *Put Your Groove On.*

"Place Your Hands." The Learning Station, *Get Funky and Musical Fun.*

"Please Stand Up." Mr. Al, *Mr. Al a Carte.*

"Pop-Up/Sit Down." Harper, Monty, *The Great Green Squishy Mean Concert CD.*

"Put Your Finger in the Air." Greg and Steve, *Playing Favorites*; Guthrie, Woody, *Nursery Days*; Guthrie, Woody, *Woody's 20 Grow Big Songs*; McGrath, Bob, *Sing Along with Bob #2*; Seeger, Pete, *For Kids and Just Plain Folks*; Silberg, "Miss Jackie," *Lollipops and Spaghetti.*

"Put Your Finger On." Parachute Express, *Feel the Music.*

"Put Your Groove On." Mr. Al, *Mr. Al Concert Live*; Mr. Al, *Put Your Groove On.*

"Put Your Hands in the Air." Palmer, Hap, *So Big.*

"Put Your Little Foot." Beall, Pamela, and Susan Nipp, *Wee Sing Fun 'n' Folk.*

"Put Your Little Hand In." Fite, Stephen, *Cool to Be in School.*

"Put Your Thumb in the Air." Scruggs, Joe, *Deep in the Jungle.*

"Razzama Tazzama." Allard, Peter and Ellen, *Raise the Children.*

"Reach for the Sky." Beall, Pamela, and Susan Nipp, *Wee Sing Children's Songs and Fingerplays.*

"Ready for a Good Time." Greg and Steve, *Ready, Set, Move!*

"Ready, Set, Move!" Greg and Steve, *Ready, Set, Move!*

"Rhythm in My Fingers." Gill, Jim, *Moving Rhymes for Modern Times.*

"Rhythm, Rhythm." Beall, Pamela, and Susan Nipp, *Wee Sing Games, Games, Games.*

"Rig a Jig Jig." Cassidy, Nancy, *Nancy Cassidy's KidsSongs*; McGrath, Bob, *Sing Along with Bob #2*; McGrath, Bob, and Katherine Smithrim, *Songs and Games for Toddlers*; Raven, Nancy, *Hop, Skip, and Sing.*

"Rock and Roll Body Parts." Mr. Al, *Mr. Al a Carte.*

"Rock n' Roll Journey." The Learning Station, *Rock n' Roll Songs That Teach.*

"Rock with Me." Greg and Steve, *Fun and Games.*

"Running down the Hill." Berkner, Laurie, *Under a Shady Tree.*

"Scratch Your Head." Colleen and Uncle Squaty, *Sing-a-Move-a-Dance.*

"See-Saw." Colleen and Uncle Squaty, *Sing-a-Move-a-Dance.*

"Shake a Friend's Hand." Peterson, Carole, *Stinky Cake.*

"Shake a Toe." Raffi, *Bananaphone.*

"Shake It." Colleen and Uncle Squaty, *Rumble to the Bottom.*

"Shake It Up." Fite, Stephen, *Gobs of Fun.*

"Shake It Up." Mr. Al, *Rockin' the Alphabet.*

"Shake My Sillies Out." Cassidy, Nancy, *Nancy Cassidy's KidsSongs*; McGrath, Bob, *Sing Along with Bob #2*; Raffi, *More Singable Songs*; Raffi, *Raffi in Concert*; Various Artists, *A Child's Celebration of Silliest Songs.*

"Shimmy Shake." Greg and Steve, *Ready, Set, Move!*

"Show Me!" Frezza, Rebecca, *Tall and Small.*

"Silly Willy." Feldman, Jean, *Dr. Jean Sings Silly Songs.*

"Simon Says." Greg and Steve, *We All Live Together*, vol. 3.

"Simon Says." The Learning Station, *Get Funky and Musical Fun.*

"Simon Says." Trout Fishing in America, *InFINity*; Trout Fishing in America, *My Best Day.*

"Sing-a-Move-a-Dance." Colleen and Uncle Squaty, *Sing-a-Move-a-Dance.*

"Slap Happy." The Learning Station, *La Di Da La Di Di Dance with Me.*

"Sliding, Rolling and Jumping." Gill, Jim, *Moving Rhymes for Modern Times.*

"Sodeo." Raffi, *More Singable Songs.*

"Spaghetti Legs." Gill, Jim, *Jim Gill Sings the Sneezing Song and Other Contagious Tunes.*

"Spin." Rudnick, Ben, *Fun and Games.*

"Spin Again." Gill, Jim, *Jim Gill Sings Do Re Mi on His Toe Leg Knee.*

"Spin Around." Alsop, Peter, *Uh-Oh!*

"Stand Up!" Cosgrove, Jim, *Mr. Stinky Feet's Road Trip.*

"Stop and Go." LaFond, Lois, *Turning It Upside Down.*

"Strollin' down the Road." Gill, Jim, *Moving Rhymes for Modern Times.*

"Sunscreen." The Learning Station, *Seasonal Songs in Motion.*

"Super Kid." Kinder, Brian, *One More Time.*

"Super Mom." Nagler, Eric, *Improvise with Eric Nagler.*

"Take Your Little Hand." Silberg, "Miss Jackie," *Sing It Again Please.*

"The Tempo Marches On." Gill, Jim, *Jim Gill Sings Do Re Mi on His Toe Leg Knee.*

"Ten Fingers." Allard, Peter and Ellen, *Sing It! Say It! Stamp It! Sway It!* vol. 2.

"Tennessee Wig Walk." Zanes, Dan, *House Party.*

"Tetes, Espaules." Raffi, *Rise and Shine.*

"That's the Way It Goes." Allard, Peter and Ellen, *Sing It! Say It! Stamp It! Sway It!* vol. 2.

"'Til the Music Stops." Allard, Peter and Ellen, *Sing It! Say It! Stamp It! Sway It!* vol. 1.

"Toes, Knees, Shoulders, and Head." Kimmy Schwimmy, *Kimmy Schwimmy Music*, vol. 1.

"Tommy Thumb." Colleen and Uncle Squaty, *Fingerplays, Movement and Story Songs*; Peterson, Carole, *Stinky Cake*; Sharon, Lois, and Bram, *Great Big Hits 2*.

"Tony Chestnut." The Learning Station, *Tony Chestnut and Fun Time Action Songs*.

"A Tooty Ta." Feldman, Jean, *Dr. Jean and Friends*; Mr. Al, *Dance like This*; Mr. Al, *Mr. Al Concert Live*.

"To-Ro-March." Ungar, Jay, and Lyn Hardy, *A Place to Be*.

"Touch Your Nose." Avni, Fran, *Artichokes and Brussel Sprouts*; Avni, Fran, *Little Ears: Songs for Reading Readiness*.

"Tummy Tango." Greg and Steve, *Kids in Motion*.

"Turn Around." LaFond, Lois, *Turning It Upside Down*.

"Turn Around Game." Scruggs, Joe, *Late Last Night*.

"Use Your Own Two Feet." Fink, Cathy, and Marcy Marxer, *A Cathy & Marcy Collection for Kids*; Marxer, Marcy, *Jump Children*.

"Walk Walk." Peterson, Carole, *Tiny Tunes*.

"Walkin' Shoes." Peterson, Carole, *Tiny Tunes*.

"Walking Can Be Fun." The Learning Station, *Children Love to Sing and Dance*.

"Walking, Walking." Beall, Pamela, and Susan Nipp, *Wee Sing Children's Songs and Fingerplays*; Beall, Pamela, and Susan Nipp, *Wee Sing for Baby*.

"A Walking We Will Go." Greg and Steve, *We All Live Together*, vol. 5.

"When You Are One." McGrath, Bob, and Katherine Smithrim, *Songs and Games for Toddlers*.

"Where Is Thumbkin?" Beall, Pamela, and Susan Nipp, *Wee Sing Children's Songs and Fingerplays*; McGrath, Bob, *Sing Along with Bob #1*.

"Wiggle." Alsop, Peter, *Uh-Oh!*

"Wiggle My Toe." Scruggs, Joe, *Late Last Night*.

"The Wiggle Song." Peterson, Carole, *Sticky Bubble Gum*.

"Wiggle Wobble." Greg and Steve, *We All Live Together*, vol. 1.

"Wiggle Worm." Mayer, Hans, *Stars of the Swing Set*.

"Wiggle Your Fingers." Allard, Peter and Ellen, *Sing It! Say It! Stamp It! Sway It!* vol. 2.

"Wiggle Your Knees Boogie." Mr. Al, *Mr. Al a Carte*.

"Wiggles, Jiggles, and Giggles." Fite, Stephen, *Wiggles, Jiggles, and Giggles*.

"Willowbee." Beall, Pamela, and Susan Nipp, *Wee Sing Games, Games, Games*.

"Willy Dilly Diddle Hop Camilly." The Learning Station, *Seasonal Songs in Motion*.
"Wobbly Song." Walker, Graham, *Fiddlesticks*.

Dancing

"The Ants in Your Pants Dance." The Chenille Sisters, *Teaching Hippopotami to Fly!*
"At the Codfish Ball." The Chenille Sisters, *1, 2, 3 for Kids*; Lithgow, John, *Singin' in the Bathtub*; Muldaur, Maria, *Animal Crackers in My Soup*.
"Dance." Harper, Jessica, *Hey, Picasso*.
"Dance Around." Guthrie, Woody, *Nursery Days*; Guthrie, Woody, *Woody's 20 Grow Big Songs*; Raven, Nancy, *Singing, Prancing, and Dancing*.
"Dance Around." Ralph's World, *Green Gorilla, Monster, and Me*.
"Dance, Dance, Dance." Chapin, Tom, *Around the World and Back Again*.
"Dance like This." Mr. Al, *Dance like This*; Mr. Al, *Mr. Al Concert Live*.
"Dance Medley." Greg and Steve, *We All Live Together*, vol. 4.
"Dance on My Shoes." Milkshake, *Happy Songs*.
"Dance on One Leg." Big Jeff, *Big Jeff and His Middle-Sized Band*.
"Dance with Me." Frezza, Rebecca, *Road Trip*.
"Dancin' Machine." Greg and Steve, *Rockin' down the Road*; Greg and Steve, *We All Live Together*, vol. 3.
"Dancin' with Happy Feet." SteveSongs, *Morning til Night*.
"Dancing." Sprout, Jonathan, *Dr. Music*.
"Do the Bird." Grunsky, Jack, *Follow the Leader*; Grunsky, Jack, *Jack in the Box 2*.
"Don't Make Me Dance." Chapin, Tom, *Some Assembly Required*.
"Earth Dance." Grunsky, Jack, *Like a Flower to the Sun*.
"Fancy Pants Dance." Cosgrove, Jim, *Pick Me! Pick Me!*
"Get the Rhythm." Harper, Jessica, *Nora's Room*.
"The Good Night Waltz." Zanes, Dan, *Family Dance*.
"Goofy Hat Dance." Greg and Steve, *Fun and Games*.
"Hand Dance." Feldman, Jean, *Is Everybody Happy?*
"Hand Jive." Fite, Stephen, *Wiggles, Jiggles, and Giggles*.
"Hip to Hop." Harper, Jessica, *Nora's Room*.
"I Can Dance." Trout Fishing in America, *Family Music Party*; Trout Fishing in America, *Mine!*
"I Really Like to Dance." Berkner, Laurie, *Buzz Buzz*.
"Jig Along Home." Guthrie, Woody, *Woody's 20 Grow Big Songs*; Guthrie, Woody and Arlo, *This Land Is Your Land*; Raffi, *Corner Grocery Store*; Rosenthal, Phil, *Folksongs and Bluegrass for Children*; Rosenthal, Phil, *The Green Grass Grew All Around*; Strausman, Paul, *Rainbows, Stones, and Dinosaur Bones*.

"Journey Dance." Pirtle, Sarah, *Magical Earth.*

"Knees Up Mother Brown." Raffi, *Raffi in Concert.*

"La Di Da La Di Di." The Learning Station, *La Di Da La Di Di Dance with Me.*

"Let's Dance." Fite, Stephen, *Gobs of Fun.*

"Let's Dance." Ode, Eric, *Trash Can.*

"Let's Shake." Zanes, Dan, *Catch That Train!*

"List of Dances." Gill, Jim, *Jim Gill Makes It Noisy in Boise, Idaho.*

"A Little Polka." Bartles, Joanie, *Put On Your Dancing Shoes.*

"Magical Waltz." Miss Amy, *Underwater.*

"Mockingbird Polka." Fink, Cathy, and Marcy Marxer, *All Wound Up!*

"Molly's Dance." Magical Music Express, *Friendship Stew.*

"My Heart (Does a Little Dance)." Bartles, Joanie, *Put On Your Dancing Shoes.*

"Now We're Dancing." The Learning Station, *Children Love to Sing and Dance.*

"One Big Dance." Stotts, Stuart, *One Big Dance.*

"Oogie Woogie Boogie." Bartles, Joanie, *Put On Your Dancing Shoes.*

"Partner Dance." Peterson, Carole, *Stinky Cake.*

"Pig Latin Polka Dance." Fink, Cathy, and Marcy Marxer, *Scat like That.*

"Razz-Ma-Tazz." Parachute Express, *Don't Blink.*

"Reggae Dancin'." Various Artists, *Caribbean Playground.*

"Rock and Roll Freeze Dance." Palmer, Hap, *So Big.*

"Rock and Roll Polka." Fink, Cathy, and Marcy Marxer, *Air Guitar.*

"Shakin' Everywhere." Gill, Jim, *Jim Gill's Irrational Anthem.*

"Silly Dance Contest." Gill, Jim, *Jim Gill Sings the Sneezing Song and Other Contagious Tunes.*

"Sing and Dance." Grunsky, Jack, *Dancing Feet*; Grunsky, Jack, *Sing and Dance.*

"Skip to My Lou." Beall, Pamela, and Susan Nipp, *Wee Sing and Play*; Feldman, Jean, *Nursery Rhymes and Good Ol' Times*; Fink, Cathy, *When the Rain Comes Down*; Greg and Steve, *We All Live Together*, vol. 1; Mitchell, Elizabeth, *You Are My Sunshine*; Raffi, *Raffi Radio*; Raven, Nancy, *Hop, Skip, and Sing*; Rosenthal, Phil, *The Paw Paw Patch*; Rudnick, Ben, *Emily Songs*; Seeger, Pete, *Pete Seeger's Family Concert*; Various Artists, *A Child's Celebration of Folk Music*; Various Artists, *A Child's Celebration of Song*; Zanes, Dan, *Family Dance.*

"Swing Your Partner." Gill, Jim, *Moving Rhymes for Modern Times.*

"Waltzing with Bears." Herdman, Priscilla, *Stardreamer*; Knight, Tom, *Don't Kiss a Codfish*; Rosen, Gary, *Teddy Bears' Picnic.*

"What Dance You Wanna Do?" Colleen and Uncle Squaty, *Sing-a-Move-a-Dance.*

"When Daddy Starts to Dance." Pease, Tom, *Daddy Starts to Dance*; Stotts, Stuart, *One Big Dance*.

"You Can Dance." LaFond, Lois, *One World*.

Moving

"Best Friends." SteveSongs, *On a Flying Guitar*.

"Goodbye Good Friend." Vitamin L, *Every Moment!*

"I Don't Want to Go." Thaddeus Rex, *We Wanna Rock*.

"I Like Where I Am." Harper, Jessica, *Rhythm in My Shoes*.

"Justin." Scruggs, Joe, *Abracadabra*.

"Moving." Roberts, Justin, *Not Naptime*.

"Moving Day." Harley, Bill, *One More Time*; Harley, Bill, *There's a Pea on My Plate*.

"Tomorrow We're Moving Away." Strausman, Paul, *Rainbows, Stones, and Dinosaur Bones*.

Music

"All over My Home Town." Strausman, Paul, *Rainbows, Stones, and Dinosaur Bones*.

"Boom, Boom." Milkshake, *Bottle of Sunshine*.

"Clap, Snap, and Whistle." Byers, Kathy, *Do You Wish You Could Fly?*

"Crazy Song." Yosi, *Monkey Business*.

"Dishpan Jam." LaFond, Lois, *Lois LaFond and the Rockadiles*.

"Dr. Music." Sprout, Jonathan, *Dr. Music*.

"Everybody Has Music Inside." Greg and Steve, *We All Live Together*, vol. 4.

"Everything Is Music." Harley, Bill, *Down in the Backpack*.

"The Fine Friends Are Here." Zanes, Dan, *Catch That Train!*

"The Finger Band." Beall, Pamela, and Susan Nipp, *Wee Sing Children's Songs and Fingerplays*.

"First You Make a Note." Kinnoin, Dave, *Daring Dewey*.

"The Frog's Party." Walker, Mary Lu, *The Frog's Party*.

"Gonna Have a Good Time." Rosenshontz, *Share It*.

"I Feel Music." The Dream Project, *We've All Got Stories*.

"I'm in the Mood." Raffi, *Rise and Shine*.

"Introduction to the Blues." Knight, Tom, *The Classroom Boogie*.

"Is There Anybody Here?" Sharon, Lois, and Bram, *One Elephant, Deux Éléphants*.

"Let's Make Music." Dana, *Dana's Best Sing and Play-a-Long Tunes*.

"Let's Make Some Noise." Raffi, *Everything Grows*.

"Making Good Noise." Chapin, Tom, *Making Good Noise*.

"Making Music." Tickle Tune Typhoon, *Hearts and Hands*.

"Mama Don't Allow." Arnold, Linda, *Happiness Cake*; Hullabaloo, *Sing Along with Sam*; Old Town School of Folk Music, *Wiggleworms Love You*; Rosenthal, Phil, *Folksongs and Bluegrass for Children*; Rymer, Brady, *Every Day Is a Birthday*.

"Me-tronome." Allard, Peter and Ellen, *Good Kid*.

"Mi Cuerpo." Stotts, Stuart, and Tom Pease, *Celebrate: A Song Resource*.

"Mi Cuerpo Hace Musica." Pirtle, Sarah, *The Wind Is Telling Secrets*.

"Milkshake." Milkshake, *Bottle of Sunshine*.

"Music." Grunsky, Jack, *Sing and Dance*.

"The Music Box." Fink, Cathy, and Marcy Marxer, *Pillow Full of Wishes*.

"Music Farm." Various Artists, *World Playground 2*.

"Music in My Mother's House." Stotts, Stuart, *One Big Dance*.

"Music Is a Lovely Language." Various Artists, *Hear and Gone in 60 Seconds*.

"Music Is Magic." Magical Music Express, *Music Is Magic*.

"Music Makes Me Feel Better." LaFond, Lois, *Lois LaFond and the Rockadiles*.

"One Little Song." Stotts, Stuart, and Tom Pease, *Celebrate: A Song Resource*.

"Out in the Garage." Daddy A Go Go, *Big Rock Rooster*.

"Rock around the World." Pease, Tom, *I'm Gonna Reach!*; Stotts, Stuart, *Are We There Yet?*

"Rock 'n Roll Teddy Bear." Rosenshontz, *Rock 'n Roll Teddy Bear*; Rosenshontz, *Rosenshontz Greatest Hits*.

"Rockadile Rock." LaFond, Lois, *Lois LaFond and the Rockadiles*.

"Samba." Grunsky, Jack, *Jack in the Box 1*; Various Artists, *Hear and Gone in 60 Seconds*.

"The Singing Tree." Pirtle, Sarah, *Magical Earth*.

"Street Beat." Grunsky, Jack, *Follow the Leader*; Grunsky, Jack, *Jack in the Box 2*.

"The Troubadour." Chapin, Tom, *Around the World and Back Again*.

"Turn On the Music." Palmer, Hap, *Turn On the Music*.

"We Have a Song." Kinnoin, Dave, *Daring Dewey*.

"We Wanna Rock." Thaddeus Rex, *We Wanna Rock*.

"Your Hands." Grunsky, Jack, *Follow the Leader*; Grunsky, Jack, *Playground*.

"Your Song." Thaddeus Rex, *We Wanna Rock*.

Musical Instruments

"Air Guitar." Fink, Cathy, and Marcy Marxer, *Air Guitar*.

"The Bamboo Flute." Grunsky, Jack, *Playground*.

"The Band." Harper, Jessica, *Inside Out*.

"The Bandshell Right Next to the Zoo." Lithgow, John, *Farkle and Friends*.

"Bang on the Pan." Chapin, Tom, *Making Good Noise.*

"Banjo." Kinder, Brian, *One More Time.*

"A Banjo Jamboree." Ode, Eric, *Grandpa's Truck.*

"Banjo Song." Fink, Cathy, *When the Rain Comes Down*; Fink, Cathy, and Marcy Marxer, *A Cathy & Marcy Collection for Kids.*

"The Battle of the Bands." Daddy A Go Go, *Mojo A Go Go.*

"Big Brass Band." Grammer, Red, *Can You Sound Just like Me?*

"Boy Meets Drum." Harper, Jessica, *Rhythm in My Shoes.*

"Cello." Grunsky, Jack, *Playground.*

"Come Follow the Band." Sharon, Lois, and Bram, *Sing A to Z.*

"D Is for Drums." They Might Be Giants, *Here Come the ABCs.*

"Dads Who Rock." Daddy A Go Go, *Eat Every Bean and Pea on Your Plate.*

"Didgeridoo." Shontz, Bill, *The Day I Read a Book.*

"Drumming the House." Gill, Jim, *Moving Rhymes for Modern Times.*

"Electric Guitar." Stotts, Stuart, *Are We There Yet?*

"Guitar Box Band." Pelham, Ruth, *Under One Sky.*

"Guitars from Mars." Daddy A Go Go, *Big Rock Rooster.*

"Hippo Hurray." Arnold, Linda, *Favorites in the Key of Fun.*

"I Am a Fine Musician." Peterson, Carole, *Sticky Bubble Gum.*

"I Love Playing the Kazoo." Chapin, Tom, *Making Good Noise.*

"I Spy." The Learning Station, *Get Funky and Musical Fun.*

"I'd Rather Lead a Band." Lithgow, John, *Farkle and Friends.*

"In Our Band." Knight, Tom, *The Classroom Boogie.*

"Johnny Glockenspiel." Chapin, Tom, *Zag Zig.*

"Kazoo Song." Cosgrove, Jim, *Bop Bop Dinosaur.*

"The Kitchen Percussion Song." The Chenille Sisters, *1, 2, 3 for Kids.*

"The Magic Whistle." Paxton, Tom, *I've Got a Yo-Yo.*

"The Mandolin Song." Rosenshontz, *Share It.*

"The Mouse Band." Grunsky, Jack, *Sing and Dance.*

"A Mozart Duet." Chapin, Tom, *In My Hometown.*

"The Music Store." Rosenshontz, *Share It.*

"Music Teacher Blues." Gemini, *The Best of Gemini.*

"Musical Animal." Grammer, Red, *Down the Do-Re-Mi.*

"My B-A-N-J-O." Chapin, Tom, *Making Good Noise.*

"The Night We Made It Noisy in Boise, Idaho." Gill, Jim, *Jim Gill Makes It Noisy in Boise, Idaho.*

"Not Your Father's." Harper, Jessica, *Hey, Picasso.*

"Old MacDonald Had a Band." Raffi, *Singable Songs for the Very Young*.
"On a Flying Guitar." SteveSongs, *On a Flying Guitar*.
"The Orchestra." Beall, Pamela, and Susan Nipp, *Wee Sing and Pretend*.
"People All over the World." Stotts, Stuart, *Are We There Yet?*
"Percussion Band." Grunsky, Jack, *Follow the Leader*; Grunsky, Jack, *Jack in the Box 2*.
"Piano." Tucker, Nancy, *Glad That You Asked*.
"Play My Drum." Strausman, Paul, *Camels, Cats, and Rainbows*.
"Play the Band." Peterson, Carole, *Tiny Tunes*.
"Pots and Pans." Boynton, Sandra, *Dog Train*.
"The Ragtime Dance." Chapin, Tom, *Zag Zig*.
"Rat-Tat-Tat-Tat-Tattoo." Parachute Express, *Doctor Looney's Remedy*.
"Rock and Roll MacDonald." Scruggs, Joe, *Deep in the Jungle*.
"Rock Band." Beall, Pamela, and Susan Nipp, *Wee Sing and Pretend*.
"Rock 'n' Roll Rhythm Band." Greg and Steve, *We All Live Together*, vol. 5.
"Rock 'n Roll Teddy Bear." Rosen, Gary, *Teddy Bears' Picnic*.
"Sammy the Dog." Ralph's World, *Happy Lemon*.
"Saxophone." Knight, Tom, *Don't Kiss a Codfish*.
"Strings on My Banjo." Gill, Jim, *Jim Gill Makes It Noisy in Boise, Idaho*.
"Sunny Day Rainy Day Anytime Band." Ralph's World, *At the Bottom of the Sea*.
"Teddy Rockin'." Shontz, Bill, *Teddy Bear's Greatest Hits*.
"This Old Guitar." Tucker, Nancy, *Happy as a Clam*.
"Treehouse Orchestra." Ralph's World, *The Amazing Adventures of Kid Astro*.
"Ukulele—O." Foote, Norman, *If the Shoe Fits*.
"What Is a Didjeridoo?" Chapin, Tom, *Around the World and Back Again*.
"You Just Improvise." Nagler, Eric, *Improvise with Eric Nagler*.
"You're in the Jug Band." Stotts, Stuart, and Tom Pease, *Celebrate: A Song Resource*.

Singing

"All God's Critters." McCutcheon, John, *Howjadoo*. (Same song as "A Place in the Choir.")
"The Audition." SteveSongs, *Marvelous Day!*
"Bella Bella Tula Monga." Harley, Bill, *I Wanna Play*.
"Don't Forget to Sing." Gemini, *The Best of Gemini*, vol. 2.
"Don't Make Me Sing Along." Simmons, Al, *The Celery Stalks at Midnight*.
"Down the Do-Re-Mi." Grammer, Red, *Down the Do-Re-Mi*.
"Dr. DoReMi." Arnold, Linda, *Happiness Cake*.
"Escala Musical: Musical Scale." Hinojosa, Tish, *Cada Niño: Every Child*.

"Get Ready, Get Set, Sing!" Barchas, Sarah, *Get Ready, Get Set, Sing!*

"The Harmony Song." The Chenille Sisters, *1, 2, 3 for Kids.*

"Hey Dum Diddeley Dum." Cassidy, Nancy, *Nancy Cassidy's KidsSongs*; Sharon, Lois, and Bram, *Great Big Hits.*

"Hi Dee Ho." Cosgrove, Jim, *Pick Me! Pick Me!*

"Hum." Big Jeff, *Big Jeff and His Middle-Sized Band.*

"I Knew a Young Girl (La Lee Lee)." Cosgrove, Jim, *Bop Bop Dinosaur.*

"I Like to Sing." Harley, Bill, *I Wanna Play.*

"I Like to Sing." Stotts, Stuart, *Are We There Yet?*

"It Goes . . ." Frezza, Rebecca, *Tall and Small.*

"Jay Jilly Jango." Parachute Express, *Who's Got a Hug?*

"Let Us Sing Together." Beall, Pamela, and Susan Nipp, *Wee Sing Sing-Alongs.*

"Let's Sing a Song." Foote, Norman, *1000 Pennies.*

"Love to Sing." Magical Music Express, *Music Is Magic.*

"Making Moosic." Moo, Anna, *Making Moosic.*

"A Place in the Choir." Abell, Timmy, *The Farmer's Market*; Grammer, Red, *Down the Do-Re-Mi*; Knight, Tom, *Don't Kiss a Codfish*; Staines, Bill, *The Happy Wanderer.* (Same song as "All God's Critters.")

"Same Song." Allard, Peter and Ellen, *Good Kid.*

"Scat like That." Fink, Cathy, and Marcy Marxer, *Scat like That.*

"Sing." Harper, Jessica, *Hey, Picasso.*

"Sing Along Stew." Arnold, Linda, *Sing Along Stew.*

"Sing and Dance." Grunsky, Jack, *Dancing Feet*; Grunsky, Jack, *Sing and Dance.*

"Sing from Your Heart." Knight, Tom, *Easy as Pie*; McMahon, Elizabeth, *Waltzing with Fireflies.*

"Sing Together." Beall, Pamela, and Susan Nipp, *Wee Sing Sing-Alongs.*

"Sing When the Spirit Says Sing." McGrath, Bob, *Sing Along with Bob #2*; Tickle Tune Typhoon, *Hearts and Hands.* (Same song as "The Spirit Song" and "You Gotta Sing.")

"Sing Your Way Home." Beall, Pamela, and Susan Nipp, *Wee Sing Sing-Alongs.*

"Singalong, Longasing." Chapin, Tom, *Making Good Noise.*

"Sing-Along Song." Parachute Express, *Sunny Side Up.*

"Sing-a-Move-a-Dance." Colleen and Uncle Squaty, *Sing-a-Move-a-Dance.*

"Singing in the Bathtub." The Chenille Sisters, *1, 2, 3 for Kids*; Simmons, Al, *Something Fishy at Camp Wiganishie.*

"Singing Policeman." Foote, Norman, *Pictures on the Fridge.*

"Song in My Tummy." Berkner, Laurie, *Under a Shady Tree.*

"Songbirds." Grunsky, Jack, *Follow the Leader*; Grunsky, Jack, *Jack in the Box 1*.
"The Spirit Song." The Learning Station, *Tony Chestnut and Fun Time Action Songs*. (Same song as "Sing When the Spirit Says Sing" and "You Gotta Sing.")
"Sweet Harmony." Frezza, Rebecca, *Tall and Small*.
"The Swing Along Song." Dana, *Dana's Best Sing and Swing-a-Long Tunes*.
"This Song Is for the Birds." Staines, Bill, *The Happy Wanderer*.
"Time to Sing." Raffi, *One Light One Sun*; Raffi, *Raffi in Concert*.
"Woodland Chorus." Shontz, Bill, *Animal Tales*.
"You Gotta Sing." Cassidy, Nancy, *Nancy Cassidy's KidsSongs*; Raffi, *More Singable Songs*. (Same song as "Sing When the Spirit Says Sing" and "The Spirit Song.")
"You'll Sing a Song and I'll Sing a Song." McGrath, Bob, *Sing Along with Bob #2*; Raffi, *Corner Grocery Store*; Various Artists, *cELLAbration! A Tribute to Ella Jenkins*.

Yodeling

"A-E-I-O and U." Fink, Cathy, and Marcy Marxer, *Scat like That*.
"Austrian Folk Song." Byers, Kathy, *'Round the Campfire*. (Same song as "Once an Austrian Went Yodeling.")
"Grandma Slid down the Mountain." Fink, Cathy, *Grandma Slid down the Mountain*; Fink, Cathy, and Marcy Marxer, *A Cathy & Marcy Collection for Kids*.
"How Does He Yodel?" Riders in the Sky, *Harmony Ranch*.
"A Kid and a Goat." Foote, Norman, *If the Shoe Fits*.
"Let's All Sing a Yodeling Song." Various Artists, *cELLAbration! A Tribute to Ella Jenkins*.
"Little Pony Hoo." Green Chili Jam Band, *Starfishing*.
"Once an Austrian Went Yodeling." Beall, Pamela, and Susan Nipp, *Wee Sing Silly Songs*; Miss Amy, *Wide, Wide World*. (Same song as "Austrian Folk Song.")
"Pony Ride." Colleen and Uncle Squaty, *Rumble to the Bottom*.
"Rosie the Cow." Walker, Graham, *Knobbledee Knees*.
"3 Happy Cows." Lonnquist, Ken, *Sci-Fi Hi-Fi*.
"Ukulele Blue Yodel." Colleen and Uncle Squaty, *Sing-a-Move-a-Dance*.
"Uncle Squaty Went Yodeling." Colleen and Uncle Squaty, *Fingerplays, Movement and Story Songs*.
"Weggis Zue." Beall, Pamela, and Susan Nipp, *Wee Sing around the World*.
"The Yodel Polka." Fink, Cathy, *Grandma Slid down the Mountain*.

"Yodeling." Gill, Jim, *Jim Gill's Irrational Anthem.*
"The Yodeling Song." Silberg, "Miss Jackie," *Joining Hands with Other Lands.*

Names

"Chicken Joe." Trout Fishing in America, *My World.*
"The Dog That Went to Yale." Simmons, Al, *The Truck I Bought from Moe.*
"Everybody Eats When They Come to My House." Lithgow, John, *Singin' in the Bathtub*; Pease, Tom, *Daddy Starts to Dance*; Sharon, Lois, and Bram, *Great Big Hits 2.*
"Everybody Has a Name." Avni, Fran, *Little Ears: Songs for Reading Readiness.*
"Fifteen Animals." Boynton, Sandra, *Philadelphia Chickens.*
"Four Boys Named Jordan." Harper, Jessica, *Inside Out.*
"Hey, Lolly Lolly." Beall, Pamela, and Susan Nipp, *Wee Sing Sing-Alongs.*
"Hicketty Picketty Bumble Bee." Peterson, Carole, *Tiny Tunes.*
"I Had a Friend." Berkner, Laurie, *Buzz Buzz.*
"I Hate My Name." Charette, Rick, *Where Do My Sneakers Go at Night?*
"I Know a Tom." Various Artists, *cELLAbration! A Tribute to Ella Jenkins.*
"I've Got a Dog and My Dog's Name Is Cat." Polisar, Barry Louis, *Family Concert*; Polisar, Barry Louis, *Old Dog, New Tricks.*
"John Jacob Jingleheimer Schmidt." Beall, Pamela, and Susan Nipp, *Wee Sing Children's Songs and Fingerplays*; Beall, Pamela, and Susan Nipp, *Wee Sing in the Car*; McGrath, Bob, *Sing Along with Bob #2*; Sharon, Lois, and Bram, *School Days*; Various Artists, *A Child's Celebration of Silliest Songs.*
"Lisa Lee Elizabeth." Harper, Monty, *Imagine That.*
"Miss Molly Crackerjack." Ralph's World, *The Amazing Adventures of Kid Astro.*
"My Father's Friends." Del Bianco, Lou, *When I Was a Kid.*
"My Name Begins with a Letter." Avni, Fran, *Little Ears: Songs for Reading Readiness.*
"My Name Game." Grunsky, Jack, *Follow the Leader*; Grunsky, Jack, *Jack in the Box 2.*
"My Name Is . . ." Miss Amy, *Underwater.*
"The Name Game." Bartels, Joanie, *Sillytime Magic*; The Chenille Sisters, *The Big Picture and Other Songs for Kids*; Sharon, Lois, and Bram, *Great Big Hits 2*; Sharon, Lois, and Bram, *Sing A to Z.*
"The Name Song." Daddy A Go Go, *Cool Songs for Cool Kids.*
"The Name Song." Ralph's World, *Ralph's World.*
"Names." Jenkins, Ella, *Growing Up with Ella Jenkins.*
"Patalina Matalina." Feldman, Jean, *Dr. Jean and Friends*; Feldman, Jean, *Dr. Jean Sings Silly Songs.*

"Tappy Tappy." The Learning Station, *Literacy in Motion.*
"Tuna Fish." Madsen, Gunnar, *Ants in My Pants!*
"Willoughby Wallaby Woo." Cassidy, Nancy, *Nancy Cassidy's KidsSongs*; McGrath, Bob, *Sing Along with Bob #1*; Raffi, *Singable Songs for the Very Young.*
"Yon Yonson." Beall, Pamela, and Susan Nipp, *Wee Sing in the Car*; Ralph's World, *Peggy's Pie Parlor.*
"Your Name Backwards." Trout Fishing in America, *InFINity.*
"Your Name Is . . ." McGrath, Bob, and Katherine Smithrim, *Songs and Games for Toddlers.*
"Zachary Zach." Foote, Norman, *If the Shoe Fits.*

Nighttime

"After the Fuss." Livingston, Bob, *Open the Window.*
"The Camper's Lullaby." Banana Slug String Band, *Wings of Slumber.*
"Camping Tonight." Haynes, Sammie, *Nature's ABCs.*
"Cowlit Night." Raffi, *Bananaphone.*
"Down the Railroad Track." Lonnquist, Ken, *Welcome 2 Kenland.*
"Evening Time." Zanes, Dan, *Night Time!*
"Go into the Night." Banana Slug String Band, *Penguin Parade.*
"I Love the Dark." Knight, Tom, *The Classroom Boogie.*
"I Sneaked into the Kitchen in the Middle of the Night." Polisar, Barry Louis, *Family Concert*; Polisar, Barry Louis, *Family Trip.*
"In the Evening." Zanes, Dan, *Family Dance.*
"It's a Quiet Night." Charette, Rick, *A Little Peace and Quiet.*
"Late at Night When I'm Hungry." Charette, Rick, *Bubble Gum.*
"Moon upon the Left." Herdman, Priscilla, *Stardreamer.*
"Moonlit Town." Zanes, Dan, *Catch That Train!*
"Mother Nature's Lullaby." Banana Slug String Band, *Wings of Slumber.*
"Night Creatures." Tickle Tune Typhoon, *Singing Science.*
"Night Owl." Zanes, Dan, *Night Time!*
"Nocturnal." Jonas, Billy, *What Kind of Cat Are You?!*
"Nocturnal." Lonnquist, Ken, *Earthy Songs.*
"Nocturnal Animals." Banana Slug String Band, *Dirt Made My Lunch.*
"This Starry Night." Harper, Jessica, *40 Winks*; Harper, Jessica, *Hey, Picasso.*
"Twink a Link." Feldman, Jean, *Dr. Jean Sings Silly Songs.*
"When the Busy Day Is Done." Chapin, Tom, *Zag Zig.*
"Where Do My Sneakers Go at Night?" Charette, Rick, *Where Do My Sneakers Go at Night?*

Noise

"I've Got a Friend (He Won't Be Quiet)." Trout Fishing in America, *My Best Day*.
"My Mother's Snoring." Lonnquist, Ken, *The Lost Songs of Kenland*.
"Nora's Room." Harper, Jessica, *Nora's Room*.
"Very Bear-y to Roar." Kinnoin, Dave, *Dunce Cap Kelly*.

Nonsense

"Ain't We Crazy." Various Artists, *A Child's Celebration of Silliest Songs*.
"Bo Bo See Wattin' Tattin." Grammer, Red, *Red Grammer's Favorite Sing Along Songs*.
"Boom, Boom, Ain't It Great to Be Crazy." Arnold, Linda, *Favorites in the Key of Fun*; Arnold, Linda, *Sing Along Stew*; Beall, Pamela, and Susan Nipp, *Wee Sing Silly Songs*; Cassidy, Nancy, *Nancy Cassidy's KidsSongs*; McGrath, Bob, *Sing Along with Bob #2*; Raffi, *Corner Grocery Store*.
"Boy Who Cried Wolf Sheepishly." Ralph's World, *Happy Lemon*.
"Buckeye Jim." Ives, Burl, *Burl Ives Sings Little White Duck*; Zanes, Dan, *Rocket Ship Beach*.
"Cindy." Beall, Pamela, and Susan Nipp, *Wee Sing Fun 'n' Folk*.
"Corner Grocery Store." Raffi, *Corner Grocery Store*.
"Doo-Wacka-Doo." Parachute Express, *Sunny Side Up*.
"Down by the Bay." Arnold, Linda, *Sing Along Stew*; Barchas, Sarah, *If I Had a Pony*; Beall, Pamela, and Susan Nipp, *Wee Sing in the Car*; Beall, Pamela, and Susan Nipp, *Wee Sing Silly Songs*; Cassidy, Nancy, *Nancy Cassidy's KidsSongs*; Greg and Steve, *Playing Favorites*; Palmer, Hap, *Two Little Sounds*; Pullara, Steve, *One Potato, Two Potato*; Raffi, *Singable Songs for the Very Young*; Roth, Kevin, *Dinosaurs and Dragons*; Roth, Kevin, *Travel Song Sing Alongs*.
"E, I, Addie Addie, O." Paxton, Tom, *I've Got a Yo-Yo*.
"Fooba Wooba John." Cassidy, Nancy, *Nancy Cassidy's KidsSongs*; Ives, Burl, *Burl Ives Sings Little White Duck*; Zanes, Dan, *Family Dance*.
"Fooba Wooba/Turkey in the Straw." Pease, Tom, *I'm Gonna Reach!*
"Giddyup!" Howdy, Buck, *Giddyup!*
"Goofy Old MacDonald." Peterson, Carole, *H.U.M.—All Year Long*.
"Hopalong Peter." Garcia, Jerry, and David Grisman, *Not for Kids Only*.
"A Horse Named Bill." Garcia, Jerry, and David Grisman, *Not for Kids Only*; Hinton, Sam, *Whoever Shall Have Some Good Peanuts*.
"I Am Slowly Going Crazy." Allard, Peter and Ellen, *Pizza Pizzaz*.
"I Asked My Mom." Raven, Nancy, *Hop, Skip, and Sing*.
"The 'I Eat Kids' Klezmer Polka." Polisar, Barry Louis, *Old Enough to Know Better*.

"I Know an Old Lady." Abell, Timmy, *I Know an Old Lady*; Feldman, Jean, *Keep On Singing and Dancing with Dr. Jean*; The Learning Station, *Here We Go Loopty Loo*; The Learning Station, *Literacy in Motion*; Peter, Paul, and Mary, *Peter, Paul, and Mommy, Too*; Roth, Kevin, *Travel Song Sing Alongs*; Roth, Kevin, *Unbearable Bears*; Silberg, "Miss Jackie," *Lollipops and Spaghetti*.

"I'm a Nut." Beall, Pamela, and Susan Nipp, *Wee Sing Silly Songs*; Feldman, Jean, *Keep On Singing and Dancing with Dr. Jean*.

"It Ain't Gonna Rain." Penner, Fred, *Rhyme a Word or Two*. (Same song as "Ain't Gonna Rain No More.")

"The Land of Silly." Beall, Pamela, and Susan Nipp, *Wee Sing and Pretend*.

"Little Liza Jane." McGrath, Bob, *Sing Along with Bob #2*; Rosenthal, Phil, *Turkey in the Straw*; Sharon, Lois, and Bram, *Name Games*.

"The Lollipop Tree." Silberg, "Miss Jackie," *Lollipops and Spaghetti*; Silberg, "Miss Jackie," *Sing It Again Please*.

"Oh Me, Oh My." Raffi, *More Singable Songs*.

"Old Dan Tucker." Beall, Pamela, and Susan Nipp, *Wee Sing Fun 'n' Folk*.

"Old Joe Clark." Beall, Pamela, and Susan Nipp, *Wee Sing Fun 'n' Folk*; Raven, Nancy, *People and Animal Songs*; Zanes, Dan, *House Party*. (Same song as "Rock, Old Joe [Old Joe Clark].")

"Patalina Matalina." Feldman, Jean, *Dr. Jean and Friends*; Feldman, Jean, *Dr. Jean Sings Silly Songs*.

"Pig on Her Head." Berkner, Laurie, *Buzz Buzz*.

"Plenty of Room." Chapin, Tom, *Family Tree*.

"Polly Wolly Doodle." Beall, Pamela, and Susan Nipp, *Wee Sing Fun 'n' Folk*; Beall, Pamela, and Susan Nipp, *Wee Sing in the Car*; Cassidy, Nancy, *Nancy Cassidy's KidsSongs*; Old Town School of Folk Music, *Wiggleworms Love You*; Penner, Fred, *Rhyme a Word or Two*; Rosenthal, Phil, *The Paw Paw Patch*; Various Artists, *A Child's Celebration of Song*; Various Artists, *Folk Playground*; Zanes, Dan, *Rocket Ship Beach*.

"The Pretzel Store." Berkner, Laurie, *Buzz Buzz*.

"Ribberitz." Allard, Peter and Ellen, *Sing It! Say It! Stamp It! Sway It!* vol. 2.

"Risseldy, Rosseldy." Beall, Pamela, and Susan Nipp, *Wee Sing Silly Songs*.

"Rock Old Joe (Old Joe Clark)." Fink, Cathy, *When the Rain Comes Down*. (Same song as "Old Joe Clark.")

"Silly Lullaby." Boynton, Sandra, *Philadelphia Chickens*.

"Silly Song." Harper, Monty, *The Great Green Squishy Mean Concert CD*.

"Silly Song." Livingston, Bob, *Open the Window*.

"Something I Ate." Harper, Monty, *Jungle Junk!*

"Something in My Shoe." Raffi, *Rise and Shine*; Simmons, Al, *Something Fishy at Camp Wiganishie.*

"Stinky Cake." Peterson, Carole, *Stinky Cake.*

"Turkey in the Straw." Abell, Timmy, *Little Red Wagon*; Barchas, Sarah, *If I Had a Pony*; Beall, Pamela, and Susan Nipp, *Wee Sing Fun 'n' Folk*; Rosenthal, Phil, *Turkey in the Straw*; Sharon, Lois, and Bram, *One Elephant, Deux Éléphants.*

"When I Went Out." Avni, Fran, *Artichokes and Brussel Sprouts*; Avni, Fran, *Tuning into Nature.*

"Wish They'd Find a Home." Moo, Anna, *Anna Moo Crackers.*

"The Wrong Song." Gill, Jim, *Jim Gill Sings Do Re Mi on His Toe Leg Knee.*

"You Can't Rollerskate in a Buffalo Herd." Ralph's World, *Ralph's World.*

Nursery Rhymes

"ABC Nursery Rhyme Game." Beall, Pamela, and Susan Nipp, *Wee Sing in the Car.*

"Alphabet Medley." Sharon, Lois, and Bram, *Sing A to Z.*

"Baa Baa Black Sheep." Beall, Pamela, and Susan Nipp, *Wee Sing Animals, Animals, Animals*; Beall, Pamela, and Susan Nipp, *Wee Sing Nursery Rhymes and Lullabies*; McGrath, Bob, *Sing Along with Bob #1*; Raffi, *Singable Songs for the Very Young*; Ralph's World, *At the Bottom of the Sea.*

"Crooked House." Walker, Graham, *Knobbledee Knees.*

"Curly-Locks." Silberg, "Miss Jackie," *The Complete Sniggles, Squirrels, and Chicken Pox*; Silberg, "Miss Jackie," *Sing about Martin.*

"Diddle Doodle." Walker, Graham, *Jumpety Jump.*

"Father Goose." Zanes, Dan, *Rocket Ship Beach.*

"Georgie Porgie." Beall, Pamela, and Susan Nipp, *Wee Sing Nursery Rhymes and Lullabies.*

"Hey Diddle Diddle." Beall, Pamela, and Susan Nipp, *Wee Sing Nursery Rhymes and Lullabies*; Feldman, Jean, *Nursery Rhymes and Good Ol' Times*; Silberg, "Miss Jackie," *The Complete Sniggles, Squirrels, and Chicken Pox*; Silberg, "Miss Jackie," *Sing about Martin.*

"Hickety, Pickety, My Black Hen." Beall, Pamela, and Susan Nipp, *Wee Sing Nursery Rhymes and Lullabies.*

"Hickory Dickory Dock." Barchas, Sarah, *Get Ready, Get Set, Sing!*; Beall, Pamela, and Susan Nipp, *Wee Sing Children's Songs and Fingerplays*; Beall, Pamela, and Susan Nipp, *Wee Sing Nursery Rhymes and Lullabies*; Feldman, Jean, *Nursery Rhymes and Good Ol' Times.*

"Hickory Dickory Dock." SteveSongs, *On a Flying Guitar.*

"Hot Cross Buns." Beall, Pamela, and Susan Nipp, *Wee Sing Nursery Rhymes and Lullabies.*

"Humpty Dumpty." Beall, Pamela, and Susan Nipp, *Wee Sing Nursery Rhymes and Lullabies*; Feldman, Jean, *Nursery Rhymes and Good Ol' Times*; Old Town School of Folk Music, *Wiggleworms Love You*.

"Humpty Dumpty." Kaye, Mary, *I Sang It Just for You*.

"Humpty Dumpty." Scruggs, Joe, *Bahamas Pajamas*.

"Humpty's at It Again." Roberts, Justin, *Way Out*.

"Hush Little Baby." Sharon, Lois, and Bram, *Great Big Hits 2*; Sharon, Lois, and Bram, *Sing A to Z*.

"I Had a Little Nut Tree." Beall, Pamela, and Susan Nipp, *Wee Sing Nursery Rhymes and Lullabies*; Hinton, Sam, *Whoever Shall Have Some Good Peanuts*; Rosenthal, Phil, *Folksongs and Bluegrass for Children*; Rosenthal, Phil, *The Green Grass Grew All Around*.

"Jack and Jill." Beall, Pamela, and Susan Nipp, *Wee Sing Children's Songs and Fingerplays*; Beall, Pamela, and Susan Nipp, *Wee Sing Nursery Rhymes and Lullabies*; Feldman, Jean, *Nursery Rhymes and Good Ol' Times*; Sharon, Lois, and Bram, *Mainly Mother Goose*; Sharon, Lois, and Bram, *Sleepytime*.

"Jack Be Nimble." Feldman, Jean, *Nursery Rhymes and Good Ol' Times*; McGrath, Bob, and Katherine Smithrim, *Songs and Games for Toddlers*.

"Jack Sprat." Beall, Pamela, and Susan Nipp, *Wee Sing Nursery Rhymes and Lullabies*.

"Lavender's Blue." Beall, Pamela, and Susan Nipp, *Wee Sing around the World*; Cassidy, Nancy, *Nancy Cassidy's KidsSongs*; Sharon, Lois, and Bram, *Mainly Mother Goose*.

"Lazy Mary, Will You Get Up?" Bartels, Joanie, *Morning Magic*.

"Let's Read and Rock." Greg and Steve, *Ready, Set, Move!*

"Little Bo-Peep." Beall, Pamela, and Susan Nipp, *Wee Sing Nursery Rhymes and Lullabies*.

"Little Boy Blue." Beall, Pamela, and Susan Nipp, *Wee Sing Nursery Rhymes and Lullabies*; Feldman, Jean, *Nursery Rhymes and Good Ol' Times*.

"Little Jack Horner." Beall, Pamela, and Susan Nipp, *Wee Sing Nursery Rhymes and Lullabies*; Feldman, Jean, *Nursery Rhymes and Good Ol' Times*.

"Little Miss Muffet." Beall, Pamela, and Susan Nipp, *Wee Sing Nursery Rhymes and Lullabies*; Feldman, Jean, *Nursery Rhymes and Good Ol' Times*; Silberg, "Miss Jackie," *The Complete Sniggles, Squirrels, and Chicken Pox*; Silberg, "Miss Jackie," *Sing about Martin*.

"Living in a Pumpkin Shell." Foote, Norman, *Foote Prints*.

"London Bridge." Beall, Pamela, and Susan Nipp, *Wee Sing and Play*; Dana, *Dana's Best Travelin' Tunes*; Feldman, Jean, *Nursery Rhymes and Good Ol' Times*; McGrath, Bob, *Sing Along with Bob #2*.

"Mary Had a Little Lamb." Beall, Pamela, and Susan Nipp, *Wee Sing Nursery Rhymes and Lullabies*; Feldman, Jean, *Nursery Rhymes and Good Ol' Times*; McGrath, Bob, *Sing Along with Bob #2*; Old Town School of Folk Music, *Wiggleworms Love You*; Rosenthal, Phil, *The Paw Paw Patch*; Sharon, Lois, and Bram, *Mainly Mother Goose*; Sharon, Lois, and Bram, *Name Games*.

"Mary, Mary." Beall, Pamela, and Susan Nipp, *Wee Sing Nursery Rhymes and Lullabies*.

"Mockingbird." Peter, Paul, and Mary, *Peter, Paul, and Mommy*.

"Mother Goose Songs." Ives, Burl, *Burl Ives Sings Little White Duck*.

"The Muffin Man." Beall, Pamela, and Susan Nipp, *Wee Sing and Play*; Feldman, Jean, *Nursery Rhymes and Good Ol' Times*; Greg and Steve, *We All Live Together*, vol. 2; Jenkins, Ella, *Songs Children Love to Sing*; McGrath, Bob, *Sing Along with Bob #2*.

"Mulberry Bush." The Learning Station, *Seasonal Songs in Motion*.

"Nursery in Overdrive." Dana, *Dana's Best Sing and Swing-a-Long Tunes*.

"Nursery Mudley." Foote, Norman, *Foote Prints*.

"Nursery Rhyme Rap." Feldman, Jean, *Dr. Jean and Friends*.

"Nursery Rhyme Rock and Roll." Harper, Monty, *Jungle Junk!*

"Nursery Rhyme Song." Beall, Pamela, and Susan Nipp, *Wee Sing Silly Songs*.

"Nursery Rhymes." Scruggs, Joe, *Abracadabra*.

"Nursery Session." Foote, Norman, *If the Shoe Fits*.

"Oh Dear, What Can the Matter Be?" Sharon, Lois, and Bram, *Mainly Mother Goose*; Sharon, Lois, and Bram, *Sleepytime*.

"Old King Cole." Beall, Pamela, and Susan Nipp, *Wee Sing Nursery Rhymes and Lullabies*; McGrath, Bob, *Sing Along with Bob #2*; Sharon, Lois, and Bram, *Name Games*.

"Old King Cole Revisited." Cosgrove, Jim, *Bop Bop Dinosaur*.

"Old Mother Hubbard." Silberg, "Miss Jackie," *The Complete Sniggles, Squirrels, and Chicken Pox*.

"Oleanna." Berkner, Laurie, *Victor Vito*.

"Out the Window." Allard, Peter and Ellen, *Sing It! Say It! Stamp It! Sway It!* vol. 2. (Same song as "Throw It out the Window.")

"Pat-a-Cake." Beall, Pamela, and Susan Nipp, *Wee Sing Nursery Rhymes and Lullabies*.

"Pease Porridge Hot." Beall, Pamela, and Susan Nipp, *Wee Sing for Baby*; Beall, Pamela, and Susan Nipp, *Wee Sing Nursery Rhymes and Lullabies*; Old Town School of Folk Music, *Wiggleworms Love You*.

"Peter Piper." Silberg, "Miss Jackie," *The Complete Sniggles, Squirrels, and Chicken Pox*; Silberg, "Miss Jackie," *Sing about Martin*.

"Polly Put the Kettle On." Beall, Pamela, and Susan Nipp, *Wee Sing Nursery Rhymes and Lullabies*.

"Pop! Goes the Weasel." Barchas, Sarah, *If I Had a Pony*; Beall, Pamela, and Susan Nipp, *Wee Sing and Play*; Beall, Pamela, and Susan Nipp, *Wee Sing Children's Songs and Fingerplays*; Beall, Pamela, and Susan Nipp, *Wee Sing for Baby*; Old Town School of Folk Music, *Wiggleworms Love You*; Sharon, Lois, and Bram, *Great Big Hits*; Sharon, Lois, and Bram, *Mainly Mother Goose*; Walker, Graham, *Jumpety Jump*.

"Pussycat, Pussycat." Beall, Pamela, and Susan Nipp, *Wee Sing Nursery Rhymes and Lullabies*.

"Rhyme the Rhyme." Mr. Al, *Dance like This*.

"Ride a Cock-Horse." Beall, Pamela, and Susan Nipp, *Wee Sing Nursery Rhymes and Lullabies*.

"Ring around the Rosie." Beall, Pamela, and Susan Nipp, *Wee Sing Children's Songs and Fingerplays*.

"Rock 'n' Roll Mother Goose." Rymer, Brady, *Every Day Is a Birthday*.

"Rock-a-Bye Baby." Beall, Pamela, and Susan Nipp, *Wee Sing for Baby*.

"Rockin' Roll Nursery Rhymes." The Learning Station, *Rock n' Roll Songs That Teach*.

"Rosy, My Posy." Beall, Pamela, and Susan Nipp, *Wee Sing for Baby*.

"Rub-a-Dub-Dub." Beall, Pamela, and Susan Nipp, *Wee Sing Nursery Rhymes and Lullabies*.

"Sing a Song of Sixpence." Beall, Pamela, and Susan Nipp, *Wee Sing Nursery Rhymes and Lullabies*.

"The Story Book Ball." Muldaur, Maria, *On the Sunny Side*.

"There Was a Crooked Man." Beall, Pamela, and Susan Nipp, *Wee Sing Nursery Rhymes and Lullabies*.

"This Little Pig Went to Market." Beall, Pamela, and Susan Nipp, *Wee Sing Nursery Rhymes and Lullabies*.

"Three Blind Mice." Beall, Pamela, and Susan Nipp, *Wee Sing Sing-Alongs*; McGrath, Bob, *Sing Along with Bob #2*; Various Artists, *Grandma's Patchwork Quilt*.

"Three Little Kittens." Beall, Pamela, and Susan Nipp, *Wee Sing Nursery Rhymes and Lullabies*; Feldman, Jean, *Nursery Rhymes and Good Ol' Times*.

"Throw It out the Window." Beall, Pamela, and Susan Nipp, *Wee Sing Silly Songs*; Rudnick, Ben, *Emily Songs*; Trout Fishing in America, *Big Trouble*; Trout Fishing in America, *Family Music Party*. (Same song as "Out the Window.")

"To Market, To Market." Beall, Pamela, and Susan Nipp, *Wee Sing for Baby*; Beall, Pamela, and Susan Nipp, *Wee Sing Nursery Rhymes and Lullabies*.

"Wee Willie Winkie." Silberg, "Miss Jackie," *The Complete Sniggles, Squirrels, and Chicken Pox.*

"Willy Winky." Walker, Graham, *Fiddlesticks.*

Occupations

"A Ballet Dancing Truck Driver." Fink, Cathy, and Marcy Marxer, *Changing Channels.*

"Everyone Can Be a Helper." Palmer, Hap, *Can a Cherry Pie Wave Goodbye?*

"For Now I'll Just Be Me." Fite, Stephen, *We're Just like Crayons.*

"Horse of a Different Hue." Ode, Eric, *I Love My Shoes.*

"How'd You Like to Do That?" Chapin, Tom, *Around the World and Back Again.*

"I Can Be Almost Anything I Try." Charette, Rick, *Alligator in the Elevator.*

"I Got a Job." Jenkins, Ella, *Growing Up with Ella Jenkins.*

"I Want to Be a Farmer." Raven, Nancy, *Hop, Skip, and Sing.*

"I Work All Day." Grunsky, Jack, *Like a Flower to the Sun.*

"Occupations." The Learning Station, *Children Love to Sing and Dance.*

"What Does Your Mama Do?" Fink, Cathy, *Grandma Slid down the Mountain*; Pease, Tom, *Boogie! Boogie! Boogie!*

"What'cha Gonna Be." Kinder, Brian, *Again.*

"Whatchagonnabe?" McCutcheon, John, *Bigger Than Yourself.*

"When I Grow Up." The Chenille Sisters, *The Big Picture and Other Songs for Kids.*

"When I Grow Up." Foote, Norman, *1000 Pennies.*

"When I Grow Up." Frezza, Rebecca, *Music in My Head.*

"When I Grow Up." Harley, Bill, *Monsters in the Bathroom.*

Opposites

"Fast Monkey." SteveSongs, *Marvelous Day!*

"Opposite Day." SteveSongs, *Marvelous Day!*

"The Opposite Song." Feldman, Jean, *Keep On Singing and Dancing with Dr. Jean.*

"Opposite Words Are Fun." Charette, Rick, *Alligator in the Elevator.*

"Opposites." Greg and Steve, *Fun and Games.*

"Opposites." The Learning Station, *Rock n' Roll Songs That Teach.*

"Opposites." Rosen, Gary, *Pet Sounds*; Various Artists, *Hear and Gone in 60 Seconds.*

"Say the Opposite." Palmer, Hap, *Can a Cherry Pie Wave Goodbye?*

"Up! Up! Up!" Buchman, Rachel, *Hello Everybody!*

Optimism

"Accentuate the Positive." Rosenshontz, *Uh-Oh!*

"The Bright Side." Vitamin L, *Walk a Mile.*

"Building a Better World." Allard, Peter and Ellen, *Sing It! Say It! Stamp It! Sway It!* vol. 3.

"Children of the Future." Sprout, Jonathan, *On the Radio.*

"Every Moment." Vitamin L, *Every Moment!*

"If You Believe." Grunsky, Jack, *Jack in the Box 1.*

"Just Keep Goin' On." Various Artists, *World Playground.*

"Just Look Up." Various Artists, *Folk Playground.*

"Keep on the Sunnyside." Zanes, Dan, *Rocket Ship Beach.*

"Let's Make a Better World." The Dream Project, *We've All Got Stories.*

"My Best Day." Trout Fishing in America, *InFINity*; Trout Fishing in America, *My Best Day.*

"Never End." Milkshake, *Happy Songs.*

"New World Coming." Sharon, Lois, and Bram, *Sing A to Z.*

"No One Knows for Sure." Alsop, Peter, *Wha' D'Ya Wanna Do?*

"One World." LaFond, Lois, *One World.*

"Right Side Up." Moo, Anna, *Moochas Gracias.*

"Roots and Shoots Everywhere." Raffi, *Let's Play.*

"Seeds." Gemini, *The Best of Gemini*, vol. 2.

"Stand Up." Sprout, Jonathan, *Kid Power.*

"Sun Showers." Rudnick, Ben, *Fun and Games.*

"We the Children." Parachute Express, *Doctor Looney's Remedy.*

"We'll Make the World AOK." Charette, Rick, *Popcorn and Other Songs to Munch On.*

"Won't Let the Rain Keep Fallin'." Frezza, Rebecca, *Tall and Small.*

Outer Space (see also Imaginary Characters/Creatures—Aliens)

"Backyard Spaceship." Roberts, Justin, *Way Out.*

"Blast Off." SteveSongs, *On a Flying Guitar.*

"Cow Planet." Boynton, Sandra, *Dog Train.*

"Galactic Real Estate." Lonnquist, Ken, *Sci-Fi Hi-Fi.*

"Kablaam." Thaddeus Rex, *Martian Television Invasion.*

"Kid Astro." Ralph's World, *The Amazing Adventures of Kid Astro.*

"Meteors/The Perseid." McCutcheon, John, *Summersongs.*

"Milky Way." Cosgrove, Jim, *Ooey Gooey.*

"Milky Way." Harley, Bill, *Down in the Backpack.*
"Planet Bruno." Chapin, Tom, *Some Assembly Required.*
"Planet Mirth." Lonnquist, Ken, *The Circus Kenlando.*
"Rocket." Lonnquist, Ken, *The Circus Kenlando.*
"Rocket Ship Man." Rudnick, Ben, *Blast Off!*
"Rocket Ship Trip." Walker, Graham, *Jumpety Jump.*
"Rocketship." Roberts, Justin, *Yellow Bus.*
"Roundy Round." Harper, Monty, *Take Me to Your Library.*
"Space Dog." Frezza, Rebecca, *Road Trip.*
"Space Is Going to Be Fun." LaFond, Lois, *I Am Who I Am.*
"Space Song." Milkshake, *Bottle of Sunshine.*
"Spinning Around." SteveSongs, *On a Flying Guitar.*
"Turning and Turning." Frezza, Rebecca, *Tall and Small.*
"Zoom." Stotts, Stuart, and Tom Pease, *Celebrate: A Song Resource.*
"Zoom." Various Artists, *Hear and Gone in 60 Seconds.*
"Zoom Zoom Zoom." McGrath, Bob, and Katherine Smithrim, *Songs and Games for Toddlers.*

Aurora Borealis

"Aurora." McCutcheon, John, *Wintersongs.*

Moon

"Full Moon Walk." Rymer, Brady, *Every Day Is a Birthday.*
"The Girl and Mister Moon." Lonnquist, Ken, *The Lost Songs of Kenland*; Lonnquist, Ken, *The Switcher-On of Stars.*
"Good Night Mistress Moon." Diamond, Charlotte, *Diamonds and Daydreams.*
"Hey, Mr. Moonlight." Rymer, Brady, *I Found It!*
"I See the Moon." Pease, Tom, *I'm Gonna Reach!*
"I'd Like to Visit the Moon." The Chenille Sisters, *1, 2, 3 for Kids.*
"The Ladybug and the Moon." Roth, Kevin, *Travel Song Sing Alongs.*
"Last Night the Moon Was Full." Roberts, Justin, *Not Naptime.*
"The Man Who Ran Away with the Moon." Foote, Norman, *If the Shoe Fits.*
"The Moon." Herdman, Priscilla, *Stardreamer.*
"Moon and Me." Harley, Bill, *Play It Again*; Harley, Bill, *You're in Trouble.*
"Moon Moon Moon." Berkner, Laurie, *Victor Vito.*
"Moon, My Dad and Me." Fink, Cathy, and Marcy Marxer, *Blanket Full of Dreams.*
"The Moon Song." Penner, Fred, *Sing with Fred*; Penner, Fred, *What a Day!*

"Move with the Moon." Pirtle, Sarah, *Heart of the World*.

"Mr. Man in the Moon." Charette, Rick, *A Little Peace and Quiet*.

"My Moon Song." Rymer, Brady, *Look at My Belly*.

"Our Next-Door Neighbor, the Moon." Chapin, Tom, *In My Hometown*.

"Rachel and the Moon." Alsop, Peter, *Stayin' Over*.

"Singing to the Moon." Banana Slug String Band, *Wings of Slumber*.

Planets

"Guitars from Mars." Daddy A Go Go, *Big Rock Rooster*.

"Nine Planets." Roberts, Justin, *Not Naptime*.

"Planet Jive." Tickle Tune Typhoon, *Singing Science*.

"Planet Poem." Feldman, Jean, *Is Everybody Happy?*

"The Solar System." Knight, Tom, *The Library Boogie*.

Stars

"Constellation Cowboy." Tickle Tune Typhoon, *Singing Science*.

"Constellations." Livingston, Bob, *Open the Window*.

"Every Little Star." Fink, Cathy, and Marcy Marxer, *Pocket Full of Stardust*.

"The First Star Lullaby." Herdman, Priscilla, *Stardreamer*.

"Little Star." Knight, Tom, *Don't Kiss a Codfish*.

"Look out Your Window." Harley, Bill, *The Town around the Bend*.

"Starlight." Atkinson, Lisa, *The Elephant in Aisle Four*.

"Starlight, Star Bright." Arnold, Linda, *Favorites in the Key of Fun*; Beall, Pamela, and Susan Nipp, *Wee Sing for Baby*; Grammer, Red, *Hello World*; McGrath, Bob, and Katherine Smithrim, *Songs and Games for Toddlers*.

"The Stars Are Coming Out like Popcorn." The Chenille Sisters, *Teaching Hippopotami to Fly!*; Pease, Tom, *Wobbi-Do-Wop!*

"Stars over Wyoming." Banana Slug String Band, *Goin' Wild*.

"Swinging on a Star." Bartels, Joanie, *Sillytime Magic*; Lithgow, John, *Singin' in the Bathtub*; Pease, Tom, *Boogie! Boogie! Boogie!*; Rudnick, Ben, *Fun and Games*. (Same song as "Would You Like to Swing on a Star?")

"The Switcher-On of Stars." Lonnquist, Ken, *The Circus Kenlando*; Lonnquist, Ken, *The Switcher-On of Stars*.

"Twinkle Twinkle Little Star." Avni, Fran, *Little Ears: Songs for Reading Readiness*; Beall, Pamela, and Susan Nipp, *Wee Sing Children's Songs and Fingerplays*; Beall, Pamela, and Susan Nipp, *Wee Sing for Baby*; Beall, Pamela, and Susan Nipp, *Wee Sing Nursery Rhymes and Lullabies*; Cassidy, Nancy, *Nancy Cassidy's KidsSongs*; Dana, *Dana's Best Sing and Swing-a-Long Tunes*;

Feldman, Jean, *Nursery Rhymes and Good Ol' Times*; Herdman, Priscilla, *Stardreamer*; McGrath, Bob, *Sing Along with Bob #2*; McGrath, Bob, and Katherine Smithrim, *Songs and Games for Toddlers*; Raffi, *One Light One Sun*; Raffi, *Quiet Time*; Rosenthal, Phil, *Turkey in the Straw*; Sharon, Lois, and Bram, *One Elephant, Deux Éléphants*; Tickle Tune Typhoon, *All of Us Will Shine*; Tickle Tune Typhoon, *Patty-Cakes and Peek-a-Boos*.
"Wonder What It's Like to Be a Star." Silberg, "Miss Jackie," *Touched by a Song*.
"Would You Like to Swing on a Star?" Muldaur, Maria, *On the Sunny Side*; Various Artists, *A Child's Celebration of Folk Music*. (Same song as "Swinging on a Star.")

Sun

"Gettin' Our Energy from the Sun." Pease, Tom, *Daddy Starts to Dance*.
"Great Big Sun." Roberts, Justin, *Great Big Sun*.
"Just like the Sun." Berkner, Laurie, *Under a Shady Tree*.
"Look! Look! The Sun Woke Up!" Sweet Honey in the Rock, *I Got Shoes*.
"Mister Sun." Cassidy, Nancy, *Nancy Cassidy's KidsSongs*; McGrath, Bob, *Sing Along with Bob #1*; Raffi, *Singable Songs for the Very Young*; Sharon, Lois, and Bram, *Sing A to Z*.
"Mr. Sun, Sun." Roth, Kevin, *Dinosaurs and Dragons*.
"One Light, One Sun." Barchas, Sarah, *Bridges across the World*; Raffi, *Evergreen, Everblue*; Raffi, *One Light One Sun*.
"Solar Energy Shout." Banana Slug String Band, *Dirt Made My Lunch*.
"Star Sun." Scruggs, Joe, *Bahamas Pajamas*.
"Sunny Old Sun." Zanes, Dan, *House Party*.

Patience

"Five More Minootsa." Pullara, Steve, *A Big Bowl of Musicroni*.
"Five More Minutes." Polisar, Barry Louis, *Old Enough to Know Better*.
"Hold Your Horses." Byers, Kathy, *Do You Wish You Could Fly?*
"Hum." Big Jeff, *Big Jeff and His Middle-Sized Band*.
"I Don't Wanna Wait." Harley, Bill, *Big Big World*; Harley, Bill, *One More Time*.
"Patience." Diamond, Charlotte, *Charlotte Diamond's World*.
"Patience." Grammer, Red, *Be Bop Your Best!*
"Patience." Sprout, Jonathan, *Dr. Music*.
"Waiting." Kaye, Mary, *Spin Your Web*.
"Waiting." Walker, Mary Lu, *The Frog's Party*.
"Wave Bye-Bye." Boynton, Sandra, *Dog Train*.

Peace

"Chickens for Peace." Alsop, Peter, *Take Me with You*.

"Down by the Riverside." Raffi, *Bananaphone*; Zanes, Dan, *Night Time!*

"Everyone Can Be a Winner." Vitamin L, *Swingin' in the Key of L*.

"Find a Peaceful Thought." Arnold, Linda, *Make Believe*; Various Artists, *Peace Is the World Smiling*.

"Hands." Fink, Cathy, and Marcy Marxer, *Air Guitar*.

"I'm Not Going to Chase the Cat Today." Harper, Jessica, *Rhythm in My Shoes*.

"Kid's Peace Song." Alsop, Peter, *Take Me with You*.

"Let's Live Peacefully." Arnold, Linda, *Favorites in the Key of Fun*; Arnold, Linda, *Peppermint Wings*.

"Make Peace." Various Artists, *Peace Is the World Smiling*.

"Nobody's Chasin' Nobody." Harper, Jessica, *A Wonderful Life*.

"One Crane." Pease, Tom, *Wobbi-Do-Wop!*; Stotts, Stuart, *Are We There Yet?*

"One Earth." Arnold, Linda, *Happiness Cake*.

"Paz y Libertad." Pirtle, Sarah, *Magical Earth*.

"Peace." Barchas, Sarah, *Bridges across the World*.

"Peace in Twelve Languages." Knight, Tom, *The Classroom Boogie*.

"Peace Is the World Smiling." Various Artists, *Peace Is the World Smiling*.

"Peace on Earth." Pease, Tom, *Daddy Starts to Dance*; Stotts, Stuart, *One Big Dance*.

"Peace Round." Pease, Tom, *Boogie! Boogie! Boogie!*

"Peace Song." Walker, Mary Lu, *The Frog's Party*.

"Peace to the Children." Cosgrove, Jim, *Pick Me! Pick Me!*

"Peace Will Come." Fink, Cathy, and Marcy Marxer, *Air Guitar*; Paxton, Tom, *Your Shoes, My Shoes*.

"Peace Will Dawn." Abell, Timmy, *Little Red Wagon*.

"A Song of Peace." Staines, Bill, *One More River*.

"Teaching Peace." Grammer, Red, *Teaching Peace*.

"Tree of Life." Pirtle, Sarah, *Heart of the World*.

"With Two Wings." Grammer, Red, *Teaching Peace*.

"Zum Gali Gali." Beall, Pamela, and Susan Nipp, *Wee Sing around the World*.

Perseverance

"Anything Is Possible." Bartles, Joanie, *Put On Your Dancing Shoes*.

"Big Ned." Del Bianco, Lou, *A Little Bit Clumsy*.

"Endurance." Vitamin L, *Walk a Mile*.

"Everybody Makes Mistakes." Knight, Tom, *The Classroom Boogie*.

"Go for It." Rosenshontz, *Rock 'n Roll Teddy Bear*.

"Go for It." Various Artists, *Hear and Gone in 60 Seconds*.

"Halfway Through." Parachute Express, *Doctor Looney's Remedy*.

"High Hopes." Arnold, Linda, *Sing Along Stew*.

"I Can, I Will, I'll Try." Frezza, Rebecca, *Music in My Head*.

"I Think I Can." Kaye, Mary, *Mouse Jamboree*.

"If at First." Foote, Norman, *Foote Prints*.

"If You Want to Fly." SteveSongs, *Marvelous Day!*

"Is There Anybody Here." Sharon, Lois, and Bram, *One Elephant, Deux Éléphants*.

"Let 'Em Laugh." Alsop, Peter, *Take Me with You*.

"Look at What I Can Do." Strausman, Paul, *The World's Big Family*.

"Look Ma, No Hands." Rosenshontz, *Uh-Oh!*

"The Love of the Game." Harley, Bill, *One More Time*; Harley, Bill, *There's a Pea on My Plate*.

"Mighty Big Plans." Scruggs, Joe, *Bahamas Pajamas*.

"A Mozart Duet." Chapin, Tom, *In My Hometown*.

"Musical Animal." Grammer, Red, *Down the Do-Re-Mi*.

"One More Try." Atkinson, Lisa, *The One and Only Me*.

"Perseverance." Grammer, Red, *Be Bop Your Best!*

"Pluggin' Away." Alsop, Peter, *Pluggin' Away*.

"A Swing Tune." The Chenille Sisters, *The Big Picture and Other Songs for Kids*.

"Try." Milkshake, *Happy Songs*.

"Try, Try Again." Arnold, Linda, *Circus Magic*.

"Yes I Can." The Learning Station, *Seasonal Songs in Motion*.

"You Can Do It." Palmer, Hap, *Turn On the Music*.

"You Can Do It If You Try." Penner, Fred, *Fred's Favourites*; Penner, Fred, *Sing with Fred*.

Pirates

"Captain T." Kinder, Brian, *One More Time*.

"Don't Shake Hands with a One-Eyed Pirate." Madsen, Gunnar, *Ants in My Pants!*

"Going over the Sea." Sharon, Lois, and Bram, *Everybody Sing!*

"Pirate Song." Arnold, Linda, *Happiness Cake*.

"Pirate Song." Harley, Bill, *Big Big World*; Harley, Bill, *One More Time*.

"The Pirate Song." Peterson, Carole, *H.U.M.—All Year Long*.

"The Pirate Song." SteveSongs, *Little Superman*.

"Pirates." Milkshake, *Play!*

"A Pirate's Life." Fink, Cathy, and Marcy Marxer, *Scat like That*.

"Three Pirates." Raven, Nancy, *Hop, Skip, and Sing*.

"Tropeo the Pirate." Harper, Monty, *Take Me to Your Library*.

Plants

"Giant Kelp Forest." Banana Slug String Band, *Slugs at Sea*.

"Give Plants a Chance." Banana Slug String Band, *Singing in Our Garden*.

"I Know a Little Pussy." Sharon, Lois, and Bram, *Sleepytime*.

"I'm a Little Seed." Peterson, Carole, *Tiny Tunes*.

"Little Seed." Guthrie, Woody, *Woody's 20 Grow Big Songs*.

"My Roots Go Down." Pease, Tom, *Wobbi-Do-Wop!*; Pirtle, Sarah,
    Two Hands Hold the Earth.

"Oats and Beans and Barley." Raffi, *Baby Beluga*. (Same song as "Oats, Peas, Beans.")

"Oats, Peas, Beans." Beall, Pamela, and Susan Nipp, *Wee Sing and Play*;
    Buchman, Rachel, *Sing a Song of Seasons*; Raven, Nancy, *Jambalaya!*; Raven,
    Nancy, *Nancy Raven Sings Her Favorites*. (Same song as "Oats and Beans and
    Barley.")

"Photosynthesize Me." Lonnquist, Ken, *Earthy Songs*; Lonnquist, Ken, *Sci-Fi Hi-Fi*.

"Plant a Seed." Allard, Peter and Ellen, *Sing It! Say It! Stamp It! Sway It!* vol. 2.

"Planting Rice." Raven, Nancy, *The House We Live In*, vols. 1 and 2.

"Poison Ivy." Gill, Jim, *Jim Gill Sings the Sneezing Song and Other Contagious Tunes*.

"Pumpkin Song." Walker, Mary Lu, *The Frog's Party*.

"Pussy Willow Riddle." Buchman, Rachel, *Hello Everybody!*

"Roots, Stems, Leaves." Banana Slug String Band, *Dirt Made My Lunch*; Banana
    Slug String Band, *Singing in Our Garden*.

"The Seed Cycle." Beall, Pamela, and Susan Nipp, *Wee Sing and Play*.

"Seed in the Ground." Kaldor, Connie, *A Duck in New York City*.

"That's Botany." Tickle Tune Typhoon, *Singing Science*.

"There's More to a Seed." Ode, Eric, *Grandpa's Truck*.

Flowers

"Dandelion." Rosen, Gary, *Tot Rock*.

"Dandelions." Atkinson, Lisa, *I Wanna Tickle the Fish*.

"Each of Us Is a Flower." Diamond, Charlotte, *10 Carrot Diamond*.

"Flowers." Tickle Tune Typhoon, *All of Us Will Shine*.

"4000 Roses." Harper, Jessica, *A Wonderful Life.*

"I Papaveri (The Poppy Song)." Chapin, Tom, *Around the World and Back Again.*

"Pluckin' the Petals." Harper, Jessica, *A Wonderful Life.*

"Sunflower." Raffi, *Quiet Time*; Raffi, *Raffi Radio.*

"Tulips and Daisies." Avni, Fran, *Tuning into Nature.*

"White Coral Bells." Beall, Pamela, and Susan Nipp, *Wee Sing Sing-Alongs*;
    Berkner, Laurie, *Victor Vito*; Herdman, Priscilla, *Daydreamer.*

"Wild Mountain Thyme." Zanes, Dan, *Night Time!*

"Wildflowers." Diamond, Charlotte, *My Bear Gruff.*

Mushrooms

"Mushroom Umbrella." Walker, Mary Lu, *The Frog's Party.*

Pumpkins

"Libby Lou's Pumpkin." Ode, Eric, *Grandpa's Truck.*

"The Pumpkin Man." McCutcheon, John, *Autumnsongs*; Various Artists,
    Grandma's Patchwork Quilt.

"Twenty Pumpkins." Barchas, Sarah, *Get Ready, Get Set, Sing!*

Trees

"The Apple Seed." Silberg, "Miss Jackie," *Touched by a Song.*

"The Apple Tree." Peterson, Carole, *H.U.M.—All Year Long.*

"Apple Tree." Roberts, Justin, *Great Big Sun.*

"Arbutus Baby." Raffi, *Let's Play.*

"The Birch Tree." Raven, Nancy, *Friends and Family.*

"Branching Out." Herdman, Priscilla, *Daydreamer*; Pease, Tom, *I'm Gonna Reach!*

"C Is for Conifers." They Might Be Giants, *Here Come the ABCs.*

"Can You Imagine?" Berkner, Laurie, *Whaddaya Think of That?*

"Coconut Tree." Walker, Graham, *Jumpety Jump.*

"Colors." McCutcheon, John, *Autumnsongs.*

"Don't Needle Me." Tucker, Nancy, *Escape of the Slinkys.*

"Everything That's Made of Wood." Trout Fishing in America, *InFINity.*

"Falling Leaves." Charette, Rick, *Toad Motel.*

"Giving Tree." Parachute Express, *Don't Blink.*

"The Green Grass Grows All Around." Barchas, Sarah, *If I Had a Pony*; Beall,
    Pamela, and Susan Nipp, *Wee Sing Silly Songs*; Buchman, Rachel, *Sing a Song
    of Seasons*; Greg and Steve, *Rockin' down the Road*; Hinton, Sam, *Whoever*

Shall Have Some Good Peanuts; The Learning Station, *Seasonal Songs in Motion*; Roth, Kevin, *Travel Song Sing Alongs*.

"I Had a Little Nut Tree." Beall, Pamela, and Susan Nipp, *Wee Sing Nursery Rhymes and Lullabies*; Hinton, Sam, *Whoever Shall Have Some Good Peanuts*; Rosenthal, Phil, *Folksongs and Bluegrass for Children*; Rosenthal, Phil, *The Green Grass Grew All Around*.

"I'm a Tree." Banana Slug String Band, *Dirt Made My Lunch*; Banana Slug String Band, *Singing in Our Garden*.

"Know Your Oaks." Stotts, Stuart, and Tom Pease, *Celebrate: A Song Resource*.

"Lambeth Children." Raven, Nancy, *Singing, Prancing, and Dancing*.

"A Little Acorn." The Chenille Sisters, *The Big Picture and Other Songs for Kids*.

"Little Tree." Lonnquist, Ken, *Earthy Songs*; Lonnquist, Ken, *Welcome 2 Kenland*.

"The Lollipop Tree." Silberg, "Miss Jackie," *Lollipops and Spaghetti*; Silberg, "Miss Jackie," *Sing It Again Please*.

"Magnolia." Hinojosa, Tish, *Cada Niño: Every Child*.

"Mahogany Tree." Pirtle, Sarah, *Magical Earth*.

"Many Pretty Trees All around the World." Jenkins, Ella, *Songs Children Love to Sing*.

"Mustard Tree." Del Bianco, Lou, *A Little Bit Clumsy*.

"My Tree." Grunsky, Jack, *Jack in the Box 2*; Grunsky, Jack, *World Safari*.

"My Tree." Stotts, Stuart, *Are We There Yet?*

"Nani Wale Na Hala (Pretty Hala Trees)." Beall, Pamela, and Susan Nipp, *Wee Sing around the World*.

"Sacred Trees." Tickle Tune Typhoon, *Hearts and Hands*.

"The Singing Tree." Pirtle, Sarah, *Magical Earth*.

"There's a Hole in the Middle of the Tree." Avni, Fran, *Tuning into Nature*.

"Tree Climbing." Mayer, Hans, *Stars of the Swing Set*.

"Tree Dancin'." Tickle Tune Typhoon, *Circle Around*.

"A Tree Is Just a Tree." Kaldor, Connie, *A Poodle in Paris*.

"Tree Song." Troubadour, *On the Trail*.

"Trees." Avni, Fran, *Tuning into Nature*.

"Trees." Green Chili Jam Band, *Magic Bike*.

"Under a Shady Tree." Berkner, Laurie, *Under a Shady Tree*.

"Up in a Tree." Lonnquist, Ken, *Welcome 2 Kenland*.

"What Falls in the Fall?" Berkner, Laurie, *Whaddaya Think of That?*

"What Kind of Tree Are You?" Diamond, Charlotte, *Diamond in the Rough*.

"When I Climb the Tallest Tree." Charette, Rick, *A Little Peace and Quiet*.

"Willows." Lonnquist, Ken, *The Switcher-On of Stars*.

Playing

"All I Wanna Do Is Play." Ralph's World, *Peggy's Pie Parlor.*

"Boogie Woogie Chase." Chapin, Tom, *In My Hometown.*

"Bottle of Sunshine." Milkshake, *Bottle of Sunshine.*

"Come and Play Catch with Me." Paxton, Tom, *I've Got a Yo-Yo.*

"Daddy Be a Horsie." Palmer, Hap, *Peek-a-Boo.*

"Do You Want to Play in My Playground." Coffey, James, *Come Ride Along with Me.*

"End O' Nintendo." Lonnquist, Ken, *Sci-Fi Hi-Fi.*

"The Fever." Daddy A Go Go, *Monkey in the Middle.*

"Games." Sprout, Jonathan, *Dr. Music.*

"Going Out to Play." Silberg, "Miss Jackie," *The Complete Sniggles, Squirrels, and Chicken Pox.*

"Goofin' Around." Lonnquist, Ken, *Welcome 2 Kenland.*

"Gotcha Last." Del Bianco, Lou, *Lost in School.*

"Hip Hip Hooray." Kinder, Brian, *Again.*

"Hopscotch." Parachute Express, *Friends, Forever Friends.*

"Hopscotch." Rudnick, Ben, *Fun and Games.*

"I Like to Swing." Buchman, Rachel, *Hello Everybody!*

"In My Closet." Scruggs, Joe, *Ants.*

"In My Playground." Greg and Steve, *Fun and Games.*

"Jumping in the Leaves." Nagler, Eric, *Improvise with Eric Nagler.*

"Let's Go Out and Play." SteveSongs, *Morning til Night.*

"Let's Play." Arnold, Linda, *Peppermint Wings.*

"Let's Play." Grunsky, Jack, *Follow the Leader*; Grunsky, Jack, *Jack in the Box 2.*

"Let's Play." Raffi, *Let's Play.*

"New Games." Alsop, Peter, *Pluggin' Away.*

"Peek-a-Boo." Palmer, Hap, *Peek-a-Boo.*

"Piggy Back Ride." Penner, Fred, *Sing with Fred.*

"Playground." Grunsky, Jack, *Playground.*

"Playground." Mayer, Hans, *Stars of the Swing Set.*

"Playground." Ralph's World, *The Amazing Adventures of Kid Astro.*

"Red Rover." Scruggs, Joe, *Abracadabra.*

"See-Saw." Colleen and Uncle Squaty, *Sing-a-Move-a-Dance.*

"Somebody Come and Play." Sharon, Lois, and Bram, *Sing A to Z.*

"A Swing Tune." The Chenille Sisters, *The Big Picture and Other Songs for Kids.*

"Swinging in the Grapevine Swing." Jenkins, Ella, *Growing Up with Ella Jenkins.*

"Swingset." Ralph's World, *Green Gorilla, Monster, and Me.*

"We're in the Sandbox." SteveSongs, *Morning til Night.*
"What Will We Do." Old Town School of Folk Music, *Wiggleworms Love You.*

Pollution (see also Ecology/Nature)

"The Beach Song." Magical Music Express, *Music Is Magic.*
"A Better Place to Live." Sprout, Jonathan, *Kid Power.*
"Brown Air." Banana Slug String Band, *Adventures on the Air Cycle.*
"Bubble, Bubble." Lonnquist, Ken, *Earthy Songs.*
"Can You Imagine?" Berkner, Laurie, *Whaddaya Think of That?*
"Garbage." Rosenshontz, *Share It.*
"The Garbage Monster." Knight, Tom, *Don't Kiss a Codfish.*
"Gettin' Our Energy from the Sun." Pease, Tom, *Daddy Starts to Dance.*
"Green Up!" Shontz, Bill, *Animal Tales.*
"Heal the Bay." Alsop, Peter, *Pluggin' Away.*
"Hole in the Ozone." Shontz, Bill, *Animal Tales.*
"Keep It Green." Harley, Bill, *Big Big World.*
"Litterbug." Sprout, Jonathan, *On the Radio.*
"Oo Ee." Magical Music Express, *Music Is Magic.*
"Ozone." Lonnquist, Ken, *Earthy Songs.*
"Pick It Up!" Ode, Eric, *I Love My Shoes.*
"See the Beauty." Vitamin L, *Everyone's Invited!*
"Sing a Whale Song." Chapin, Tom, *Moonboat.*
"We Are Not Alone." Raffi, *Evergreen, Everblue.*
"What's the Matter with Us?" Raffi, *Evergreen, Everblue.*
"Who Made This Mess?" Harley, Bill, *Big Big World*; Pease, Tom, *Wobbi-Do-Wop!*

Procrastination

"Procrastination." Diamond, Charlotte, *My Bear Gruff.*
"Tomorrow." Polisar, Barry Louis, *Family Concert*; Polisar, Barry Louis, *Teacher's Favorites.*

Questions

"Ask Someone Who Knows." Chapin, Tom, *Great Big Fun for the Very Little One.*
"Because." Miss Amy, *Wide, Wide World.*
"Can a Cherry Pie Wave Goodbye?" Palmer, Hap, *Can a Cherry Pie Wave Goodbye?*
"Can a Jumbo Jet Sing the Alphabet?" Palmer, Hap, *Can a Jumbo Jet Sing the Alphabet?*

"Curiosity." Frezza, Rebecca, *Music in My Head*.

"Everyone Can Be a Helper." Palmer, Hap, *Can a Cherry Pie Wave Goodbye?*

"How Many Days?" Harper, Monty, *Imagine That*.

"I Don't Know." Lonnquist, Ken, *Sci-Fi Hi-Fi*.

"I Want to Know." Sprout, Jonathan, *Kid Power*.

"I Want to Know." Vitamin L, *Walk a Mile*.

"Mommy, What If . . ." Sharon, Lois, and Bram, *Great Big Hits*.

"Questions." Chapin, Tom, *Some Assembly Required*.

"Quien: Who." Hinojosa, Tish, *Cada Niño: Every Child*.

"These Are the Questions." Rosen, Gary, *Pet Sounds*; Rosenshontz, *Rosenshontz Greatest Hits*; Rosenshontz, *Tickles You!*

"What Could You Use?" Palmer, Hap, *Can a Jumbo Jet Sing the Alphabet?*

"What If a Zebra Had Spots?" Polisar, Barry Louis, *Old Dog, New Tricks*.

"Where Do All Things Come From?" Yosi, *Under a Big Bright Yellow Umbrella*.

"Where Will I Go?" Alsop, Peter, *Stayin' Over*.

"Who Knows." Scruggs, Joe, *Deep in the Jungle*.

"Why Do You Ask?" Tucker, Nancy, *Glad That You Asked*.

"Why, Oh Why?" Guthrie, Woody, *Songs to Grow On for Mother and Child*; Kirk, John, and Trish Miller, *The Big Rock Candy Mountain*.

"The Wonder Song." Roth, Kevin, *Travel Song Sing Alongs*.

"Yes, No, Maybe So." Gill, Jim, *Jim Gill Sings Do Re Mi on His Toe Leg Knee*.

"You've Got to Ask." Harley, Bill, *I Wanna Play*.

Radio

"Late Night Radio." Brown, Greg, *Bathtub Blues*.

"Mom and the Radio." Harley, Bill, *Down in the Backpack*.

"You Can't Say 'Psbpsbpsb' on the Radio." Polisar, Barry Louis, *Naughty Songs for Boys and Girls*.

Rainbows

"Arco Iris." Barchas, Sarah, *¡Piñata! and More*.

"Colors of the Rainbow." Allard, Peter and Ellen, *Pizza Pizzaz*.

"The First Time I Saw a Rainbow." Charette, Rick, *Popcorn and Other Songs to Munch On*.

"Gonna Be a Rainbow." Pease, Tom, *Wobbi-Do-Wop!*; Stotts, Stuart, and Tom Pease, *Celebrate: A Song Resource*.

"I Can Sing a Rainbow." Old Town School of Folk Music, *Wiggleworms Love You*; Penner, Fred, *Sing with Fred*.

"Over the Rainbow." Grammer, Red, *Hello World*; Penner, Fred, *Sing with Fred*; Tickle Tune Typhoon, *Hearts and Hands*; Various Artists, *A Child's Celebration of Song*; Zanes, Dan, *Rocket Ship Beach*.

"Rainbow in the Sky." Byers, Kathy, *Do You Wish You Could Fly?*

"Rainbow Parachute Sky." Parachute Express, *Who's Got a Hug?*

"Rainbow 'round Me." Pelham, Ruth, *Under One Sky*; Stotts, Stuart, and Tom Pease, *Celebrate: A Song Resource*.

"Rainbows." LaFond, Lois, *I Am Who I Am*; LaFond, Lois, *Turning It Upside Down*.

"Rainbows All over My Room." Strausman, Paul, *Rainbows, Stones, and Dinosaur Bones*.

Recreation/Sports

"50 Things That I Can Do Instead of Watch TV." Fink, Cathy, and Marcy Marxer, *Changing Channels*.

"Gobs of Fun." Fite, Stephen, *Gobs of Fun*.

"In the Great Outdoors." Charette, Rick, *Toad Motel*.

"Instead of Watching My TV." Rymer, Brady, *Every Day Is a Birthday*.

"It's Raining." Mayer, Hans, *Just a Little Hug*.

"My Way Home." Raffi, *Corner Grocery Store*.

"The Sports Song." Daddy A Go Go, *Big Rock Rooster*.

"Two Hands." Ode, Eric, *Grandpa's Truck*.

"Wha' D'Ya Wanna Do?" Alsop, Peter, *Wha' D'Ya Wanna Do?*

"What Do You Do on a Rainy Day?" Rosen, Gary, *Tot Rock*.

Baseball

"At the Dinosaur Baseball Game." Arnold, Linda, *Favorites in the Key of Fun*; Arnold, Linda, *Peppermint Wings*.

"Baseball." Milkshake, *Play!*

"Baseball Dreams." Ralph's World, *At the Bottom of the Sea*.

"The Baseball Kids." Paxton, Tom, *I've Got a Yo-Yo*.

"Baseball on the Block." McCutcheon, John, *Family Garden*.

"Cryin' in the Dugout." Daddy A Go Go, *Eat Every Bean and Pea on Your Plate*.

"Give Me a Hit." Del Bianco, Lou, *When I Was a Kid*.

"Hard Ball." Trout Fishing in America, *My World*.

"Hope I Make It." McCutcheon, John, *Springsongs*.

"I Caught It (The Baseball Song)." Charette, Rick, *Chickens on Vacation*.

"I Love Baseball." Cosgrove, Jim, *Ooey Gooey*.

"Not So Good at Baseball." Polisar, Barry Louis, *Old Enough to Know Better*.

"Right Field." Peter, Paul, and Mary, *Peter, Paul, and Mommy, Too*.

"Take Me Out to the Ball Game." Beall, Pamela, and Susan Nipp, *Wee Sing in the Car*; McGrath, Bob, *Sing Along with Bob #1*; Old Town School of Folk Music, *Wiggleworms Love You*; Palmer, Hap, *Can a Jumbo Jet Sing the Alphabet?*; Pullara, Steve, *Hop like a Frog*; Raffi, *One Light One Sun*.

"Take Me Out to the Ballgame/Bravo, Bravissimo." Sharon, Lois, and Bram, *Great Big Hits 2*.

"World Series '57." McCutcheon, John, *Autumnsongs*.

Basketball

"Slam Dunk." Lonnquist, Ken, *The Circus Kenlando*.

Bowling

"The Bowling Song." Raffi, *One Light One Sun*.

"Bowling with You." Milkshake, *Play!*

Camping/Camps

"Camp Wiganishie." Simmons, Al, *Something Fishy at Camp Wiganishie*.

"The Camper's Lullaby." Banana Slug String Band, *Wings of Slumber*.

"Campfire." McCutcheon, John, *Autumnsongs*.

"Camping in the Wilderness." McCutcheon, John, *Summersongs*.

"Camping Tonight." Haynes, Sammie, *Nature's ABCs*.

"Day Camp." Roberts, Justin, *Way Out*.

"Goin' Campin'." Beall, Pamela, and Susan Nipp, *Wee Sing in the Car*.

"S'mores." Howdy, Buck, *Giddyup!*

"S'Mores." Parachute Express, *Doctor Looney's Remedy*.

Fishing (see also Fish)

"The Crawdad Song." Beall, Pamela, and Susan Nipp, *Wee Sing Fun 'n' Folk*; Hinton, Sam, *Whoever Shall Have Some Good Peanuts*; Mitchell, Elizabeth, *You Are My Sunshine*; Old Town School of Folk Music, *Wiggleworms Love You*; Raven, Nancy, *People and Animal Songs*; Various Artists, *A Child's Celebration of Folk Music*; Various Artists, *Folk Playground*.

"Fishin'." McCutcheon, John, *Springsongs*.

"Goin' Fishin'." Rosenshontz, *Family Vacation.*

"Going Bass Fishing." Moo, Anna, *Anna Moo Crackers.*

"Have You Ever Been Fishing?" Feldman, Jean, *Keep On Singing and Dancing with Dr. Jean.*

"Ro, Ro Til Fiskeskjaer (Row, Row to the Fishing Spot)." Beall, Pamela, and Susan Nipp, *Wee Sing around the World.*

"Something Fishy." Kinder, Brian, *One More Time.*

"Starfishing." Green Chili Jam Band, *Starfishing.*

Hiking/Walking

"Everybody Walks a Dog." Pullara, Steve, *Hop like a Frog.*

"A Friend, a Laugh, a Walk in the Woods." Crow, Dan, *A Friend, a Laugh, a Walk in the Woods.*

"Full Moon Walk." Rymer, Brady, *Every Day Is a Birthday.*

"The Happy Wanderer." Byers, Kathy, *'Round the Campfire*; Dana, *Dana's Best Travelin' Tunes*; Staines, Bill, *The Happy Wanderer.* (Same song as "I Love to Go Wandering.")

"Hiking up the Mountains." Charette, Rick, *Toad Motel.*

"Hold On Tight." McGrath, Bob, and Katherine Smithrim, *Songs and Games for Toddlers.*

"I Love to Go Wandering." McMahon, Elizabeth, *Magic Parade.* (Same song as "The Happy Wanderer.")

"Let's Take a Walk." Beall, Pamela, and Susan Nipp, *Wee Sing for Baby.*

"On the Trail." Troubadour, *On the Trail.*

"Pack Up Your Hot Dog." Beall, Pamela, and Susan Nipp, *Wee Sing in the Car.*

"Walk around My Street." Pullara, Steve, *Spinning Tails.*

"Walk around the World." Grunsky, Jack, *Like a Flower to the Sun.*

"Walk It While You Talk It." Harper, Jessica, *Inside Out.*

"Walk Outside." Crow, Dan, *A Friend, a Laugh, a Walk in the Woods.*

"Walk Outside." Raffi, *One Light One Sun.*

"Walk, Walk, Walk." Raffi, *Rise and Shine.*

"Walking." Palmer, Hap, *Peek-a-Boo.*

"Walking in the Woods." Barchas, Sarah, *If I Had a Pony.*

Hunting

"The Bear Hunt." The Learning Station, *Here We Go Loopty Loo.*

"Billy Barlow." Raven, Nancy, *People and Animal Songs.*

"Bird Dog." McCutcheon, John, *Autumnsongs*.

"The Cool Bear Hunt." Feldman, Jean, *Dr. Jean Sings Silly Songs*.

"Grey Goose." Ives, Burl, *Burl Ives Sings Little White Duck*; Zanes, Dan, *Catch That Train!*

"Groundhog." Hinton, Sam, *Whoever Shall Have Some Good Peanuts*.

"A-Hunting We Will Go." Beall, Pamela, and Susan Nipp, *Wee Sing and Play*.

"Robin the Bobbin." Hinton, Sam, *Whoever Shall Have Some Good Peanuts*.

"Tally Ho." Arnold, Linda, *Make Believe*.

"Three Men Went A-Hunting." Garcia, Jerry, and David Grisman, *Not for Kids Only*.

"Wee Weary Deer." Trout Fishing in America, *Family Music Party*; Trout Fishing in America, *My World*.

Juggling

"The Juggler." Knight, Tom, *Don't Kiss a Codfish*.

Riding

"Coming 'round the Mountain." Feldman, Jean, *Nursery Rhymes and Good Ol' Times*. (Same song as "She'll Be Comin' 'round the Mountain.")

"Donkey Riding." Allard, Peter and Ellen, *Sing It! Say It! Stamp It! Sway It!* vol. 1; Raven, Nancy, *Hop, Skip, and Sing*.

"Giddyup Pony." Diamond, Charlotte, *Charlotte Diamond's World*.

"Horse and Buggy." Sweet Honey in the Rock, *All for Freedom*.

"I Have a Horse." Barchas, Sarah, *Get Ready, Get Set, Sing!*

"Ladies Ride." Old Town School of Folk Music, *Wiggleworms Love You*. (Same song as "This Is the Way the Ladies Ride.")

"Over the River and Through the Woods." Beall, Pamela, and Susan Nipp, *Wee Sing Children's Songs and Fingerplays*; Rosenthal, Phil, *The Green Grass Grew All Around*.

"Pony Ride." Colleen and Uncle Squaty, *Rumble to the Bottom*.

"Ride That Pony." Feldman, Jean, *Is Everybody Happy?*

"Riding in the Buggy." Rosenthal, Phil, *Folksongs and Bluegrass for Children*; Rosenthal, Phil, *Turkey in the Straw*.

"Riding in the Buggy/Tideo." Sharon, Lois, and Bram, *Sing A to Z*.

"She'll Be Comin' 'round the Mountain." Arnold, Linda, *Sing Along Stew*; Beall, Pamela, and Susan Nipp, *Wee Sing Sing-Alongs*; Berkner, Laurie, *Whaddaya Think of That?*; Cassidy, Nancy, *Nancy Cassidy's KidsSongs*; Dana, *Dana's Best Travelin' Tunes*; Greg and Steve, *We All Live Together*, vol. 2; The Learning Station, *All-Time Children's Favorites*; McGrath, Bob, *Sing Along* with Bob #1; Seeger, Pete, *Pete Seeger's Family Concert*; Sharon, Lois, and Bram, *Everybody Sing!*; Sharon, Lois, and Bram, *Great Big Hits*; Sharon, Lois, and Bram, *One Elephant, Deux Éléphants*; SteveSongs, *Marvelous Day!*; Various Artists, *A Child's Celebration of Folk Music*. (Same song as "Coming 'round the Mountain.")

"This Is the Way the Ladies Ride." Beall, Pamela, and Susan Nipp, *Wee Sing Children's Songs and Fingerplays*; Beall, Pamela, and Susan Nipp, *Wee Sing for Baby*. (Same song as "Ladies Ride.")

"This Is the Way We Ride." Colleen and Uncle Squaty, *Rumble to the Bottom*.

"The Trail Song." Chapin, Tom, *Moonboat*.

"Trot, Trot, Trot." Beall, Pamela, and Susan Nipp, *Wee Sing for Baby*.

Skateboarding

"Skateboard." Scruggs, Joe, *Deep in the Jungle*.

Skating

"Fly." McCutcheon, John, *Wintersongs*.

"The Inline Skaters." Pullara, Steve, *Hop like a Frog*.

"Roller Skating." Penner, Fred, *Sing with Fred*.

"Seven Silly Squirrels." Avni, Fran, *Little Ears: Songs for Reading Readiness*; Avni, Fran, *Tuning into Nature*.

Soccer

"The Love of the Game." Harley, Bill, *One More Time*; Harley, Bill, *There's a Pea on My Plate*.

"Susie Is a Rocker." Paxton, Tom, *I've Got a Yo-Yo*.

Surfing

"Hey Johnny-O." Hullabaloo, *Sing Along with Sam*.

"Surfin' in My Imagination." Ralph's World, *At the Bottom of the Sea*.

Swimming

"Aye, Aye Captain." The Learning Station, *La Di Da La Di Di Dance with Me*.

"Jenning's Pond." Knight, Tom, *Easy as Pie*.

"Splish Splash." Mayer, Hans, *Just a Little Hug*.

"Splishin' and Splashin.'" Diamond, Charlotte, *Charlotte Diamond's World*.

"Swimming Hole." McCutcheon, John, *Summersongs*.

"Swimming Pool." Trout Fishing in America, *Mine!*

"Swimming Song." The Learning Station, *Tony Chestnut and Fun Time Action Songs.*

"Swimmy Swim." Buchman, Rachel, *Sing a Song of Seasons*; Guthrie, Woody, *Songs to Grow On for Mother and Child.*

Recycling (see also Ecology/Nature; Pollution)

"Beautiful Things." Avni, Fran, *Tuning into Nature.*

"Brown Gold." Chapin, Tom, *Some Assembly Required.*

"Clean Machine." Chapin, Tom, *This Pretty Planet*; Chapin, Tom, *Zag Zig.*

"Garbage Sale—Pass It On." Avni, Fran, *Tuning into Nature.*

"Good Garbage." Chapin, Tom, *Mother Earth*; Chapin, Tom, *This Pretty Planet.*

"Habitat." Knight, Tom, *Easy as Pie.*

"It Really Isn't Garbage." Tucker, Nancy, *Escape of the Slinkys.*

"Own Backyard." McCutcheon, John, *Summersongs.*

"R-E-C-Y-C-L-E." Chapin, Tom, *This Pretty Planet*; Chapin, Tom, *Zag Zig.*

"Re-Cycle!" Knight, Tom, *Don't Kiss a Codfish.*

"Recycle Depot." Avni, Fran, *Tuning into Nature.*

"Recycle Hokey Pokey." Pirtle, Sarah, *Heart of the World.*

"Solar Energy Shout." Banana Slug String Band, *Dirt Made My Lunch.*

"Someone's Gonna Use It." Chapin, Tom, *Family Tree*; Chapin, Tom, *This Pretty Planet.*

"The Whole Earth Anthem." Fink, Cathy, and Marcy Marxer, *Air Guitar.*

Rivers

"All the Rivers Flow Down." Grunsky, Jack, *Jack in the Box 1*; Grunsky, Jack, *World Safari.*

"Bamboo." Grunsky, Jack, *Playground.*

"Down the River." Rosenthal, Phil, *The Green Grass Grew All Around.*

"Lady River." Yosi, *Monkey Business.*

"Muhheakunnuk." Chapin, Tom, *In My Hometown.*

"Mysteries of the Nile." Moo, Anna, *Anna Moo Crackers.*

"The Nile Is Wild." Lonnquist, Ken, *Earthy Songs*; Lonnquist, Ken, *Sci-Fi Hi-Fi.*

"River Flow." Ralph's World, *Green Gorilla, Monster, and Me.*

"The River in Your Town." Haynes, Sammie, *Nature's ABCs.*

"River Song." Banana Slug String Band, *Dirt Made My Lunch.*

"River Song." Green Chili Jam Band, *Starfishing.*

"The Rivers of Texas." Raven, Nancy, *Friends and Family.*

"Rivers of the World." Tickle Tune Typhoon, *Singing Science*.
"Roll along Yellowstone." Banana Slug String Band, *Goin' Wild*.
"Sailin' Up, Sailin' Down." Seeger, Pete, *Pete Seeger's Family Concert*.
"Sailing to the Sea." Chapin, Tom, *Great Big Fun for the Very Little One*; Chapin, Tom, *Mother Earth*.
"A Shenandoah Lullaby." Garcia, Jerry, and David Grisman, *Not for Kids Only*.
"Sittin' by the River." Magical Music Express, *Friendship Stew*.
"So Sang the River." Staines, Bill, *One More River*.
"Spooky River." Lonnquist, Ken, *Earthy Songs*.
"Up the River." Grunsky, Jack, *Sing and Dance*; Grunsky, Jack, *World Safari*.

Robots

"Mr. Robot." Kimmy Schwimmy, *Kimmy Schwimmy Music*, vol. 1.
"Robot Farm." Big Jeff, *Big Jeff and His Middle-Sized Band*.

Rocks and Minerals

"I Collect Rocks." Simmons, Al, *Something Fishy at Camp Wiganishie*.
"A Rock Blocks the Walk." Beall, Pamela, and Susan Nipp, *Wee Sing and Pretend*.
"Rocks in My Pockets." Various Artists, *Hear and Gone in 60 Seconds*.
"Skip a Rock." Foote, Norman, *Pictures on the Fridge*.

Rounds

"All around the World." Fink, Cathy, and Marcy Marxer, *Pillow Full of Wishes*.
"Are You Sleeping?" Beall, Pamela, and Susan Nipp, *Wee Sing Sing-Alongs*. (Same song as "Frère Jacques.")
"Arirang." Raven, Nancy, *Friends and Family*.
"The Beach Song." Magical Music Express, *Music Is Magic*.
"Bedtime Round." Chapin, Tom, *Billy the Squid*; Chapin, Tom, *Great Big Fun for the Very Little One*.
"Belly Button (Round)." Boynton, Sandra, *Philadelphia Chickens*.
"Black Socks." Fink, Cathy, and Marcy Marxer, *Scat like That*; Harley, Bill, *Monsters in the Bathroom*; Harley, Bill, *Play It Again*.
"Catches." Chapin, Tom, *Moonboat*.
"Chairs to Mend." Beall, Pamela, and Susan Nipp, *Wee Sing Sing-Alongs*; Raven, Nancy, *You Gotta Juba*.
"Come Follow." Beall, Pamela, and Susan Nipp, *Wee Sing Sing-Alongs*; Sharon, Lois, and Bram, *Everybody Sing!*

"Dinosaur Round." Boynton, Sandra, *Rhinoceros Tap*.

"'Doo-Doo' Is a Bad Word." Polisar, Barry Louis, *Juggling Babies*.

"Down by the Station." Beall, Pamela, and Susan Nipp, *Wee Sing Children's Songs and Fingerplays*; Beall, Pamela, and Susan Nipp, *Wee Sing Sing-Alongs*; Sharon, Lois, and Bram, *Great Big Hits*; Sharon, Lois, and Bram, *Name Games*.

"Fish and Chips and Vinegar." Sharon, Lois, and Bram, *Great Big Hits*; Sharon, Lois, and Bram, *School Days*. (Same song as "One Bottle o' Pop.")

"Frère Jacques." Barchas, Sarah, *Bridges across the World*; Beall, Pamela, and Susan Nipp, *Wee Sing around the World*; Raffi, *Corner Grocery Store*. (Same song as "Are You Sleeping?")

"The Frog in the Bog." Beall, Pamela, and Susan Nipp, *Wee Sing Fun 'n' Folk*.

"Frog Round." Beall, Pamela, and Susan Nipp, *Wee Sing Sing-Alongs*.

"The Frog's Song." Magical Music Express, *Friendship Stew*.

"Grasshoppers Three." Beall, Pamela, and Susan Nipp, *Wee Sing Fun 'n' Folk*.

"Grow in Your Own Way." Chapin, Tom, *Moonboat*.

"Hey Ho! Nobody Home." Beall, Pamela, and Susan Nipp, *Wee Sing Sing-Alongs*; Raven, Nancy, *You Gotta Juba*.

"I Love the Mountains." Beall, Pamela, and Susan Nipp, *Wee Sing in the Car*; Beall, Pamela, and Susan Nipp, *Wee Sing Sing-Alongs*; Byers, Kathy, *'Round the Campfire*.

"Kookaburra." Barchas, Sarah, *Bridges across the World*; Beall, Pamela, and Susan Nipp, *Wee Sing Sing-Alongs*; Staines, Bill, *The Happy Wanderer*.

"Let Us Sing Together." Beall, Pamela, and Susan Nipp, *Wee Sing Sing-Alongs*.

"Little Tommy Tinker." Beall, Pamela, and Susan Nipp, *Wee Sing Sing-Alongs*; Sharon, Lois, and Bram, *Name Games*; Sharon, Lois, and Bram, *One Elephant, Deux Éléphants*.

"Love Round." Tickle Tune Typhoon, *Patty-Cakes and Peek-a-Boos*.

"Make New Friends." Beall, Pamela, and Susan Nipp, *Wee Sing Sing-Alongs*; Sweet Honey in the Rock, *All for Freedom*.

"Matthew, Mark, Luke and John." Herdman, Priscilla, *Stardreamer*; Sharon, Lois, and Bram, *Sleepytime*.

"Oh How Lovely Is the Evening." Barchas, Sarah, *Bridges across the World*; Beall, Pamela, and Susan Nipp, *Wee Sing Sing-Alongs*.

"One Bottle o' Pop." Beall, Pamela, and Susan Nipp, *Wee Sing Silly Songs*; Strausman, Paul, *Camels, Cats, and Rainbows*. (Same song as "Fish and Chips and Vinegar.")

"One Earth." Arnold, Linda, *Happiness Cake*.

"One More Round." Harper, Jessica, *A Wonderful Life*.

"Peace Round." Pease, Tom, *Boogie! Boogie! Boogie!*

"A Ram Sam Sam." Beall, Pamela, and Susan Nipp, *Wee Sing Sing-Alongs*.

"Reuben and Rachel." Beall, Pamela, and Susan Nipp, *Wee Sing Sing-Alongs*.

"Rounds." Chapin, Tom, *Family Tree*.

"Row, Row, Row Your Boat." Beall, Pamela, and Susan Nipp, *Wee Sing Sing-Alongs*.

"Russian Lullaby." The Chenille Sisters, *1, 2, 3 for Kids*.

"Scotland's Burning." Beall, Pamela, and Susan Nipp, *Wee Sing Sing-Alongs*.

"Seasons." Magical Music Express, *Music Is Magic*.

"Sing a Round." Magical Music Express, *Music Is Magic*.

"Sing Together." Beall, Pamela, and Susan Nipp, *Wee Sing Sing-Alongs*.

"Slimy Mud." Magical Music Express, *Music Is Magic*.

"Sweet Potato Round." Raven, Nancy, *Jambalaya!*

"Sweetly Sings the Donkey." Beall, Pamela, and Susan Nipp, *Wee Sing Animals, Animals, Animals*; Beall, Pamela, and Susan Nipp, *Wee Sing Sing-Alongs*.

"Tender Shepherd." McCutcheon, John, *Howjadoo*.

"There Is Thunder." Beall, Pamela, and Susan Nipp, *Wee Sing Children's Songs and Fingerplays*.

"This Pretty Planet." Chapin, Tom, *Family Tree*; Chapin, Tom, *This Pretty Planet*.

"This Pretty Planet II." Chapin, Tom, *This Pretty Planet*.

"Three Blind Mice." Beall, Pamela, and Susan Nipp, *Wee Sing Sing-Alongs*.

"Tue Tue." Harley, Bill, *There's a Pea on My Plate*.

"The Upward Trail." Beall, Pamela, and Susan Nipp, *Wee Sing in the Car*.

"White Coral Bells." Beall, Pamela, and Susan Nipp, *Wee Sing Sing-Alongs*; Berkner, Laurie, *Victor Vito*.

"Why Shouldn't My Goose?" Beall, Pamela, and Susan Nipp, *Wee Sing Sing-Alongs*.

"Wild Bird Round." Lonnquist, Ken, *The Circus Kenlando*; Lonnquist, Ken, *Earthy Songs*; Lonnquist, Ken, *The Switcher-On of Stars*.

Royalty

"The Duchess at Tea." Sharon, Lois, and Bram, *School Days*.

"Englebert the Elephant." Paxton, Tom, *Goin' to the Zoo*.

"The Frog Song." Harper, Monty, *The Great Green Squishy Mean Concert CD*.

"King Karacticus." Kirk, John, and Trish Miller, *The Big Rock Candy Mountain*.

"King Midas." Kaye, Mary, *I Sang It Just for You*.

"The King of Caliber." Harley, Bill, *Down in the Backpack*.

"La La Land." Lonnquist, Ken, *Sci-Fi Hi-Fi*.

"Lavender's Blue." Beall, Pamela, and Susan Nipp, *Wee Sing around the World*; Cassidy, Nancy, *Nancy Cassidy's KidsSongs*; Sharon, Lois, and Bram, *Mainly Mother Goose.*

"The Noble Duke of York." Beall, Pamela, and Susan Nipp, *Wee Sing and Play.*

"Old King Cole." Beall, Pamela, and Susan Nipp, *Wee Sing Nursery Rhymes and Lullabies*; McGrath, Bob, *Sing Along with Bob #2*; Sharon, Lois, and Bram, *Name Games.*

"Old King Cole Revisited." Cosgrove, Jim, *Bop Bop Dinosaur.*

"The Princess and the Farmer's Son." Harper, Monty, *Imagine That.*

"Princess and the Pea." Lonnquist, Ken, *The Lost Songs of Kenland.*

"Princess Di's Distress." Chapin, Tom, *Moonboat.*

"Princess Power." Miss Amy, *Wide, Wide World.*

"The Silliest Dream." Fink, Cathy, and Marcy Marxer, *Pocket Full of Stardust.*

"Sing a Song of Sixpence." Beall, Pamela, and Susan Nipp, *Wee Sing Nursery Rhymes and Lullabies.*

Safety (see also Accidents)

"Be Sensible, Be Smart, Be Safe." Coffey, James, *I Love Toy Trains.*

"Better Say No." Rosenshontz, *Family Vacation*; Rosenshontz, *Rosenshontz Greatest Hits.*

"Buckle Up." Scruggs, Joe, *Traffic Jams.*

"I Need a Hand." Rudnick, Ben, *Emily Songs.*

"I've Got a Secret." Fink, Cathy, and Marcy Marxer, *Help Yourself.*

"Leave It There." Stotts, Stuart, and Tom Pease, *Celebrate: A Song Resource.*

"Left Right Left." Stotts, Stuart, and Tom Pease, *Celebrate: A Song Resource.*

"My Body." Alsop, Peter, *Wha' D'Ya Wanna Do?*

"My Body Belongs to Me." Tickle Tune Typhoon, *All of Us Will Shine*; Tickle Tune Typhoon, *Healthy Beginnings.*

"The Name and Address Song." Fink, Cathy, and Marcy Marxer, *Help Yourself.*

"Never Talk to Strangers." Fink, Cathy, and Marcy Marxer, *Help Yourself.*

"No Way!" Magical Music Express, *Music Is Magic.*

"Nothing Too Scary." Stotts, Stuart, and Tom Pease, *Celebrate: A Song Resource.*

"Playin' It Safe." Tickle Tune Typhoon, *Healthy Beginnings.*

"Put Your Helmet On." Harley, Bill, *There's a Pea on My Plate.*

"Safe at Home." McCutcheon, John, *Bigger Than Yourself.*

"Safe Kids." Rosen, Gary, *Cookin'.*

"Safe Not Sorry." Fite, Stephen, *Monkey Business.*

"Safety Break." Greg and Steve, *Kidding Around.*

"Say No to Strangers." The Learning Station, *Seasonal Songs in Motion.*

"Seat Belt On." McGrath, Bob, and Katherine Smithrim, *Songs and Games for Toddlers.*

"Stop, Look and Listen." Coffey, James, *Come Ride Along with Me.*

"Stop, Look and Listen." Fink, Cathy, and Marcy Marxer, *Help Yourself.*

"Take Care of Your Body." Stotts, Stuart, and Tom Pease, *Celebrate: A Song Resource.*

"Thinking Safety." Tickle Tune Typhoon, *Healthy Beginnings.*

"Watch Out." Harley, Bill, *You're in Trouble.*

Schools

"Back to School Again." Mr. Al and Stephen Fite, *Back to School Again.*

"Back to School Bop." Mr. Al, *Mr. Al a Carte.*

"Bad Day Today." Del Bianco, Lou, *Lost in School.*

"Barney Ate My Homework." Paxton, Tom, *Your Shoes, My Shoes.*

"Cool in School." Harley, Bill, *Play It Again*; Harley, Bill, *You're in Trouble.*

"Cool to Be in School." Fite, Stephen, *Cool to Be in School.*

"Day Care Blues." Trout Fishing in America, *Big Trouble*; Trout Fishing in America, *My Best Day.*

"Don't Make Me." Chapin, Tom, *Family Tree.*

"Down in the Backpack." Harley, Bill, *Down in the Backpack.*

"Dracula Came to Our School." Avni, Fran, *I'm All Ears: Sing into Reading.*

"Ducks Hatching." SteveSongs, *Marvelous Day!*

"Dunce Cap Kelly." Kinnoin, Dave, *Dunce Cap Kelly.*

"Excuses." Troubadour, *On the Trail.*

"Field Trip." Ode, Eric, *I Love My Shoes.*

"First Day." Scruggs, Joe, *Even Trolls Have Moms.*

"The First 12 Days of School." Feldman, Jean, *Keep On Singing and Dancing with Dr. Jean.*

"Four Boys Named Jordan." Harper, Jessica, *Inside Out.*

"Gnarly Dude." Alsop, Peter, *Take Me with You.*

"Graduation Day." Foote, Norman, *1000 Pennies.*

"His Name Is Ty." Chapin, Tom, *In My Hometown.*

"Homework Blues." Del Bianco, Lou, *Lost in School.*

"Hundredth Day of School." Fite, Stephen, *Monkey Business.*

"I Don't Believe You're Going to the Bathroom." Polisar, Barry Louis, *Old Enough to Know Better.*

"I Don't Wanna Go to School." Polisar, Barry Louis, *Family Concert*; Polisar, Barry Louis, *Teacher's Favorites.*

"I Don't Wanna Go to School Today." Daddy A Go Go, *Mojo A Go Go.*

"I Think I'm Too Old to Be a Preschool Teacher Blues." Mr. Al, *Dance like This.*

"I Went to School One Morning." Buchman, Rachel, *Sing a Song of Seasons.*

"I've Got a Teacher, She's So Mean." Polisar, Barry Louis, *Family Concert*; Polisar, Barry Louis, *Teacher's Favorites.*

"It Makes Me Jump." Fite, Stephen, *Cool to Be in School.*

"Kindergarten Wall." Herdman, Priscilla, *Daydreamer*; McCutcheon, John, *Mail Myself to You.*

"Letter to Mr. Brown." Alsop, Peter, *Take Me with You.*

"Magical Art Room." Lonnquist, Ken, *Sci-Fi Hi-Fi.*

"Music Teacher Blues." Gemini, *The Best of Gemini.*

"My Teacher Cracked Me Up." Charette, Rick, *Popcorn and Other Songs to Munch On.*

"New Kid." Lonnquist, Ken, *Sci-Fi Hi-Fi.*

"New Kid in School." McCutcheon, John, *Autumnsongs.*

"No School Today." Harley, Bill, *You're in Trouble.*

"Our School." Barchas, Sarah, *Get Ready, Get Set, Sing!*

"Our School Rap." Grunsky, Jack, *Jack in the Box 1.*

"Please Don't Bring a Tyrannosaurus to Show and Tell." Scruggs, Joe, *Late Last Night.*

"Pray for Snow." Gemini, *The Best of Gemini.*

"The Principle." McCutcheon, John, *Bigger Than Yourself.*

"Red Rover." Scruggs, Joe, *Abracadabra.*

"School." Milkshake, *Bottle of Sunshine.*

"School Days." Grunsky, Jack, *Sing and Dance.*

"School Glue." Scruggs, Joe, *Abracadabra.*

"School Shoes." Kinder, Brian, *A Kid like You.*

"Science Fair." Trout Fishing in America, *My World.*

"Simple Act of Kindness." Kinnoin, Dave, *Getting Bigger.*

"There's a Dog in the School." Stotts, Stuart, and Tom Pease, *Celebrate: A Song Resource.*

"Tommy Hook." Shontz, Bill, *The Day I Read a Book.*

"Twins." Fink, Cathy, and Marcy Marxer, *Nobody Else like Me.*

"Two Good Reasons." Diamond, Charlotte, *Charlotte Diamond's World.*

"Victoria Village School." Grunsky, Jack, *Playground.*

"Welcome to Our Classroom." Knight, Tom, *The Classroom Boogie.*

"Welcome to School." Fite, Stephen, *Havin' Fun and Feelin' Groovy.*

"Zchool." Lonnquist, Ken, *Sci-Fi Hi-Fi.*

Sea and Seashore (see also Fish)

"At the Bottom of the Sea." Ralph's World, *At the Bottom of the Sea.*

"At the Seaside." Buchman, Rachel, *Sing a Song of Seasons.*

"The Beach Song." Magical Music Express, *Music Is Magic.*

"Blue Planet." Banana Slug String Band, *Slugs at Sea.*

"Castillo de Arena." Frezza, Rebecca, *Music in My Head.*

"Cowtown." Yosi, *Monkey Business.*

"Diving in the Deep Blue Ocean." Harper, Monty, *Take Me to Your Library.*

"Down at the Sea Hotel." Brown, Greg, *Bathtub Blues.*

"Down by the Ocean." Allard, Peter and Ellen, *Sing It! Say It! Stamp It! Sway It!* vol. 2.

"Down by the Sea." Grammer, Red, *Down the Do-Re-Mi.*

"Estuary Life." Banana Slug String Band, *Slugs at Sea.*

"Giant Kelp Forest." Banana Slug String Band, *Slugs at Sea.*

"Goin' to the Coral Reef." Arnold, Linda, *Splash Zone.*

"Hide and Seek/Las Escondidas." Arnold, Linda, *Splash Zone.*

"Hold On or Go with the Flow." Arnold, Linda, *Splash Zone.*

"Home on the Sea." Tickle Tune Typhoon, *Singing Science.*

"I Am the Rolling Sea." Arnold, Linda, *Splash Zone.*

"If It Were Up to Me." Hullabaloo, *Sing Along with Sam.*

"Life on the Shore." Banana Slug String Band, *Slugs at Sea.*

"Ocean Communities." Banana Slug String Band, *Slugs at Sea.*

"Ocean Rap." Banana Slug String Band, *Slugs at Sea.*

"Out on the Beach." Harper, Monty, *Take Me to Your Library.*

"Rainbow City." Arnold, Linda, *Splash Zone.*

"Rocky Shore Symphony." Arnold, Linda, *Splash Zone.*

"Rocky Shore Wonders." Arnold, Linda, *Splash Zone.*

"Rumble Hula." Colleen and Uncle Squaty, *Rumble to the Bottom.*

"Sandcastle." Charette, Rick, *A Little Peace and Quiet.*

"Sandcastle." Roberts, Justin, *Meltdown!*

"Sea Shell." McGrath, Bob, and Katherine Smithrim, *Songs and Games for Toddlers.*

"Sea Shell, Sea Shell." Peterson, Carole, *H.U.M.—All Year Long.*

"See the Sea." Various Artists, *A Child's Celebration of Folk Music.*

"She Waded in the Water." Beall, Pamela, and Susan Nipp, *Wee Sing Silly Songs.*

"So Happy under the Sea." Coffey, James, *I Love Toy Trains.*

"Splash Zone." Arnold, Linda, *Splash Zone.*

"That's a Habitat." Arnold, Linda, *Splash Zone.*

"There's a Hole in the Bottom of the Sea." Beall, Pamela, and Susan Nipp, *Wee Sing Silly Songs*; Grammer, Red, *Red Grammer's Favorite Sing Along Songs*; Howdy, Buck, *Skidaddle!*; Various Artists, *A Child's Celebration of Silliest Songs*.
"Tide Pool Boogie." Banana Slug String Band, *Adventures on the Air Cycle*; Banana Slug String Band, *Slugs at Sea*.
"Tropical Song." Boynton, Sandra, *Rhinoceros Tap*.
"We're on Our Way." SteveSongs, *Marvelous Day!*
"When the Tide Goes Out." Diamond, Charlotte, *Charlotte Diamond's World*.
"Woo-Woo." Milkshake, *Bottle of Sunshine*.

Seasons

"Country Life." Kirk, John, and Trish Miller, *The Big Rock Candy Mountain*.
"The Country Life/Red Haired Boy." McMahon, Elizabeth, *Tea Party Shuffle*.
"Dance of the Seasons." Grunsky, Jack, *Dancing Feet*; Grunsky, Jack, *Sing and Dance*.
"Hello Winter." Diamond, Charlotte, *Diamonds and Dragons*.
"I Can't Wait for Spring." Pirtle, Sarah, *The Wind Is Telling Secrets*.
"If You Feel It." The Learning Station, *Seasonal Songs in Motion*.
"The Moon's Lullaby." Pirtle, Sarah, *Two Hands Hold the Earth*.
"Mother Earth's Routine." Chapin, Tom, *Mother Earth*; Chapin, Tom, *This Pretty Planet*.
"Pumpkin Town." Pirtle, Sarah, *The Wind Is Telling Secrets*.
"The Season Song." Strausman, Paul, *Camels, Cats, and Rainbows*.
"Seasons." Avni, Fran, *Tuning into Nature*.
"Seasons." Palmer, Hap, *Can Cockatoos Count by Twos?*
"Seasons for Us All." SteveSongs, *Morning til Night*.
"A Season's Lullaby." Banana Slug String Band, *Wings of Slumber*.
"Sing a Song of Seasons." Buchman, Rachel, *Sing a Song of Seasons*.
"Summer Time Winter Time." Colleen and Uncle Squaty, *Fingerplays, Movement and Story Songs*.
"Winter Dreams." McMahon, Elizabeth, *Blue Sky Sparklin' Day*.

Autumn/Fall

"Colors." McCutcheon, John, *Autumnsongs*.
"Dear Old Woolly Bear." McMahon, Elizabeth, *Waltzing with Fireflies*.
"Falling Leaves." Charette, Rick, *Toad Motel*.
"Five Little Leaves." Avni, Fran, *Tuning into Nature*; Buchman, Rachel, *Sing a Song of Seasons*.

"I Like the Fall." Buchman, Rachel, *Sing a Song of Seasons*.

"It's Fall." McCutcheon, John, *Autumnsongs*.

"It's Fall Again." The Learning Station, *Seasonal Songs in Motion*.

"Jumping in the Leaves." Nagler, Eric, *Improvise with Eric Nagler*.

"Rise and Shine." McMahon, Elizabeth, *Tea Party Shuffle*.

"Seasons." Magical Music Express, *Music Is Magic*.

"Sing a Song of September." Silberg, "Miss Jackie," *The Complete Sniggles, Squirrels, and Chicken Pox*; Silberg, "Miss Jackie," *Sing about Martin*.

"What Falls in the Fall." Berkner, Laurie, *Whaddaya Think of That?*

"When It's Autumn." Peterson, Carole, *H.U.M.—All Year Long*.

Spring

"April Fool." McCutcheon, John, *Springsongs*.

"Frog on a Log." McCutcheon, John, *Springsongs*.

"Goodbye Winter, Hello Spring." Silberg, "Miss Jackie," *The Complete Sniggles, Squirrels, and Chicken Pox*; Silberg, "Miss Jackie," *Sing about Martin*.

"Peepers." Walker, Mary Lu, *The Frog's Party*.

"Pom Na Tu Ri (Spring Outing)." Mitchell, Elizabeth, *You Are My Little Bird*.

"Snow in April." McCutcheon, John, *Springsongs*.

"Spring!" Stotts, Stuart, and Tom Pease, *Celebrate: A Song Resource*.

"Spring Fever." McCutcheon, John, *Springsongs*.

"Spring Is Here." The Learning Station, *Seasonal Songs in Motion*.

"Ten Robins." Kaye, Mary, *Spin Your Web*.

"Waiting (Song for Spring)." Grunsky, Jack, *Sing and Dance*.

"Welcome Back Mrs. Robin." McMahon, Elizabeth, *Magic Parade*.

Summer

"Bed in Summer." Buchman, Rachel, *Sing a Song of Seasons*.

"I Love Summer." McCutcheon, John, *Summersongs*.

"The Kid Who Hates Summer." McCutcheon, John, *Summersongs*.

"Selling Lemonade." Madsen, Gunnar, *Old Mr. Mackle Hackle*.

"Summer Is A-Coming." McCutcheon, John, *Springsongs*.

"Summertime Is Here." Madsen, Gunnar, *Old Mr. Mackle Hackle*.

"Summertime Song." Moo, Anna, *Moochas Gracias*.

"Summertime's Here." Kinnoin, Dave, *Getting Bigger*.

"Where the Blackberries Grow." Foote, Norman, *1000 Pennies*.

Winter (see also Weather—Snow)

"Alberta Postcard." Trout Fishing in America, *My Best Day*.

"Big Ned." Del Bianco, Lou, *A Little Bit Clumsy*.

"The Earth Is Still Sleeping." McMahon, Elizabeth, *Waltzing with Fireflies*.

"Going Out to Play." Silberg, "Miss Jackie," *The Complete Sniggles, Squirrels, and Chicken Pox*.

"Hibernation." McCutcheon, John, *Wintersongs*.

"I Can Make a Snowman." Peterson, Carole, *H.U.M.—All Year Long*.

"I Like to Be Cold and Wet." Troubadour, *On the Trail*.

"Let's Play in the Snow." Buchman, Rachel, *Sing a Song of Seasons*.

"Put Another Log on the Fire (Winter Song)." Grunsky, Jack, *Sing and Dance*.

"Ring Those Bells." Peterson, Carole, *H.U.M.—All Year Long*.

"Sleigh Bells." Barchas, Sarah, *Bridges across the World*.

"Smells like Winter." Byers, Kathy, *Do You Wish You Could Fly?*

"Snowman." Rosenshontz, *Family Vacation*.

"Snowman's Café." McMahon, Elizabeth, *Tea Party Shuffle*.

"So Cold Outside." Avni, Fran, *Artichokes and Brussel Sprouts*; Avni, Fran, *Tuning into Nature*.

"Soup." McCutcheon, John, *Wintersongs*.

"Take a Toboggan Ride." Charette, Rick, *Toad Motel*.

"Tommy Don't Lick That Pipe." McCutcheon, John, *Wintersongs*.

"Winter Sleep." Rosenthal, Phil, *Animal Songs*.

"Winter's Come and Gone." Mitchell, Elizabeth, *You Are My Little Bird*.

"Wintersong." McCutcheon, John, *Wintersongs*.

Self Concept/Self-Esteem

"ABC of Me." Milkshake, *Bottle of Sunshine*.

"Alive and Dreaming." Raffi, *Evergreen, Everblue*.

"All about Me." Silberg, "Miss Jackie," *Sing It Again Please*.

"All of These Things." Hullabaloo, *Sing Along with Sam*.

"Be Yourself." Magical Music Express, *Music Is Magic*.

"The Beauty Shop." Vitamin L, *Every Moment!*

"Be-Bop Your Best." Grammer, Red, *Be Bop Your Best!*

"Believe in Yourself." Greg and Steve, *Kidding Around*.

"Costume Party." Alsop, Peter, *Pluggin' Away*.

"C-R-A-Z-Y." Harley, Bill, *I Wanna Play*.

"Create Your Own Way." Green Chili Jam Band, *Starfishing*.

"Different Drum." Scruggs, Joe, *Ants*.

"Digging for Diamonds." Grammer, Red, *Hello World*.

"Everybody Is Somebody." Various Artists, *Peace Is the World Smiling*.

"Express Yourself." Vitamin L, *Swingin' in the Key of L*.

"For Now I'll Just Be Me." Fite, Stephen, *We're Just like Crayons*.

"Francie Had a Football." Palmer, Hap, *Turn On the Music*.

"Glad to Be Me." Allard, Peter and Ellen, *Good Kid*.

"Good Kid." Allard, Peter and Ellen, *Good Kid*.

"Got to Be Good to Your Self." LaFond, Lois, *Lois LaFond and the Rockadiles*.

"A Great Idea That's All Your Own." Charette, Rick, *Popcorn and Other Songs to Munch On*.

"Healthy Beginnings." Tickle Tune Typhoon, *Healthy Beginnings*.

"Help Yourself." Fink, Cathy, and Marcy Marxer, *Help Yourself*.

"I Am a Person." Pirtle, Sarah, *Two Hands Hold the Earth*.

"I Am Special." Magical Music Express, *Music Is Magic*.

"I Am Who I Am." LaFond, Lois, *I Am Who I Am*; LaFond, Lois, *Lois LaFond and the Rockadiles*.

"I Believe in Me." Tickle Tune Typhoon, *Hearts and Hands*.

"I Believe Myself." Fink, Cathy, and Marcy Marxer, *Help Yourself*.

"I Can Be Almost Anything I Try." Charette, Rick, *Alligator in the Elevator*.

"I Can Do It by Myself." Moo, Anna, *Making Moosic*.

"I Can Do That." Parachute Express, *Sunny Side Up*.

"I Can If I Wanna." Alsop, Peter, *Pluggin' Away*.

"I Can Swing by Myself." Daddy A Go Go, *Cool Songs for Cool Kids*.

"I Like What I Like." Green Chili Jam Band, *Coconut Moon*.

"I Think You're Wonderful." Grammer, Red, *Teaching Peace*.

"I Wanna Be." Del Bianco, Lou, *Lost in School*.

"I Wanna Be Tall." Milkshake, *Happy Songs*.

"I Want to Be Strong." The Dream Project, *We've All Got Stories*.

"I'm Not Perfect." Berkner, Laurie, *Victor Vito*.

"I'm Not Small." Harley, Bill, *Monsters in the Bathroom*; Sharon, Lois, and Bram, *One Elephant, Deux Éléphants*; Sharon, Lois, and Bram, *Sleepytime*.

"I'm Shining." Green Chili Jam Band, *Starfishing*.

"I'm So Big." Stotts, Stuart, and Tom Pease, *Celebrate: A Song Resource*.

"I'm the Only Me." Chapin, Tom, *Some Assembly Required*.

"In My Heart." The Chenille Sisters, *The Big Picture and Other Songs for Kids*.

"It Takes Each One to Make This World a Little Bit Better." Barchas, Sarah, *Bridges across the World*.

"It's Great Being Me." Penner, Fred, *What a Day!*

"I've Got the Power." Magical Music Express, *Friendship Stew*.

"Keep a Little Light." Gemini, *The Best of Gemini*, vol. 2.

"The Kid behind the Mirror." Paxton, Tom, *Your Shoes, My Shoes*.

"The King of My Mountain." Trout Fishing in America, *It's a Puzzle*.

"Listen to Your Heart." Grammer, Red, *Be Bop Your Best!*

"Lucky." Lonnquist, Ken, *The Circus Kenlando*.

"The Magic Key." Arnold, Linda, *Peppermint Wings*.

"Magic Wings." Pirtle, Sarah, *Heart of the World*.

"My Roots Go Down." Pease, Tom, *Wobbi-Do-Wop!*; Pirtle, Sarah, *Two Hands Hold the Earth*.

"My Way." Craig n Co., *Rock n Together*.

"Myself, My People, My World." Barchas, Sarah, *Bridges across the World*.

"No One's Normal." Alsop, Peter, *Pluggin' Away*.

"Nobody Else like Me." Fink, Cathy, and Marcy Marxer, *Help Yourself*; Fink, Cathy, and Marcy Marxer, *Nobody Else like Me*.

"Nobody Else like Me." Walker, Mary Lu, *The Frog's Party*.

"Number One." Fink, Cathy, and Marcy Marxer, *Bon Appétit!*

"The One and Only Me." Atkinson, Lisa, *The One and Only Me*.

"The Power in Me." Fink, Cathy, and Marcy Marxer, *Changing Channels*.

"Princess Power." Miss Amy, *Wide, Wide World*.

"Say Hey." Pease, Tom, *Daddy Starts to Dance*.

"See Me Beautiful." Grammer, Red, *Teaching Peace*.

"Shine Out." Tickle Tune Typhoon, *Hearts and Hands*.

"Shine Shine Shine!" Peterson, Carole, *Stinky Cake*.

"Snowflake." Greg and Steve, *Rockin' down the Road*.

"Someone like Me." Harper, Jessica, *40 Winks*.

"Somewhere Deep Inside." Sprout, Jonathan, *Kid Power*.

"Special Me." Feldman, Jean, *Dr. Jean and Friends*.

"Still the Same Me." Sweet Honey in the Rock, *Still the Same Me*.

"That's Me." Milkshake, *Happy Songs*.

"That's My Thang!" Alsop, Peter, *Pluggin' Away*.

"There's a River Flowing in My Soul." The Dream Project, *We've All Got Stories*.

"Things That I Like." Ralph's World, *Happy Lemon*.

"The Things You Do." Ode, Eric, *Trash Can*.

"Think for Yourself." Vitamin L, *Walk a Mile*.

"This Little Light of Mine." Arnold, Linda, *Sing Along Stew*; Cassidy, Nancy, *Nancy Cassidy's KidsSongs*; The Dream Project, *We've All Got Stories*; Howdy, Buck, *Giddyup!*; Magical Music Express, *Music Is Magic*; McGrath, Bob, *Sing Along with Bob #1*; Mitchell, Elizabeth, *You Are My Flower*; Pease, Tom, *I'm Gonna Reach!*; Raffi, *Rise and Shine*; Various Artists, *I'm Gonna Let It Shine*.

"Treasure Every Step." Haynes, Sammie, *Nature's ABCs*.

"True to Myself." Pirtle, Sarah, *Heart of the World*.

"Way Down Deep." Sweet Honey in the Rock, *Still the Same Me*.

"We're Great!" Feldman, Jean, *Just for Fun!*

"We've All Got Stories." The Dream Project, *We've All Got Stories*.

"What's the Matter with You?" Harley, Bill, *Monsters in the Bathroom*.

"Whatever You Choose." Raffi, *Raffi Radio*.

"When You've Got a Heart." Kinnoin, Dave, *Getting Bigger*.

"Who Am I?" Vitamin L, *Every Moment!*

"Who Are You?" Lonnquist, Ken, *The Lost Songs of Kenland*.

"Why I'm Here in This World." Tucker, Nancy, *Happy as a Clam*.

"With These Hands." Vitamin L, *Swingin' in the Key of L*.

"You Are Special Don't You Know?" Kimmy Schwimmy, *Kimmy Schwimmy Music*, vol. 1.

"You Can Be." LaFond, Lois, *Lois LaFond and the Rockadiles*; LaFond, Lois, *One World*.

"You Can Be a Giant." Atkinson, Lisa, *I Wanna Tickle the Fish*.

Senses

"Any Way I Can." LaFond, Lois, *Turning It Upside Down*.

"Feel It, Shake It." Strausman, Paul, *Blue Jay, Blue Jay!*

"5 Senses." Lonnquist, Ken, *Sci-Fi Hi-Fi*.

"Seeing with My Ears." Pelham, Ruth, *Under One Sky*.

"Sensitive Person." Dana, *Dana's Best Sing and Swing-a-Long Tunes*.

Hearing

"All the Sounds." The Learning Station, *Seasonal Songs in Motion*.

"I'm All Ears." Avni, Fran, *I'm All Ears: Sing into Reading*; Avni, Fran, *Little Ears: Songs for Reading Readiness*.

"Just Listen." Allard, Peter and Ellen, *Raise the Children*.

"Sounds." Strausman, Paul, *Blue Jay, Blue Jay!*

"Sounds Like." Harper, Jessica, *A Wonderful Life*.

Sight

"Blue Jay." Strausman, Paul, *Blue Jay, Blue Jay!*
"Brown Bear, Brown Bear, What Do You See?" Greg and Steve, *Playing Favorites.*
"Get Me Some Glasses." Roberts, Justin, *Meltdown!*
"Harry's Glasses." Fink, Cathy, and Marcy Marxer, *Nobody Else like Me.*

Smell

"Mmm, It Smells So Good." Buchman, Rachel, *Hello Everybody!*
"Smelly Feet." Foote, Norman, *Shake a Leg.*
"Smelly Jellies." Kinnoin, Dave, *Getting Bigger.*
"A Song about Smells." Penner, Fred, *What a Day!*
"Stinky Feet." Cosgrove, Jim, *Stinky Feet.*
"You Can Tell a Boy by the Smell." Thaddeus Rex, *We Wanna Rock.*

Shadows

"Shadow." Kaye, Mary, *Spin Your Web.*
"Shadow Dancing." Greg and Steve, *Kids in Motion.*
"Shadow Song." Walker, Graham, *Knobbledee Knees.*
"The Shape of My Shadow." Crow, Dan, *A Friend, a Laugh, a Walk in the Woods.*
"Where Is My Shadow?" Del Bianco, Lou, *When I Was a Kid.*

Shapes

"All around the Circle." Allard, Peter and Ellen, *Sing It! Say It! Stamp It! Sway It!* vol. 2.
"Jig Along Shapes." Palmer, Hap, *Can a Jumbo Jet Sing the Alphabet?*
"The Shape Game." Parachute Express, *Sunny Side Up.*
"Shape Man." Barchas, Sarah, *Get Ready, Get Set, Sing!*
"The Shapes That Surround You." Palmer, Hap, *Can a Jumbo Jet Sing the Alphabet?*
"Something 'bout a Circle." Parachute Express, *Don't Blink.*
"The Town of Round." Polisar, Barry Louis, *Old Enough to Know Better.*

Sharing

"The Giving Song." The Learning Station, *Literacy in Motion.*
"If Only." Chapin, Tom, *Zag Zig.*
"I'll Share with You." Mayer, Hans, *Stars of the Swing Set.*

"A Piece of Pie." Moo, Anna, *Moochas Gracias*.

"Share It!" Rosenshontz, *Rosenshontz Greatest Hits*; Rosenshontz, *Share It*.

"Sharing." Fink, Cathy, and Marcy Marxer, *Changing Channels*.

"The Sharing Song." Raffi, *Singable Songs for the Very Young*.

"Sittin' Down to Eat." Harley, Bill, *Big Big World*; Harley, Bill, *Play It Again*.

"Something to Share (Song for UNICEF)." Grunsky, Jack, *Sing and Dance*.

"The Way It Should Be." Rymer, Brady, *Look at My Belly*.

"We Don't Have to Share." Polisar, Barry Louis, *Family Trip*.

"Whoever Shall Have Some Good Peanuts." Fink, Cathy, *When the Rain Comes Down*; Hinton, Sam, *Whoever Shall Have Some Good Peanuts*.

Shyness

"Can't Let Go Blues." Frezza, Rebecca, *Tall and Small*.

"His Name Is Ty." Chapin, Tom, *In My Hometown*.

"I Know Your Face." Pelham, Ruth, *Under One Sky*.

"Say Hi!" Grammer, Red, *Teaching Peace*.

Size

"Big, Bigger, Biggest." Jenkins, Ella, *Growing Up with Ella Jenkins*.

"Big Kids." Lithgow, John, *Singin' in the Bathtub*.

"Bigger, Bigger, Bigger." Alsop, Peter, *Stayin' Over*.

"Dawn Puccini." Del Bianco, Lou, *A Little Bit Clumsy*.

"Giant in Little Bitty Town." Kimmy Schwimmy, *Kimmy Schwimmy Music*, vol. 1.

"I Wanna Be Tall." Milkshake, *Happy Songs*.

"I'm Not Small." Harley, Bill, *Monsters in the Bathroom*; Sharon, Lois, and Bram, *One Elephant, Deux Éléphants*; Sharon, Lois, and Bram, *Sleepytime*.

"I'm Not Too Short." Tucker, Nancy, *Glad That You Asked*.

"King Kong Chair." Charette, Rick, *King Kong Chair*.

"Now Tall, Now Small." Beall, Pamela, and Susan Nipp, *Wee Sing Children's Songs and Fingerplays*.

"So Big." Palmer, Hap, *So Big*.

"Tall and Small." Frezza, Rebecca, *Tall and Small*.

"Thumbelina." Kaye, Mary, *Mouse Jamboree*.

"Thumbelina." Raffi, *Rise and Shine*.

"Very, Very Tall." Old Town School of Folk Music, *Wiggleworms Love You*.

"You Can Be a Giant." Atkinson, Lisa, *I Wanna Tickle the Fish*.

Special Places

"Happy Place." Rosenshontz, *Share It.*
"Hideaway." Ralph's World, *Green Gorilla, Monster, and Me.*
"Hiding Places." Troubadour, *On the Trail.*
"A Little Peace and Quiet." Charette, Rick, *A Little Peace and Quiet.*
"My Room." LaFond, Lois, *I Am Who I Am.*
"My Tree." Stotts, Stuart, *Are We There Yet?*
"Place to Be." Ungar, Jay, and Lyn Hardy, *A Place to Be.*

Spiders

"Anansi." Raffi, *Corner Grocery Store.*
"Arachnids." Tickle Tune Typhoon, *Singing Science.*
"Daddy Long Legs." Strausman, Paul, *Blue Jay, Blue Jay!*
"The Eensy Weensy Spider." Barchas, Sarah, *Get Ready, Get Set, Sing!*; Beall,
     Pamela, and Susan Nipp, *Wee Sing Animals, Animals, Animals*; Beall, Pamela,
     and Susan Nipp, *Wee Sing around the World*; Beall, Pamela, and Susan Nipp,
     Wee Sing Children's Songs and Fingerplays; Raffi, *Let's Play*; Scruggs, Joe,
     Deep in the Jungle; Sharon, Lois, and Bram, *Great Big Hits*; Silberg, "Miss
     Jackie," *Peanut Butter, Tarzan, and Roosters.* (Same song as "Incey Wincey
     Spider" and "The Itsy Bitsy Spider.")
"Hey, Mr. Spider." Arnold, Linda, *Make Believe.*
"The Incey Wincey Spider." McGrath, Bob, *Sing Along with Bob #1.* (Same song
     as "The Eensy Weensy Spider" and "The Itsy Bitsy Spider.")
"Itchy Squishy Spider." Pullara, Steve, *One Potato, Two Potato.*
"The Itsy Bitsy Spider." Avni, Fran, *Little Ears: Songs for Reading Readiness*;
     Bartels, Joanie, *Bathtime Magic*; Dana, *Dana's Best Sing and Play-a-Long
     Tunes*; Feldman, Jean, *Is Everybody Happy?*; Feldman, Jean, *Nursery Rhymes
     and Good Ol' Times*; Ralph's World, *At the Bottom of the Sea.* (Same song as
     "The Eensy Weensy Spider" and "Incey Wincey Spider.")
"Itsy Spider." Alsop, Peter, *Uh-Oh!*
"Little Miss Muffet." Beall, Pamela, and Susan Nipp, *Wee Sing Nursery Rhymes
     and Lullabies*; Feldman, Jean, *Nursery Rhymes and Good Ol' Times*; Silberg,
     "Miss Jackie," *The Complete Sniggles, Squirrels, and Chicken Pox*; Silberg,
     "Miss Jackie," *Sing about Martin.*
"Little Spider." Walker, Graham, *Fiddlesticks.*
"Miss Muffet/The Eensy Weensy Spider." Sharon, Lois, and Bram, *Everybody
     Sing!*; Sharon, Lois, and Bram, *Mainly Mother Goose.*
"Six Tiny Spiders." Atkinson, Lisa, *The Elephant in Aisle Four.*
"Spider and the Fly." Lonnquist, Ken, *Sci-Fi Hi-Fi.*

"Spider and the Fly." Tucker, Nancy, *Escape of the Slinkys*.

"Spider Dan." Foote, Norman, *Pictures on the Fridge*.

"Spider on the Floor." Raffi, *Singable Songs for the Very Young*.

"Spider's Web." Diamond, Charlotte, *10 Carrot Diamond*.

"Spin Spider Spin." Crow, Dan, *The Giggling Dragon*.

"Spin Spider Spin." Knight, Tom, *The Classroom Boogie*.

Spiritual

"Ain't Gonna Let Nobody Turn Me 'Round." Various Artists, *I'm Gonna Let It Shine*.

"All Night All Day." Beall, Pamela, and Susan Nipp, *Wee Sing Children's Songs and Fingerplays*; Byers, Kathy, *'Round the Campfire*.

"Amen." Sweet Honey in the Rock, *All for Freedom*.

"Cumbayah." Sweet Honey in the Rock, *All for Freedom*. (Same song as "Kumbaya.")

"Down by the Riverside." Raffi, *Bananaphone*; Zanes, Dan, *Night Time!*

"Five Hundred Miles." Byers, Kathy, *'Round the Campfire*.

"Get on Board, Little Children." Beall, Pamela, and Susan Nipp, *Wee Sing Sing-Alongs*; Tickle Tune Typhoon, *Patty-Cakes and Peek-a-Boos*; Various Artists, *I'm Gonna Let It Shine*.

"Guide My Feet." Various Artists, *I'm Gonna Let It Shine*.

"Heav'n Heav'n." Beall, Pamela, and Susan Nipp, *Wee Sing Sing-Alongs*.

"He's Got the Whole World in His Hands." Beall, Pamela, and Susan Nipp, *Wee Sing Sing-Alongs*; Cassidy, Nancy, *Nancy Cassidy's KidsSongs*; Gemini, *The Best of Gemini*, vol. 2; Raffi, *Rise and Shine*.

"Hold On (Keep Your Eyes on the Prize)." Various Artists, *I'm Gonna Let It Shine*.

"I Got Shoes." Sweet Honey in the Rock, *I Got Shoes*.

"I Want to Be Ready." Jenkins, Ella, *Sharing Cultures with Ella Jenkins*.

"I'm Gonna Sit at the Welcome Table." Various Artists, *I'm Gonna Let It Shine*.

"I'm on My Way." Byers, Kathy, *'Round the Campfire*.

"Jacob's Ladder." Beall, Pamela, and Susan Nipp, *Wee Sing Sing-Alongs*.

"Kumbaya." Beall, Pamela, and Susan Nipp, *Wee Sing Sing-Alongs*; Byers, Kathy, *'Round the Campfire*; Cassidy, Nancy, *Nancy Cassidy's KidsSongs*; Raffi, *Baby Beluga*; Various Artists, *A Child's Celebration of the World*. (Same song as "Cumbayah.")

"Meeting at the Building." Sweet Honey in the Rock, *All for Freedom*.

"Michael Row the Boat Ashore." Beall, Pamela, and Susan Nipp, *Wee Sing Sing-Alongs*; Cassidy, Nancy, *Nancy Cassidy's KidsSongs*; Grunsky, Jack,

Playground; Raffi, *Bananaphone*; Seeger, Pete, *For Kids and Just Plain Folks*; Various Artists, *Sing Along with Putumayo*.

"Nobody Knows the Trouble I've Seen." Beall, Pamela, and Susan Nipp, *Wee Sing Sing-Alongs*.

"Rocka My Soul." Beall, Pamela, and Susan Nipp, *Wee Sing Sing-Alongs*.

"Swing Low, Sweet Chariot." Arnold, Linda, *Sing Along Stew*; Beall, Pamela, and Susan Nipp, *Wee Sing Sing-Alongs*; Raffi, *Corner Grocery Store*.

"This Train." Coffey, James, *I Love Toy Trains*.

"Train Is A-Comin'." Beall, Pamela, and Susan Nipp, *Wee Sing Fun 'n' Folk*.

"We Shall Overcome." Various Artists, *I'm Gonna Let It Shine*.

"Welcome Table." Zanes, Dan, *Catch That Train!*

"We're Almost Home." Sweet Honey in the Rock, *Still the Same Me*.

"When the Saints Go Marching In." Beall, Pamela, and Susan Nipp, *Wee Sing Sing-Alongs*; McGrath, Bob, *Sing Along with Bob #1*.

"The Wilderness." Jenkins, Ella, *Songs Children Love to Sing*.

Stores/Markets/Restaurants

"At the Grocery Store." Atkinson, Lisa, *The One and Only Me*.

"Corner Grocery Store." Raffi, *Corner Grocery Store*.

"Deli." Gemini, *The Best of Gemini*.

"The Elephant in Aisle Four." Atkinson, Lisa, *The Elephant in Aisle Four*.

"The Farmer's Market." Abell, Timmy, *The Farmer's Market*.

"Fascination Café." Foote, Norman, *Foote Prints*.

"Filling Up a Shopping Cart." Charette, Rick, *King Kong Chair*.

"Gertie's Birdseed Diner." Chapin, Tom, *In My Hometown*.

"Home Dairy Bakery." McMahon, Elizabeth, *Blue Sky Sparklin' Day*.

"Let's Go to the Market." Greg and Steve, *We All Live Together*, vol. 5.

"Linstead Market." Zanes, Dan, *Family Dance*.

"Maria and Don Cheech's Pizzaria." Pullara, Steve, *A Big Bowl of Musicroni*.

"The Marketplace." Lonnquist, Ken, *The Circus Kenlando*.

"Mr. McWhizwidget's Fix It Up Shop." Parachute Express, *Doctor Looney's Remedy*.

"Peggy's Pie Parlor Polka." Ralph's World, *Peggy's Pie Parlor*.

"Pizza Hut." Feldman, Jean, *Just for Fun!*

"Spaghetti Worms and Meatballs." Yosi, *What's Eatin' Yosi?*

"Supermarket Tango." Grunsky, Jack, *Dancing Feet*; Grunsky, Jack, *Jack in the Box 1*.

"Thrift Shop." Zanes, Dan, *Family Dance*.

"What's on the List?" Fite, Stephen, *Gobs of Fun*.

Storytelling (see also Books/Reading)

"Gup!" Raven, Nancy, *The House We Live In*, vols. 1 and 2.
"It's Been a Big Day." Foote, Norman, *If the Shoe Fits*.
"The Ragtime Dance." Chapin, Tom, *Zag Zig*.
"Storyteller." Grunsky, Jack, *Jack in the Box 2*.
"Stretchin' the Truth." Kinnoin, Dave, *Dunce Cap Kelly*.
"Tell Me a Story." Frezza, Rebecca, *Tall and Small*.
"Too Much Snow in Tokyo." Harper, Jessica, *Rhythm in My Shoes*.
"The Troubadour." Chapin, Tom, *Around the World and Back Again*.
"Uh Huh." Tickle Tune Typhoon, *Hearts and Hands*.

Teddy Bears

"Bear You Loved." Roth, Kevin, *Unbearable Bears*.
"Fixing Freddy." Parachute Express, *Who's Got a Hug?*
"Freddy Bear the Teddy Bear." Ralph's World, *Ralph's World*.
"Ha-Ha Thisaway." Raffi, *Everything Grows*.
"House at Pooh Corner." Shontz, Bill, *Teddy Bear's Greatest Hits*; Various Artists, *A Child's Celebration of Song*.
"I Could Spend a Happy Moment." Rosen, Gary, *Teddy Bears' Picnic*.
"Invisible Bear." Shontz, Bill, *Teddy Bear's Greatest Hits*.
"Lines Written by a Bear of Very Little Brain." Rosen, Gary, *Teddy Bears' Picnic*.
"Lullaby for Teddy-O." Herdman, Priscilla, *Stardreamer*.
"Me and My Teddy Bear." Shontz, Bill, *Teddy Bear's Greatest Hits*.
"My Best Friend Lars." Magical Music Express, *Music Is Magic*.
"My Teddy Bear." Kinder, Brian, *Again*.
"Oh the Butterflies Are Flying." Rosen, Gary, *Teddy Bears' Picnic*.
"Party Teddy Bears." Rosenshontz, *Family Vacation*.
"Rock 'n Roll Teddy Bear." Rosen, Gary, *Teddy Bears' Picnic*; Rosenshontz, *Rock 'n Roll Teddy Bear*; Rosenshontz, *Rosenshontz Greatest Hits*.
"Sing Ho! for the Life of a Bear/Teddy Bears' Picnic." Rosen, Gary, *Teddy Bears' Picnic*.
"Talkin' to My Teddy." Fink, Cathy, and Marcy Marxer, *Pocket Full of Stardust*.
"Teddy Bear." Arnold, Linda, *Favorites in the Key of Fun*; Arnold, Linda, *Make Believe*.
"Teddy Bear." Beall, Pamela, and Susan Nipp, *Wee Sing Children's Songs and Fingerplays*.
"Teddy Bear." McCutcheon, John, *Mail Myself to You*.

"Teddy Bear." Palmer, Hap, *Peek-a-Boo*.

"Teddy Bear Ball." Palmer, Hap, *Peek-a-Boo*; Palmer, Hap, *Turn On the Music*.

"Teddy Bear Hug." Raffi, *Everything Grows*.

"The Teddy Bear Jamboree." Rosen, Gary, *Tot Rock*.

"Teddy Bear King." Arnold, Linda, *Peppermint Wings*.

"Teddy Bear King's Waltz." Arnold, Linda, *Favorites in the Key of Fun*.

"Teddy Bear Lullaby." Mayer, Hans, *Just a Little Hug*.

"Teddy Bear Playtime." Palmer, Hap, *So Big*.

"The Teddy Bear Song." Greg and Steve, *Fun and Games*.

"The Teddy Bear Song." Knight, Tom, *Don't Kiss a Codfish*.

"Teddy Bear's Parade." Shontz, Bill, *Teddy Bear's Greatest Hits*.

"Teddy Bears' Picnic." Arnold, Linda, *Circus Magic*; Atkinson, Lisa, *The One and Only Me*; Garcia, Jerry, and David Grisman, *Not for Kids Only*; Rosenshontz, *Tickles You!*; Rosenthal, Phil, *Folksongs and Bluegrass for Children*; Roth, Kevin, *Travel Song Sing Alongs*; Roth, Kevin, *Unbearable Bears*; Shontz, Bill, *Teddy Bear's Greatest Hits*; Trout Fishing in America, *Big Trouble*.

"Teddy Rockin'." Kinnoin, Dave, *Getting Bigger*.

"Teddy Rockin'." Shontz, Bill, *Teddy Bear's Greatest Hits*.

"Teddybear Waltz." Atkinson, Lisa, *I Wanna Tickle the Fish*.

"3 Cheers for Pooh." Rosen, Gary, *Teddy Bears' Picnic*.

Teeth

"Braces." Sprout, Jonathan, *On the Radio*.

"Brush Three Times a Day." Byers, Kathy, *Do You Wish You Could Fly?*

"Brush Your Teeth." Cassidy, Nancy, *Nancy Cassidy's KidsSongs*; Fink, Cathy, *Grandma Slid down the Mountain*; Fink, Cathy, and Marcy Marxer, *A Cathy & Marcy Collection for Kids*; Raffi, *Singable Songs for the Very Young*.

"Brush Your Teeth." Daddy A Go Go, *Cool Songs for Cool Kids*.

"The Dentist Is Your Smile's Best Friend." Silberg, "Miss Jackie," *Touched by a Song*.

"Here Come My Teeth." Rymer, Brady, *Look at My Belly*.

"I Brush My Teeth." Silberg, "Miss Jackie," *Sing It Again Please*.

"I Lost the Tooth." Roberts, Justin, *Way Out*.

"I Sure Have Got a Loose Tooth." Charette, Rick, *Bubble Gum*.

"Little White Star." McCutcheon, John, *Family Garden*.

"Loose Tooth." Chapin, Tom, *Zag Zig*.

"Loose Tooth." Foote, Norman, *1000 Pennies*.

"Loose Tooth." Harper, Monty, *The Great Green Squishy Mean Concert CD*.

"Loose Tooth." Sprout, Jonathan, *Kid Power*.

"Loose Tooth." Troubadour, *On the Trail*.

"Loose Tooth Blues." Gemini, *The Best of Gemini*.

"Looth Tooth." Grunsky, Jack, *Jack in the Box 2*.

"My Dentist Is an Awfully Nice Man." Polisar, Barry Louis, *Old Enough to Know Better*.

"My Gums Grow Teeth." Alsop, Peter, *Uh-Oh!*

"My Tooth Is Gone." Strausman, Paul, *Rainbows, Stones, and Dinosaur Bones*.

"My Tooth It Is Wiggling." Allard, Peter and Ellen, *Pizza Pizzaz*.

"Pearly White Waltz." Tickle Tune Typhoon, *All of Us Will Shine*.

"So Long, You Old Tooth." Brown, Greg, *Bathtub Blues*.

"Teeth." Charette, Rick, *King Kong Chair*.

"Time to Brush Our Teeth." Rymer, Brady, *Look at My Belly*.

"Tooth Fairy." Kaye, Mary, *Mouse Jamboree*.

"Tooth Fairy." Rosenshontz, *Family Vacation*.

"Tooth Fairy Song." Troubadour, *On the Trail*.

"Toothless." Green Chili Jam Band, *Starfishing*.

"Us Kids Brush Our Teeth." Alsop, Peter, *Stayin' Over*.

"Wiggle Wiggle Wiggle." Fink, Cathy, and Marcy Marxer, *Air Guitar*.

"Wiggle Wobble Tooth." Cosgrove, Jim, *Ooey Gooey*.

Telephones

"Bananaphone." Raffi, *Bananaphone*; Various Artists, *A Child's Celebration of Song 2*; Various Artists, *Sing Along with Putumayo*.

"Hang Up and Drive." Daddy A Go Go, *Eat Every Bean and Pea on Your Plate*.

"I'm on the Phone." Pease, Tom, *Wobbi-Do-Wop!*

"Telephone." Berkner, Laurie, *Buzz Buzz*.

Television

"Dad Threw the TV out the Window." Fink, Cathy, and Marcy Marxer, *Changing Channels*; Harley, Bill, *Play It Again*; Harley, Bill, *You're in Trouble*.

"50 Things That I Can Do Instead of Watch TV." Fink, Cathy, and Marcy Marxer, *Changing Channels*.

"I Caught Daddy Watching Cartoons." Daddy A Go Go, *Big Rock Rooster*.

"Instead of Watching My TV." Rymer, Brady, *Every Day Is a Birthday*.

"Martian Television Invasion." Thaddeus Rex, *Martian Television Invasion*.

"Time Vacuum." Lonnquist, Ken, *Welcome 2 Kenland*.

"Turn It Off, Change the Channel, Leave the Room." Fink, Cathy, and Marcy Marxer, *Changing Channels*.

"Turn Off the TV." Atkinson, Lisa, *The Elephant in Aisle Four*.

"You Get a Little Extra When You Watch T.V." Alsop, Peter, *Wha' D'Ya Wanna Do?*

Thankfulness

"Gratitude." Grammer, Red, *Be Bop Your Best!*

"I Want to Say Thanks." Vitamin L, *Everyone's Invited!*

"The Little Blue Dot." Pullara, Steve, *Spinning Tails*.

"Mahalo." Berkner, Laurie, *Under a Shady Tree*.

"Mi-gwetch Ah-ki." Pirtle, Sarah, *Heart of the World*.

"Thank You." Arnold, Linda, *Happiness Cake*.

"Thank You." Fink, Cathy, and Marcy Marxer, *Pocket Full of Stardust*.

"Thank You for All That You Do." Allard, Peter and Ellen, *Sing It! Say It! Stamp It! Sway It!* vol. 3.

"A Thank You Song." Charette, Rick, *Bubble Gum*.

"Thanks a Lot." Herdman, Priscilla, *Stardreamer*; Raffi, *Baby Beluga*; Raffi, *Quiet Time*.

"We Give Thanks." Fite, Stephen, *Monkey Business*.

Tickling

"I'm Not Ticklish." The Chenille Sisters, *The Big Picture and Other Songs for Kids*.

"Sam the Tickle Man." Rosenshontz, *Tickles You!*

"Tickle My Toes." Roberts, Justin, *Yellow Bus*.

"Tickle Song." Grammer, Red, *Red Grammer's Favorite Sing Along Songs*.

"Tickle Time." Boynton, Sandra, *Rhinoceros Tap*.

"Tickle Toe." Gill, Jim, *Jim Gill Makes It Noisy in Boise, Idaho*.

"Tickle You Blue." Harper, Monty, *Jungle Junk!*

Tools

"Bling Blang." Guthrie, Woody, *Songs to Grow On for Mother and Child*; Guthrie, Woody, *Woody's 20 Grow Big Songs*; Guthrie, Woody and Arlo, *This Land Is Your Land*; Old Town School of Folk Music, *Wiggleworms Love You*; Simmons, Al, *Something Fishy at Camp Wiganishie*; Various Artists, *Sing Along with Putumayo*.

"Bumping Up and Down." McGrath, Bob, and Katherine Smithrim, *Songs and Games for Toddlers*; Raffi, *Singable Songs for the Very Young*.

"I Can Work with One Hammer." Greg and Steve, *Fun and Games*.

"I Got My Axe." Simmons, Al, *Something Fishy at Camp Wiganishie*.

"Peter Hammers." Beall, Pamela, and Susan Nipp, *Wee Sing Children's Songs and Fingerplays*.

"What Could You Use?" Palmer, Hap, *Can a Jumbo Jet Sing the Alphabet?*

Toys (see also Dolls; Teddy Bears)

"Amanda Schlupp." Palmer, Hap, *Turn On the Music*.

"Bop Bop Dinosaur." Cosgrove, Jim, *Bop Bop Dinosaur*.

"A Crazy Machine." Harper, Jessica, *Rhythm in My Shoes*.

"Doctor Tinker Tinker." Sharon, Lois, and Bram, *Mainly Mother Goose*.

"I Love Toy Trains." Coffey, James, *Come Ride Along with Me*; Coffey, James, *I Love Toy Trains*.

"I'm a Top." Beall, Pamela, and Susan Nipp, *Wee Sing and Pretend*.

"I've Got a Yo-Yo." Paxton, Tom, *I've Got a Yo-Yo*.

"It's Gone." Trout Fishing in America, *It's a Puzzle*.

"Jack-in-the-Box." Beall, Pamela, and Susan Nipp, *Wee Sing and Pretend*.

"Jack-in-the-Box." Palmer, Hap, *So Big*.

"Little Blue Engine." Beall, Pamela, and Susan Nipp, *Wee Sing and Pretend*.

"The Little Engine That Could." Ives, Burl, *Burl Ives Sings Little White Duck*.

"Lovey and Me." Palmer, Hap, *Peek-a-Boo*.

"The Marvelous Toy." Atkinson, Lisa, *I Wanna Tickle the Fish*; Paxton, Tom, *Goin' to the Zoo*; Peter, Paul, and Mary, *Peter, Paul, and Mommy*; Various Artists, *A Child's Celebration of Song 2*.

"Mr. McWhizwidget's Fix It Up Shop." Parachute Express, *Doctor Looney's Remedy*.

"My Brother Threw Up on My Stuffed Toy Bunny." Alsop, Peter, *Wha' D'Ya Wanna Do?*; Polisar, Barry Louis, *Family Concert*; Polisar, Barry Louis, *Family Trip*.

"My Wooden Train." Coffey, James, *I Love Toy Trains*.

"Roll That Ball." Beall, Pamela, and Susan Nipp, *Wee Sing and Play*.

"Rubber Blubber Whale." Diamond, Charlotte, *Diamonds and Dragons*; McCutcheon, John, *Howjadoo*.

"Super Duper Turbo Toaster Toy Construction Set." Big Jeff, *Big Jeff*.

"Three Little Pigs." Avni, Fran, *Artichokes and Brussel Sprouts*.

"The Toy Museum." Berkner, Laurie, *Victor Vito*.

"Toy Train." Coffey, James, *I Love Toy Trains*.
"Yellow Crayon." Guthrie, Woody, *Nursery Days*.
"Yo Yo Rodeo." Green Chili Jam Band, *Coconut Moon*.

Transportation/Travel

"Do You Wanna Go?" Roberts, Justin, *Great Big Sun*.
"Family Vacation." Rosenshontz, *Family Vacation*.
"Going for a Ride." Barchas, Sarah, *Get Ready, Get Set, Sing!*
"Going to Grandma's." Abell, Timmy, *Little Red Wagon*.
"Hi Ho We're Rolling Home." Abell, Timmy, *The Farmer's Market*.
"Hold Your Horses." Byers, Kathy, *Do You Wish You Could Fly?*
"How 'bout You?" Ode, Eric, *I Love My Shoes*.
"I Know I'm Gonna Drive a Car." Frezza, Rebecca, *Road Trip*.
"Let's Go." Alsop, Peter, *Take Me with You*.
"Let's Go Riding." Grammer, Red, *Can You Sound Just like Me?*
"Long Way Home." Chapin, Tom, *Family Tree*.
"Magical Madcap Tour." Harper, Monty, *Take Me to Your Library*.
"Me, Myself and I." Kimmy Schwimmy, *Kimmy Schwimmy Music*, vol. 1.
"On a Vacation." The Chenille Sisters, *Teaching Hippopotami to Fly!*; Various Artists, *A Child's Celebration of the World*.
"Sailing to the Sea." Chapin, Tom, *Great Big Fun for the Very Little One*; Chapin, Tom, *Mother Earth*.
"Sounds." Strausman, Paul, *Blue Jay, Blue Jay!*
"World of Make Believe." Parachute Express, *Feel the Music*.

Airplanes

"Airplane." Beall, Pamela, and Susan Nipp, *Wee Sing and Pretend*.
"The Airplane Song." Berkner, Laurie, *Whaddaya Think of That?*
"Look at Me, I'm an Airplane." Mayer, Hans, *Just a Little Hug*.
"Riding in an Airplane." Raffi, *One Light One Sun*.
"We're Flying." Bartels, Joanie, *Travelin' Magic*.

Automobiles

"Adventures in Carpool." Daddy A Go Go, *Cool Songs for Cool Kids*.
"Are We There Yet?" Big Jeff, *Big Jeff*.
"Are We There Yet?" Cosgrove, Jim, *Mr. Stinky Feet's Road Trip*.
"Are We There Yet?" Madsen, Gunnar, *Ants in My Pants!*

"Are We There Yet?" Stotts, Stuart, *Are We There Yet?*

"Are We There Yet?" Trout Fishing in America, *InFINity*.

"The Awful Hilly Daddy-Willie Trip." McCutcheon, John, *Mail Myself to You*; Various Artists, *Grandma's Patchwork Quilt*.

"Back Seat Drivers." Dana, *Dana's Best Travelin' Tunes*.

"Beep Beep." Bartels, Joanie, *Travelin' Magic*.

"Buckle Up." Scruggs, Joe, *Traffic Jams*.

"Car Car." Bartels, Joanie, *Travelin' Magic*; Mitchell, Elizabeth, *You Are My Sunshine*. (Same song as "Car Song" and "Riding in My Car.")

"Car Song." Raven, Nancy, *Singing, Prancing, and Dancing*. (Same song as "Car Car" and "Riding in My Car.")

"Cow in the Car." Dana, *Dana's Best Travelin' Tunes*.

"Cruisin' Along." Beall, Pamela, and Susan Nipp, *Wee Sing in the Car*.

"Daddy's Car." Haynes, Sammie, *Nature's ABCs*.

"Drive My Car." Berkner, Laurie, *Under a Shady Tree*.

"Drivin' in My Car." Ralph's World, *Ralph's World*.

"Driving Here, Driving There." Gill, Jim, *Jim Gill Sings Do Re Mi on His Toe Leg Knee*.

"Driving in My Car." Allard, Peter and Ellen, *Good Kid*.

"The Driving Song." Byers, Kathy, *Do You Wish You Could Fly?*

"Going through the Car Wash." Charette, Rick, *Popcorn and Other Songs to Munch On*.

"Grandma's House Tonight." Harper, Monty, *Take Me to Your Library*.

"Hang Up and Drive." Daddy A Go Go, *Eat Every Bean and Pea on Your Plate*.

"In the Car." Roberts, Justin, *Yellow Bus*.

"It's My Mother and My Father and My Sister and the Dog." Polisar, Barry Louis, *Family Trip*.

"John Brown's Chevy." Beall, Pamela, and Susan Nipp, *Wee Sing in the Car*.

"Late Night Radio." Brown, Greg, *Bathtub Blues*.

"Little Blue Chevy." Various Artists, *Hear and Gone in 60 Seconds*.

"My Old Jalopy." Parachute Express, *Who's Got a Hug?*

"The Never Ending Road." Simmons, Al, *The Truck I Bought from Moe*.

"New Car." McCutcheon, John, *Mail Myself to You*.

"On the Road to Where We're Going." Bartels, Joanie, *Travelin' Magic*.

"On the Way Home." Knight, Tom, *The Library Boogie*.

"The People in the Car." Scruggs, Joe, *Traffic Jams*.

"Race Car." Beall, Pamela, and Susan Nipp, *Wee Sing and Pretend*.

"Ridin' in the Car." The Chenille Sisters, *Teaching Hippopotami to Fly!*

"Ridin' in the Car." Dana, *Dana's Best Travelin' Tunes*.

"Riding in My Car." Greg and Steve, *Rockin' down the Road*; Guthrie, Woody, *Nursery Days*; Guthrie, Woody, *Woody's 20 Grow Big Songs*; Guthrie, Woody and Arlo, *This Land Is Your Land*; Old Town School of Folk Music, *Wiggleworms Love You*; Various Artists, *A Child's Celebration of Folk Music*. (Same song as "Car Car" and "Car Song.")

"Road Trip." Cosgrove, Jim, *Mr. Stinky Feet's Road Trip*.

"Road Trip." Frezza, Rebecca, *Road Trip*.

"Slug Bug." Cosgrove, Jim, *Mr. Stinky Feet's Road Trip*.

"Speed Bump Blues." Scruggs, Joe, *Traffic Jams*.

"Take a Ride." Frezza, Rebecca, *Tall and Small*.

"This Old Car." Seeger, Pete, *For Kids and Just Plain Folks*.

"We Lost Our Car . . . in the Parking Lot." Pullara, Steve, *Hop like a Frog*.

"What Color Is Your Mini-Van?" Cosgrove, Jim, *Mr. Stinky Feet's Road Trip*.

Ballooning

"Big Balloon." Pullara, Steve, *Spinning Tails*.

"Hot Air Balloon." Charette, Rick, *Alligator in the Elevator*.

"Up in a Balloon." Raven, Nancy, *People and Animal Songs*.

Bicycles

"Banana Seat Bike." Ralph's World, *Peggy's Pie Parlor*.

"Bicycle Cowboy." Tickle Tune Typhoon, *All of Us Will Shine*.

"Bicycle Song." Gemini, *The Best of Gemini*.

"Get on My Bike." Charette, Rick, *Chickens on Vacation*.

"I Can, I Will, I'll Try." Frezza, Rebecca, *Music in My Head*.

"Magic Bike." Green Chili Jam Band, *Magic Bike*.

"My Bicycle." Sprout, Jonathan, *Kid Power*.

"One Speed Bike." Lonnquist, Ken, *Welcome 2 Kenland*.

"Pickle Bicycle." Kinder, Brian, *A Kid like You*.

"Put Your Helmet On." Harley, Bill, *There's a Pea on My Plate*.

"Ride My Bicycle." Magical Music Express, *Music Is Magic*.

"Ride My Bike." Paxton, Tom, *I've Got a Yo-Yo*.

"Ride on My Bike." Moos, Anna, *When I Was a Child*.

"Riding My Bicycle." McMahon, Elizabeth, *Waltzing with Fireflies*.

"Riding My Bike." McCutcheon, John, *Summersongs*.

"Rolleo Rolling Along." Bartels, Joanie, *Travelin' Magic*.

"Taking Off My Training Wheels." Roberts, Justin, *Meltdown!*

Boats

"Barges." Byers, Kathy, *'Round the Campfire*.

"Big Ship Sails." Jenkins, Ella, *Sharing Cultures with Ella Jenkins*.

"A Capital Ship." Chapin, Tom, *Mother Earth*.

"Don'ta Rocka Da Boat." Pullara, Steve, *A Big Bowl of Musicroni*.

"Great Big Boat." Various Artists, *Caribbean Playground*.

"Gum Tree Canoe." Raven, Nancy, *You Gotta Juba*.

"Happy World, Happy Sailors." Yosi, *Monkey Business*.

"Little Boat." Ungar, Jay, and Lyn Hardy, *A Place to Be*.

"Mingulay Boat Song." Grammer, Red, *Red Grammer's Favorite Sing Along Songs*.

"Moonboat." Chapin, Tom, *Moonboat*.

"Paddle My Canoe." Grunsky, Jack, *Playground*; Grunsky, Jack, *World Safari*.

"River Flow." Ralph's World, *Green Gorilla, Monster, and Me*.

"Roll On." Guthrie, Woody, *Nursery Days*.

"Row, Row, Row Adventure." The Learning Station, *Seasonal Songs in Motion*.

"Row, Row, Row Your Boat." Beall, Pamela, and Susan Nipp, *Wee Sing and Pretend*; Beall, Pamela, and Susan Nipp, *Wee Sing Sing-Alongs*; McGrath, Bob, and Katherine Smithrim, *Songs and Games for Toddlers*; Raffi, *Quiet Time*; Raffi, *Rise and Shine*.

"Sailin'." McMahon, Elizabeth, *Tea Party Shuffle*.

"Sailing." Parachute Express, *Don't Blink*.

"Sailing." Trout Fishing in America, *InFINity*; Trout Fishing in America, *My Best Day*.

"Sailing in the Boat." Rosenthal, Phil, *Folksongs and Bluegrass for Children*; Rosenthal, Phil, *Turkey in the Straw*.

"Somos El Barco." Harley, Bill, *50 Ways to Fool Your Mother*; McCutcheon, John, *Mail Myself to You*; Pease, Tom, *I'm Gonna Reach!*; Seeger, Pete, *Pete Seeger's Family Concert*; Tucker, Nancy, *Happy as a Clam*.

Buses

"The Bus Song." Cassidy, Nancy, *Nancy Cassidy's KidsSongs*. (Same song as "The People on the Bus" and "The Wheels on the Bus.")

"Don't Miss the Bus." Chapin, Tom, *In My Hometown*.

"People on the Bus." The Learning Station, *All-Time Children's Favorites*. (Same song as "The Bus Song" and "The Wheels on the Bus.")

"The Wheels on the Bus." Arnold, Linda, *Sing Along Stew*; Barchas, Sarah, *Get Ready, Get Set, Sing!*; Bartels, Joanie, *Travelin' Magic*; Beall, Pamela, and Susan Nipp, *Wee Sing in the Car*; Feldman, Jean, *Nursery Rhymes and Good*

Ol' Times; McGrath, Bob, *Sing Along with Bob #1*; Old Town School of Folk Music, *Wiggleworms Love You*; Raffi, *Rise and Shine*; Sharon, Lois, and Bram, *School Days*; Silberg, "Miss Jackie," *Peanut Butter, Tarzan, and Roosters*. (Same song as "The Bus Song" and "The People on the Bus.")
"Yellow Bus." Charette, Rick, *King Kong Chair*.
"Yellow Bus." Roberts, Justin, *Yellow Bus*.

Construction Equipment

"Dumptruck." Ralph's World, *The Amazing Adventures of Kid Astro*.
"Great Machine." Allard, Peter and Ellen, *Sing It! Say It! Stamp It! Sway It!* vol. 3.
"Hard Workin' Crane." Coffey, James, *I Love Toy Trains*.
"My Big Machine." Coffey, James, *Come Ride Along with Me*.

Jeeps

"A Little Red Jeep." Charette, Rick, *Toad Motel*.

Motorcycles

"Listen to the Motorcycle." Beall, Pamela, and Susan Nipp, *Wee Sing in the Car*.
"Motorcycle." Beall, Pamela, and Susan Nipp, *Wee Sing and Pretend*.

Subways

"The MTA Song." Rudnick, Ben, *Blast Off!*
"The Subway Song." Paxton, Tom, *I've Got a Yo-Yo*.

Taxis

"The Magic Taxi." Knight, Tom, *Don't Kiss a Codfish*.

Tractors

"Hayride." Howdy, Buck, *Giddyup!*

Trains

"ABC Train." Barchas, Sarah, *Get Ready, Get Set, Sing!*
"Aboard a Train." Coffey, James, *Come Ride Along with Me*.
"All Aboard." Lonnquist, Ken, *Welcome 2 Kenland*.
"Animal Train." Coffey, James, *Animal Groove*; Coffey, James, *I Love Toy Trains*.
"Big Train A Comin'." Coffey, James, *I Love Toy Trains*.

"Boxcar Boogie." Coffey, James, *I Love Toy Trains*.

"Catch That Train!" Zanes, Dan, *Catch That Train!*

"Choo Choo Blues." Coffey, James, *Come Ride Along with Me*.

"Choo Choo Boogaloo." Various Artists, *A Child's Celebration of Song 2*; Zanes, Dan, *Catch That Train!*

"Choo Choo Train." Ralph's World, *Ralph's World*.

"Choo-Choo Line." Fite, Stephen, *Gobs of Fun*.

"Chugga Chugga Choo Choo." Strausman, Paul, *Blue Jay, Blue Jay!*

"Circus Train." Arnold, Linda, *Circus Magic*.

"Clickety Clack." Cosgrove, Jim, *Ooey Gooey*.

"Countin' Cars on the Sleepytime Train." Fink, Cathy, and Marcy Marxer, *Pocket Full of Stardust*.

"Counting Those Railroad Cars." Coffey, James, *My Mama Was a Train*.

"Dog Train." Boynton, Sandra, *Dog Train*.

"Down by the Station." Beall, Pamela, and Susan Nipp, *Wee Sing Children's Songs and Fingerplays*; Beall, Pamela, and Susan Nipp, *Wee Sing Sing-Alongs*; Coffey, James, *I Love Toy Trains*; Coffey, James, *My Mama Was a Train*. (Same song as "Pufferbellies.")

"Engine Engine." McGrath, Bob, and Katherine Smithrim, *Songs and Games for Toddlers*.

"Five Big Dump Trucks." Beall, Pamela, and Susan Nipp, *Wee Sing in the Car*.

"Freedom Train." Coffey, James, *I Love Toy Trains*; Sweet Honey in the Rock, *I Got Shoes*; Various Artists, *World Playground 2*.

"Freight Train." Garcia, Jerry, and David Grisman, *Not for Kids Only*; Kirk, John, and Trish Miller, *The Big Rock Candy Mountain*; Mitchell, Elizabeth, *You Are My Flower*.

"Guysborough Railway." Zanes, Dan, *Night Time!*

"I Love Big Trains." Coffey, James, *I Love Toy Trains*.

"I Love Toy Trains." Coffey, James, *Come Ride Along with Me*; Coffey, James, *I Love Toy Trains*.

"I'm a Big Old Train." Big Jeff, *Big Jeff*.

"I'm a Train." Coffey, James, *My Mama Was a Train*.

"I'm an Engineer." Coffey, James, *Come Ride Along with Me*.

"I've Been Working on the Railroad." Beall, Pamela, and Susan Nipp, *Wee Sing Sing-Alongs*; Berkner, Laurie, *Buzz Buzz*; Coffey, James, *Come Ride Along with Me*; Coffey, James, *I Love Toy Trains*; Feldman, Jean, *Nursery Rhymes and Good Ol' Times*; Greg and Steve, *Playing Favorites*; McGrath, Bob, *Sing Along with Bob #2*; Raffi, *More Singable Songs*.

"I've Been Working on the Railroad/Choo Choo Shoes." Roth, Kevin, *Train Songs and Other Tracks.*

"Layin' Down Those Railroad Ties." Coffey, James, *Come Ride Along with Me.*

"Legends of the Rails." Coffey, James, *I Love Toy Trains.*

"Little Blue Engine." Beall, Pamela, and Susan Nipp, *Wee Sing and Pretend.*

"The Little Engine That Could." Ives, Burl, *Burl Ives Sings Little White Duck.*

"Little Red Caboose." Bartels, Joanie, *Travelin' Magic*; Beall, Pamela, and Susan Nipp, *Wee Sing Fun 'n' Folk*; Berkner, Laurie, *Buzz Buzz*; Coffey, James, *My Mama Was a Train*; Old Town School of Folk Music, *Wiggleworms Love You*; Sweet Honey in the Rock, *All for Freedom*; Various Artists, *A Child's Celebration of Song.*

"The Little Toy Train." Roth, Kevin, *Train Songs and Other Tracks.*

"Make Believe Town." Pullara, Steve, *Spinning Tails.*

"Monkey and the Engineer." Rudnick, Ben, *Emily Songs.*

"Morningtown Ride." Cassidy, Nancy, *Nancy Cassidy's KidsSongs*; Diamond, Charlotte, *Diamonds and Daydreams*; Raffi, *Baby Beluga*; Raven, Nancy, *Nancy Raven Sings Her Favorites*; Raven, Nancy, *Singing, Prancing, and Dancing.*

"My Mama Was a Train." Coffey, James, *My Mama Was a Train.*

"My Wooden Train." Coffey, James, *I Love Toy Trains.*

"New River Train." Coffey, James, *My Mama Was a Train*; Fink, Cathy, *Grandma Slid down the Mountain*; Raffi, *More Singable Songs*; Raven, Nancy, *Hop, Skip, and Sing*; Roth, Kevin, *Train Songs and Other Tracks.*

"Nine Hundred Miles." Coffey, James, *My Mama Was a Train.*

"Old MacDonald Had a Train." Coffey, James, *I Love Toy Trains.*

"One More Train." Coffey, James, *I Love Toy Trains.*

"Pufferbellies." Sharon, Lois, and Bram, *Great Big Hits*; Sharon, Lois, and Bram, *Name Games.* (Same song as "Down by the Station.")

"The Railroad Cars Are Coming." Beall, Pamela, and Susan Nipp, *Wee Sing Fun 'n' Folk.*

"Rock Island Line." Coffey, James, *My Mama Was a Train*; Zanes, Dan, *Family Dance.*

"Rock-Motion Choo Choo." Greg and Steve, *We All Live Together*, vol. 1.

"Signal Lights." Coffey, James, *Come Ride Along with Me.*

"The Song about Trains." Knight, Tom, *Easy as Pie.*

"Stop, Look and Listen." Coffey, James, *Come Ride Along with Me.*

"The Sunrise." Moos, Anna, *When I Was a Child.*

"Thanks Again." Coffey, James, *I Love Toy Trains.*

"That Little Red Caboose behind the Train." Coffey, James, *My Mama Was a Train.*

"Toy Train." Coffey, James, *I Love Toy Trains*.

"The Train." Beall, Pamela, and Susan Nipp, *Wee Sing Children's Songs and Fingerplays*.

"The Train." Harper, Jessica, *A Wonderful Life*.

"The Train." Mr. Al, *Mr. Al a Carte*.

"This Train." Coffey, James, *I Love Toy Trains*.

"Train Going Home." Roth, Kevin, *Train Songs and Other Tracks*.

"Train Is A-Comin'." Beall, Pamela, and Susan Nipp, *Wee Sing Fun 'n' Folk*.

"Train Medley." Yosi, *Under a Big Bright Yellow Umbrella*.

"The Train of Beauty (Le Train de Beauté)." Roth, Kevin, *Train Songs and Other Tracks*.

"The Train Song." Haynes, Sammie, *Nature's ABCs*.

"The Train Song." Rosenthal, Phil, *Folksongs and Bluegrass for Children*; Rosenthal, Phil, *The Green Grass Grew All Around*.

"Train Song." Scruggs, Joe, *Abracadabra*.

"The Trans Canadian Super Continental Special Express." Penner, Fred, *Fred's Favourites*; Penner, Fred, *Storytime*.

"The Wabash Cannonball." Beall, Pamela, and Susan Nipp, *Wee Sing Fun 'n' Folk*; Cassidy, Nancy, *Nancy Cassidy's KidsSongs*; Coffey, James, *My Mama Was a Train*; Grammer, Red, *Red Grammer's Favorite Sing Along Songs*; Zanes, Dan, *House Party*.

"What Do You Hear?" Coffey, James, *My Mama Was a Train*.

"Workin' in the Railway Yard." Coffey, James, *My Mama Was a Train*.

Trucks

"Big Red Fire Truck." Harper, Monty, *The Great Green Squishy Mean Concert CD*.

"Big Toe Truck." Scruggs, Joe, *Traffic Jams*.

"Big Truck." Frezza, Rebecca, *Music in My Head*.

"18 Wheels on a Big Rig." Ralph's World, *At the Bottom of the Sea*; Trout Fishing in America, *Family Music Party*; Trout Fishing in America, *Mine!*

"Grandpa's Truck." Ode, Eric, *Grandpa's Truck*.

"I Like Trucks." Parachute Express, *Don't Blink*.

"Monster Trucks." Cosgrove, Jim, *Pick Me! Pick Me!*

"Mr. Trucker." Cosgrove, Jim, *Mr. Stinky Feet's Road Trip*.

"Pickup Hiccup Truck." Cosgrove, Jim, *Bop Bop Dinosaur*.

"The Truck I Bought from Moe." Simmons, Al, *The Truck I Bought from Moe*.

"Trucks." Berkner, Laurie, *Victor Vito*.

"Trucks." Strausman, Paul, *Blue Jay, Blue Jay!*

Treehouses

"Tree House." Scruggs, Joe, *Ants*.

"Treehouse." Arnold, Linda, *Peppermint Wings*.

"The Treehouse." Pirtle, Sarah, *The Wind Is Telling Secrets*.

Twins/Triplets

"Triplets." Lithgow, John, *Singin' in the Bathtub*.

"Twins." Fink, Cathy, and Marcy Marxer, *Nobody Else like Me*.

The United States of America

"Driving Here, Driving There." Gill, Jim, *Jim Gill Sings Do Re Mi on His Toe Leg Knee*.

"Fifty States." Fink, Cathy, and Marcy Marxer, *Scat like That*.

"The Git Down Towns." Daddy A Go Go, *Mojo A Go Go*.

"Gobble across the USA." Cosgrove, Jim, *Mr. Stinky Feet's Road Trip*.

"Rockin' the U.S.A." Greg and Steve, *Rockin' down the Road*.

"State Laughs." Chapin, Tom, *Great Big Fun for the Very Little One*; Chapin, Tom, *Moonboat*; Kirk, John, and Trish Miller, *The Big Rock Candy Mountain*.

"This Land Is Your Land." Byers, Kathy, *'Round the Campfire*; Grammer, Red, *Red Grammer's Favorite Sing Along Songs*; Greg and Steve, *Rockin' down the Road*; Guthrie, Woody and Arlo, *This Land Is Your Land*; Seeger, Pete, *For Kids and Just Plain Folks*; Seeger, Pete, *Pete Seeger's Family Concert*; Strausman, Paul, *The World's Big Family*.

"Travelin' the USA." Various Artists, *Hear and Gone in 60 Seconds*.

"The United States." Beall, Pamela, and Susan Nipp, *Wee Sing in the Car*.

"What Did Delaware?" Beall, Pamela, and Susan Nipp, *Wee Sing Silly Songs*.

California

"California." Gill, Jim, *Moving Rhymes for Modern Times*.

Florida

"Florida." Moo, Anna, *Anna Moo Crackers*.

Hawaii

"Haleakala." Crow, Dan, *A Friend, a Laugh, a Walk in the Woods*.

"Hawaiian Cowboy Song." Raven, Nancy, *The House We Live In*, vols. 1 and 2.

"The Hukilau Song." Various Artists, *cELLAbration! A Tribute to Ella Jenkins*.

"I'll Be Dreaming of Hawaii." Fink, Cathy, and Marcy Marxer, *Pillow Full of Wishes*.
"This Little Island." Banana Slug String Band, *Wings of Slumber*.

Idaho

"The Night We Made It Noisy in Boise, Idaho." Gill, Jim, *Jim Gill Makes It Noisy in Boise, Idaho*.

Illinois

"The Pizza That Ate Chicago." Paxton, Tom, *Your Shoes, My Shoes*.

Louisiana

"Crazy Cajun Stomp." Bartles, Joanie, *Put On Your Dancing Shoes*.
"Critter Jambalaya." Coffey, James, *Animal Groove*.
"Mardi Gras Mambo." Various Artists, *Latin Playground*; Various Artists, *World Playground*.

New York

"A Duck in New York City." Kaldor, Connie, *A Duck in New York City*.
"Erie Canal." Berkner, Laurie, *Buzz Buzz*; Grammer, Red, *Red Grammer's Favorite Sing Along Songs*; Hullabaloo, *Sing Along with Sam*; Zanes, Dan, *Rocket Ship Beach*.
"Lady of the Light." Silberg, "Miss Jackie," *Joining Hands with Other Lands*; Silberg, "Miss Jackie," *Touched by a Song*.
"Sidewalks of New York." Zanes, Dan, *Rocket Ship Beach*.

Ohio

"Oh Hey Oh Hi Hello." Gill, Jim, *Jim Gill Makes It Noisy in Boise, Idaho*.

Texas

"I'm Going to Leave Old Texas Now." Riders in the Sky, *Saddle Pals*. (Same song as "Old Texas.")
"Long Tall Texan." Greg and Steve, *Rockin' down the Road*.
"Old Texas." Beall, Pamela, and Susan Nipp, *Wee Sing and Pretend*; Cassidy, Nancy, *Nancy Cassidy's KidsSongs*; Raven, Nancy, *The House We Live In*, vols. 1 and 2. (Same song as "I'm Going to Leave Old Texas Now.")
"Paddy on the Railroad/Dance Your Way to Texas." Fink, Cathy, and Marcy Marxer, *All Wound Up!*
"The Rivers of Texas." Raven, Nancy, *Friends and Family*.

Wisconsin

"Wisconsin Dairy Polka." Colleen and Uncle Squaty, *1, 2, 3, Four-Ever Friends*.
"World Series '57." McCutcheon, John, *Autumnsongs*.

Wyoming

"Old Faithful." Banana Slug String Band, *Goin' Wild*.
"Stars over Wyoming." Banana Slug String Band, *Goin' Wild*.
"Walking in the Tetons." Banana Slug String Band, *Goin' Wild*.

Video Games

"End O' Nintendo." Lonnquist, Ken, *Sci-Fi Hi-Fi*.
"The Fever." Daddy A Go Go, *Monkey in the Middle*.

Volcanoes

"Old St. Helen." Jonas, Billy, *What Kind of Cat Are You?!*
"Volcano Land." Lonnquist, Ken, *Earthy Songs*.

Wagons

"Bumping Up and Down." McGrath, Bob, and Katherine Smithrim, *Songs and Games for Toddlers*; Pullara, Steve, *One Potato, Two Potato*; Raffi, *Singable Songs for the Very Young*. (Same song as "Little Red Wagon.")
"Holey Old Wagon." Haynes, Sammie, *Nature's ABCs*.
"Little Old Wagon." Peterson, Carole, *Sticky Bubble Gum*.
"Little Red Wagon." Abell, Timmy, *Little Red Wagon*.
"Little Red Wagon." Buchman, Rachel, *Hello Everybody!*; Old Town School of Folk Music, *Wiggleworms Love You*.
"Little Red Wagon." Cosgrove, Jim, *Pick Me! Pick Me!*
"Little Red Wagon." Fite, Stephen, *Wiggles, Jiggles, and Giggles*.

Water

"Adventures of a Water Drop." Knight, Tom, *The Classroom Boogie*.
"Listen to the Water." Allard, Peter and Ellen, *Raise the Children*; Avni, Fran, *Tuning into Nature*; Diamond, Charlotte, *My Bear Gruff*; McGrath, Bob, and Katherine Smithrim, *Songs and Games for Toddlers*.
"Water." Fink, Cathy, and Marcy Marxer, *Bon Appétit!*

"Water." Lonnquist, Ken, *Earthy Songs*; Lonnquist, Ken, *Welcome 2 Kenland*.

"Water." Polisar, Barry Louis, *Teacher's Favorites*.

"Water." Various Artists, *Hear and Gone in 60 Seconds*.

"Water Cycle." Pirtle, Sarah, *Heart of the World*.

"Water Cycle." SteveSongs, *Marvelous Day!*

"Water Cycle Boogie." Banana Slug String Band, *Singing in Our Garden*; Banana Slug String Band, *Slugs at Sea*.

"Water Cycle Song." Grunsky, Jack, *Like a Flower to the Sun*.

"The Water Fountain." Rosen, Gary, *Tot Rock*.

"Water Goes 'round the World." Tickle Tune Typhoon, *Singing Science*.

"Water Wheel Song." Lonnquist, Ken, *Earthy Songs*.

"We Need Water." Diamond, Charlotte, *Charlotte Diamond's World*.

"The Wheel of Water." Chapin, Tom, *Mother Earth*; Chapin, Tom, *This Pretty Planet*.

Weather

"Don't Blame the Weatherman." Daddy A Go Go, *Mojo A Go Go*.

"It's a Rainy Day." Diamond, Charlotte, *My Bear Gruff*.

"It's a Very Good Day." Stotts, Stuart, and Tom Pease, *Celebrate: A Song Resource*.

"It's Raining, It's Pouring." Simmons, Al, *Something Fishy at Camp Wiganishie*.

"Raindrops and Lemon Drops." Scruggs, Joe, *Traffic Jams*.

"Weather Song." Feldman, Jean, *Dr. Jean and Friends*.

"What You Gonna Wear?" Fink, Cathy, and Marcy Marxer, *Help Yourself*.

"What's the Weather Outside?" Fite, Stephen, *Havin' Fun and Feelin' Groovy*.

Clouds

"The Clouds." Beall, Pamela, and Susan Nipp, *Wee Sing for Baby*.

"Clouds." Frezza, Rebecca, *Music in My Head*.

"Clouds." Moos, Anna, *When I Was a Child*.

"A Corner of a Cloud." Ode, Eric, *Grandpa's Truck*.

"I Want to Be a Cloud." Kaldor, Connie, *A Duck in New York City*.

"In the Clouds." Berkner, Laurie, *Buzz Buzz*.

"Puffy Clouds." Foote, Norman, *If the Shoe Fits*.

Rain

"After It Rains." Berkner, Laurie, *Under a Shady Tree*.

"Ain't Gonna Rain No More." Rosenthal, Phil, *Turkey in the Straw*. (Same song as "It Ain't Gonna Rain.")

"Ame, Ame (Rain Song)." Beall, Pamela, and Susan Nipp, *Wee Sing around the World*.

"Clean Rain." Raffi, *Evergreen, Everblue*.

"The Clouds Are Sleeping Over." Lonnquist, Ken, *Sci-Fi Hi-Fi*.

"Ducks Like Rain." Raffi, *Rise and Shine*.

"I Love to Walk in the Rain." Muldaur, Maria, *Animal Crackers in My Soup*.

"I'm a Little Raindrop." Rymer, Brady, *I Found It!*

"It Ain't Gonna Rain." Penner, Fred, *Rhyme a Word or Two*. (Same song as "Ain't Gonna Rain No More.")

"It's a Rainy Day." Charette, Rick, *Alligator in the Elevator*.

"It's Raining." Mayer, Hans, *Just a Little Hug*.

"It's Raining, It's Pouring." Beall, Pamela, and Susan Nipp, *Wee Sing Children's Songs and Fingerplays*; McGrath, Bob, and Katherine Smithrim, *Songs and Games for Toddlers*.

"It's Raining, It's Pouring (Big Thunder, Dark Cloud)." Grunsky, Jack, *Sing and Dance*; Grunsky, Jack, *World Safari*.

"Japanese Rain Song." Barchas, Sarah, *Bridges across the World*.

"Leaky Umbrella." Gill, Jim, *Jim Gill Sings the Sneezing Song and Other Contagious Tunes*.

"Let It Rain." Cosgrove, Jim, *Bop Bop Dinosaur*.

"Little Raindrop." Roberts, Justin, *Great Big Sun*.

"Mushroom Umbrellas." Walker, Mary Lu, *The Frog's Party*.

"100 Raindrops." Harper, Jessica, *A Wonderful Life*.

"Puddle Stomping!" Moo, Anna, *Moochas Gracias*.

"Puddles." Diamond, Charlotte, *My Bear Gruff*.

"Rain." Kaye, Mary, *Mouse Jamboree*.

"Rain Rain." Silberg, "Miss Jackie," *The Complete Sniggles, Squirrels, and Chicken Pox*; Silberg, "Miss Jackie," *Sing about Martin*.

"Rain, Rain, Go Away." Beall, Pamela, and Susan Nipp, *Wee Sing Children's Songs and Fingerplays*; McGrath, Bob, and Katherine Smithrim, *Songs and Games for Toddlers*; Old Town School of Folk Music, *Wiggleworms Love You*.

"Rain Song." Colleen and Uncle Squaty, *1, 2, 3, Four-Ever Friends*.

"The Rain Song." Mr. Al and Stephen Fite, *Back to School Again*.

"Rainbow in the Sky." Byers, Kathy, *Do You Wish You Could Fly?*

"Raining Cats and Dogs." LaFond, Lois, *One World*.

"Raining like Magic." Raffi, *Let's Play*.

"Rainstorm." Strausman, Paul, *Blue Jay, Blue Jay!*

"Rainy Day." Milkshake, *Bottle of Sunshine*.

"Rainy Day." Rudnick, Ben, *Emily Songs*.

"Rhythm of the Rain." Bartles, Joanie, *Put On Your Dancing Shoes*.

"Robin in the Rain." Raffi, *Singable Songs for the Very Young*.

"Rubber Boots and Raincoats." Kaldor, Connie, *A Poodle in Paris*.

"Shango." Barchas, Sarah, *Bridges across the World*.

"Showers in the Rain." Allard, Peter and Ellen, *Raise the Children*.

"Splash!" Peterson, Carole, *Sticky Bubble Gum*.

"There Is Thunder." Beall, Pamela, and Susan Nipp, *Wee Sing Children's Songs and Fingerplays*.

"Under a Big Bright Yellow Umbrella." Yosi, *Under a Big Bright Yellow Umbrella*.

"Water in the Rain Clouds." Silberg, "Miss Jackie," *The Complete Sniggles, Squirrels, and Chicken Pox*; Silberg, "Miss Jackie," *Sing about Martin*.

"What Do You Do on a Rainy Day?" Rosen, Gary, *Tot Rock*.

"Where Do the Animals Go When It Rains?" Buchman, Rachel, *Baby and Me*.

Snow (see also Seasons—Winter)

"Bob and Bob." Trout Fishing in America, *My Best Day*.

"I Can Make a Snowman." Peterson, Carole, *H.U.M.—All Year Long*.

"I'm a Little Snowflake." Berkner, Laurie, *Whaddaya Think of That?*

"I'm a Little Snowman." Peterson, Carole, *H.U.M.—All Year Long*.

"In the Freezer." Scruggs, Joe, *Traffic Jams*.

"No School Today." Harley, Bill, *You're in Trouble*.

"Pray for Snow." Gemini, *The Best of Gemini*.

"Shoveling." Chapin, Tom, *Family Tree*.

"Snow in April." McCutcheon, John, *Springsongs*.

"Snow Song." Buchman, Rachel, *Hello Everybody!*

"Snow Song." Walker, Mary Lu, *The Frog's Party*.

"Snowflake, Snowflake." Peterson, Carole, *H.U.M.—All Year Long*.

"Snowflakes." The Learning Station, *Seasonal Songs in Motion*.

"Snowflakes (Are Dancing)." Pullara, Steve, *Spinning Tails*.

"Snowing." Sprout, Jonathan, *On the Radio*.

"Snowman." Rosenshontz, *Family Vacation*.

"Snowman's Café." McMahon, Elizabeth, *Tea Party Shuffle*.

"Snowy Day." Rosenthal, Phil, *Turkey in the Straw*.

"Waiting for Snow." McCutcheon, John, *Wintersongs*.

Wind

"Gentle Wind." Lonnquist, Ken, *The Lost Songs of Kenland*; Lonnquist, Ken, *The Switcher-On of Stars*.

"I Am the Wind." Penner, Fred, *Fred's Favourites*.
"Let the Wild Wind Blow." Paxton, Tom, *Goin' to the Zoo*.
"Mr. Wind." Foote, Norman, *Pictures on the Fridge*.
"The North Wind." Mitchell, Elizabeth, *You Are My Little Bird*.
"Wind." Avni, Fran, *Artichokes and Brussel Sprouts*; Avni, Fran, *Tuning into Nature*.
"The Wind." Grunsky, Jack, *Like a Flower to the Sun*.
"The Wind." Peterson, Carole, *Stinky Cake*.
"The Wind Is Telling Secrets." Pirtle, Sarah, *The Wind Is Telling Secrets*.
"The Windy Day." McMahon, Elizabeth, *Blue Sky Sparklin' Day*.

Wishes (see also Dreams)

"The Banana Wish Song." Fink, Cathy, and Marcy Marxer, *Pillow Full of Wishes*.
"Baseball Dreams." Ralph's World, *At the Bottom of the Sea*.
"Big Things Come from Little Things You Do." Palmer, Hap, *So Big*.
"Chasing after Moonbeams." Lonnquist, Ken, *The Lost Songs of Kenland*.
"Dream, Dream." The Dream Project, *We've All Got Stories*.
"Dream Maker." Roth, Kevin, *Unbearable Bears*.
"Dreamer." Green Chili Jam Band, *Magic Bike*.
"Everything's Possible." Fink, Cathy, and Marcy Marxer, *Nobody Else like Me*.
"Genie Fish." Lonnquist, Ken, *Sci-Fi Hi-Fi*.
"Gold." Sprout, Jonathan, *Dr. Music*.
"Grow in Your Own Sweet Way." Chapin, Tom, *Moonboat*.
"Happy Ever After." Dana, *Dana's Best Rock and Roll Fairy Tales*.
"Happy Talk." Arnold, Linda, *Favorites in the Key of Fun*; Harper, Jessica, *Inside Out*.
"Here's One Wish." Fink, Cathy, and Marcy Marxer, *Bon Appétit!*
"Horse of a Different Hue." Ode, Eric, *I Love My Shoes*.
"I Wish I Was." Rosenshontz, *Tickles You!*
"If I Had One Wish." Charette, Rick, *Bubble Gum*.
"If I Was in Charge." Alsop, Peter, *Pluggin' Away*.
"A Kid like Me." Fink, Cathy, and Marcy Marxer, *Nobody Else like Me*.
"The Leprechaun Song." Walker, Graham, *Cats' Night Out*.
"Live in Your Imagination." Grunsky, Jack, *Jack in the Box 2*.
"Make a Wish." Fink, Cathy, and Marcy Marxer, *Pillow Full of Wishes*.
"May There Always Be Sunshine." Allard, Peter and Ellen, *Raise the Children*; Charette, Rick, *King Kong Chair*; Diamond, Charlotte, *10 Carrot Diamond*; Feldman, Jean, *Keep On Singing and Dancing with Dr. Jean*; Fink, Cathy, and Marcy Marxer, *Nobody Else like Me*; Gemini, *The Best of Gemini*, vol. 2;

Gill, Jim, *Jim Gill Sings the Sneezing Song and Other Contagious Tunes*; Gill, Jim, *Jim Gill's Irrational Anthem*; Pease, Tom, *Boogie! Boogie! Boogie!*; Pirtle, Sarah, *Two Hands Hold the Earth*; Raffi, *Let's Play*; Raven, Nancy, *The House We Live In*, vols. 1 and 2.

"Mole in the Ground." Staines, Bill, *One More River*; Zanes, Dan, *Rocket Ship Beach*.

"One Dream." Diamond, Charlotte, *Diamonds and Daydreams*.

"One Wish." Milkshake, *Bottle of Sunshine*.

"Peppermint Wings." Arnold, Linda, *Favorites in the Key of Fun*.

"Rainbow's End/Pot of Gold." Fink, Cathy, and Marcy Marxer, *Pillow Full of Wishes*.

"Save One Wish for You." Fink, Cathy, and Marcy Marxer, *Pillow Full of Wishes*.

"Sing a Whale Song." Chapin, Tom, *Moonboat*.

"Starlight, Star Bright." Arnold, Linda, *Favorites in the Key of Fun*; Grammer, Red, *Hello World*.

"Way Out." Roberts, Justin, *Way Out*.

"What Do You Want (To Know)." Livingston, Bob, *Open the Window*.

"A Wish." Fite, Stephen, *Gobs of Fun*.

"Wish for Tomorrow." Fink, Cathy, and Marcy Marxer, *Pocket Full of Stardust*.

"Wishing Well." McMahon, Elizabeth, *Blue Sky Sparklin' Day*.

Wordplay

"Alphabet Lost and Found." They Might Be Giants, *Here Come the ABCs*.

"The Alphabet Song." Bartels, Joanie, *Sillytime Magic*.

"The Animal Song." Tucker, Nancy, *Happy as a Clam*.

"Apples and Bananas." Cassidy, Nancy, *Nancy Cassidy's KidsSongs*; Crow, Dan, *Dan Crow Live*; Crow, Dan, *Oops!*; Pease, Tom, *Boogie! Boogie! Boogie!*; Raffi, *One Light One Sun*; Raffi, *Raffi in Concert*; Various Artists, *A Child's Celebration of Silliest Songs*.

"Apples, Bananas, Peaches, and Tomatoes." Palmer, Hap, *Two Little Sounds*.

"Big Toe Truck." Scruggs, Joe, *Traffic Jams*.

"Baa Baa, Little ABC Star." Yosi, *Monkey Business*.

"Bear to the Left." Jonas, Billy, *What Kind of Cat Are You?!*

"The Billboard Song." Harley, Bill, *Monsters in the Bathroom*.

"Bingo." Beall, Pamela, and Susan Nipp, *Wee Sing Animals, Animals, Animals*; Beall, Pamela, and Susan Nipp, *Wee Sing Children's Songs and Fingerplays*; Coffey, James, *Animal Groove*; Feldman, Jean, *Nursery Rhymes and Good Ol' Times*; Fite, Stephen, *Monkey Business*; Greg and Steve, *We All Live Together*, vol. 4; McGrath, Bob, *Sing Along with Bob #2*; Old Town School of Folk Music, *Wiggleworms Love You*; Peterson, Carole, *H.U.M.—All Year Long*;

Raven, Nancy, *Hop, Skip, and Sing*; Sharon, Lois, and Bram, *Great Big Hits 2*; Sharon, Lois, and Bram, *Name Games*.

"The Body Song." Nagler, Eric, *Improvise with Eric Nagler*.

"Buckaroo." Howdy, Buck, *Skidaddle!*

"Buttons Button." Tucker, Nancy, *Glad That You Asked*.

"California." Gill, Jim, *Moving Rhymes for Modern Times*.

"Change the Baby." Scruggs, Joe, *Ants*.

"The Gentlemen Are Dancing on Their Toes." Harper, Monty, *Imagine That*.

"The Gnu Song." Lithgow, John, *Singin' in the Bathtub*.

"The Guy Who Couldn't Make a Rhyme." Daddy A Go Go, *Eat Every Bean and Pea on Your Plate*.

"Hickory, Dickory, Dock." Palmer, Hap, *Two Little Sounds*.

"Horse Blues." Tucker, Nancy, *Happy as a Clam*.

"The Horse Went Around." Beall, Pamela, and Susan Nipp, *Wee Sing Silly Songs*.

"I Am Slowly Going Crazy." Allard, Peter and Ellen, *Pizza Pizzaz*.

"I C U." They Might Be Giants, *Here Come the ABCs*.

"I Like to Eat Pepperoni Pizza." Fite, Stephen, *Gobs of Fun*.

"I Like to Read." Mayer, Hans, *See You Later, Alligator*.

"I. M. 4. U." Fink, Cathy, and Marcy Marxer, *Scat like That*; Simmons, Al, *The Celery Stalks at Midnight*.

"I Was Glad." Tucker, Nancy, *Glad That You Asked*.

"I'm My Own Grandpa." Abell, Timmy, *Little Red Wagon*; Kirk, John, and Trish Miller, *The Big Rock Candy Mountain*; Ralph's World, *Peggy's Pie Parlor*; Various Artists, *A Child's Celebration of Silliest Songs*.

"John Brown's Baby." Beall, Pamela, and Susan Nipp, *Wee Sing Silly Songs*.

"L M N O." They Might Be Giants, *Here Come the ABCs*.

"Language Discrepancies." Green Chili Jam Band, *Magic Bike*.

"Little Peter Rabbit." Beall, Pamela, and Susan Nipp, *Wee Sing Animals, Animals, Animals*; Beall, Pamela, and Susan Nipp, *Wee Sing Children's Songs and Fingerplays*; McGrath, Bob, *Sing Along with Bob #2*.

"Mairzy Doats." Bartels, Joanie, *Sillytime Magic*; Muldaur, Maria, *Swingin' in the Rain*; Nagler, Eric, *Improvise with Eric Nagler*; Sharon, Lois, and Bram, *Sing A to Z*.

"My Hand on My Head." Beall, Pamela, and Susan Nipp, *Wee Sing Silly Songs*.

"My Hat It Has Three Corners." Beall, Pamela, and Susan Nipp, *Wee Sing Silly Songs*.

"The Name Game." Bartels, Joanie, *Sillytime Magic*; The Chenille Sisters, *The Big Picture and Other Songs for Kids*; Sharon, Lois, and Bram, *Great Big Hits 2*; Sharon, Lois, and Bram, *Sing A to Z*.

"Nobody." Trout Fishing in America, *Big Trouble*.

"One Little Letter." Rymer, Brady, *I Found It!*

"Pepperoni Pizza." Feldman, Jean, *Dr. Jean Sings Silly Songs.*

"Piano." Tucker, Nancy, *Glad That You Asked.*

"Pig Latin Polka Dance." Fink, Cathy, and Marcy Marxer, *Scat like That.*

"R-U-O-K." Magical Music Express, *Friendship Stew.*

"Sailing." Trout Fishing in America, *InFINity*; Trout Fishing in America, *My Best Day.*

"See You Later, Alligator." Mayer, Hans, *See You Later, Alligator.*

"Starfishing." Green Chili Jam Band, *Starfishing.*

"There's a Starfish Hidden under My Bed." Avni, Fran, *I'm All Ears: Sing into Reading*; Avni, Fran, *Little Ears: Songs for Reading Readiness.*

"Tinkerboxer." Parachute Express, *Friends, Forever Friends.*

"Two Kinds of Seagulls." Chapin, Tom, *Mother Earth*; Chapin, Tom, *This Pretty Planet.*

"Vegetation Migration/Celery Stalks at Midnight." Simmons, Al, *The Celery Stalks at Midnight.*

"What Kind of Cat Are You?!" Jonas, Billy, *What Kind of Cat Are You?!*

"What Did Delaware?" Beall, Pamela, and Susan Nipp, *Wee Sing Silly Songs.*

"What Do You Say?" Haynes, Sammie, *Nature's ABCs.*

"Wiggle the Wool." Colleen and Uncle Squaty, *Fingerplays, Movement and Story Songs.*

"Willoughby Wallaby Woo." Cassidy, Nancy, *Nancy Cassidy's KidsSongs*; McGrath, Bob, *Sing Along with Bob #1*; Raffi, *Singable Songs for the Very Young.*

"Word Play." Craig n Co., *Rock n Together.*

"You Are What You Eat." Shontz, Bill, *Animal Tales.*

"Your Name Backwards." Trout Fishing in America, *InFINity.*

"Zag Zig." Chapin, Tom, *Great Big Fun for the Very Little One*; Chapin, Tom, *Zag Zig.*

"Zip Zip." Scruggs, Joe, *Abracadabra.*

Zoos

"The Bandshell Right Next to the Zoo." Lithgow, John, *Farkle and Friends.*

"Don't Kiss a Codfish." Knight, Tom, *Don't Kiss a Codfish.*

"Goin' to the Zoo." Beall, Pamela, and Susan Nipp, *Wee Sing Animals, Animals, Animals.*

"Goin' to the Zoo." Paxton, Tom, *Goin' to the Zoo*; Peter, Paul, and Mary, *Peter, Paul, and Mommy*; Raffi, *Singable Songs for the Very Young.*

"Let's Go to the Zoo." Raven, Nancy, *Hop, Skip, and Sing.*

"Lost in the Zoo." Dana, *Dana's Best Sing and Play-a-Long Tunes.*

"Rockin' at the Zoo." Arnold, Linda, *Favorites in the Key of Fun*; Arnold, Linda, *Happiness Cake.*

"Tickle a Tiger." Ralph's World, *Ralph's World*.
"Zany School." Palmer, Hap, *Turn On the Music*.
"Zchool." Lonnquist, Ken, *Sci-Fi Hi-Fi*.
"The Zoo Was Having a Party." Kaldor, Connie, *A Poodle in Paris*.

Resources

Many of the recordings in this book can be found at many major online bookstores, such as Amazon.com and Barnesandnoble.com.

The following websites also carry many of the recordings found in this book:

CD Baby: www.cdbaby.com
KiddoMusic: www.kiddomusic.com
North Side Music: www.northsidemusicwi.com
Songs for Teaching: www.songsforteaching.com

Bill Shontz's Children's Music Hall of Fame features downloads of several recordings found in this book: http://www.billshontz.com/cmhof.html.

The following companies handle a set roster of recording artists:

Casablanca Kids: www.casablancakids.com
A Gentle Wind: www.gentlewind.com
Music for Little People: www.musicforlittlepeople.com
Putumayo Kids: http://www.putumayo.com/playground.html
Rounder Kids: www.rounderkids.com

Individual Artist Websites

Many artists have their own websites. In most cases, you can purchase their products directly from these websites or, sometimes, you will be directed to a vendor that carries their products. As of the writing of this book, the following artists have websites that contain ordering information:

Abell, Timmy: www.timmyabell.com

Allard, Peter and Ellen: www.peterandellen.com

Alsop, Peter: www.peteralsop.com

Avni, Fran: www.franavni.com

Banana Slug String Band: www.bananaslugstringband.com

Barchas, Sarah: www.highhavenmusic.com

Bartels, Joanie: www.joaniebartels.com

Beall, Pamela, and Susan Nipp: www.weesing.com

Berkner, Laurie: www.twotomatoes.com

Big Jeff: www.bigjeffmusic.com

Boynton, Sandra: www.sandraboynton.com

Byers, Kathy: www.kathybyers.com

Cassidy, Nancy: www.nancycassidymusic.com

Chapin, Tom: http://members.aol.com/chapinfo/tc/

Charette, Rick: http://www.pinepoint.com/rick.html

The Chenille Sisters: www.cantoorecords.com

Coffey, James: www.jamescoffey.com

Colleen and Uncle Squaty: http://colleenanduncleesquaty.com

Cosgrove, Jim: www.jimcosgrove.com

Craig n Co.: www.craignco.com

Crow, Dan: www.dancrow.com

Daddy A Go Go: www.daddyagogo.com

Dana: www.swiggleditties.com

Del Bianco, Lou: www.findlou.com

Diamond, Charlotte: www.charlottediamond.com

Feldman, Jean: www.drjean.org

Fink, Cathy, and Marcy Marxer: www.cathymarcy.com

Fite, Stephen: www.melodyhousemusic.com

Foote, Norman: www.normanfoote.com

Frezza, Rebecca: www.bigtruckmusic.com

Gemini: www.geminichildrensmusic.com

Gill, Jim: www.jimgill.com

Grammer, Red: www.redgrammer.com

Green Chili Jam Band: http://kumo.swcp.com/
      kidzmusic/

Greg and Steve: www.gregandsteve.com

Grunsky, Jack: www.jackgrunsky.com

Harley, Bill: www.billharley.com
Harper, Jessica: www.jessicaharper.com
Harper, Monty: www.montyharper.com
Haynes, Sammie: www.sammiehaynes.com
Hinojosa, Tish: www.mundotish.com
Howdy, Buck: www.buckhowdy.com
Hullabaloo: www.hullabalooband.com
Jenkins, Ella: www.ellajenkins.com
Jonas, Billy: www.billyjonas.com
Kaldor, Connie: www.conniekaldor.com
Kaye, Mary: www.marykayemusic.com
Kimmy Schwimmy: www.kimmyschwimmy.com
Kinder, Brian: www.kindersongs.com
Kinnoin, Dave: www.songwizard.com
Kirk, John, and Trish Miller: www.johnandtrish.com
Knight, Tom: www.tomknight.com
LaFond, Lois: www.loislafond.com
The Learning Station: www.learningstationmusic.com
Lithgow, John: www.johnlithgow.com
Livingston, Bob: www.texasmusic.org
Lonnquist, Ken: www.kenland.com
Madsen, Gunnar: www.gunnarmadsen.com
Marxer, Marcy: www.cathymarcy.com
Mayer, Hans: www.hansmayer.com
McCutcheon, John: www.folkmusic.com
McDermott, Joe: www.joemcdermottmusic.com
McGrath, Bob: www.bobmcgrath.com
McMahon, Elizabeth: www.mrsmcpuppet.com
Milkshake: www.milkshakemusic.com
Miss Amy: www.missamykids.com
Mitchell, Elizabeth: www.youaremyflower.org
Moo, Anna: www.annamoo.com
Mr. Al: www.mralmusic.com
Muldaur, Maria: www.mariamuldaur.com
Nagler, Eric: www.ericnagler.com
Ode, Eric: www.ericode.com
Old Town School of Folk Music: www.oldtownschool.org

Palmer, Hap: www.happalmer.com
Parachute Express: www.parachuteexpress.com
Paxton, Tom: www.tompaxton.com
Pease, Tom: www.tompease.com
Penner, Fred: www.fredpenner.com
Peterson, Carole: www.macaronisoup.com
Pirtle, Sarah: www.sarahpirtle.com
Polisar, Barry Louis: www.barrylou.com
Pullara, Steve: www.coolbeansmusic.com
Raffi: www.raffinews.com
Ralph's World: www.ralphsworld.com
Raven, Nancy: www.lizardsrockmusic.com
Riders in the Sky: www.ridersinthesky.com
Roberts, Justin: www.justinroberts.org
Rosen, Gary: www.garyrosenkidsmusic.com
Rosenthal, Phil: www.americanmelody.com
Roth, Kevin: www.kevinrothmusic.com
Rudnick, Ben: www.benrudnickandfriends.com
Rymer, Brady: www.bradyrymer.com
Sharon, Lois, and Bram: www.casablancakids.com
Shontz, Bill: www.billshontz.com
Silberg, "Miss Jackie": www.jackiesilberg.com
Simmons, Al: www.alsimmons.com
Sprout, Jonathan: www.jonsprout.com
Staines, Bill: http://www.acousticmusic.com/staines
SteveSongs: www.stevesongs.com
Stotts, Stuart: www.stuartstotts.com
Sweet Honey in the Rock: www.sweethoney.com
Thaddeus Rex: www.thaddeusrex.com
They Might Be Giants: www.tmbg.com
Tickle Tune Typhoon: www.tickletunetyphoon.com
Trout Fishing in America: www.troutmusic.com
Tucker, Nancy: www.nancytucker.biz
Vitamin L: www.vitaminl.org
Walker, Graham: www.grahamwalker.ca
Yosi: www.yosimusic.com
Zanes, Dan: www.danzanes.com

Rob Reid is a full-time instructor at the University of Wisconsin–Eau Claire specializing in children's literature and literature for adolescents. He is the author of several ALA Editions books including *Family Storytime; Something Funny Happened at the Library; Cool Story Programs for the School-Age Crowd; Children's Jukebox;* and *Something Musical Happened at the Library*. He is a regular contributor to *Book Links* magazine and *LibrarySparks* magazine, and he has an online column for the Children's Literature Network titled Heart of a Child. He is a recent recipient of the Wisconsin Librarian of the Year. In addition to teaching and writing, Reid visits schools and libraries as a children's humorist, using storytelling, musical activities, and wordplay to make reading come alive for children.